Slaves and Englishmen

THE EARLY MODERN AMERICAS

Peter C. Mancall, Series Editor

Volumes in the series explore neglected aspects of
early modern history in the western hemisphere.
Interdisciplinary in character, and with a special
emphasis on the Atlantic World from 1450 to 1850,
the series is published in partnership with the
USC-Huntington Early Modern Studies Institute.

SLAVES

── AND ──

ENGLISHMEN

HUMAN BONDAGE IN THE EARLY
MODERN ATLANTIC WORLD

MICHAEL GUASCO

PENN

UNIVERSITY OF PENNSYLVANIA PRESS

PHILADELPHIA

Published by
University of Pennsylvania Press
Philadelphia, Pennsylvania 19104-4112
www.upenn.edu/pennpress

Printed in the United States of America on acid-free paper
10   9   8   7   6   5   4   3   2   1

Library of Congress Cataloging-in-Publication Data

Guasco, Michael, 1968–
    Slaves and Englishmen : human bondage in the early
modern Atlantic world / Michael Guasco. — 1st ed.
        p. cm. — (Early modern Americas)
    Includes bibliographical references and index.
    ISBN 978-0-8122-4578-3 (hardcover : alk. paper)
    1. Slavery—Atlantic Ocean Region—History.
2. Slavery—United States—History—Colonial period,
ca. 1600–1775.   3. Slavery—Great Britain—History.
4. Atlantic Ocean Region—History—17th century.
5. United States—History—Colonial period, ca. 1600–1775.
6. Great Britain—Colonies—America—History—17th
century.   I. Title.   II. Series: Early modern Americas.
HT867.G83 2014
306.3'62—dc23

                                            2013024699

For Suz

CONTENTS

The Problem of Slavery in Pre-Plantation America

Perhaps it is best to begin with the familiar: In 1619, a Flemish privateer called the *White Lion* dropped anchor off Point Comfort at the eastern extremity of the English settlement in Virginia. Captain Jope and his men had suffered greatly on their return voyage from the West Indies and when the ship arrived in the Chesapeake the pirates were short on palatable food and potable water. It may be that Jope and his men had been at sea longer than anticipated or that his provisions had spoiled as a result of exposure to rough weather or rotted as a result of improper storage. These things happen. Of course, Jope and his men could also have been unusually hungry and thirsty because of the extra mouths they had stored away somewhere in the belly of their ship, for one Englishman reported that on board were "not any thing but 20. and odd Negroes, w[hich] the Governo[r] and Cape Marchant bought for victualle."[1] By the time he departed, Jope had fresh provisions and water and had reduced the number of mouths on board by striking a bargain with the leaders of the English settlement, an exchange that resulted in the first documented arrival of African peoples in Virginia. For Captain Jope and his men, it was clear sailing as they set out for familiar European waters. For the colonists and the newly purchased Africans, not to mention the historians who have studied both, matters quickly became much more complicated.

Almost a generation later, another story unfolded: In the wake of the Pequot War in New England in 1637, Massachusetts officials ordered seventeen Pequot Indians—fifteen boys and two women—to be sent out of New England. English Puritans had taken hundreds of captives in the wake of their triumphs in battle at Mistick and the Great Swamp. Subsequently, they put some Pequot men to death and divided the survivors among the English soldiers, their Narragansett allies, or assigned them to the Connecticut and Massachusetts colonies. The seventeen women and boys, however, were placed on board the Salem-built craft of Captain Peirce and earmarked for sale in the remote English colony of Bermuda. For some reason, Captain Peirce missed his landing and continued on to the West Indies. Once there, Peirce landed his cargo on the tiny Puritan outpost off the coast of Nicaragua at Providence Island where, by a stroke of the Providence Island Company's pen, English officials transformed the rebel Pequots into "cannibal negroes," condemned to serve out their lives in slavery in Anglo-America's first true slave society.[2]

Twenty years later, a third, almost certainly less well-known event occurred in the English Atlantic: During the late 1650s, Parliament received two petitions on behalf of more than seventy Englishmen claiming that they were "freeborn people of this nation now in slavery" in Barbados. In response, Parliament conducted a brief debate, although some members protested that the petitions had been introduced through irregular channels. Those who were directly implicated by name or as property holders in Barbados were particularly defensive. Martin Noel of Staffordshire noted that he traded into those parts and to the best of his knowledge the work was indeed hard, "but none are sent without their consent" and those who went "were civilly used, and had horses to ride on." Besides, Noel added, they were commonly contracted for five years and did not work as hard as the petitioners claimed because "the work is mostly carried on by the Negroes." Other Parliamentarians were not so certain that the grievances were false. Hugh Boscawen of Cornwall made a particularly compelling argument when he warned that if Englishmen lost the right to a trial or to petition Parliament "our lives will be as cheap as those negroes. They look upon them as their goods, horses, &c., and rack them only to make their time out of them, and cherish them to perform their work." For that reason alone, Boscawen "would have [Parliament] consider the trade of buying and selling men."[3]

These often-told tales (at least in certain circles) are important parts of early Anglo-American history and, of course, they are stories about slavery—or at least they appear to be so. Numerous historians have argued that the arrival of a small shipload of Africans in early Virginia, while certainly an important chapter in the history of the circulation of African peoples in the broader Atlantic world, does not really tell us much about slavery in Anglo-America because "no law yet enshrined African slavery in either

Maryland or Virginia, and the laws that referred to black people were scattered and miscellaneous."[4] It still is not clear if the two dozen or so Africans were actually held as slaves. Certainly, there was no law of slavery in England or its colonies at this time. As a result, the events of 1619 often appear in historical narratives designed to emphasize the fluidity of colonial society and to show the opportunities that existed for the earliest generation of African peoples to assert themselves in English colonies.[5] Some historians have set aside the question of slavery entirely and have focused their attention instead on the English encounter with African peoples or on whether early modern Anglo-Americans subscribed to some version of anti-black prejudice.[6]

Different historical lights have also been cast on the story of the Pequot Indian slaves. Indian slavery is currently a vibrant area of scholarly inquiry, but the Pequot story rarely receives more than a brief mention because scholars are much more likely to look at other times and places in order to understand the broad outlines of this underappreciated subject.[7] Those scholars who do consider the sale of the Pequot captives into slavery rightly use this event to demonstrate the constancy of the classical notion that individuals captured in a "just war" could be justly enslaved.[8] In this regard, the punishment suffered by these prisoners of war was not particularly new or surprising. Other scholars, however, see in the story an early example of something totally new coming to fruition in the colonies, such as the encroachment of plantation slavery among the English in the Americas and the racialization of non-European peoples that was ongoing early in the seventeenth century and would only intensify with time.[9] As with the "20. and odd Negroes," the "cannibal negroes" have been used in a variety of ways to suit the demands of scholarly inquiry.

And what about the Britons who became slaves? Certainly some scholars have been inclined to sympathize with the aggrieved Barbadians.[10] There is little doubt that a term of service on Barbados, whether as an indentured servant, a convict laborer, or a slave, was hazardous under even the best of circumstances and brutalizing and life-shortening under the worst. Yet scholars have generally been hesitant to take the petitioners at their word. The language of slavery, it has been argued, is more properly thought of as rhetorical flourish in this instance than an accurate characterization of the status of a group of convicts who were transported for their crimes.[11] Their plight, real or imagined, has nonetheless proved to be fruitful fodder for historians interested in uncovering the early relationship between servitude and slavery, the difficulties faced by planters who were desperate for laborers to fuel their expanding agricultural enterprises, and the willingness of officials to stretch the bounds of customary English labor arrangements to maximize their control over what could become a dangerous population if completely unfettered.[12]

Although there are countless ways to use these disparate stories from different parts of the early English Atlantic world, they are nonetheless linked by slavery. Unfortunately, characterizing anything as "slavery" or anyone in particular as a "slave" during the first half century of English colonialism tends to produce more confusion than clarity because, from a strictly technical point of view, slavery was not legal in the English-speaking world before the mid-seventeenth century. Barbados and Virginia both enacted important legislation in 1661 to rectify that situation, and subsequent generations of scholars have dutifully taken that date as a convenient starting point for documenting the development of slavery as a key social and economic institution in the English Atlantic world. From that date forward, it is relatively easy to trace the growth of England's plantation complex and the transformation of colonial societies from the mid-Atlantic southward as ever larger numbers of bound Africans began pouring into the Chesapeake and West Indies. By the dawn of the eighteenth century, slavery was fully buttressed by positive law, firmly entrenched in Anglo-American society and culture, and Great Britain was well on its way to becoming the dominant slave-trading power in the world.

Before the 1660s, Africans may have seeped into the colonies and may have been held in perpetual bondage, but slavery was neither systematic nor routine. On some level, there is no disputing the rather loose hold slavery had in the English Atlantic world. Yet, it is equally difficult to ignore the fact that Englishmen wrote about slavery with surprising frequency in the hundred or so years before the practice became commonplace. The English engaged slavery in a variety of ways. English travelers and commentators sometimes simply noted slavery's prevalence throughout the world or thought about it as a historical phenomenon that was interesting because, they claimed, it no longer factored into English society and culture. In that regard, the English were often passive observers. At other times, English mariners and merchants bought and sold slaves, seemingly eager to embrace human bondage as a means of achieving greater wealth and status. Thinking about who could be enslaved, and under what circumstances, occupied the attention of more than a few writers, theorists, and legislators. And there were actual "English" slaves themselves, the thousands of English men (and they were mostly men) who were captured and transformed into brute laborers by the Catholic and Muslim powers in the Mediterranean and elsewhere. Slaves and slavery were everywhere.

It is well worth asking, however, whether slavery really mattered. One reason so many different historical narratives have been constructed around the three stories that began this work—stories in which Indians became "negroes," Europeans become slaves, and Africans became (perhaps) servants—is that we have rarely devoted as much attention to the meaning of human bondage as we have to the origins of racial slavery in the early Anglo-Atlantic world. Works abound on the meaning of blackness in the early modern Atlantic world, but the number of scholars who have thought deeply about slavery apart from the effort to explain either the origins of the transatlantic plantation system or the origins of modern racism is small. This book seeks to redress that oversight by demonstrating that slavery was not only central to how the English interacted with people and places throughout the Atlantic world, but also that early English colonialism was necessarily shaped by English ideas about slavery and the willingness to take advantage of human bondage to construct and preserve English colonies during the first half century of overseas settlement.

To that end, the first chapter of this book is concerned with the early modern English understanding of, and experience with, human bondage long before the practice became an integral part of England's colonial endeavors. A careful reading of contemporary sources reveals that English men and women knew a great deal more about slavery than we tend to assume. Slavery was recognizable throughout early modern English society, in part, because the idea pervaded the most important texts available to the educated elite. In addition, although it had not existed as a legal institution for several centuries, a number of discrete manifestations of human bondage encouraged Tudor-Stuart English men and women to think and write about slavery in familiar terms. Some people even seem to have imagined that England would be a better place if slavery were reintroduced as a living institution. Although this idea proved to be impractical, the language and image of slavery in pre-colonial England was both widespread and familiar, something that would inform the idea of slavery in subtle but powerful ways in subsequent decades.

If there continued to be some debate about the real presence of slavery in England, Chapter 2 leaves little doubt about the pervasiveness of human bondage throughout the world. Even as many of their countrymen were able to think and write about slavery from a comfortable remove, thousands of Englishmen were coming face-to-face with human bondage as they spread out across the globe during the late sixteenth and early seventeenth centuries. And regardless of where they traveled, English observers routinely noted both the presence of slaves and the important role played by slavery in non-English settings. Because they came from a place largely untouched by the actual practice of slavery, noting its pervasiveness in foreign lands was an easy way to set the English apart from and above the people and nations they encountered in Europe, Asia, and Africa. It is important to note, however, early English impressions of slavery as it existed beyond England's borders were not determined by racial—or even proto-racial—conceits. Initial English accounts of the nature of slavery in Africa are therefore worth scrutinizing because they highlight how the pursuit of economic gain at the expense of European competitors, particularly the Portuguese, played a larger role in how English merchants and mariners encountered and interacted with African peoples than did any abstract anti-black ideology or any persistent interest in the emerging transatlantic slave trade.

The complicated relationship between Englishmen and Africans in the broader Atlantic world during the late sixteenth century comes in for fuller treatment in Chapter 3. The Atlantic world was tainted by the stain of slavery from an early date and the number of captive Africans being transported across the ocean in the holds of European ships was on the rise as English sailors began to traverse the seas in greater numbers. Although a loose link between Africans and slavery already existed in the minds of early modern Englishmen, the English were much more likely to make a direct connection between the descendants of African peoples and the opprobrious practice of slavery when they happened to be in Spain's Atlantic empire. English pirates and privateers, particularly when they operated in the West Indies, were among the first of their nation to conceive of, and treat, Africans as simple commodities. At the same time, the English acceptance of racial slavery in this context in no way prevented them from engaging Africans as translators, concubines, shipmates, soldiers, intermediaries, and more. Indeed, they had little choice; Spain's Atlantic world would have been impenetrable and incomprehensible to the English without African allies. Thus, although Englishmen in Africa and the Spanish colonies can be accused of callousness toward Africans, they do not seem to have wedded themselves to an intransigent view of dark-skinned peoples.

The English did not immediately accept either that Africans were necessarily best suited to slavery or that the definitive slave in the Atlantic world was most easily identified by the color of his or her skin. Crucially, just as Englishmen were becoming more familiar with the practice of slavery and the enslavement of African peoples, they were confronted by the harsh prospect that they, too, were legitimate candidates for human bondage under the right circumstances. Chapter 4 reveals that Tudor and early Stuart Englishmen devoted a great deal of attention to explaining what it meant to be English and repeatedly emphasized that theirs was a heritage colored by the efforts of others to enslave Englishmen and subjugate the English nation. When, beginning in the late sixteenth century, tens of thousands of English mariners and merchants were captured and enslaved in other parts of the world, Englishmen scrutinized these developments and nervously identified an emerging threat to their national integrity. Because some English slaves escaped or were ransomed, former slaves were able to publish firsthand accounts that cultivated fearful stereotypes and generated shocking images, which were disseminated throughout the land in royal proclamations, in sermons, and on stage. Nothing else did as much to shape the way the general English public thought about slavery, especially what it meant to be enslaved, before the elaboration of England's Atlantic plantation complex in the mid-seventeenth century.

The final two chapters of this book follow these separate threads to the English colonial world, particularly during the first half of the seventeenth century. In the half century after the settlement of Jamestown, slavery and other forms of human bondage could be found in every English colony, but *how* slavery manifested itself between 1607 and the mid-seventeenth century was quite different from the condition at the heart of the race-based plantation labor system that would prevail in a later era. Africans, Indians, and Europeans all could be (and were) subjected to enslavement in early America, but the reasons why individuals from each of these groups might be enslaved varied greatly. So, too, did the meaning of slavery itself. Slavery was often only loosely related to the need for labor during the early seventeenth century. The meaning of slavery was more closely connected to the question of what it meant to be English in the Atlantic world, especially with regard to the practice of holding fellow English men and women in bondage, but this attitude also impacted Indians. When Anglo-American colonists held Africans in bondage, however, they had a much harder time explaining their actions. Of course, the manifestation of racial slavery in the early English colonies was consistent with the prevailing customs of Spain and Portugal's Atlantic world. It should hardly be surprising that characteristic features of Iberian and Iberian Atlantic slavery were present in the English colonies before the institution was defined in positive law. The presence of free blacks, the tacit acceptance of racial intermixture, and the effort to integrate African peoples into the Christian community—all things that would be discouraged later—are revealing evidence of the lingering influence of what Englishmen had been witnessing and experiencing in the Americas since the late sixteenth century. It may have looked a bit different from what would be commonplace later, but slavery was present in the English colonies from the beginning.

This brings us back to the stories recounted at the beginning of this book. About fifty years ago the historian Winthrop Jordan quipped, "[W]ere [it] possible to poll the inhabitants of Jamestown, Virginia, concerning their reaction to those famous first 'twenty Negars' who arrived in 1619 I would be among the first to be at the foot of the gangplank, questionnaire in hand."[13] Judging by the response to his seminal study over subsequent decades and the important place the date "1619" has played in scholarly enterprises, a number of people would love to know the results of such a survey.[14] I, for one, would especially like to know what those early Anglo-Virginians thought about slavery in general terms, not just as it may have applied to the new arrivals. We know, of course, that racial slavery would ultimately become a characteristic feature of every English colony in the Americas and the defining institution in virtually every settlement south of the Potomac River and throughout the West Indies. Yet, English peoples neither thought about nor used slavery during the early modern era in ways that were consistent with how things would stand at the end of the seventeenth century. The cultural, intellectual, and legal worlds out of which English colonists emerged prepared them to think about human bondage in different ways and under different circumstances. Few historians will challenge the notion that Anglo-American slavery came to full fruition in England's colonies during the last half of the seventeenth century, but it is important to acknowledge that slavery was not simply invented out of whole cloth, in situ, by people trying to figure out how to do things for the first time.

It is customary these days to distinguish between "slave societies" and "societies with slaves" as a way of measuring the relative impact slavery had on local and regional cultures and economies.[15] By this measure, no English slave societies existed before the plantation revolution reconfigured

English America in a way that would make some of those settlements largely unrecognizable to their founders. A good case could even be made that, before the mid-seventeenth century, most English colonies barely even qualified as "societies with slaves," possessing as they did a supply of primarily European laborers and lacking even a rudimentary infrastructure for employing and managing bound African slaves. In raw economic and demographic terms, the institution of slavery and the presence of African peoples were equally unimpressive and bordering on insignificant. Regardless, it is the central premise of this work that both African peoples and slavery—often quite apart from each other—were central to the articulation of an Anglo-Atlantic world in the century before 1660. Englishmen repeatedly defined themselves and their nation in ways that can only be understood if one takes seriously the idea that, even without plantations and even without large numbers of bound Africans living in their midst, slavery mattered. It may have been possible, while in England, to imagine that theirs was that exceptionally rare thing in the early modern era: neither a slave society nor a society with slaves, but a society epitomized by its commitment to the ideals of liberty and freedom. That, at least, is what early modern Englishmen liked to think and what we sometimes choose to think about them. Once they set sail into the Atlantic world and beyond, however, there was little doubt that slavery was ubiquitous.

Long before the establishment of English colonies in the Americas, the subsequent arrival of African peoples to those colonies, and the creation of plantations dedicated to the production of staple crops, England was already wrestling with the pressing problem of slavery. Ideas about slavery were varied in early modern England, but human bondage was perceived by many people to be a serious issue that bore down on them as individuals and as a nation. As such, when Englishmen thought and wrote about slavery during this period, they were typically much more concerned about the possibility of their own enslavement than they were with the condition of African or Indian peoples. By the standards established in eighteenth-century British America and by historians of the mature plantation complex, early modern Englishmen imagined slavery in exceedingly loose terms. Without a doubt, English conceptions of slavery were wide ranging and often incoherent, but the diffuse nature of English ideas also provides a clear guide for understanding the logic of human bondage in the early English colonies. Eventually, the diversity of experiences and excess of precedents that created the problem of how to deal with both slavery and African peoples in the early Anglo-American social order would be simplified. Numerous scholars have worked that problem out. It is important, however, to try to make sense of those ideas and experiences that framed the earliest English colonial efforts and social relations among Europeans, Africans, and indigenous Americans in the New World. Before we move on to the question of how things changed, it is incumbent upon us to grapple with how things stood before the seemingly irresistible power of the plantation complex, with its attendant demographic and economic considerations, overwashed the Anglo-Atlantic world. If we want to make sense of the "20. and odd Negroes," the Pequot "cannibal negroes," or the petitioners who claimed that they had been reduced to slavery, we need to think about these stories as a reflection of the English Atlantic world *as it was* rather than as what it would become. We need to know as much about the "before" as we do the "after."

CHAPTER 1

The Nature of a Slave: Human Bondage in Early Modern England

Such as have made forfeit of themselves
By vicious courses, and their birthright lost
'Tis not injustice they are marked for slaves.[1]

In late 1583 Sir Francis Walsingham, Queen Elizabeth's principal secretary, dispatched a thirty-year-old Oxford cleric named Richard Hakluyt to France to search out information that could be used to promote royal support for the development of English colonies abroad. Walsingham, who had been a backer of Martin Frobisher's voyages of discovery during the 1570s and would give aid to John Davis during the 1580s, was one among a growing number of luminaries who believed that England needed to accelerate its overseas activities. Elizabethan England faced an array of challenges. Nearby, colonization efforts in Ireland had recently entered a much more violent stage as the English struggled to put down a series of local rebellions, particularly those that had plagued the Munster Plantation during the previous fifteen years. England's northern frontier was hardly more secure as the apparent machinations of Mary, Queen of Scots, and her Catholic allies encouraged the view that Elizabeth's grasp on the throne was tentative, at best. The Catholic threat to Tudor rule in England was especially vivid across the English Channel, where thousands of Protestants had recently been killed by rampaging Catholic mobs during the St. Bartholomew's Day Massacre in 1572. The revolt of Dutch Calvinists against the Spanish Habsburgs may have loomed even larger as English shipping and, especially, its woolen industry were hamstrung by a surge in piracy and the closing of traditional trading ports like Antwerp. And, of course, there was Spain, with whom England would soon enough be at war because of all of these things. Walsingham was but one among many English leaders who believed that England was endangered and it was therefore with a great sense of urgency and a desire to ensure England's very survival that he commanded Hakluyt to learn all he could about the world beyond the western horizon.[2]

Despite outward appearances, Hakluyt was an obvious choice for the job. As the namesake of his older and more renowned cousin, young Hakluyt was already connected to a group of people urging the nation to take a more active role in the Americas and throughout the world. During the 1570s, he had begun to gather information about the Northwest Passage from foreign authorities, including the celebrated mapmakers Abraham Ortelius and Gerard Mercator. In 1581, Hakluyt engaged both Walsingham and Sir Francis Drake, who had only recently returned from his circumnavigation, in discussions about establishing a lectureship in navigation. A year later, he made an even bigger mark when he published *Divers Voyages Touching the Discovery of America*, a collection of accounts edited and translated by Hakluyt himself designed to promote overseas colonization.[3] Hakluyt may have been working in the shadows of other writers, translators, and editors, such as Richard Eden and Richard Willes, and may not have been as celebrated as some of his contemporaries, such as John Dee and Sir Philip Sidney, but he was nonetheless a man on the rise.[4]

Upon returning from his fact-finding mission in 1584, Hakluyt sat down and composed "A particuler discourse concerninge the greate necessitie and manifolde commodyties that are like to growe to this Realme of Englande by the Westerne discoveries lately attempted" or, as it is more commonly known, "A Discourse of Western Planting." Hakluyt's "Discourse," which he presented to Walsingham and Queen Elizabeth in October, precisely detailed the need for a more comprehensive overseas policy based on the acquisition and settlement of permanent colonies in the Americas. He claimed that colonization was the only way to stem the tide of Spanish expansionism, that it would project Protestant Christianity into a region where the Catholic Church presently exercised a spiritual monopoly, and that it would generate innumerable economic and demographic rewards. Central to Hakluyt's argument was the idea that North American colonies would be the engine of England's rise to national greatness, just as overseas conquests had aided Spain's emergence as a global power during the previous century.

Considering Spain and Portugal's grip on the Americas, just how England could dislodge the Catholic powers would seem to have been problematic. Not so, Hakluyt argued. The secret, he suggested, lay not simply in English power but in the inherent weaknesses in Spanish colonial policies characterized by "more then barbarous and savage endeles cruelties." Rehashing a litany of accusations, largely drawn (often verbatim) from Bartolomé de las Casas's *Brevíssima relación de la destruycíon de las yndias* (1552), which had been translated and published in English as *The Spanish Colonie* in 1583, Hakluyt claimed that a "people kepte in subjection desire nothinge more then freedome. And like as a little passage geven to water it maketh his own way, so give but a small meane to such kepte in tyranie, they will make their own way to libertie, which way may easely be made." Because Spain ruled "the Indies with all pride and tyranie," Indians and Africans would "joyne with us or any other moste willinglye to shake of[f] their moste intollerable yoke." Indeed, they "have begonne to doo yt already in divers places where they were lordes heretofore." With English encouragement to help root out their oppressors, it would be "like as when people of contrarie nature at the sea enter into Gallies, where men are tied as slaves, all yell and crye with one voice *liberta, liberta*, as desirous of libertie & freedomme." Because the Spanish could only lay claim during their tenure to have "exercised moste outragious and more then Turkishe cruelties in all the West Indies," and future English colonialism would be characterized by "humanitie, curtesie, and freedomme," a foreign policy premised on the establishment of English colonies in the Americas could only succeed.[5]

Hakluyt's references here to the brutality of the Spanish conquest have subsequently become familiar elements of the notorious Black Legend and a predictable part of a document that was drafted at a time when so many Englishmen believed that their lives and liberties were imperiled.[6] Less familiar are his uses of the language of slavery, galleys, Turkish cruelties, and the intolerable yoke of bondage. But as striking as Hakluyt's choice of words may seem in retrospect, they were unremarkable for the period and likely would not have confused English readers had this private document been distributed more widely. Indeed, Hakluyt could toss about references to these different forms of human bondage without explanation because he understood that both his immediate audience and the English public at large had well-formed and often quite sophisticated ideas about slavery. A few prescient souls were able to perceive the developing plantation system on the horizon, involving as it did a commitment to chattel slavery, but few people living at the time thought about slavery as a labor system or a way of organizing human populations in terms of superficial phenotypical categories. Both the received wisdom of the ages and contemporary experience suggested that slavery could manifest itself in a variety of ways and that it was a characteristic feature in many parts of the world. It was hardly shocking, then, when Hakluyt claimed that Spanish America was besotted by slavery.

Slavery, for all intents and purposes, was alive and well in England even if actual slaves were hard to find. Slavery lived in England's most important texts: the Christian Bible, where bondage was both a defining spiritual theme and an acknowledged historical condition, and the classical works being read in both Latin and newly fashionable English translations by England's educated elite. Slavery also existed in English society as a contemporary social issue that manifested itself, variously, in the lingering vestiges of manorial villeinage, in intermittent proposals to expand galley slavery, and even as a practical solution to a range of social ills that plagued the nation. Thus, when English men and women wrote or talked about slavery, when they heard references to it from the pulpit or from government officials, they were not necessarily inclined to dream up something far off, foreign, or characterized by groups of people whose race, nation, ethnicity, or religion set them apart. Instead, slavery made Englishmen think, and worry, about themselves as individuals and a nation whose personal liberty and collective autonomy hung in the balance.

*   *   *

Sixteenth-century Englishmen liked to claim that they were uniquely free, yet slavery was undoubtedly an integral part of their national story. In particular, the idea of slavery resonated in English religious and intellectual circles. Indeed, it would have been difficult to avoid the issue, if only because slavery pervaded the nation's most ubiquitous text, the Christian Bible. Literate English men and women may have been especially aware of the specific contents of the Bible as a result of the publication of the Geneva Bible in English in 1560.[7] The Geneva Bible was laced with references to slaves and slavery and established human bondage as an apt metaphor for the complete submission of humankind and particular individuals to God. Throughout the book of Exodus, one could read of the children of Israel who "sighed for the[ir] bondage and cryed" (2:23) in an Egypt so miserable and cruel that when Moses told them that Yahweh would free them of their burdens and lead them to a better place they could not listen, "for anguish of spirit & for cruel bondage" (Exodus 6:9). But even as the Bible could be read as a story of liberation, of God freeing his chosen people from slavery, the Old Testament also granted tacit justification for the legality of human bondage, provided it conformed to certain religious precepts. The book of Leviticus, for example, made it clear that slaves should come from foreign nations and that "ye shal take them as inheritance for your children after you, to possesse them by inheritance, ye shal use their labours for ever: but over your brethren the children of Israel ye shal not rule one over another with crueltie" (Leviticus 25:44–46).[8] The New Testament, particularly the letters of Paul, also endorsed slavery as a legitimate human institution and contained injunctions that upheld the status quo, such as the assertion that slaves must "counte their masters worthie of all honour, that the Name of God, and *his* doctrine be not evil spoken of" (1 Timothy 6:1).[9] Resistance to earthly slavery, in this instance, was an affront to God.

Other often-cited religious authorities similarly elaborated on the subject of slavery. Most notably, within the Christian tradition, theologians debated whether either the condition or the institution of slavery was natural. St. Augustine of Hippo's conception of slavery as a consequence of man's fall from a state of innocence was typical of the views expressed by the early church fathers and those who followed them during the first millennium. In the *City of God*, a work first published in English in 1610, Augustine recounted that, before man's fall from a state of grace, God made man "reasonable," and wished for human beings to rule "onely over the unreasonable, not over man, but over beastes." Servitude was only subsequently "layde upon the backe of transgression. And therefore in all the scriptures wee never reade the word, *Servant*, untill such time as that just man *Noah* . . . layd it as a curse upon his offending sonne. So that it was guilt, and not nature that gave originall unto that name." Slavery, in Augustine's schema, was brought upon mankind not by God's design but by man's actions. Slavery was therefore a natural condition insofar as human beings no longer lived in a world of God's original design.[10]

The centerpiece of Augustine's explanation for slavery—the "transgression" to which he referred—was Noah's curse. According to Genesis 9:21–27, as it appeared in the 1560 edition of the Bible, Noah became intoxicated on the ark and "was uncovered in ye middes of his tent. And when Ham the father of Canaan sawe the nakednes of his father, he tolde his two brethren without. Then toke Shem and Japeth a garment and put it upon bothe their

shulders and went backward, and covered the nakednes of their father."
When Noah awoke "from his wine, and knewe what his yonger sonne had
done unto him" he said "Cursed *be* Canaan: servant of servantes shall he be
unto his brethren. He said moreover, Blessed *be* the Lord God of Shem, and
let Canaan be his servant." In case there was any doubt about the severity of
the punishment, a marginal notation was attached to the phrase "servant
of servantes" reading: "That is, a moste vile slave."[11]

Whether St. Augustine's work was read widely in England, his characterization of slavery as a product of sinfulness remained the dominant strain
of thought within Christian theology for more than a thousand years and
Augustine continued to influence English theologians well into the seventeenth century.[12] Western Europeans also leaned heavily on secular sources.
In the twelfth century, Europeans famously rediscovered Aristotle's *Politics*, a
work that was subsequently influential in the thirteenth-century writings of
St. Thomas Aquinas, who incorporated many of Aristotle's ideas into Christian thought. Aristotle's treatment of the subject of slavery in his *Politics*, ultimately translated into English from an older French source, was therefore
doubly important in early modern England. Here, readers could learn that
slavery was not only natural, it was part of a "universal natural pattern" in
which those with the capacity to reason should rule over those whose "function is the use of their bodies and nothing better can be expected of them."
Aristotle even declared that it was "nature's purpose to make the bodies of
free men to differ from those of slaves, the latter strong enough to be used for
necessary tasks, the former erect and useless for that kind of work, but well
suited for the life of a citizen of the state."[13]

Working within the confines of Augustinian doctrine, Aquinas maintained the presumption that slavery could not have existed before the Fall,
yet he allowed that natural disparities existed among individuals based on
sex, age, strength, and wisdom. Aquinas believed that "the condition of men
in the state of nature was not more honourable than the condition of the
angels. Yet among the angels some lord over others." Hierarchy and dominion almost certainly existed in a state of nature, something repeatedly urged
in Tudor sermons on the ever popular theme of obedience.[14] Therefore, the
emergence of full-fledged slavery and mastery, much less dependency and
bondage, in the post-lapsarian world could only be viewed as a logical extension of things and not necessarily inconsistent with, much less contrary to,
natural design. In rationalizing the legitimacy of slavery this way, Aquinas
challenged Roman and earlier Christian ideas, both of which suggested that

slavery was inconsistent with natural law. Aquinas therefore lined up much more closely with Aristotle in his assertion that slavery was in accord with what he called the second intention of nature and that it ultimately benefited both masters and slaves.[15]

The influence of the Bible and Christian thought clearly shaped the meaning of slavery throughout Tudor and early Stuart society, even as they often did so on the continent as well. Nonetheless, other intellectual reference points shaped English society's ideas and attitudes about slavery, many of which tended to characterize slavery as commonplace but not necessarily a product of natural law. Most elite Englishmen, for example, including not only many gentry and professionals but also a few of the "middling sort," were remarkably well-informed about human bondage through their university or grammar school education in the classics. Legal and political slavery were important themes in the writings of Sallust and Cicero, whose works were routinely used in the instruction of Latin.[16] Livy's *Romane Historie* and Tacitus's *Germania* were also fundamental and popular reference sources for English knowledge about classical slavery. Indeed, both works were laced with references to slaves performing mundane tasks; they considered how people fell into a state of bondage or, in Livy's case, might be manumitted, and they commented on the propriety of slavery as an institution. Significantly, they were not available only in their original language; these works also underwent English translations near the end of Elizabeth's reign, which allowed the texts to reach an even wider audience.[17]

For educated Englishmen—a small but rapidly growing cohort in the last decades of the sixteenth century—the essence of classical slavery was contained in the Roman *Digest*, a collection of legal writings compiled by the Roman Emperor Justinian during the sixth century. Here readers could discover the rather straightforward convention that there were three classes of men: "free men, and set against those slaves and the third class, freedmen, that is, those who had stopped being slaves." These categories, however, were a product of civil society. Roman law was premised on the idea that slavery was legitimate insofar as it could be legalized, but it was also essentially unnatural. Thirteenth-century jurist Henri de Bracton [Henry of Bratton] articulated this idea clearly when he wrote that servitude was "an institution of the *jus gentium*, by which, contrary to nature, one person is subjected to the dominion of another." By this logic, the bondman could actually be a free man because "with respect to the *jus gentium* they are bonds, [but] free with respect to the *jus naturale*." Educated Englishmen, whose knowledge of bondage had been primarily informed by Latin texts, therefore were instructed with the idea (and presumably accepted) that the essence of slavery involved being *in potestate domini*, in the possession of another. The Roman *Digest* also encouraged the view that, although human bondage was against nature (i.e., it could not exist in a perfect world), it could be justified under the law and reasonably applied in appropriate circumstances. Fundamentally, then, it was an idea of slavery that had nothing to do with harsh physical treatment, essential or superficial differences in character or appearance, or labor demands.[18]

The Roman *Digest* was also central to emerging English, and broader European, conceptions of freedom. According to Roman law, "Manumission means sending out of one's hand, that is, granting freedom. For whereas one who is in slavery is subjected to the hand (*manus*) and power of another, on being sent out of hand he is freed of that power. All of which originated from the *jus gentium*, since, of course, everyone would be born free by the natural law, and manumission would not be known when slavery was unknown."[19] From this perspective, freedom was incomprehensible without reference to its antithesis in history, law, and social status. All free humans were therefore more accurately termed "freed" humans in recognition of the larger and longer history of human bondage out of which the much more recent innovations, such as the concepts of freedom and liberty, emerged.[20]

The idea that slavery was an unnatural condition, a product of the law of man rather than the law of nature, was also supported in other popular contemporary texts. The French political theorist Jean Bodin, for one, provided a clear analysis of both the history and the inherent problems of slavery in his *Six Bookes of a Commonweale*, a work that first appeared in England in 1606. Bodin was concerned with whether slavery could exist in a commonwealth or, to be more specific, whether a commonwealth could endure as long as it condoned slavery. Like a growing number of authors of his day, Bodin's treatment began with the Aristotelian conclusion that slavery was natural. Bodin, however, contrasted this view with the contention that lawyers, "who measure the law not by the discourses or decrees of Philosophers, but according to the common sense and capacitie of the people, hold servitude to be directly contrarie unto nature." He acknowledged that slavery appeared at first glance to be natural, based on its ancient and seemingly universal history, but slavery was also fundamentally irrational. For example, slavery "is well agreeing unto nature" when a strong, ignorant man yields his obedience unto a wise and feeble man. But what could be more unnatural than for "wise men to serve fools, men of understanding to serve the ignorant, and the good to serve the bad?"[21] This possibility elicited some of the strongest language a century earlier in Thomas More's *Utopia* when he ridiculed the idea that "a lumpyshe blockhedded churle" with "no more wytte than an asse" could possess "manye wyse and good men in subjection and bondage" simply because he was wealthy. Conversely, give gold "to the moste vile slave and abject dryvell of all his housholde, then shortly after he shal go into the service of his servaunt."[22] If slavery were theoretically natural, then, it could manifest itself in a fashion that ran contrary to nature.

Theological, philosophical, and legal treatises kept slavery alive in the minds of many early modern Englishmen, but they tell us little on their own about slavery's resonance in contemporary society. What gave these printed sources real significance, then, was the conviction that slavery, natural or otherwise, was not simply an abstract consideration. Englishmen believed they could speak with authority about human bondage, in part, because it was an important piece of their national story. In 1576 the English cleric William Harrison was commissioned to write a *Description of Britain* for Raphael Holinshed's *Chronicles of England, Scotlande and Ireland*.[23] Harrison's task was to provide a historical overview of England and Scotland down to 1066, and the story he had to tell was nothing short of a catalog of successive waves of invasion, violence, and subjugation. "Manie sorts of people," he claimed, "have come in hither and settled themselves here in this Ile." The island's first inhabitants were "a parcell of the linage and posteritie of Japhet, brought in by Samothes [1,910 years] after the creation of Adam." After several hundred years, "Albion the giant . . . repaired hither with a companie of his owne race proceeding from Cham" and reduced Japhet's descendants "into miserable servitude and most extreame thraldome." The giants of Albion were subsequently conquered by "Brute the sonne of *Sylvius* with a great traine of the posteritie of the dispersed Trojans. . . ." The Romans came next, and "with them came all maner of vice and vicious living, all riot and excesse of behaviour into our countrie." The Scots, "a people mixed of the Scithian and Spanish blood" who were "given to the eating of mans flesh," also plagued Britain around the time of Christ. The Saxons soon followed, having been "sent for by *Vortiger*" in the fifth century "to serve him in his warres against the Picts" (a people about whom Harrison claimed to know little except that "they were setled in this Ile long before the time of *Severus*, yea of *Caesar*"). In time, the Saxons managed to get "possession of the whole, or at the leastwise the greatest part of our countrie; the Britons in the meane season being driven either into Wales and Cornwall, or altogither out of the Iland to seeke new habitations."

Matters hardly improved during the eleventh century, Harrison observed, when the Danes and Norman French descended on the British Isles. The Danes, who invaded Britain under the leadership of Canute in 1015, were characterized by their "lordlinesse, crueltie, and insatiable desire of riches, beside their detestable abusing of chast[e] matrons, and young virgins (whose husbands and parents were daile inforced to become their drudges and slaves . . .)." In their wake came the Normans, "a people mixed with Danes" who "were so cruellie bent to our utter subversion and overthrow, that in the beginning it was lesse reproch to be accounted a slave than an Englishman, or a drudge in anie filthie businesse than a Britaine." Harrison lamented: "Oh how miserable was the estate of our countrie under the French and Normans, wherein the Brittish and English that remained, could not be called to any function in the commonwealth. . . . Oh what numbers of all degrees of English and Brittish were made slaves and bondmen, and bought and sold as oxen in open market!" The ancient Britons were particularly devastated. Had not Edward the Confessor, the penultimate Anglo-Saxon king of England, "permitted the remnant of their women to joine in mariage with the Englishmen . . . their whole race" would have died off and "thereby the memorie of the Britons utterlie have perished among us."[24]

Harrison's work was emblematic of the patriotic zeal increasingly evident in the historical works being produced by sixteenth-century Englishmen. Tudor and Stuart scholars believed that an ancient and honorable past was a critical part of their collective effort to characterize England as a great and free nation. Harrison's story reveals, however, that it was difficult to determine what *exactly* constituted the core of the English or British past. Should Tudor Englishmen emphasize that the first inhabitant of their island was a grandson of Noah (Samothes) or the son of Neptune (Albion)? Perhaps there was more honor in Brutus, reputedly the grandson of Aeneas and liberator of enslaved Trojans? What about the Anglo-Saxons and Norman French? Each group offered a way of establishing the antiquity and greatness of the English nation by linking England directly with a Bibilical, Greek, or Roman past.[25] However scholars may have gone about their historical reconstructions, though, there seemed to be no denying that subjugation, captivity, and slavery were integral components of England's national story.

If slavery was part of England's past, as Harrison's narrative suggested, it also appeared in a number of guises during the early modern era, including the defining religious conflict of the time. The English cleric and ardent nationalist John Bale liked to imagine that England was the new Holy Land in his attacks on the Roman church. He censured Catholic bishops and characterized the English as a people "cruelly enslaved by the tyrannical papists, who made them suffer far more than the Israelites did when enslaved by Pharoah." In his anti-French tract, the English bishop John Aylmer prayed that the God who defended his children of Israel from their enemies might "defend us from the slavery and misery of that proude nacyon, that cruel people, and tiranous rulers."[26] Slavery also factored into the overheated rhetoric generated by English patriots in their struggles against the continental Catholic powers. During the Anglo-Spanish War (1585–1604), Elizabeth rallied her nation by warning that Spain and the papacy were preparing to invade England and to "overthrow our most happy estate and flourishing commonweal, and to subject the same to the proud, servile and slavish government of foreigners and strangers." Worse still, Elizabeth suggested, the pope was plotting to incite the English "to betray and yield themselves, their parents, kindred, and children . . . to be subjects and slaves to aliens and strangers." The conflict between England and Spain, between Protestants and Catholics, was easily couched as a struggle between freedom and slavery and it fed into the notion that the English were, ipso facto, anti-slavery.[27]

References to human bondage in religious and political contexts could not have had the same rhetorical force without the myths of English freedom and the struggle against enslavement that pervaded competing versions of English history. Indeed, one argument for the resiliency of the so-called "British History"—the mythohistorical narrative that identified England's forebears with ancient Greece—was that it lent credence to the assertion that the English were God's chosen people. Like the biblical Jews, the British History emphasized that the English nation had emerged from a state of bondage in the Mediterranean and had continued to struggle against re-enslavement ever since the arrival of the English in Albion. As the twelfth-century chronicler Geoffrey of Monmouth told the story, Brutus had led the enslaved Trojans against their Greek captors. Their decision to resist entailed great hardship, but the Trojans preferred to "have their liberty, rather than remain under the yoke of . . . slavery, even if pampered there by every kind of wealth." In the poet Michael Drayton's panegyric to the "God-like *Brute* . . . of the race of *Troy*," the hero returned to Greece only to find his Trojan cousins enslaved and

there, by *Pandrasus* kept, in sad and servile awe.
Who when they knew young *Brute*, & that brave shape they saw,
They humbly him desire, that he a meane would bee,
From those imperious Greeks, his countrymen to free.[28]

Geoffrey's *History* can be read as a narrative retelling of the ongoing
struggle of a people, of ancient and noble heritage, to resist the efforts of successive waves of enemies to enslave them. Geoffrey devoted significant attention to
Julius Caesar, who is said to exclaim that "[t]hose Britons come from the
same race as we do, for we Romans are descended from Trojan stock. . . . All
the same, unless I am mistaken, they have become very degenerate when
compared with us." When Caesar demanded the capitulation of the Britons,
however, King Cassivelaunus refused on the grounds that to do so would
signal an end to British liberty and freedom, in both the political and physical meanings of the terms. And in a dramatic statement of defiance, the king
of the Britons (or, perhaps more accurately, Geoffrey) rebuked Caesar, asserting that "[i]t is friendship which you should have asked of us, not slavery. For
our part we are more used to making allies than to enduring the yoke of
bondage. We have become so accustomed to the concept of liberty that we
are completely ignorant of what is meant by submitting to slavery." Eventually, of course, the Britons were overawed, but not before they repelled the
Romans on two separate occasions. For this, Geoffrey lauded England's ancestors, who "went on resisting the man whom the whole world could not
withstand. They were ready to die for their fatherland and for their liberty."[29]
Subsequently, during Arthur's reign, Geoffrey characterizes Roman efforts in
battle as "their utmost [effort] to deprive you of your freedom." "No doubt,"
Arthur contends, "they imagined, when they planned to make your country
pay them tribute and to enslave you yourselves, that they would discover in
you the cowardice of Eastern peoples." Thus, Arthur's many victories were
not simply evidence of English martial valor or courage. Arthur's victories
were cast by Geoffrey as a defense of English liberty and part of the ongoing
struggle to prevent the (re)enslavement of Englishmen by foreign powers.[30]

   The anti-slavery theme of Geoffrey's *History* continued to operate in later
works written in the tradition of the British History, especially in accounts of
the Norman Conquest and the reign of King John. Perhaps one of the more
well-known traditions of this era was the equation of William the Conqueror's
rise to power with the imposition of the Norman Yoke. The English antiquarian and historian William Camden, although he questioned many aspects of

the British History, lauded Britons' resistance to bondage once they were confined to Wales, where "with like honour of fortitude, for many hundred years repelled the yoke of both the English and Norman slavery." Antiquarian William Lambarde, among others, associated specific regions of England with freedom and the Conquest. Lambarde wrote in his *Perambulation of Kent* that the common people were no "more free, and jolly" than in Kent because "Kent was never vanquished by the Conquerour, . . . [and] there were never any bondmen . . . in Kent." Lambarde also cited the medieval contention that "it is holden sufficient for a man to avoide the objection of bondage, to say, that his father was born in the Shyre of Kent."[31] And, on the theme of Kentish liberty, Michael Drayton wrote:

> O noble *Kent*, quoth he, this praise doth the belong,
> The hard'st to be controld, impatientest of wrong.
> Who, when the *Norman* first with pride and horror sway'd,
> Threw'st off the servile yoke upon the *English* lay'd;
> And with a high resolve, most bravely didst restore
> That liberties so long enjoy'd before.
> Not suffring forraine Lawes should thy free Customes bind,
> Then onely showd'st thy selfe of th' ancient *Saxon* kind.
> Of all the *English* Shires be thou surnam'd the Free,
> And formost ever plac't, when they reckned bee.[32]

The British History was well known and often cited in sixteenth-century England, but a growing number of historians and antiquarians, like Camden, questioned its veracity. Based on linguistic and other documentary evidence, a competing "Anglo-Saxon History" emerged that offered a somewhat different but certainly no less heroic story about the relationship between the English nation and human bondage. Anglo-Saxonists rooted the English past in northern Europe rather than in Greece. With Tacitus as his guide, William Camden extolled English freedoms by recounting how, while the Roman period witnessed the enslavement of the British to Roman invaders, "Germany had shaken off the yoke of obedience, and yet were defended by a river only, and not by the Ocean." To be sure, ancient Britons stood up against the Romans who had kept them as "captives and slaves" and "vowed to recover and resume their liberty."[33] But even more honor could be found among Anglo-Saxon forebears, who had not only put up a good fight but also had triumphed in their efforts to remain free. Unlike the Britons, who had been conquered by the Romans, the Anglo-Saxonist Richard Verstegan remembered, Germans "were never subdued by any, for albeit the Romans with exceedingly great cost, losse & long trooble, might come to bee the comaunders of some parte thereof; yet of the whole never."[34]

Whether ancient Britons had been enslaved or Anglo-Saxons had always been free, the moral of these stories remained the same: "The nature of our nation is free, stout, haultaine, prodigall of life and bloud," boasted Sir Thomas Smith in the 1560s, "contumelie, beatings, servitude and servile torment and punishment it will not abide." William Harrison echoed Smith in his preface to Holinshed's *Chronicles* by claiming that Englishmen cherished freedom to such a degree that they would sooner suffer death than "yield our bodies unto such servile halings and tearings as are used in other countries." For this reason, Harrison claimed, "our condemned prisoners [go] cheerfully to their deaths, for our nation . . . cannot in any wise digest to be used as villeins and slaves, in suffering continually beating, servitude, and servile torments." Englishmen detested slavery so much, Harrison added, that "if any [slaves] came hither from other realms, so soon as they set foot on land they become so free of condition as their masters, whereby all note of servile bondage is utterly removed from them."[35] As far as English patriots were concerned, there was no overstating the case: one could not be both English and a slave, England was the fountainhead of liberty, and where there was England, there could be no slavery.

English scholars may have disagreed on the particulars, but their collective effort to chart the history of England contributed to a language of slavery and a broader understanding of human bondage in early modern England. Competing arguments continued to circulate about whether slavery was an institution buttressed by natural law, as the Aristotelian tradition would have it, or the law of man, as the Roman *Digest* characterized the situation. However, Englishmen uniformly celebrated their national rejection of slavery and liked to claim that England itself was enlivened by the struggle against slavery. But just how widely did these ideas circulate? Historical and antiquarian writings could inform popular conceptions of human bondage to a limited degree.[36] Therefore, *how* people may have developed thoughts about slavery, including both what it meant to be a slave and what slavery entailed for a society as a whole, must be conceptualized beyond the important but limited confines of religious and intellectual traditions.

*   *   *

Whatever rhetoric existed about the sacrosanct freedoms of Englishmen, there was a remarkable disparity between the pious proclamations made for public and transnational consumption and social practice in English cities and the countryside. The mythological freeborn Englishman who would rather suffer death than endure bondage actually inhabited a society where human bondage was perpetuated by conscious design. Indeed, just as Tudor Englishmen were increasingly inclined to insist that they were unique in both a global and European context in their commitment to liberty, there was a perceptible rise in the incidences of human bondage within England and some serious discussion that the nation could benefit from the application of certain kinds of slavery in unique circumstances.

If slavery was rare in Tudor England, it had been much more common in earlier eras. As late as the eleventh century, at least 25,000 slaves, roughly 10 percent of the total population, could be found scattered throughout England.[37] In certain counties, such as Cornwall and Gloucester, the number of slaves was significant, perhaps comprising more than 20 percent of the population. Even so, it is difficult to argue that the plight of slaves in medieval England was exceptionally harsh. The use of slaves (*nativi* or *servi*) in agricultural labor had been common throughout the medieval period, yet the social and economic status of slaves in England does not appear to have been all that different from the lower orders of free society (the *villani*, *bordarii*, and *cotarii*). Human bondage may therefore have been an even more galling issue to the English because they were a favored target for slave traders during the medieval period. The future St. Patrick, who was born in southwestern England, was famously taken and sold into slavery in Ireland while still a teenager. The Venerable Bede, writing in the eighth century, reported that the soon-to-be Pope Gregory the Great was first introduced to Englishmen in a Roman slave market when he came across "some boys put up for sale, with fair complexions, handsome faces, and lovely hair" who identified themselves as Britons. William of Malmesbury, a twelfth-century Benedictine monk and historian, recorded that some medieval English rulers were "in the habit of purchasing companies of slaves in England, and sending them into Denmark; more especially the girls, whose beauty and age rendered them more valuable." In the northern regions, according to eleventh- and twelfth-century English chroniclers, "whoever seemed suitable for work" by invading Scots, was "driven bound before the enemy" and "Scotland was filled with English slaves."[38]

During the twelfth and thirteenth centuries, largely as a result of long-term economic, social, and religious transformations, Anglo-Norman lords unfettered their enslaved plowmen and oxherds.[39] Similarly, the practice of preying on English men and women to serve as slaves in foreign lands also diminished. Nonetheless, a perpetual and an inheritable unfree status continued to characterize the lives of many of the lower orders of late medieval English society. Rather than liberating their slaves outright, masters simply reclassified many of their bondmen as serfs.[40] Parallel to this transition from slavery to serfdom was the simultaneous reduction in status under the law of a group of people categorized as free in the *Domesday Book* at the end of the eleventh century—the *villani*. Serfdom and villeinage, terms often imprecisely used interchangeably, actually have distinct points of origin in the English past. Serfs, in general, were the descendants of enslaved peoples from the Conquest Era (those listed as *nativi*, or the unfree by birth, in the *Domesday Book*). Thus, although the medieval legal scholar Andrew Horn characterized villeins rather innocuously in the late fourteenth century as "cultivators of the fee, dwelling in upland villages," he pitied the plight of serfs who, as "*servi a servando,*"could not own anything in their own name—"they do not know in the evening what service they will do in the morning, and there is nothing certain in their services. The lords may put them in fetters and in the stocks, may imprison, beat and chastise them at will, saving their lives and limbs." If legal slavery perished in medieval England, then, human bondage involving physical and psychological coercion, as well as other traditional characteristics of unfreedom, persisted.[41]

Although some observers continued to emphasize distinctions between the originally free villeins and the serfs who descended from slaves, these subtleties became increasingly irrelevant as the customary exactions of legal unfreedom were applied to both groups in the late medieval period. Even in Horn's lifetime, English lords expected villeins to labor on their behalf, pay death duties (*heriot*), pay their lords upon the marriage of a son or daughter (*merchet*), pay for permission to sell livestock (*toll*), and pay an annual tax (*arbitrary tallage*). English lords treated villeins and serfs equally as chattel. Lords, or masters, could even exercise the customary prerogative common to all slave cultures of selling their bondmen. Certainly, some villeins benefited from protective rights that prevented them from lapsing into a state of categorical slavery. Despite the common-law notion that the property of bondmen was ultimately the lord's property, many villeins also acquired their own property and defended it in their own name, according to the medieval doctrine of possession.[42] Still, their legal status placed them in a precarious position and there was often little they could do to protect themselves from persistent or opprobrious lords.

Technically, villeins were not slaves, but many of those who remained in the archaic condition seem to have believed there was little in their status to distinguish them from that lowliest of conditions. Bondmen and their sympathizers were quite vocal about the abuses they suffered and repeatedly pointed out the problem of reconciling the rights of freeborn Englishmen with the rights of English lords over their human property. In the fourteenth century, Geoffrey Chaucer asserted in the homily of the Parson's Tale that bondage was not a natural condition and condemned those who "taken they of hire bond-men amercimentz [i.e., a discretionary penalty or fine], whiche myghten moore resonably be cleped extorcions than amercimentz. Of which amercimentz and raunsonynge of boonde-men somme lordes stywardes seyn that it is rightful, for as muche as a cherl hath no termporeel thing that it ne is his lordes."[43] John Fitzherbert reiterated this point in 1523 when he mentioned that despite manumissions, "in some places bondemen conynue as yet." Worse, he continued, "there be many freman taken as bondmen, and their lands and goodes taken from them so that they shal nat be able to sue for remedy, to prove them selfe fre of blode." Fortunately, for sixteenth-century bondmen, Tudor monarchs generally sympathized with villeins and several blanket manumissions were issued during the era as the Crown sought to clear the landscape of the remnants of a system of perpetual and inheritable bondage.[44]

Precisely because of the perception that there was a relationship between villeinage and slavery, aggrieved Englishmen, many of whom found themselves subject to the whims of others because of their tainted bloodlines, were able to find recourse to justice in the Court of Common Requests, a body that was frequently referred to as the "Court of Poor Men's Cases." In *Netheway v. Gorge* (1534) the Court of Requests was confronted with a case that exemplified the plight of bondmen who, according to tradition, had no right to personal property. Sir Edward Gorge, lord of the manor of Walton in Somersetshire, dispatched an agent to purchase an ox from the plaintiff, William Netheway. Gorge's agent agreed to pay 29s. for the ox, but when Netheway demanded payment the money was withheld. Gorge informed the court that the plaintiff was his bondman and, therefore, the ox was already his property. The court conceded the legitimacy of this claim, but it also recognized that public opinion forbade the enforcement of the dated notions of villeinage. Thus, the royal commissioners pressured the defendant in this case to pay the full value of the disputed ox.[45]

In other words, although the government was clearly inclined to side with supposed bondmen, based in great part on the increasingly powerful notion of the presumptive freedom of Englishmen, the continuing legitimacy of villeinage under the law allowed for abuses during the Tudor era. In 1535, John Bourchier, who would become the first Earl of Bath a year later, seized goods valued at £400 from a man named Burde. Bourchier made no pretense of purchase in this case; as in the case of *Netheway v. Gorge*, this was just another example of the legal spoilation of a purported bondman. In response, then, Burde petitioned the Council of the West in 1539, which ordered the restitution of the disputed goods. The first Earl of Bath had died the previous year, but his son took up the fight by not only disregarding the order but also seizing additional items in October 1540. Eventually the plaintiff petitioned King Henry VIII directly and in February 1541 the order to pay for the seized items was endorsed by a writ of Privy Seal from Hampton Court. Still, the earl refused to comply until the threat of a fine prompted him to restore the goods in 1544. Even so, in the less assured political climate following Henry's death in 1547 and the subsequent downfall of Protector Somerset in 1549, the earl once again seized horses and cattle from Burde. In this last instance, before the records fall silent, the Earl of Bath defended his actions by emphasizing that he and his father had been within their rights all along because the ancestor who had enfranchised Burde's ancestor had exceeded his legal right—he could actually only liberate for the term of his own life; upon his death, though, the subsequent Earls of Bath could legally reclaim the family's legacy.[46]

The Bourchier family was not the first to claim that the manumissions of a previous generation were nonbinding. In the case of *Carter v. the Abbot of Malmesbury* in 1500, the plaintiff complained to the Court of the Star Chamber that he could not be held against his will because his grandfather had been liberated. The Abbot of Malmesbury, who seized Carter, threw him in prison, and confiscated his substantial holdings in sheep and cattle, defended his actions by claiming that Carter was not free man but a "vylleyne and bondman regardaunt." Carter, however, produced witnesses to corroborate his claim he had been treated cruelly and that his grandfather had been manumitted. Although the records again fall silent, it seems likely that Carter succeeded in passing the litmus test of descent. Without absolute proof that the ancestors of the person claimed were villeins, no English lord could hold an individual in bondage. Even if servile linkage was established, the maternal line of descent was disallowed and only one male was considered insufficient evidence. At the same time, one free male progenitor typically cleared an entire family of the stain of bondage. In effect, the burden of proving whether an individual was bound or free was increasingly falling in the hands of the lords. The presumption of freedom was clearly ascendant in sixteenth-century England.[47]

The language used by the Abbot of Malmesbury reveals an important distinction concerning the present condition of bondmen in Tudor England. Legal differentiation among different kinds of bondmen that had existed in the past furthered the widespread notion that there were no slaves in England by the sixteenth century. Most, if not all, slaves had in fact been manumitted, or enserfed, nearly four centuries earlier and few people remained in an actual state of either serfdom or villeinage. Nonetheless, some English writers were careful to specify the precise nature of the bondmen that could be found in Tudor society. Sir Thomas Smith, Queen Elizabeth's occasional ambassador to France and Secretary of State in the 1570s, produced an entire chapter on the subject in his *De Republia Anglorum*. Smith declared that, according to Roman tradition, there were two kinds of bondmen, "one which were called *servi*, [who] were bought for money, taken in warre, left by succession, or purchased by other kinde and lawful acquisition, or else borne of their bonde women and called *vernae*." Collectively, Smith noted, these people were known in England as "villeins in gross," while the others were called "*adscripticij glebae*, or *agri censii*. These were not bond to the person, but to the mannor or place, and did followe him who had the manors. Those in our lawe are called villaines [regardants]." For the benefit of his continental audience, Smith claimed that he never encountered any of the first type in the realm, and of the second kind, "so few there be, that it is not almost worth the speaking. But our lawe doth acknowledge them in both those sorts."[48] Smith conceded, then, that slavery existed in England although only in a theoretical sense or as a legal artifact.

Although the distinction between two different legal categories of unfreedom were useful in court cases and commentaries penned for foreign and domestic audiences, English villeins saw little in the subtle distinction between "villeinage in gross" and "villeinage regardant" to soothe their souls. Those at the bottom of the social and economic ladder prided themselves as much as elites on England's mythical national commitment to liberty and they were not above reminding their countrymen about the anachronistic role of bondage in English society. During the spring and summer of 1549, for example, East Anglia erupted in one of the most sustained popular uprisings in Tudor England. Kett's Rebellion, as it came to be known, began when Norfolk villagers leveled the hedges of a landlord who had enclosed a portion of the common land. The uprising was sustained, however, by a deeper concern with local issues and the perception that there was a notable absence of "good government" responsive to the needs of all people. To make their grievances clear, the rebels submitted twenty-nine articles, one of which was the brash declaration that "all bonde men . . . be made ffre for god made all ffre with his precious blode sheddying."[49] Smith may have comforted himself with the notion that human bondage was exceedingly rare, but the Norfolk rebels thought otherwise.

Kett's Rebellion was not really about slavery, of course, but the inclusion of this one brief statement attests to the scope of popular notions of English freedoms, and human bondage, during the sixteenth century. Like the western shires of Gloucester and Somerset, the East Anglian counties of Norfolk and Suffolk were the main centers of the lingering vestiges of villeinage in Tudor England.[50] One of the most important families in the region was the Howards, the dukes of Norfolk. The Howard family fell from power in 1546 when the third duke of Norfolk was attainted, which led to the family's lands reverting to the Crown. Subsequently, twenty-six heads of families from four Suffolk manors, formerly held by the Howards, petitioned Protector Somerset for manumission. The bondmen complained about how they had been treated by the Duke of Norfolk, who had "spoiled your said oratours of any their landes and tenementes, goddes and cattalles . . . with such extremitie void of any compassion pietie or reason." Bondmen were not allowed "to marrye accordyng to the lawes of god ne yet to sette any of their children to schoole or to any kynde of learnyng without exaccions and fines."[51]

The grievances of Tudor bondmen ultimately bore fruit. More than forty-six former Howard family villeins would find their way to freedom through a series of manumissions enacted after 1550.[52] Aggrieved bondmen were often successful because their interests paralleled the desire of the Tudor government to put to rest for good the last vestiges of serfdom in England. Throughout the sixteenth century, on a number of occasions, the Crown made individual or sweeping manumissions, or attempted to compel English lords to free the bondmen in their possession. Tudor monarchs, however, often met fierce resistance when they tried to convince English lords to free their bondmen. In 1538, Henry VIII's minister, Thomas Cromwell, requested the Earl of Arundel to manumit one of his bondmen. Arundel resisted, however, responding that Thomas Goodfreye "is in truth my bondman, as all his progenitors have been, and if I made him free it would be to the prejudice of my inheritance for ever. I should be glad to gratify you otherwise in a better thing." Cromwell was equally unsuccessful in convincing Dr. John London to manumit the Alweyes family, bondmen in his college's possession in Colern. London, who had previously been encouraged in this endeavor by Sir Henry Long and the Bishop of Winchester, protested that the college's governing statutes would allow him to "alienate neither land nor bondmen." But, even if he could liberate the family, he was not inclined to do so because the head of the family, the "reve and overseer of my college wood, wastes the woods and conceals the rents." London, it seems, believed that some people deserved bondage.[53]

Although Tudor monarchs sympathized with the plight of their bound subjects, they rarely did more than issue polite requests for the manumission of villeins not in the Crown's possession. In 1507, Henry VII stretched the limit of prerogative when he granted a charter for three new Welsh counties that proclaimed a general manumission for the local *nativi*. This exceptional case of a Tudor monarch liberating his subjects' property angered some of his lords, who expressed their displeasure when they subsequently rejected the general bill *concernes Manumissionem sevorum vocat. Bondmen*.[54] Thus, the best hope for bondmen with aspirations of free status was for the estate to which they were bound to fall into royal hands. In 1550, Edward VI commissioned Sir Richard Sakevile, chancellor of Augmentations, to manumit "those vyllaynes and nefes aswell regardant to our honours lordeshippes and mannours as otherwyse in gros not yet manumysed and dyscharged of their bondage." Later, Sakevile came to terms with William Cuckoo, "bocher," and his brother John, "villeins regardant" to the manor of Ersham. After paying £3.6.8, "William and John and their *sequela*" were manumitted and given rights to their goods and lands. Although they had to pay for their freedom, and although manumissions were often compulsory, evidence suggests that Tudor monarchs were eager to destroy villeinage once and for all in part because of the perception that it was a form of domestic slavery. In what may have been the most important reason of all, simply "hating slavery (*servituti odientes*)" moved Edward VI to manumit four Suffolk men in 1551.[55]

Elizabeth followed in the footsteps of her father and half-brother when she attempted to resolve the status of "divers and sundry of our poor faithful and loyal subjects" who had been "born bond in blood and regardant to divers and sundry our manors and possessions within our realm of England."

In 1574, she ordered that the bondmen in four counties be "enfranchised and made free, with their children and sequels." In 1575, Elizabeth licensed Sir Henry Lee, a minor courtier at the time, to free additional bondmen. Lee's first order of business was to determine how much money the queen's villeins would be required to pay for their freedom. Once Lee and the bondmen in question came to an agreement, a charter of manumission was drawn up espousing the firm belief that "God created all men free by nature, and the law of man placed some under the yoke of servitude." Thus, it would be "a pious thing, and acceptable to God and consonant with Christian charity" to free all bondmen. To this end, and for the greater good of his own and the royal coffers, Lee rounded up and manumitted at least 137 families, comprising nearly 500 individuals, between 1575 and 1580.[56]

Tudor initiatives like these aside, unfree Englishmen—villeins—continued to inhabit England well into the sixteenth century and they continued to be preyed upon by dissolute lords. One English lord, Edward Stafford, even went so far as to try to seize the mayor of Bristol, Richard Cole, as his villein during the 1580s. Still, the continuing presence of a small number of villeins did not diminish the widespread notion that England was, by nature, a free nation. In 1567, for example, Cartwright's Case in the Star Chamber addressed the possibility of holding a Russian in bondage. Cartwright "brought a slave from Russia . . . for which he was questioned; and it was resolved that England was too pure an air for slaves to breathe in." England was hardly unique in asserting its "free air," but the case did demonstrate the powerful belief among jurists that everyone under common law was free by nature of their Englishness. At the same time, the notion that the English nation was free did not necessarily mean that human bondage was entirely unacceptable. As the Cartwright ruling asserted, England was no place for slaves, but the relics of medieval forms of human bondage could not be totally destroyed so long as English freedom also included the right of individuals to defend their ownership of human property.[57]

The history of domestic bondage in the sixteenth century highlights the paradoxical relationship between Englishness and slavery, for what offended most during this period was not the propriety of slavery but the arbitrary nature of a system of human bondage based entirely on descent. How, Englishmen might wonder, was it possible to be born both free (by virtue of being born in England) and in bondage (by descent)? Repeated references to the idea that God had created human beings free and that only the law could take that away undermined villeinage, especially when bondmen could assert that their condition was tantamount to slavery. Moreover, if England was, by nature or tradition, a free nation, then the continuing existence of villein-age—an institution that defined some people as unfree by birth alone—was a troublesome indicator that the barrier between slavery and Englishness was not as impenetrable as national mythologizers would have it. In this light, the Tudor government's manumission efforts in the sixteenth century could be interpreted not simply as a scheme to extort those with no rights or a gener-ous plan to liberate individual bondman—as they surely were—but as a much bigger effort to free England, once and for all, from the stain of natural slavery. If English men and women were to be enslaved, there had better be a good reason why and neither birth nor lineage made any sense in the increas-ingly ideologically charged climate of the day.

*　*　*

The religious and intellectual legacy of slavery and decaying domestic institu-tions like manorial villeinage were not the only ways that Englishmen may have experienced bondage, or imagined slavery, in a domestic setting. En-glishmen were also able to witness and experience slavery as a penal institution during the sixteenth century. Penal slavery, however, differed from villeinage in a number of crucial ways. Unlike villeins, penal slaves were not born into bondage, rather they were reduced to slavery as a form of punishment result-ing from their own actions. Penal slavery was clearly punitive, but it is even more interesting because it was also envisaged, in some circles, as a progres-sive form of individual improvement and social control. The idea of slavery as a positive, virtue-instilling institution was most clearly revealed in Thomas More's *Utopia*, which first appeared in a number of Latin editions after 1516. Subsequently, two English translations by Ralph Robinson were published in England in 1551 and 1556. Although More's text was not explicitly concerned with the subject of human bondage, he addressed the subject thoroughly. In particular, as a result of his critique of the arbitrary and harsh punishments suffered by common thieves (which included the death penalty) More sug-gested alternative ways of dealing with criminal behavior. In this vein, in Book One, More lauded the more humane and practical punishment of com-mon criminals in Persia among a group of people styled the "Polylerites."[58] Instead of death, thieves in this fictional land were condemned to be "com-mon servauntes to the common wealth." Lest there be any confusion about the degraded status of these "serving men," as they are termed in Robinson's

English translation, these criminals were clearly marked. They were to be "apparailed in one coloure," their hair was "rounded a lytlte above the eares. And the typpe of one eare is cut off." Moreover, Polylerites rigidly constrained bondmen whom they "locked in theyr chambers" at night, whipped for indolence, declared that they "may touch no weapons," and threatened with death if they "intende[d] to runne awaye," much less "do it in dede." Nonetheless, bondmen were otherwise treated gently, for their "punyshement intendeth nothynge elles, but the destruction of vices, and savynge of menne: wyth so usynge, and ordering them, that they can not chuse but be good." Thus, "everye yeare divers of them be restored to their freedome: throughe the commendation of their patience."[59]

The reasonable—or "worthy and commendable" as Robinson's marginal note indicates—system of slavery More located in Persia agreed with the one More's fictional traveler, Raphael Hythloday, encountered in Utopia.[60] More treated the subject of human bondage quite carefully in Book Two, choosing even to give the subject of slavery its own section heading.[61] Utopians acquired slaves through well-defined channels. First, they did not "make bondemen of prisoners taken in battayle" unless it was a "battaylle that they foughte themselves." Second, Utopians purchased convicted criminals, or those in "other landes [who] for greate trespasses be condemned to death." A third group of slaves consisted of "their owne men," whom "they handle hardest" because "they being so godlye brought up to vertue in soo excelente a common wealth, could not for all that be refreined from misdoing." Finally, Utopians sometimes allowed a "vile drudge" from another country to "chuse of his owne free wyll to be a bondman among them." Utopian slaves, then, were men who suffered such a fate as a result of just wars, because of criminal behavior, or by choice. As More makes clear, Utopians were discriminating when it came to their slaves; neither another nation's prisoners of war nor the "bondmens children" could therefore be counted among the enslaved.[62]

More also characterized Utopian slavery as a purposeful institution, equally so for the enslaved themselves and for Utopian society as a whole. To be sure, bondage was a "miserable & wretched condition" involving "al vile service, all slavery, and drudgerie." At the same time, human bondage could also be viewed as a progressive, virtue-instilling practice that existed as much to redeem wayward individuals as it did to punish them. Because slavery was characterized as an institution that was neither accidental nor capricious, because slavery was something that bondmen could be said to have brought upon themselves by their actions, slavery was less a labor system than it was a social system. Thus, "they, which take theire bondage pacientlye, be not lefte hopeles. For after they have bene broken and tamed with long miseries, if then thei shew such repentaunce . . . theire bondage either be mitigated, or else cleane released and forgeven." And anyone who chose to enslave himself, More added, "they neither hold him against his wyll" or "send him away with emptye handes."[63]

If slavery was ideally a temporary condition for the enslaved, it was nonetheless an integral institution for the proper functioning of the Utopian social order. More imagined, for example, that slaves served a fundamental role in Utopian society by insulating the social order from instability by assigning the most pernicious tasks to slaves. Butchering, hunting, and other "laboursome toyle & base business" were performed by bondmen. Hunting and butchering were singled out as particularly unpleasant and dehumanizing endeavors because "they thinke, clemencye the genteleste affection of our nature" which would "lytle and lytle . . . decaye and peryshe" were free Utopians to perform them. The remarkable virtue of Utopians was, in an important sense, preserved by slavery. Individual slaves might be redeemed, but while they served the needs of Utopians they were a visible reminder of the barbarity and degeneracy of the outer world. Indeed, in the performance of these necessary labors, Utopian slaves were as close to brute "beastes" as humanly possible. Although redemption was the ideal, then, More did not hesitate to suggest that one distinguishing characteristic of slaves was their proximity to the animal world. Therefore, if they "doo rebell and kicke againe, then forsothe they be slayne as desperate and wilde beastes, whom neither prison nor chaine could restraine."[64]

Utopian slavery was a model of human bondage that served to instill a sense of virtue on Utopian society. The sense of honor enjoyed by freedom-loving Utopians necessitated the shame of slavery. There could be no real liberty without real slavery, even if it only served as a visible reminder of what was at stake in society. How else would Utopians appreciate what they had?[65] It was this conception of slavery, as a mechanism by which degenerate individuals could be reformed and redeemed, that was expressed most famously in Tudor society in 1547 when Parliament passed its most extreme penal measure to date, possibly authored by a young Sir Thomas Smith, to attack "idle beggars and sturdy vagabonds." With this act (which was soon repealed), slavery could be imposed on recalcitrant individuals who refused to work; any competent man "not applying them self to some honest and allowed arte, Scyence, service or Labour" could be taken for a vagabond and enslaved for two years. The master would have absolute control over the diet of his bond-men, and could "cawse the saide Slave to work by beating, cheyninge or other-wise in such worke and Labor how vyle so ever it be." The slave could also be leased, sold or bequeathed, as "any other of the master's movable goodes or Catelles." Nonetheless, this conception of slavery differed from the subse-quent New World model, primarily in its purpose, because rather than creat-ing a class of slaves to satisfy labor demands, this law was about the potential laborers themselves. With the 1547 act, Parliament intended to punish but also hoped to instill a sense of virtue, frugality, and hard work and to make workingmen out of idle men.[66]

Galley slavery was the most infamous form of penal slavery in Europe and the Mediterranean. Not surprisingly, it appeared in England, though it seems to have been talked about much more than it was used because tradi-tional oared galleys were not especially practical in the high winds and rough seas of the North Atlantic. European visitors asserted outright that the En-glish, "do not use galleys, owing to the strong tide of the ocean." Still, the English government experimented with galleys for a brief period between the 1540s and 1620s. During his later years, Henry VIII attempted to purchase a coastal defense force of ten fully equipped and furnished galleys from Em-peror Charles V. When that effort failed, subsequent monarchs simply re-commissioned galleys captured from the enemy. Late in Elizabeth's reign, England even inaugurated a modest galley-building program, leading to the construction of five vessels. Ultimately, though, English galleys were rarely used for defense. Most galleys—and there were rarely more than three suit-able for use at any one time—were thought by more practical minds to "serve in dede to lytle purpose." The *Galley Bonavolia*, which had been acquired from the French in 1563, helped chart the Thames estuary and worked as a tug during its otherwise ignoble career.[67]

Considering the checkered history of English galleys, it is remarkable how frequently galley slavery appears in the sources. Legislation and procla-mations allowing for individuals to be condemned to slavery was common during the 1540s. In 1544, the king issued a proclamation ordering alien French to leave England or they would be "sent to his grace's galleys." A year later, the ranks of galley slaves were augmented by other "such ruffians, vaga-bonds, masterless men, common players, and evil-disposed persons" who crossed the government's path. In 1548, the city of London punished Edmund Grymeston for "writing an infamous libel full of reproach" by cutting off his ears at the pillory and sentencing him "to serve in the galleys as a slave during his life." Elizabeth's royal government went even further by making some effort to raise a force of galley slaves. In 1586, Francis Walsingham pressed the queen's solicitor general to make plans to condemn the most vile criminals, "being repryved from execution" to the galleys, which would "both terrify ill disposed persons from offending, and make thos that shall hasard them selves to offend in some sorte proffitable to the common wealthe."[68]

As evidence of the power and persistence of these ideas, two seventeenth-century English knights, Sir William Monson and the reformed pirate Sir Henry Mainwaring, were particularly forthright in their articulation of the advantages of galley slavery. In a discourse on pirates submitted to King James during the 1610s, Mainwaring suggested that in order to reduce the incidence of piracy in Ireland and England, it would be "no ill policy of this State, to make them Slaves, in the nature of Galley-Slaves." "Other Christian Princes use this kind of punishment," Mainwaring noted, "and so convert it to a public profit." Moreover, he continued, "it is observable, that as many as make slaves of offenders, have not any Pirates of their Nation." Monson concurred with Mainwaring, adding that pirates and other criminals "must be shaved both head and face, and marked in the cheek with a hot iron" so that others would "take them to be the King's labourers, for so they should be termed, and not slaves." Both Monson and Mainwaring recognized that the threat of slavery—the term even, in Monson's case—would "terrify and deter them, more than the assurance of Death itself." But echoing the insights found in More's *Utopia*, they also asserted that slavery "will make men avoid sloth and pilfering and apply themselves to labour and pains." And, in a best-case scenario, "it may be a means to save many of their Souls, by giving them a long time of Repentance."[69]

Of course, galley slavery never amounted to much in Britain. In 1589, Sir John Hawkins issued a memorandum on the sea charges of the *Galley Bonavolia*, noting that the ship required 150 slaves to fill its 50 banks. Hawkins, however, did not even feel equipped to provide a budget for food expenditures for the slaves because "we are not yett in the experyence of yt."[70] On the few occasions when an English galley actually took to the sea, it was typically powered by free oarsmen. England's self-styled reputation as a place void of slaves may also have limited the creation of a large force of galley slaves. When the English government returned the captured *Galley Blanchard* to the French in 1547, for example, Henry VIII refused to return its complement of 140 enslaved Neapolitans, Spaniards, and Gascons. For a short while, the men continued to row in chains while being encouraged by English cudgels,

but Henry was advised that the galley would be "some chardge . . . con-
tynewally iff his highness do kepe her styll with her sute of forsados as she ys
nowe." Viscount Lisle, England's lord admiral, suggested instead that Henry
should "gyve fredom and liberty to the sayde forsados at the leaste to as many
as wold take yt wch I think wold be more worth to his [majesty] then the
strength of [four] gallys if ever his [majesty] shold have any more to do with
theym." Besides endearing the former galley slaves to the English monarch,
Lisle believed this measure would send a message to foreign powers who
"wolbe ever in doubt to come nere unto any of the Kyngs [majesty's] navy or
ports for feare of Rendering theym selves unto his highnes."[71]

From the perspective of a number English writers and policy makers,
then, slavery was not something that should be rejected outright because it
was inconsistent with the dignity of England. Human bondage, as most
English authors preferred to label it, was a practical solution to a number of
social ills that, if left unchecked, threatened to do even greater damage to the
integrity of English freedoms and liberties than the institution of slavery ever
could on its own. Although the most negative connotations associated with
slavery galled—most particularly its abject nature—Englishmen like Ralph
Robinson and Sir William Monson believed that the problem could be alle-
viated simply by labeling it as something else. If slavery had no place in early
modern England, a system of human bondage founded on progressive, redemptive ideals was nonetheless a tantalizing notion.

*   *   *

When Walsingham dispatched Hakluyt to Paris in 1583, neither man knew as
much about long-distance, transatlantic navigation and colonialism as they
would have liked. What they did know about and recognize when they saw it
was slavery. To men like Walsingham and Hakluyt, slavery was useful to invoke because it emphasized the precarious grip England held on liberty and
freedom, qualities they believed they enjoyed by virtue of their Protestant
religion and English national identity. As well-educated Englishmen, they
had read plenty about slavery as a result of the literary world they inhabited.
Whether they studied Latin texts or contemporary works and whether they
read secular histories or the Christian Bible, slavery was a subject that could
not be avoided without seriously distorting the sacred and secular worlds
they inhabited. That slavery had once been common but was no longer perhaps comforted some people and highlighted the triumph of English liberty

in a world otherwise bound in chains, both real and metaphorical. But English men and women were also quick to recognize that the new era of domestic and international strife in which they lived threatened to undermine all that they held dear. To be English in the late sixteenth century was tantamount to being free while for others it was not, but that luxury was by no means guaranteed.

Servitude, villeinage, and penal slavery were not the same thing as the institutional system of slavery that would develop in the Atlantic world in later years, but these practices nonetheless encouraged Englishmen to think about slavery. A few individuals also chose to reconceptualize human bondage as a practical, even pragmatic, institution linked with England's past, present, and future.[72] Certainly, in raw numbers slavery itself was ultimately of small import, but its existence and theoretical application nonetheless reveals that, even outside the bounds of religious and intellectual circles, there were domestic reference points from which Englishmen could construct ideas about human bondage. Moreover, the existence of slavery points to a disjuncture between contemporary political rhetoric concerning the inclusive English nation and the social and cultural reality in which Englishness alone might not be enough to guarantee every individual the ideological benefits of his or her own nationhood. Freedom may have been a defining element of English national identity in the era of overseas settlement, but that did not mean that villeinage could not be justified in practice or that recalcitrant Englishmen could not be forced to labor in bondage. Penal slavery, in particular, and vagrancy legislation demonstrate the readiness of Tudor authorities to compel the lower orders to labor—not for labor's sake but for that of society as a whole. Although Tudor elites might rhetorically eschew the arbitrary nature of slavery as perpetual and inheritable, nothing about slavery was deemed unreasonable if individuals brought it upon themselves, if the practice served a social purpose, or if it was directed toward stabilizing and preserving, paradoxically, the idea of freedom in England.

These domestic touchstones, however, did not exist in a vacuum. While English elites were ruminating on the practical application of domestic slavery or thinking about the relationship between Englishness and liberty, many of their fellow countrymen were coming to terms with the reality that the larger world in which they lived was rife with slavery. England was an island nation, but it was far from a world unto itself. As English travelers, merchants, soldiers, sailors, and others began to explore and learn more about distant lands, exotic cultures, and often mysterious peoples, they were struck by the seemingly countless ways human beings could be treated as brute beasts and cheap commodities. In many places, slavery was not so much contemplated as it was merely noted; in certain arenas, however, English travelers and writers could not resist the temptation to register a profound sense of disgust and horror at the sufferings of the enslaved. On the one hand, a fuller awareness of the prevalence of human bondage and the important role that slavery played throughout the world facilitated an emerging sense of English exceptionalism. On the other hand, slavery's pervasiveness on the global stage presented Englishmen with new challenges, new possibilities, and a new opportunity to define the relationship between Englishness and slavery.

Slaves the World Over: Early English Encounters with Slavery

England stepped purposely onto the global stage during the second half of the sixteenth century as its merchants, sailors, emigrants, bureaucrats, and adventurers fanned out across the globe in search of new lands, new trade routes, and new commodities. The English had not been well represented among the first wave of Europeans who pushed out into the Atlantic world during the early stages of long-distance navigation and global exploration during the late fifteenth century. That, however, changed dramatically during the Elizabethan era. In the opening pages of the 1589 edition of his *Principall Navigations*, Richard Hakluyt boasted that "in searching the most opposite corners and quarters of the world" and "in compassing the vaste globe of the earth more than once," the English "have excelled all the nations and people of her earth."[1] If Hakluyt's patriotism inclined him to overstate the case, little doubt remained about the rapidly escalating English interest in the affairs of the world. Even if they stayed at home, where they might discover many of the same new worlds in published accounts or witness foreign lands and strange peoples on stage or experience rare and unusual items as consumers, countless Englishmen were beginning to see themselves as part of an expanding and diverse world in motion. But as much as English eyes were captivated, in the words of Richard Willes in 1577, by "the different manners & fashions of divers nations, the wonderfull workes of nature, the sightes of straunge trees, fruites, foule, and beastes, [and] the infinite treasure of Pearle, Golde, [and] Silver," the English had reasons to be cautious.[2] As more wary observers were quick to recognize, the world beyond England's shores promised great rewards, but the potential dangers were many. Not least among these was slavery, a subject that never ceased to impress English authors and publishers or, apparently, simultaneously fascinate and horrify English readers.

It would have been difficult for perceptive travelers and careful readers in the early modern era to avoid the conclusion that slavery was a universal institution. Many works that appeared in print during the late Tudor and early Stuart eras spoke to the subject in a rather matter-of-fact fashion. When Jean Bodin's *Six Books of a Commonweale* appeared in English in 1606, many Englishmen were already aware of the writings of the French jurist from the Latin and French editions of his previous works. Bodin treated slavery as a widespread human institution that began "immediately after the general deluge" before it diminished for a time but was "now againe approved, by the agreement and consent of almost all nations." Regardless of religious or governmental considerations, slavery existed everywhere. From the West Indies, whose people "never heard speech of the lawes of God or man" to places characterized by greater degrees of civility or where Europeans expected to find "the holiest men that ever lived," slaves were ubiquitous. Like many of his contemporaries, Bodin concluded that human bondage—in all its possible manifestations—was the likely condition of a majority of the world's peoples. Of course, this depiction shocked no one in England, many of whom claimed that they lived in a land largely untouched by slavery even as they recognized that their situation was exceptional in that regard.[3]

Similar conclusions could be gleaned from another French author, Pierre Charron, whose treatise *Of Wisdom* was translated into English by Samson Lennard in the early seventeenth century (and subsequently reprinted eight other times before 1700). Charron declared that "the use of slaves . . . is a thing both monstrous and ignominious in the nature of man." Charron noted that the "law of *Moyses* hath permitted this as other things, . . . but not such as hath beene elsewhere: for it was neither so great, nor so absolute, nor perpetuall, but moderated within the compasse of seven yeeres at the most." Charron recognized, as most Englishmen did also, that different types of slavery existed, but that, in essence, slaves "have no power neither in their bodies nor their goods, but are wholly their masters, who may give, lend, sell, resell, exchange, and use them as beasts of services."[4] From the perspective of the enslaved, human bondage must have seemed completely arbitrary, involving as it did the total loss of self-determination, dehumanization, and emasculation. From a comfortable remove, however, slavery was more unfortunate than tragic, a comprehensible institution if only because it was so common.

But the English did not need the French to tell them about slavery. English authors were equally capable of lamenting the continued presence of human bondage and the plight of the enslaved. Slavery's pervasiveness could easily be gleaned from some of the more important geographical and historical works of the day, especially the multivolume collections issued by Richard Hakluyt and Samuel Purchas between the 1580s and 1620s. Hakluyt and Purchas sought to celebrate past English achievements and ongoing overseas activities, as well as to promote English expansionism. There were, however, important differences between Hakluyt's late sixteenth-century volumes (1582, 1589, and 1598–1600) and the even more extensive collections published by Purchas a generation later (1613, 1614, 1617, and 1625). Hakluyt devoted himself to memorializing English accomplishments and urged his countrymen to pursue evermore distant and potentially profitable voyages of discovery. He was particularly excited about the potential wealth that might be drawn from American enterprises, although the future development of large-scale plantations was arguably less important in his publications than the broader themes of commerce, exploration, and English national greatness.[5] Purchas borrowed from and extended Hakluyt's scholarly enterprise, but his selections and emendations indicate that he was both a less discriminating editor and more beholden to a particularly overweening theological perspective. Protestant providencialism, perhaps even more than any sense of English patriotism, weighed heavily on Purchas's otherwise richly detailed and varied collections and they are not necessarily the better for it.[6]

Regardless of their differences, Hakluyt and Purchas presented material that revealed the depth and breadth of slavery throughout the world. Indeed, in the opening pages of his *Hakluytus Posthumus, or, Purchas His Pilgrimes*, printed in four large volumes in 1625, Purchas reflected on the subject of bondage in religious, philosophical, and historical terms. "Christians," he noted as a kind of operating premise to his larger work, "are not their own." "Hee then that is Christs, is a new Creature, to which, bondage or freedome and other worldly respects, are meere respects and circumstances." Slavery, at least as far as the Anglican cleric Samuel Purchas would have it, needed to be understood in metaphysical terms before it could be fully appreciated as a physical condition or secular institution that bore down upon the nameless and numberless masses. Englishmen needed to appreciate their indebtedness to God—"[H]ee that denieth himselfe and his owne will, puts off the chaines of his bondage, the slavery to innumerable tyrants, [and] impious lusts"—before they could come to terms with the worldly slavery endured by so many individuals and nations.[7] Whether they did as Purchas asked, however, Englishmen encountered slavery wherever they traveled, used its presence to shape their conception of newfound peoples and places, and continued to think more carefully about how—as Englishmen—they were unique in their national antipathy for human bondage.

*   *   *

If slavery was a global phenomenon, the English did not have to travel far to find it. On the European continent, particularly in those lands that bordered the Mediterranean, slavery was a vital institution, largely as a result of internecine conflict between the Christian powers and Islam. Slavery had largely disappeared as an institution of any significant cultural or economic importance in northern Europe during the medieval era. To the south, however, slavery persisted. In Italy, large numbers of Russians, Slavs, Greeks, and Muslims were held in bondage, but sub-Saharan Africans could also be found in increasing numbers among the enslaved. European slaves from the Black Sea and Balkan regions were less common on the Iberian Peninsula, but large numbers of captured Muslims and prisoners-of-war from other parts of the Mediterranean world filled the ranks of the unfree. In both places, the pattern was much the same: An array of people, regardless of their physical appearance or religion, could be found in bondage. After the fourteenth century, non-European and largely non-Christian slaves were increasingly prevalent as physical appearance and religion began to serve as more absolute indicators of an individual's legal status. The rise of sub-Saharan African slaves was particularly important. In places where the *Reconquista* had been achieved, as in Portugal, European buyers acquired Africans through peaceful trade networks that linked southern Europe to a vibrant and extensive trans-Saharan market. By the first decade of the sixteenth century, even the recently recaptured city of Granada, once the center of Moorish civilization on the Iberian peninsula, engaged in a slave trade that was two-thirds black.[8]

But if slavery was common in southern Europe, that reality could have been missed by Englishmen who were often looking elsewhere during the early Elizabethan era. English privateers and pirates coursed Mediterranean waters in small numbers, but escalating tensions between Protestant England

and the Catholic powers made it difficult for English merchants and mariners to ply their trade in the region, at least before 1580. The English government and merchant community did, however, cast about other regions in
search of profitable trade and in the process a handful of travelers came face-
to-face with human bondage. English engagement with Russia, to pick an early
example, brought the subject of continental slavery close to home, not least
because it was the previously noted plight of a Russian slave that prompted the
Star Chamber in 1567 to declare that England was "too pure an air for slaves
to breathe in." Russia, in and of itself, interested most Englishmen to a limited degree, but of more interest was its value as a highway to places that really sparkled in the imagination of those people who dreamed of wealth and
power. Much as early Portuguese awareness of and involvement in the African
slave trade was a by-product of Portugal's effort to circumvent Africa, the
search for a northeast passage to the Indies at midcentury and curiosity about
alternate routes to Persia led to the creation of the Muscovy Company in 1555.
The Muscovy Company dispatched ships annually to Russia and controlled
English trade to the Middle East for about a generation, sending out six separate expeditions to Persia via the northern route in search of valuable silks
and spices before the Ottoman Turks curtailed the trade in 1580.[9] Russia,
therefore, provided one of the earliest opportunities for the English to witness
and write about slavery as it was practiced in contemporary settings.

Human bondage was an inescapable reality in the Russian environs described so vividly by the early trader Anthony Jenkinson, who made his first
trip to the region in 1557, and Giles Fletcher, who was sent to Russia as a special
ambassador in 1588.[10] Both Jenkinson and Fletcher located the hub of slavery
in the central Asian regions on the southern border of Russia. There, Jenkinson observed, slavery manifested itself prominently in the form of concubinage. Jenkinson even attributed some of the internal turmoil he witnessed to
the absence of "natural love among them, by reason that they are begotten of
divers women, and commonly they are the children of slaves." Slavery was so
common in Bokhara that merchants from India and Persia attended the famous bazaars, in part, to purchase Christian slaves. Even Jenkinson came
away with some slaves. When he boarded a ship on the Caspian Sea for his
return trip to Moscow, he had with him "25. Russes, which had been slaves a
long time in Tartaria, nor ever had before my comming, libertie, or meanes
to gette home, and these slaves served to rowe when neede was." Upon reach-
ing Moscow in late 1559, he demonstrated his willingness to participate in
the indigenous system of bondage and exchange by presenting some of his

slaves to the Tsar as a sign of his gratitude for the favors bestowed on English traders.[11]

Giles Fletcher's travels were not nearly as wide-ranging as those of Jenkinson, but he also provided an insightful picture of human bondage in sixteenth-century Russia. Indeed, Russian slavery may have been relatively easy for Fletcher to grasp, involving as it did categories familiar in contemporary English discourse on the subject. Fletcher was deeply interested in the plight of "the poor people that are now oppressed with intollerable servitude," such that "people for the most part . . . wishe for some forreine invasion, which they suppose to bee the onely meanes, to rid them of the heavy yoke of this tyrannous government." Everyone, in Fletcher's mind, suffered from an absence of political liberty, but he believed "that there is no servant nor bondslave more awed by his Maister, nor kept downe in more servile subjection, then the poore people are." In his description of "Novograde," Fletcher elaborated on the situation of Scythian slaves who had rebelled but were then subsequently put down by their masters with nothing more than horsewhips "to put them in remembrance of their servile condition, thereby to terrifie them, & abate their courage." Continuing to emphasize the parallels between slaves and animals, Fletcher recounted how the chastened slaves "fled altogether like sheepe before the drivers."[12] Outside Russia proper, Fletcher characterized the Tartars, or Mongols, in even less flattering terms as a people who engaged in more extensive forms of human bondage. Fletcher claimed that the "chiefe bootie the *Tartars* seeke for in all their warres, is to get store of captives, specially yong boyes, and girls, whom they sell to the *Turkes*, or other their neighbors." These eastern slave raiders, however, had little patience or compassion for their victims, such that if any of their captives "happen to tyer, or to be sicke on the way, they dash him against the ground, or some tree, and so leave him dead."[13]

English governmental affairs and commercial interests inspired curiosity about Russia and the reports of English merchants, including what they had to say about slavery, indicate that even though Russia was located nearby (at least on a global scale), geographic proximity had little bearing on cultural similarity. Russians were different and their active embrace of slavery was a clear indication of that difference. This point was made even more baldly when the English turned their attention to Ireland. Tudor and Stuart Englishmen thought and wrote about Ireland a great deal, arguably more than any other place in the world in the early modern era.[14] When they did so, they rarely had nice things to say. Collectively, Scotland, Wales, and Ireland constituted the English marchlands during the early modern era. Beginning in the eleventh century, the Norman kings inaugurated what turned out to be a protracted, grinding effort to subdue these territories and their inhabitants under Anglo-Norman rule. Medieval Scotland and Wales were less unified nations than ill-defined regions consisting of multiple hotly contested principalities and fiefdoms whose inhabitants posed a serious threat to their English neighbors. During the eleventh and twelfth centuries, Scots repeatedly invaded northern England. As a result, the English chronicler Symeon of Durham lamented, "Scotland was filled with English slaves." The invasion of 1138, John of Hexam detailed, led to the death of countless men while "the maidens and widows, naked, bound with ropes, were driven off to Scotland in crowds to the yoke of slavery."[15] The attempt by King Edward I, and other English monarchs, to subdue the Scots was partly an effort to extend English sovereignty, but English incursions were also designed to eliminate slave raiding on the northern frontier.

The situation in Ireland was different. Most Englishmen subscribed to long-held and deeply embedded derogatory ideas about the Irish people, ideas that often drew directly on the foundational writing of Gerald of Wales, the twelfth-century chronicler who had journeyed to Ireland in 1185 with an Anglo-Norman force led by the future King John. Gerald's scurrilous characterizations were the rhetorical armament of an invading army, but they proved long-lasting and his observations were translated into English and reprinted, or echoed, throughout the sixteenth and seventeenth centuries.[16] In Gerald's telling, the Irish were naked, wild, and unfriendly people who had more in common with animals than with men. Or, in the unguarded words of Andrew Trollope in a letter to Francis Walsingham written in 1581, the Irish "are not christian, civil human creatures, but heathen or rather savages and brute beasts" who "go commonly all naked." Clearly intent on making sure Walsingham did not miss the point, Trollope added that "[i]f hell were open and all the evil spirits abroad, they could never be worse than these Irish rogues—rather dogs or worse than dogs." Or, most famously, in Edmund Spenser's telling, the Irish "steal; they are cruel and bloody, full of revenge and delighting in deadly execution, licentious swearers and blasphemers, common ravishers of women and murderers of children."[17]

Of course, English observers routinely heaped scorn on all sorts of people throughout the world, but the Irish were favored targets because foreign observers could easily compare them with the English. Unlike the people and societies that might be found throughout the Mediterranean world, Asia,

Africa, or the Americas, the only thing that separated the Irish from the English was a short stretch of easily navigable water. On the surface, as Barnabe
Rich noted, "the English, Scottish, and Irish are easy to be discerned from all
the nations of the world, besides as well by the excellency of their complexions as by all the rest of their lineaments, from the crown of the head, to the
sole of the foot." All the peoples of the British Isles were more alike than unlike and therefore the supposed barbarity of the Irish people and the rudeness
of their customs were problems in need of explaining. How was it, Rich
wondered, "that a countrey scituate and seated under so temperate a Climate" could be "more uncivill, more uncleanly, more barbarous, and more
brutish . . . then any other part of the world that is knowne"?[18] Colonialism
needed to be justified, but who the Irish really were was an even bigger problem because that question could not be addressed without broaching the
larger problem of what it meant to be English, a problem that confronted
England repeatedly from the late medieval through the early modern era.[19]

Ireland therefore presented England with a series of overlapping social,
political, and cultural challenges that were worked out over the course of
many generations.[20] Predictably, English commentators addressed the subject of slavery in Ireland, but they did so in curious ways during the sixteenth
and early seventeenth centuries. Although the English had been in Ireland
since the late twelfth century, their control over the island was generally limited to the area around Dublin—the so-called Irish Pale—and often hotly
contested. During the sixteenth century, a series of local rebellions took place
that shaped English colonialism on the island. In the wake of Thomas Fitzgerald's failed rebellion in 1534, Henry VIII recommitted the English government to imposing its sovereignty on the island, even having himself declared
"king" rather than "lord" of Ireland in 1541. This effort met with stern resistance throughout the rest of the century, most famously during two large-
scale conflicts: the Second Desmond Rebellion (1579–83), which sought to
eject the English from Munster, and Tyrone's Rebellion (1594–1603), led by
the capable Hugh O'Neill, which spread outward from Ulster and nearly succeeded in defeating the English.[21] The bloody effort to impose English rule in
Ireland, and the refusal of both the Anglo-Irish and Gaelic Irish to be brought
to heel, combined therefore to create a compelling rationale for English invaders
to write about slavery.

Irish resistance to English suzerainty virtually demanded character as-
sassination in order to justify the ongoing efforts to (re)conquer the island.

Considering the ease with which English propagandists denigrated the Irish, it should come as no surprise that would-be English conquerors routinely justified the continuing effort to subdue the Irish by expressing their profound sympathy for "the country people living under the lords' absolute power as slaves." "[U]nder the sun," Sir Philip Sidney concluded in the 1570s, "there is not a nation which live more tyrannously than they do, one over the other." In 1567, English officials accused the rebellious Earl of Desmond of treating the inhabitants of Cork "as in effecte they are or were become his Thralls or Slaves." In 1592, Sir Henry Bagenal reported to Lord Burghley that because the English had allowed the local lords to maintain control of large swaths of land, Irish leaders had "been enabled to enslave all their tenants" and maintain their independence from English rule. In an even more extensive treatment, Sir John Davies, who served in Ireland as Attorney-General and, eventually, Speaker of the Irish Parliament, claimed that the problem with the Irish was not their basic nature but that "such as are oppressed and live in slavery are ever put to their shifts." Irish laws and traditions, and the oppressive rule and extortions of Irish lords, had simultaneously promoted tyranny from above and made "the tenant a very slave and villain, and in one respect more miserable than bondslaves, for commonly the bondslave is fed by his lord, but here the lord was fed by his bondslave."[22]

Because early modern Englishmen were routinely critical of slavery as it existed throughout the world, these accusations are unsurprising. In Ireland, however, slavery provided English apologists with a weapon to claim that they were actually engaged in a war to liberate the mass of poor, downtrodden Irish from the bondage that was imposed on them by their own lords. They recognized, of course, that slavery was a double-edged rhetorical sword. Barnabe Rich argued that the Irish rebellions were routinely excused by people who claimed that they wanted "to free themselves from thralldom (as they pretended)." And, indeed, Rich was correct. Hugh O'Neill justified his efforts in 1598, in part, by lamenting that "we Irishmen are exiled and made bond slaves and servitors to a strange and foreign prince, having neither joy nor felicity in anything, remaining still in captivity." But Ireland's problem, according to Rich, was not really the Irish enslaving their own people or the English holding their neighbors in a state of bondage so much as it was the absence of the restraints on the inherent cruelty of the Irish. "[W]hat subjects in Europe do live so lawless as the Irish," he queried, "when the lords and great men throughout the whole country do rather seem to be absolute than to live within the compass of subjection?" Bondage was relevant because Ireland lacked order, something that could only be rectified through the imposition of English rule.[23]

Ironically, although slavery may have been listed prominently among the reasons why the English needed to impose themselves on the Irish, it is a measure of the frustration of English proponents of the invasion of Ireland like Sir Arthur Chichester, writing to Burghley's successor, Lord Cecil, in 1602, that they were led to conclude that "their barbarism gives us cause to think them unworthy of other treatment than to be made perpetual slaves to her Majesty." Chichester, however, did not generate this recommendation without precedent. The idea that the Irish deserved to be enslaved had previously been mentioned by Gerald of Wales and it reappeared in print when Raphael Holinshed published his *Chronicles* in the 1570s, the second volume of which dealt largely with Ireland. Holinshed reported on a thirteenth-century gathering of clergymen in Ireland where the participants sought out an explanation for why Ireland "was thus plagued by the resort and repaire of strangers in among them." After some debate, the congregants concluded that "it was Gods just plague for the sinnes of the people, and especiallie bicause they used to buie Englishmen of merchants and pirats, and (contrarie to all equitie or reason) did make bondslaves of them." Divine justice "hath set these Englishmen & strangers to reduce them now into the like slaverie and bondage." It was the sinful behavior of the Irish themselves, Holinshed's *Chronicles* reported, that brought the Anglo-Norman invaders to their door. And God, not without a sense of irony, apparently meant for the Irish to be enslaved for retribution while "all the Englishmen within that land, wheresoever they were, in bondage or captivitie, should be manumissed, set free and at libertie."[24] Such was the nature of English ideas about slavery in the early modern era that the effort to rescue the Irish from slavery demanded that the Irish be reduced to slavery.

*   *   *

The presence of slavery in Russia and Ireland was important to English observers bent on emphasizing the differences between themselves and the inhabitants of other parts of Europe. It also proved to be an easy way to criticize the customary practices and cultural values of other nations. But slavery was not necessarily viewed as inherently bad or as an indicator of moral turpitude in all cases. Many Englishmen approached slavery with a kind of academic curiosity, not revulsion. The subtlety with which English travelers were willing to treat the subject of human bondage as it was practiced in foreign lands is demonstrated in the surviving accounts of the system of slavery that pervaded the Mediterranean world, especially Turkey, Syria, Persia, Jerusalem, the Levant, Egypt, Tunisia, and Morocco (much of which was, in fact, part of the Ottoman Empire). Certainly, English writers like Samuel Purchas did not hesitate to emphasize that slavery was an abject, dehumanizing, and physically punishing system. In the introduction to his 1625 work, he asserted that "the Devill hath sent the Moores with damnable Mahumetisme in their merchandizing quite thorow the East, to pervert so many Nations with thraldome of their states and persons."[25] Slavery was spiritually symbolic in Purchas's telling, but it was immediate and meaningful as an all-too-real fate suffered by countless individuals. But that was only part of the story.

Most of the English and other European travelers whose accounts were published by Hakluyt and Purchas (or separately printed) during the late sixteenth and early seventeenth centuries were careful and often quite generous observers. Thus, diligent readers could learn a great deal about the particular characteristics of Mediterranean slavery and, when they were not bemoaning the plight of their own countrymen held in bondage (something that will be discussed more fully in Chapter 4), their observations could be quite instructive. From European witnesses, then, it was clear that there were aspects of human bondage as it functioned in the Mediterranean world that conformed to expectations. Slaves were, by definition, owned or in the possession of another power. Slaves in the Mediterranean also typically originated as prisoners of war and many of these captives were Christians from southern Europe. John Locke, who traveled to Jerusalem in 1553, wrote about a battle "a fewe yeeres past" in which the victorious Turks captured a fortress "from the Emperour, in which fight were slaine three hundred Spanish souldiers, besides the rest which were taken prisoners, and made gallie slaves." George Sandys, who visited the Levant in 1610, reiterated a simple point when he noted that slaves were primarily "Christians taken in the Warres, or purchased with their money."[26] Indeed, English audiences were so familiar with this sort of observation by the seventeenth century that the point was rarely described in detail. Nothing could be less surprising than the presence of slaves who met their fate as a result of being on the losing side of a battle.

A number of subjects, however, either did not cohere with English expectations or were viewed as so fantastic that they were deemed worthy of fuller consideration. Military slavery, for example, elicited considerable attention as a distinctive form of slavery and as a peculiar practice located in one particular region of the world. English travelers in the Mediterranean world routinely commented on the large number of slave soldiers, or Janizaries, in the Ottoman Empire. The remarkably well-traveled Anthony Jenkinson, ultimately more famous for his exploits in Russia, described an elaborate procession "of Soliman the grand Turk" he witnessed into Syria in 1553 that included 16,000 Janizaries, "slaves of the Grand Signior." On a much smaller scale, slave soldiers were also incidental characters. William Biddulph, an English cleric, noted in 1600 that a local English factor "provided us with horses to ride to Aleppo, and a Janizarie, called Paravan Bashaw . . . to guard us" on the dangerous three-day journey inland. Although Biddulph praised the assistance he received from this man, he later reported, while in the vicinity of Jerusalem, that the inhabitants of a village called Lacmine "fled into the Mountaynes to dwell, for feare of the Janizaries of Damascus, who travelling that way used to take from them . . . whatsoever things else they found in their homes." Purchas registered his personal feelings about the subject at this juncture when he noted in the margin of this passage, simply, "Wretched slaverie." He also more than likely agreed with Sir Anthony Sherley's characterization from 1599 that "Janizaries (which were appointed for the safetie of the Provinces . . .) now obey no authoritie which calleth them to other Warres: but by combining themselves in a strength together, tyrannize the Countries committed to their charges."[27]

English observers were particularly intrigued by military slaves because they wielded extraordinary power and influence. Yet, just as slaves could be found in privileged positions at the top of society, exercising their will through violence, other important English sources reveal that slavery could involve utter degradation, suffering, and poverty for individuals at the other end of the social ladder. In a discussion of charity among the Turks, George Sandys acknowledged that "I have seene but few Beggers amongst them. Yet sometimes you shall meet in the streets with couples chained together by the necke, who beg to satisfie their Creditors in part, and are at the yeeres end released of their Bonds, provided that they make satisfaction if they prove afterward able." Purchas also published an account by Leo Africanus (often referred to in England as "John Leo" but born in Morocco as "al-Hasan al-Wazzan") of Moroccans who found themselves pressed between the King of Portugal on one side and the King of Fez on the other. The resulting famine and scarcity brought the people "unto such misery, that they freely offered themselves as slaves" to the Portuguese, "submitting themselves to any man, that was willing to relieve their intolerable hunger."[28] If powerful slaves like the Janiz-aries of the Ottoman Empire were frightful, the condition of those who hap-pened to lapse into a state of slavery as a result of debt or poverty, or perhaps even submitted to slavery voluntarily, was more lamentable than menacing.[29]

A slave's chances in the world depended greatly on who owned him or her. All English travelers in the Islamic world commented on the heteroge-neous nature of the local populations. William Biddulph noted that Aleppo was "inhabited by Turkes, Moores, Arabians, Jewes, Greekes, Armenians, Chelfalines, Nostranes, and people of sundry other Nations." The enslaved population, however, was described more narrowly. Sandys claimed that slaves consisted primarily of Christians taken in war or those purchased with money at any of the weekly markets "where they are to be sold as Horses in Faires: the men being rated according to their faculties, or personal abilities, as the Women for their youths and beauties." These slaves performed a num-ber of services, but if they were fortunate enough to possess a useful skill, they might eventually be able to pay for their freedom. If they were excep-tionally fortunate, Sandys added, they might be bought by a Christian. Thus, slaves at market "endeavour[ed] to allure the Christians to buy them, as ex-pecting from them a more easie servitude, and continuance of Religion: when being thrall to the Turke, they are often inforced to renounce it for their better entertainment." Regardless, Sandys suggested, quite accurately, there were well-established avenues to freedom under Islamic law. Sandys claimed that the "men-slaves may compell their Masters . . . to limit the time of their bondage, or set a price of their redemption, or else to sell them to another." If slaves were owned by a Christian master and subsequently converted to Islam, "they are discharged of their bondage; but if a Slave of a Turke, he onely is the better intreated." Those who ended up in the galleys, or in more menial tasks, seldom were released "in regard of their small number, and much employment which they have for them."[30] Slavery was an absolute con-dition, but there were still opportunities for manumission for the lucky few.

Some English observers were also clearly fascinated by the important role gender played in shaping the supply and use of slaves in the Islamic world. Gender influenced English impressions of contemporary slavery be-cause, quite unlike in England, many roles prescribed for slaves in the Muslim world were conditioned by sex.[31] Female slaves were most often depicted as concubines, or even wives. In 1574, Geffrey Ducket characterized "[b]ond-men and bondwomen [as] . . . one of the best kind of merchandise that any man may bring" to Persia. Ducket noted that when Persians purchased "any maydes or yong women, they use to feele them in all partes, as with us men doe horses." Female slaves were the absolute servants of their masters and could be sold many times over. If these women were found by their masters "to be false to him, and give her body to any other, he may kill her if he will." Not only Persians, but foreign merchants and travelers seem to have participated in the ownership of women. Ducket noted that when the visitors stayed for any length of time in one place, he "hireth a woman, or sometimes 2. or 3. during his abode there . . . for there they use to put out their women to hire, as wee doo here hackney horses."[32]

Samuel Purchas published several accounts that characterized the role of enslaved women in a similar vein. Not surprisingly, George Sandys weighed in on the subject when he noted that every man could hold "as many Concubine slaves as hee is able to keepe, of what Religion soever." From his general description of the lot of wives and concubines, Sandys concluded that he could "speake of their slaves: for little difference is there made between them." While male slaves were "rated according to their faculties, or personal abilities," women were valued "for their youths and beauties." Once a woman was purchased, her buyer examined her for "assurance (if so she be said to be) of her virginitie." Masters could then "lye with them, chastise them, exchange and sell them at their pleasure." But Christian masters were not completely void of compassion, he claimed, for he "will not lightly sell her whom he hath layne with, but give her libertie."[33] Such were the benefits that apparently accrued to women whose fate it was to be purchased for the sexual favors they were compelled to provide for their owners.

As fascinating as the subject may have been, female slavery was something that historically minded Englishmen could easily comprehend. William of Malmesbury's twelfth-century *Chronicle* recounted several examples from pre-Conquest society of the selling of female slaves out of England. Malmesbury recorded these tales as examples of the degeneracy of England before the arrival of the Normans. In one particularly offensive example, Malmesbury cited the custom, "repugnant to nature, which they adopted; namely, to sell their female servants, when pregnant by them and after they had satisfied their lust, either to public prostitution, or foreign slavery." Likewise, in another tale, Malmesbury recounted how the sister of the early eleventh-century King Canute had been killed by a lightning strike, supposedly as punishment for the king making money off the "horrid traffic" in English youths, especially girls, who were taken against their will and sold into slavery in Denmark.[34] The purchase of females had a particular symbolic power in England where, as in Islam, the significance of the enslavement of women was historically rooted in the owner's ability to exploit women's sexuality rather than the women's labor value. In addition, the use of slave women could enhance the master's power not only over slave men but also over free men because of their ability to control access to a desired commodity or destination. Male slaves never forgot that regardless of how they might define the nature of their relationship with a female slave, another man—a free male—actually exercised the ultimate authority. Within this historical context, readers needed little elaboration in the accounts printed by Hakluyt and Purchas to understand that female concubinage was an insidious form of slavery that was part and parcel of the overall interest of the male population in controlling the sexual behavior of women.[35]

The enslavement of women clearly fascinated English observers, but they were arguably even more intrigued, or perhaps repulsed, by the closely related subject of eunuchs, particularly in the Islamic world. Once again, the account by George Sandys is instructive. Sandys claimed that many of the children "that the Turkes doe buy . . . they castrate, making all smooth as the backe of the hand, (whereof divers doe dye in the cutting) who supply the uses of Nature with a Silver Quill, which they wear in their Turbants." Sandys was fascinated that eunuchs were "heere in great repute with their Masters, trusted with their States, the Government of their Women and Houses in their absence; having for the most part beene approved faithfull, wise, and couragious." Robert Withers went into even greater detail in his account of the "Grand Signiors Serraglio" from 1620. Withers was struck in particular by the role played by black eunuchs, who "goe about and doe all other businesse for the Sultanaes in the Womens lodgings, which White Eunuches cannot performe." And, in fact, black eunuchs do seem to have become especially prized possessions and influential allies by the sixteenth century in the Ottoman Empire.[36]

Eunuchs played a particularly prominent role in Purchas's volumes because they were an especially visible sign of the degeneracy he believed inundated the Mediterranean world and much of the east. Eunuchs were not merely men who had been castrated; they were agents of sexual depravity. The Withers account, for example, was preceded on the printed page by the record of the English cleric Edward Terry, who journeyed to India in 1616 to serve as Sir Thomas Roe's chaplain in the English Embassy. Like numerous other European witnesses, Terry mentioned eunuchs in passing as royal attendants, guards, and even high officials. But among his varied observations,

Terry noted at one point that nobody lived "in the Kings house but his women and Eunuches, and some little Boyes which hee keepes about him for a wicked use." At once, this comment reads as both a passing reference to the luxury in which a local ruler lived and a resounding condemnation of his detestable personal proclivities.[37] Eunuchs repelled, then, not simply because they had been physically altered, but because they were emblematic of a widespread phenomenon that reflected a broader understanding of Islam, the exotic lands to the east, and slavery.

*   *   *

As Terry's account implies, the English were quick to identify the Mediterranean as the epicenter of bondage and captivity in the world, but there were other newly encountered places that were easily characterized in like terms. The presence and roles of slaves in these less familiar, and decidedly less menacing, societies reinforced the familiar conventions that human bondage often resulted from warfare and represented a kind of perpetual captivity involving a complicated interplay between indiscriminate and potentially brutal treatment and generous opportunities for the enslaved either to exercise power through their bondage or to reclaim their lost liberty. These ideas, however, were often based on imperfect and incomplete information. Because few Englishmen traveled to either south or southeast Asia before 1600, Richard Hakluyt had little in the way of firsthand observations or written narrative accounts before he published the final edition of the *Principal Navigations*. Samuel Purchas, however, was able to extract liberally from a mixture of Spanish, Portuguese, Dutch, and English narratives and therefore included significantly more material on Asia in his volumes.[38] The English sources were a particularly rich body of material that Purchas acquired directly from the English East India Company (EIC) in 1622. The EIC had been founded in 1600 and English ships and merchants began to show up in the southeast Asian archipelago soon thereafter. Before the EIC reformed in 1613 as a joint-stock company, at least twelve separate expeditions voyaged to the region. English ships also sailed to India in 1608 and Sir Thomas Roe established the first formal embassy to the Mogul court in 1615. As a result of these contacts, Samuel Purchas had a variety of sources to draw on by the time his multivolume work was published in 1625.[39]

English ships and merchants were lured beyond the southern tip of Africa by the same promise of rich rewards in valuable commodities that dared them to chart the Russian interior and broach the Mediterranean market during the late sixteenth century. And just as they had difficulty avoiding the subject of human bondage in these regions, English observers took notice of the nature and character of slavery further east. Considering their precarious and decidedly dependent status in the region, the accounts authored by early English merchants in the Indian Ocean and Asia are particularly interesting because these Englishmen were not in the market for slaves, as their country-men would later be in Africa.[40] Equally important, unlike the accounts written about slavery in the Mediterranean world, the English who plied their trade in the Indian and Pacific Oceans were not necessarily worried that they might themselves be enslaved.[41] For this reason, the handful of English re-ports about the presence and use of slaves in this arena are generally charac-terized by a much more matter-of-fact tone than those that emanated from the Mediterranean, where the slaves that interested English commentators the most would prove to be their fellow countrymen (particularly during the seventeenth century). Still, English observers did not shy away from drawing often negative conclusions about the indigenous slave systems of south and southeast Asia.

In Java, for example, the English factor Edmund Scot commented on the tenuous existence of slaves whose masters "may execute them for any small fault." Javan elites often kept large numbers of Chinese slaves, so many that "[t]he Gentlemen of this Land are brought to bee poore, by the number of their Slaves that they keepe, which eate faster then their Pepper or Rice groweth." Scot also made at least passing reference to concubinage of a sort found in the Mediterranean world when he observed that for every wife that a free Javan married "he must keepe ten women-slaves." Scot sympathized with the plight of slaves in Java, who suffered under masters some En-glishmen characterized in the harshest terms. Javans were, in Scot's opinion, "idle" and "much given to stealing, from the highest to the lowest, and surely in times past, they have beene Man-eaters, before the Traffique was had with them by the Chynasses." An earlier account reprinted by Purchas, however, presented a less flattering view of the Chinese. Among their vices was the tendency of those who "finding their family too numerous sell their Sonnes and Daughters as Beasts, for two or three pieces of Gold (although no dearth provoke them) to everlasting separation and bondage [so that] the Kingdome is full of Slaves, not captived in warre, but of their owne free-borne."[42]

Although Scot characterized the Chinese as the most common slaves in Java, other English accounts made it clear that just as all the nations of Asia enslaved, all the people of the region were subject to enslavement. As with accounts about slavery in the Mediterranean world, just how (precisely) individuals became slaves did not elicit extended consideration. Purchas did include an account of the voyage of François Pyrard de Laval to the East Indies in 1601 who noted blithely, "Slaves are such as make themselves so, or such as they bring from other places." More commonly, European observers noted only who was enslaved rather than how he or she had been enslaved. Peter William Floris recorded in his journal that one ruler in Siam, "a mightie Kingdome and ancient," had "amongst other Slaves, two hundred and eightie Japanders." In Patania, also on the Malay Peninsula, they were "richest in Slaves of Javonians." David Middleton, an energetic captain in the service of the East India Company, described the slaves of "Pulaway" (Pula Ai), an island off the coast of Sumatra, simply and unhelpfully as "Blackes."[43] Slaves in Asia were not delineated by any one national, racial, religious, or cultural characteristic. They were, on the whole, merely the unfortunate victims of random predation or unlucky to have been on the losing side in a larger conflict. Sometimes the only thing that can be said with certainty is that they were generally outsiders.

Slavery was also part of the fabric of life in Japan, at least according to John Saris, who sailed there in the service of the EIC in 1613. Saris was among the small group of Englishmen who established a trading outpost on the small island of Hirado, located in the southwestern part of Japan. Although he departed after only a short stay, he did relate that slaves in Japan were valued primarily for the prestige they imparted on their owners, including the English. Even before the English had formally set up their factory, William Adams (whose own misfortune had led to his abandonment in Japan a decade earlier) bragged in a letter written in 1611 that he had managed to do so well for himself that "th'Emperor hath geven me a living, as in England a lordshipp, w'th 80 or 90 husbandmen that be my slaves or servauntes." Adams seems to have been deeply interested in ingratiating himself with local elites and his newly arrived countrymen, but Saris also commented somewhat favorably on the honorific value that slaves could bestow on their masters when he commented that, "[a]ccording to the custome of the countrey, I had a slave appointed to runne with a Pike before me" when he moved about the countryside. Whether Adams's husbandmen or Saris's pikeman were indeed slaves seems less important than the fact that the two Englishmen chose to characterize them as such for their intended audience of English readers.[44]

As much as Adams and Saris were impressed by their slave retinues, they and others were much more intrigued by female slaves. Saris related the tale of three men who were executed for stealing a female slave. Indeed, most of Saris's references to human bondage in Japan were to female entertainers and the men who shopped them to the nobility. The existence of sexual slavery in Japan was difficult for English observers to ignore, but Saris was equally interested in the men who facilitated the industry. "These women are the slaves of one man," Saris recounted, "who putteth a price what every man shall pay that hath to doe with any of them." These male purchasers, however, were complicated figures. "When any of these Panders die (though in their life time they were received into Company of the best, yet nowe as unworthy to rest amongst the worst)," Saris noted with morbid curiosity, "they are bridled with a bridle made of straw as you would bridle an Horse, and in the cloathes they died in, are dragged through the streetes into the fields, and there cast upon a dunghill, for dogges and fowles to devoure."[45] The men who dealt in female slaves were richly valued for the commodities they provided during their lives, but few were willing to accord them (or their memory) with any sense of dignity or honor once they ceased being useful.

Whatever they may have thought about these subjects at home, English merchants willingly adapted themselves to their local surroundings as part of a larger survival strategy that necessitated flexibility and open-mindedness.[46] Whether survival depended on slavery is open to debate, but English merchants nonetheless embraced the practice. Englishmen may have acknowledged that slavery was inconsistent with the way things operated at home, but they sometimes accepted that slavery was normative and benign when they encountered it in other places and did not automatically conclude that it was a prime indicator of social degeneracy. Not surprisingly, then, Englishmen abroad were as likely to purchase slaves for their own use as they were to criticize the practice among their hosts. During the tenth EIC voyage under the command of Thomas Best, the commander freely purchased slaves on at least two occasions as his two ships sailed off the northern tip of Sumatra in July 1613, the second time numbering "about 25 or thereabout Indeans, for to suplie the want of our men deceased." The first generation of English merchants in Japan eagerly and without shame welcomed the opportunity to purchase concubines. Richard Cocks, in a letter to his colleague Richard Wickham, openly bragged that he "bought a wench yesterday" who "must serve 5 yeares" and then either repay back the purchase price or exchange "som frendes for

her, or else remaine a p'petuall captive." Cocks continued with even more
shocking details, noting that the girl "is but 12 yeares ould, over small yet for
trade, but yow would littell thynke that I have another forthcominge that is
mor lapedeable," or ready for sexual activity. Although not all Englishmen
were as crass about the subject, many of them recognized the advantages of
buying and owning slaves in the region.[47]

*   *   *

Slavery was a global phenomenon, so only its absence in Africa would have
been surprising. Few English merchants or mariners actually visited Africa
before the last half of the sixteenth century, by which time the practice of
slavery had been somewhat altered by the predatory activities of other European merchants and slave traders. Even so, an expansive body of literature
was available for public consumption, which allowed literate Englishmen to
learn about African practices. Among the most popular works were the medieval travelogues that had originally circulated in manuscript but were subsequently translated into the vernacular during the early modern era.[48] London
printers issued an edition of *The Most Noble and Famous Travels of Marcus
Paulus* in 1579, and the most popular work of the day, *The Travels of Sir John
Mandeville,* appeared in English, in one version or another, at least six times
between 1496 and 1583.[49] Curious readers could also discover information
about Africa and Africans in the recently translated geographical works of
classical authors, including Ptolemy (1532, 1535, 1540), Pliny the Elder (1566,
1585, 1587, 1601), Herodotus (1584), and Pomponius Mela (1585, 1590). Moreover, influential Greek and Latin texts such as Ptolemy's *Geographia* and
Strabo's *De situ orbis* continued to be at the heart of university curricula.[50]
Other Europeans, especially the Portuguese, also wrote important texts that
shed light on both West and East Africa. English printers published translations of the diplomatic exchanges between agents of Portugal and Ethiopia
during the reign of Henry VIII.[51] Several other English translations of Portuguese activities in Africa and the East Indies appeared during the sixteenth
century, including Duarte Lopes's *A reporte of the kingdome of Congo* (1587).
Beyond this large body of material, promoters like Richard Hakluyt and
Samuel Purchas compiled, translated, and published numerous narrative accounts that provided detailed information about the people, societies, geography, climate, and commodities of Africa. Large parts of Africa would
remain a mystery to even the most intrepid Europeans for a long time to

come, but adventurous readers had plenty of information at their disposal during the sixteenth century.

Collectively, these authors and translators presented Africa as an exotic and mysterious place that was alternately alluring for the spiritual and material rewards it promised and terrifying for what awaited those few individuals unfortunate enough to actually go there. Most important, among the many possible lines of inquiry, classical and medieval authors did not dwell on the subject of slavery. Africa's defining characteristic was arguably its climate,

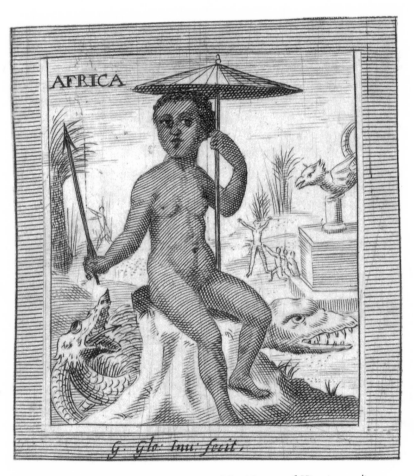

Figure 1. Detail from the lower-left quadrant of the title page of *Historia mundi: or Mercator's Atlas. Containing his cosmographical description of the fabricke and figure of the world* (London, 1635). By permission of the Folger Shakespeare Library.

which authors invariably described as unbearably hot. William Prat's 1554 translation of Johann Boemus's *Omnium gentium mores* described "the lande of *Ethiopie*" as the "neighbour to the sonne, as before al other to feale the heate." Boemus also translated "Athiopes" in a way that emphasized the point, claiming that the word derived from the Greek "*Atho* which signifieth burne and *Oph* which signifieth take hede, and that because of the approchynge nyghe to the soone [the Sun]. The countreye is continually hote." As a result, the inhabitants of Africa possessed characteristic features, most noticeably their skin color. As George Abbot observed in 1600, "All the people in general to the South, l[i]ving within the *Zona torrida*, are not onely blackish like the Moores, but are exceedingly blacke. And therefore in olde time, by an excellency, some of them were called *Nigrita*; so that to this day they are named *Negros*, and then whome, no men are blacker."[52]

Africa, numerous authorities reported, was also a land of monstrous races of men. The authoritative text on this subject was Pliny the Elder's *Historia Naturalis*, translated into English by Philemon Holland in 1601 (although an excerpted version had previously appeared in 1566). In the account of the "Æthyopians," Pliny described the existence of peoples whose differences could be relatively subtle, like the "Troglodites" who lived in caves and fed "upon the flesh of serpents" and the "Garamants" who were intriguing because they "live[d] out of wedlocke, and converse with their women in common." Some differences were quite stark: "The Blemmyi, by report, have no heads, but mouth and eies both in their breast. The Satyres besides their shape onely, have no properties nor fashions of men" and the "Himantopodes bee some of them limberlegged and tender, who naturally goe creeping by the ground." Sir John Mandeville made even more of these characters, including a passing reference to a "monstrously shaped beast" who lived in Egypt that "had the shape of a man from the navel upward, and from there downward the form of a goat, with two horns standing up on its head." South of Ethiopia, he added, was "a vast country, but it is uninhabitable because of the terrible heat of the sun." Nonetheless, there you could find "some who have only one foot" that "is so big that it will cover and shade all the body from the sun." Those who traveled farther, to India and Southeast Asia, might even come across "people whose ears are so big that they hang down to their knees," "people who walk on their hands and their feet like four-footed beasts," hermaphrodites, and people who "live just on the smell of a kind of apple."[53]

If classical and medieval sources compelled the English to imagine a world to their south inhabited by strange and monstrous beings, Christianity played no less an important role in how Europeans wrote and thought about Africa (or any other place, for that matter). First, even if English and other European authors were disinclined to explain the physical appearance of African people with reference to the so-called Curse of Ham, a number of writers did associate African peoples with the biblical passage. Boemus's *Omnium gentium mores*, which appeared in two separate English translations (in 1554 and 1555), is once again representative. Recounting the origin of the division of the world, Boemus reported that Cham, "by the reason of his naughty demeanour towarde his father" was "constrayned to departe with his wyfe and hys chyldren" and subsequently "lefte no trade or religion to his posteritie, because he none had learned of his father." If Cham and his descendants were cursed with darkness, it was clearly a spiritual rather than a physical matter. Thus, over time "some fel into errours whereout they could never unsnarle themselves" and eventually "some lived so wildely . . . that it ware harde to discerne a difference betwixte them and the beastes of the felde." John Pory noted that most of the inhabitants of Africa, excluding "some Arabians," were "thought to be descended from *Cham* the cursed son of *Noah*," but he did not elaborate on the subject any further.[54] Although there were exceptions, few domestic English authors were willing to embrace the idea that the skin color of Africans was wholly attributable to a curse handed down by Noah.

Second, and more important, Christian Europeans dreamed of Africa because of the potential presence of Prester John. An anonymous fourteenth-century Spanish Franciscan traveler, whose observations survive today as the *Book of the Knowledge of All the Kingdoms, Lands, and Lordships that Are in the World*, described Prester John as the Patriarch of Nubia and Abyssinia, which were "very great lands" with "many cities of Christians."[55] The origins of the Prester John myth date to the twelfth century when news reached Pope Eugenius III that a powerful Christian king in the East stood ready to assist European Christians in their ongoing struggles against Islam. It was unclear where this fabled king may have been located, but his rumored presence served as a rationale for voyages of discovery and other official missions to both Asia and Africa during subsequent centuries. Three hundred years after he first appeared, Prester John continued to be an enticing, if illusive, figure whose greatest legacy may have been the Portuguese effort to establish direct contact with Ethiopia.[56] Other Europeans, however, were also intrigued by stories about "the kynge of Ethiope whiche we call pretian or prest John whom they cal *Gian*," a man who, in Johann Boemus's words, was "of so great a personage and blud, that under him he hath threscoore and two other kynges."[57]

There were always serious doubts about the veracity of these legends, but even Henry IV of England had written to Prester John in 1400 asking him to lend his support to the reconquest of the Holy Land. Still, the small chance that there might be a powerful Christian kingdom to the south was too tantalizing to dismiss out of hand. Abraham Hartwell was moved to declare in his 1597 translation of Duarte Lopes's *A Report of the Kingdom of Congo*, if "*Papists* and *Protestants*" and "all *Sectaries* and *Presbyter-Johns men*" would joyne all together" they would be able "to convert the *Turkes*, the *Jewes*, the *Heathens*, the *Pagans*, and the *Infidels* that know not *God* but live still in darkenesse."[58] Yet, Prester John increasingly appeared in English sources more as a caricature designed to amuse readers than as the leader of a kingdom that might actually exist. In 1590, Edward Webbe claimed to have visited Prester John's court, where he encountered "a king of great power" and "a very bountifull Court." At the same time, he also claimed that at the court of Prester John there was "a wilde man" who was "allowed every day a quarter of mans flesh" whenever someone was executed for "some notorious offence." In addition, he declared that there was "a beast in the court of Prester John, called Arians, having four heades" that were "in shape like a wilde Cat."[59] Like Webbe, George Abbot linked Prester John with the fantastic rather than the sacred. Drawing from Pliny the Elder's *Historia Naturalis*, he noted at the end of his consideration of Prester John's kingdom that Africa "bringeth forth store of all sortes of wilde beastes," including "newe and strange shapes of beastes." These new creatures, according to Abbot, were a result of "the country being hot and full of wildernesses which have in them little water." Thus, "the beastes of all sortes are inforced to meete at those fewe watering places . . . ; where, oftentimes contrary kindes have conjunction the one with the other: so that there ariseth newe kindes or *species*, which taketh part of both."[60]

Before they went to Africa, Englishmen learned about the place and its peoples as best they could from an array of manuscript and printed sources. After the 1590s, it was increasingly likely that English readers could read accounts authored by Portuguese, Dutch, and even English merchants and sailors who had spent considerable time in the places about which they wrote. The Portuguese had been actively engaged in diplomacy, commercial exchange, and religious conversion with West Africans for more than a century before English readers and mariners began to demonstrate any serious interest in the region. Portuguese texts, even when they did not find contemporary English translators, were typically the only sources interested English readers could find before the 1550s and continued to be among the most detailed accounts available to them through the end of the century. Even when the works of authors such as Cadamosto and Barros were not mentioned directly, evidence suggests that English authors and editors like Richard Eden, Humphrey Gilbert, Richard Willes, John Pory, Hakluyt, Purchas, and others relied heavily on Portuguese sources.[61] When Portuguese accounts were read alongside some of the recently translated and very rich Dutch sources, especially Jan Huygen van Linschoten's *Itinerario*, which was translated and published in England in 1598 at the recommendation of Richard Hakluyt, English readers were able to learn a great deal about West African polities, the nature of their religious practices, and the wealth of commodities that circulated along the African littoral.[62]

Dog-headed men and the descendants of the Magi would continue to fascinate Englishmen for years to come, but increasingly the English were reading about an Africa that was of interest because it was "full of Gold and Silver, and other Commodities." As Englishmen traveled to Africa, George Abbot reported, they "found trafique into the parts of the country: where their greatest commoditie is golde, and Elephants teeth: of both which there is very good store."[63] These items were made available for trade by the numerous sophisticated polities that could be found along the West African littoral. These linguistically and culturally diverse kingdoms ranged in size from a few hundred people to tens, if not hundreds, of thousands. Although they could be difficult for Europeans to describe with precision, African societies were dynamic and often as technologically and materially sophisticated as European societies. Active, long-distance trade networks blanketed the continent. Local rulers regulated trade and moderated the commercial activities of merchants. Cloth and iron manufacturing were characteristic features of local and regional economies. There was also slavery. Although it was an institution that existed to serve different needs and was justified by different criteria than the plantation-labor institution that would subsequently come to dominate the Atlantic slave system, slavery was as pervasive in African societies as it appeared to be in other parts of the world. Of course, there was an important difference. Although enslaved Africans were exported out of Africa by European traders in small numbers to start with, and constituted a small

fraction of the value of all African exports before the seventeenth century, all
Europeans took advantage of the availability of African peoples as commodities both at home and, especially, in their Atlantic world colonies.[64]

Slavery was nothing new to the inhabitants of Africa; it was not, as one
historian notes, "an 'impact' brought in from outside." Rather, "it grew out
of and was rationalized by the African societies who participated in it."[65] Not
surprisingly, disagreements persist about the relative importance of the institution before the arrival of European ships in the fifteenth century and a
number of scholars suggest that slavery was a relatively insignificant social
and economic institution until the Portuguese, French, English, and Dutch
began exploiting African peoples. Nonetheless, slavery clearly existed in various sub-Saharan African societies as a tribute mechanism, a domestic institution, and, in rare cases, an industrial system. Thus, by the time the English
began arriving in small numbers during the late sixteenth century, nothing
would have surprised them more than the absence of slavery. Europeans were
familiar with the commodity value of African peoples from their dealings
with North Africans who had facilitated the trade in sub-Saharan Africans
into the Mediterranean and southern European worlds for several centuries
before Europeans began sailing southward.[66] The English saw slavery wherever they looked. Why should Africa be any different?

English merchants entered the African trade slowly.[67] During the 1530s
and 1540s, as many as six English expeditions touched base on the eastern
Atlantic seaboard of Africa. The most famous of these were the three expeditions to Brazil between 1530 and 1532 launched by the wealthy Plymouth merchant, William Hawkins, during which time the English captain "touched at
the river of Sestos upon the coast of Guinea, where hee traffiqued with the
negros."[68] A few decades later, however, English ships began to journey to
Africa for the express purpose of regularizing a direct trade. During the 1550s
and 1560s, when Englishmen and Africans encountered each other for the
first time in a sustained fashion, perhaps a dozen expeditions, involving as
many as 1,500 English mariners, sailed the waters between the southern coast
of England and the western shores of Africa. But as vital as the English effort
seemed to be during this early stage, the African trade presented numerous
complications for English merchants, not least of which were the devastating
mortality rates. As Richard Eden recounted about the 1558 expedition of
Thomas Wyndham, "of the sevenscore men" who set out from Plymouth,
there returned "scarcely forty, and of them many died."[69] Africa was a destination from which shocking numbers of English mariners failed to return.

The transatlantic slave trade was, in many ways, still in its infancy during the sixteenth century, but thousands of captive Africans were already being loaded onto European ships and transported across the sea to Spanish America and Brazil every year, especially after 1560.[70] In this vein, an expedition under the command of John Lok reportedly returned to England with "certayne blacke slaves" in 1555. Although a small number of sub-Saharan Africans had been in the British Isles before this date, their arrival was remarkable. According to Eden, "sum were taule and stronge men, and could well agree with owr meates and drynkes." At the same time, the "coulde and moyst ayer dooth sumwhat offende them." The difficulties and sufferings of the indigenous inhabitants of equatorial Africa transplanted to England's colder clime were not surprising: "[D]oubtlesse men that are borne in hotte regions may better abyde heate" than cold. But what about their apparent status as "slaves"? Certainly, these Africans were not slaves in the modern sense of the term. The English viewed these five men more as cultural mediators than as bondmen. William Towerson, a London merchant and commander of three well-documented expeditions to Africa (1555, 1556, and 1558) reported to a group of Africans during his first voyage that "they were in England well used, and were there kept till they could speake the language, and then they should be brought againe to be a helpe to Englishmen in this Countrey."[71] When three of the original five Africans who had been taken to England returned to Africa with Towerson on his second voyage, then, the English saw them as mechanisms that would make it easier to acquire gold, pepper, and ivory. To this end, the "slaves" proved their worth immediately. At one point, Towerson reported meeting some Africans who "would not come to us, but at the last by the perswasion of our owne Negros, one boat came to us, and with him we sent George our Negro ashore, and after he had talked with them, they came aboord our boates without feare."[72]

The characterization of the five Africans on board Lok's ships as "slaves" may have been a label of convenience rather than a true indication of their condition and, certainly, West Africans in general had little to fear from the English during their early voyages. Even so, some Englishmen clearly embraced the slave trade from an early date and accepted that it was a necessary component of successful African enterprises. In 1555, a group of English merchants petitioned Queen Mary in order to obtain free trade privileges in Guinea. They claimed that earlier English expeditions to Africa had uncovered several local rulers who were happy to trade with English ships. In addition, the "said inhabitauntes of that country offred us and our said factors ground to build uppon, if they wold make anie fortresses in their country, and further offred them assistaunce of certen slaves for those workes without anie charge."[73] These English merchants recognized the advantages of a captive labor force as well as the importance of the willing assistance of African merchants and leaders.

The rapid English embrace of African slavery, however, was demonstrated most clearly during the 1560s when four English expeditions (three of which were led by John Hawkins) sailed to the African coast, filled their holds with Africans, and sold their human cargoes in Spain's American colonies. Hawkins's first expedition, which departed England in 1562, consisted of three ships and "not above 100. men for feare of sicknesse and other inconveniences." The small fleet sailed to Sierra Leone and, "partly by sworde, and partly by other means," acquired "300. Negros at the least, besides other merchandises which that country yeeldeth." As quickly as possible, the ships sailed on to the Caribbean where they unloaded their cargo. By September 1563, they were back in England. Hawkins set sail again the following year with a slightly larger and much more powerful fleet of four ships and more than 150 men. This expedition was broadly similar to the first and succeeded in capturing or trading for 400 Africans, who they subsequently transported across the Atlantic and sold into slavery. John Lovell attempted to sail in his former commander's wake two years later when he left Plymouth with three ships, but he lacked Hawkins's skill, or good fortune, and only managed to acquire and sell a few slaves. Lovell's small fleet was largely dispirited and none-the-wealthier when it returned to England in 1567.[74]

The most notorious English expedition to Africa during the sixteenth century was the final slave-trading expedition launched and led by John Hawkins in 1567. This massive expedition was a grand scheme and represented a serious commitment to the slave trade on the part of Hawkins, numerous investors, and Queen Elizabeth herself. By contemporary standards, the fleet was impressive, consisting of six ships, including two royal warships. In a letter from Plymouth drafted shortly before his departure, Hawkins confidently assured Elizabeth that he would return from the West Indies laden with "gold, pearls and emeralds, whereof I doubt not but to bring home great abundance to the contentation of your highness and to the relief of the number of worthy servitures ready now for this pretended voyage." Departing Plymouth in October, the fleet reached Cape Verde in mid-November and proceeded to try to "obtaine some Negros," but they "got but fewe, and those with great hurt and damage to our men." Hawkins continued down the coast to Sierra Leone and prepared to give up on his grand scheme, having procured fewer than 150 slaves, when "there came to us a Negro, sent from a king, oppressed by other Kings his neighbours, desiring our aide, with promise that as many Negros as by these warres might be obtained, aswell of his part as of ours, should be at our pleasure."[75] After a disappointing start, then, things appeared to be looking more positive for the English slave traders.

Having learned the painful lesson that he could not simply dispatch his men to the coast to waylay random Africans without great difficulty, Hawkins prepared to work in consort with an African ally. Together, they attacked and set fire to a village housing approximately 8,000 people. As the inhabitants fled for their lives, Hawkins and his men managed to capture "250 persons, men, women, & children, and by our friend the king of our side, there were taken 600 prisoners, whereof we hope to have had our choise." Hawkins was disappointed, however, when "the Negro (in which nation is seldome or never found truth) . . . remooved his campe and prisoners, so that we were faine to content us with those few which we had gotten our selves." Thus, with perhaps 500 Africans on board, the English fleet set sail for the West Indies in early February. After a difficult journey, they arrived in the West Indies and "coasted from place to place, making our traffike with the Spaniards as we might, somewhat hardly, because the king had straightly commanded all his Governors in those parts, by no meanes to suffer any trade to be made with us." By the end of July, the English ships were ready to depart, but in August, off the coast of Cuba, they were caught in "an extreme storme which continued the space of foure dayes." Initially, they sought safe harbor in Florida to repair their ships, but another storm forced them westward and compelled Hawkins to seek relief at San Juan de Ulloa on the coast of Mexico near Veracruz. There, however, they soon found themselves trapped by the newly arrived Spanish *flota*. The two sides initially maintained an uneasy peace. Unfortunately for the English, the Spanish viceroy, Don Martín Enríquez, had no intention of allowing the privateers to go unchallenged. Within days, the Spanish attacked and devastated the English force. Two ships, the *Judith* and the *Minion*, managed to get past the Spanish fleet and safely out to sea, but three other ships were destroyed and a majority of the men were abandoned to their fate in New Spain. Of the roughly 400 men who set sail with Hawkins in 1567, only about 100 returned to England in 1568.[76]

Figure 2. Sketch of the arms and crest (a bound African slave) granted to Sir John Hawkins in 1568. "Miscellaneous Grants 1," fol. 148r. By permission of the College of Arms, London.

With the notable exception of these four slave-trading expeditions during the 1560s, few Englishmen went to Africa to participate in the transatlantic slave trade before the mid-seventeenth century. Hawkins's voyage was such an unmitigated financial and diplomatic disaster that there was little in it to suggest that it was worth imitating. Hawkins was even compelled to draft a very public defense of his enterprise upon his return in which the duplicity of the Spanish and bad weather featured most prominently among the list of explanations for the voyage's failure.[77] In subsequent decades, therefore, only a small number of English merchants attempted to profit from the transatlantic slave trade. In 1587, two English ships were granted safe passage by the Portuguese government to trade textiles into the Azores where they were to acquire wine that would be used for the purchase of slaves in Guinea or Angola, which would then be exchanged for sugar in Brazil. Illicit trading in black slaves was also sporadic during the early decades of the seventeenth century, though English merchants often had other more pressing interests in Africa.[78] When the Company of Adventurers of London trading to Gynney and Bynney was formed in 1618, the corporation was primarily interested in the gold trade. Although the company established a fort on the Gambia River and sponsored three voyages between 1618 and 1621, the business venture was largely unsuccessful. Eventually, the company was reorganized under the leadership of the London merchant Nicholas Crispe and granted a new monopoly as the Company of Merchants Trading to Guinea and it proceeded to establish additional outposts in Sierra Leone and along the Gold Coast. Even then, gold and lumber were more likely than slaves to be listed as the desired commodities.[79] Hawkins's disaster was a hard-learned lesson and the English government and its merchants were not quick to forget it—the slave trade was dangerous.

But if Englishmen found the slave trade to be impractical for a host of economic and geo-political reasons, they did not necessarily find slavery to be particularly disagreeable. Before 1600, a few English observers commented on the practice of slavery in both its domestic and transatlantic manifestations without passing judgment, much as their countrymen had done in other parts of the world. William Finch, a resident English merchant for a brief time in Sierra Leone early in the seventeenth century, was intrigued by a local ruler who "hath power to sell his people for slaves (which he preferred unto us)" but chose not to comment further on the subject. In describing the coastal trading activities of the "many Spaniards and Portugals resident by permission of the Negroes," Richard Rainolds recorded their practice of buying iron from French and English ships and then trading it "for Negros; which be caried continually to the West Indies in such ships as come from Spaine."[80] For the English, slavery was a characteristic feature of Africa, as it was throughout much of the world. In an era when Englishmen were inclined to argue that much of the world beyond the shores of the British Isles was epitomized by slavery, the presence of human bondage in Africa was predictable.

After 1600, largely as a result of Samuel Purchas's translation and publication of numerous Dutch sources, much more information was available about the nature of slavery in coastal West Africa. Richard Hakluyt had seen to the English translation of Linschoten's *Itinerario* soon after it had appeared in 1596, but he included little of it or anything else from Dutch sources in his *Principal Navigations*. This omission was largely a result of timing. The Dutch East India Company was not founded until 1602, at which time a number of Dutch authors began producing remarkably detailed accounts of Africa, India, the East Indies, and the Americas. Purchas therefore had at his disposal not only Linschoten, but a 1602 description of the Gold Coast by Pieter de Marees and an account of Benin possibly authored by Dierick Ruiters.[81] On Benin, then, Purchas was able to note that the Portuguese were very familiar with a certain river "not because of any great commoditie that is therein to be had; but because of the great number of slaves which are bought there, to carry to other places . . . to labour there, and to refine Sugar." In even more detail, Purchas continued, "[T]hey are very strong men, and can labour stoutly, and commonly are better slaves than those of Gabom, but those that are sold in Angola are much better."[82] With the possible exception of Andrew Battell, no English eyewitness commented as extensively as Dutch and Portuguese authorities on the precise nature and operation of slavery in Africa, but English readers were largely unaware of many of these works before the early seventeenth century.

The relative silence of English observers on the subject of slavery in Africa is perhaps not surprising considering the prevalence of what can only loosely be characterized as generic anti-slavery rhetoric in the early modern Atlantic world. Whenever and wherever the English found themselves in competition with other Europeans, they often strove to describe themselves in the most flattering terms possible. By claiming that others were the real practitioners of both slavery and the transatlantic slave trade, propagandists buttressed the dignity of the English nation by highlighting their own supposed commitment to liberty. Yet, it is also important to remember that English criticisms of slavery were rooted in the understanding by the English of the practice as epiphenomenal. Under what circumstances Africans were enslaved, or perhaps how they were treated by other Europeans, was of greater import than slavery itself. Although it dates from a slightly later period, the most famous example of a theoretically English anti-slavery critique was authored by the early Stuart merchant Richard Jobson, who, when offered "certaine young blacke women" while in West Africa, claimed that the English "were a people, who did not deale in any such commodities, neither did wee buy or sell one another, or any that had our owne shapes."[83] Jobson was not alone in his protestations. His near contemporary, Sir Thomas Roe, similarly objected to the purchase of slaves during his tenure in India. On at least two separate occasions, Roe reported, he was given the opportunity to purchase slaves. In both cases, even though he acknowledged that he could not only better their condition but quite likely save the lives of the enslaved, he asserted that he was willing to pay ransoms, "but I would not buy them as slaves." From the perspective of the sellers, Roe could do whatever he wanted with his slaves, including setting them at liberty. But Roe was so determined to avoid the perception that the English bought and sold slaves that he insisted the king be informed "that I had offered to redeeme the Prisoners for charities sake, if after his Majesty would consent to their liberty, I was ready to send him money; but to buy them as slaves, though for an houre, I would not, they should never come nor be manumised by mee, but that I desired his Majesty to pardon them upon my redemption."[84] Although something of a formality, Roe's stance reflected the desire of some Englishmen to remain above the fray.

Of course, Englishmen did buy and sell human beings because, in truth, slavery was considered perfectly defensible under appropriate circumstances, such as when people were captured in a just war. But slavery seems to have offended English sensibilities when it appeared to be rationalized by purely commercial principles. Slavery, as the jurist Sir Edward Coke allowed in the early seventeenth century, had been "ordained by constitution of Nations, That none should kill another, but that he that was taken in battell should remaine bond to his taker for ever, and to doe with him, and all that should come of him, his will and pleasure." There were, however, important conditions. Early in the sixteenth century, Thomas More had characterized slavery as a practical and beneficial institution in his *Utopia*, but he had also been careful to emphasize that the Utopians "neither make bondemen of prisoners taken in battayle, oneles it be in battaylle that they fought themselves." In his 1601 *Treatise of Commerce*, John Wheeler, secretary of the Company of Merchant Adventurers, lamented that "there are some found so subtill and cunning merchants, that they perswade and induce men to suffer themselves to bee bought and sold, and we have seene in our time enow, and too many which have made merchandise of mens soules."[85] Jobson's and Roe's protestations, in this light, reveal less an English disdain for human bondage under all circumstances than a certain queasiness with the idea of buying and selling human beings.

Other early English criticisms of slavery were equally elliptical and tended to focus on the behavior of other Europeans rather than condemn human bondage outright. English writers were more likely to castigate the Spanish and Portuguese for their treatment of African peoples than they were to express any criticism of slavery itself. The Portuguese, in particular, were frequently derided. As Robert Baker recorded in a mini-epic poem laced with classical references, Africa could be a dangerous place for the English not just because of the climate or the indigenous inhabitants but also because of the rapacity of other European traders. Baker and his shipmates sailed to Africa in 1562 to trade for gold and pepper but were routed by the natives on the Malagueta Coast, a people Baker dismissed as "slaves" and "fiends more fierce then those in hell."[86] Forgetting his misadventures, Baker returned with a second expedition only to find himself part of a group of nine men who became separated from their ships and abandoned as lost along the Gold Coast. Sustained by locals who supplied them with food and fresh water in exchange for their wares, the group eventually found itself in the neighborhood of São Jorge da Mina, a Portuguese trading fort established in the late fifteenth century. For fear of retaliation, English mariners in the past had carefully avoided the Portuguese in Africa and now Baker was forced to contemplate a dilemma. On the one hand, "Our miserie may make / them pitie us the more." But, on the other,

> Their Gallies may perhaps
>   lacke such yong men as we,
> And thus it may fall in our laps,
>   all Galeyslaves to be,
> During our life, and this
>   we shall be sure to have,
> Although we row, such meate as is
>   the allowance of a slave.
> But here we rowe and sterve,
>   our misery is so sore:
> The slave with meat inough they serve,
>   that he may teare his ore.[87]

As Baker saw the issue, the English had another option: They could throw themselves on the mercy of the native Africans and see "what friendship they

will shew." Not surprisingly, however, the wayward English were not too
keen on taking refuge with the locals:

> But what favour would ye
>   of these men looke to have:
> Who beastly savage people be,
>   farre worse then any slave?
> If Cannibals they be
>   in kind, we doe not know,
> But if they be, then welcome we,
>   to pot straight way we goe.
> They naked goe likewise,
>   for shame we cannot so:
> We cannot live after their guise,
>   thus naked for to go.
> By rootes and leaves they live,
>   as beasts doe in the wood:
> Among these heathen who can thrive,
>   with this so wilde a food?
> The piercing heate againe,
>   that scorcheth with such strength,
> Piercing our naked flesh with paine,
>   will us consume at length.[88]

Determining that their prospects were better with untrustworthy fellow
Christians than with naked Africans who lived like animals in an inhospita-
ble climate—and who might choose to make a meal of them—the nine Englishmen rowed toward the fortress. As they neared, however, they were fired
upon and forced back out to sea. Fortunately, Baker's negative assessment of
the Africans proved to be as false as his hope that the Portuguese would offer
sustenance. Once they were safely away from the Portuguese, the English
mariners were met at sea by the son of the local ruler. After Baker recounted
the plight of the lost English mariners, the African prince "[h]ad great pitie
on us" and subsequently invited the English to come ashore. As they did,
their ship was swamped, but the weakened Englishmen were rescued by their
benefactors. Here, in strikingly different language from that used earlier in
the poem, Baker commented favorably on the king's son ("a stout and valiant

man, / In whom I thinke Nature i'wis [certainly], / hath wrought all that she can") and the natives' generosity ("And gave to us, even such as they / themselves do daily eate").[89] After several days, however, the African hosts gave up trying to sustain the castaways and left them to their own devices. In the end, Baker and only two others lived long enough to be picked up by a passing French ship.

The lesson that Englishmen often learned in Africa was simple: There was more to fear from other Europeans in the region than from Africans themselves. William Towerson reported that the natives told him that "the Portugales were bad men, and that they made them slaves if they could take them, and would put yrons upon their legges." Perhaps even more frightening, Towerson noted that "as many Frenchmen or Englishmen, as they could take . . . they would hang them." Walter Wren, who wrote the narrative account of George Fenner's voyage to Africa in 1566, described a failed attempt to trade with some Portuguese merchants who, in what would prove to be a recurring theme, intended nothing more than "villainously to betray us . . . although we meant in truth and honestie, friendly to trafike with them." Richard Rainolds, writing about his trip to Guinea in 1591, made repeated references to the duplicity of the Portuguese and observed that whatever success the English were able to achieve was partly attributable to the fact that the local inhabitants "seemed to be very glad that no Portugall was come in our ship." The local ruler, he noted, "did esteeme them as people of no truth." Rainolds was inclined to agree but explained that most of the Iberians "resident in these places be banished men or fugitives, for committing most hainous crimes and incestuous acts." Not surprisingly, then, "they are of the basest behaviour that we have ever seene of these nations in any other country."[90]

By extension, Englishmen frequently authored sympathetic or even admiring comments about the Africans they encountered in Africa. Although the occasional English visitor to coastal West Africa may have dwelled on gross stereotypes that suggested sub-Saharan Africans were inferior or abnormal, most Englishmen before the mid-seventeenth century, as profit-oriented traders, seem to have been comfortable with the notion that Africans in Africa were "gentle and loving," or "very friendly and tractable." Francis Petty, who sailed with Thomas Cavendish during his circumnavigation, recounted that they stopped briefly at Sierra Leone on the outward leg of their journey where "they played and daunced all the forenoone among the Negros."[91] If Englishmen, in general, were ethnocentric and prone to characterize non-Europeans in unflattering ways, Englishmen in Africa were more pragmatic. Virtually every English voyager to Africa was involved in some sort of mercantile endeavor and therefore most written accounts dwell on matters having to do with the actual voyage, navigation, disease, and trade. When they did bother to comment on the nature or character of the local inhabitants, their observations tended to be impressionistic, even if they did take note that the natives were naked, black, and adorned with jewelry or extensive scarification. Even so, English observers rarely elaborated on these matters and often ignored them entirely.

The message from Africa was decidedly mixed. Just as they had learned elsewhere, the English found slavery to be a characteristic feature of Africa, with an internal logic they typically deemed not worth questioning. Unlike other parts of the world, other European nations were already actively engaged in the appropriation and transshipment of large numbers of indigenous inhabitants to southern Europe and the Americas where the unfortunates were destined to serve out the remainder of their days as slaves. Indigenous slave systems were remarkable and interesting to English eyes, but they did not often elicit much concern because the impact on English efforts to profit from other commercial exchanges was minimal. Some English merchants even bought into the system when they acclimated themselves to their new surroundings. Slavery in Africa was a different matter because, while English merchants may have first appeared in the region to tap into the trade in gold, pepper, ivory, and other regional commodities, the nature of slavery and the slave trade had already been changed by European actors. Slaves were more of a merchantable and potentially profitable commodity in coastal West Africa than in any other place the English visited in the early modern era. Perhaps to their credit, the first wave of English in Africa (John Hawkins apart) distanced themselves from the African slave trade. Their unwillingness to trade in human beings, however, was more an indication of the absence of reliable markets with reliable buyers than a measure of any kind of cultural revulsion to the practice or moral opposition to slavery.

* * *

Early modern Englishmen encountered slavery, regardless of whether they wanted to, wherever they traveled. Slavery was characteristic of the exotic and remote regions of the world being encountered for the first time by intrepid Englishmen in the late sixteenth and early seventeenth centuries. Locating human bondage in the Russian steppes, the Muslim world, South Asia,

China, and Africa was a useful way of emphasizing how England was not only some distance away from these places in geographic terms but also culturally distinctive. Even if these places came in for praise because of their wealth and power, the presence of slavery indicated that the inhabitants of Asia, Russia, the Islamic world, and sub-Saharan Africa lacked the same commitment to the principle of individual liberty that the English liked to claim was the hallmark of the world they inhabited at home. Slavery might also be a measure of the deficiency of a given society or culture. Slavery did not always factor into English characterizations of other nations and peoples, but even its absence was revealing. Perhaps ironically, English writers were seemingly more likely to mention slavery as a significant part of the day-to-day lives of people who lived in complex, civil societies than they were to consider the subject in settings they perceived to be uncivilized or among a people they categorized as barbarous. One way to read the rather minimal evidence of slavery in Ireland, for example, is to suggest that slavery was less a measure of incivility and savagery than it was glaring proof that a given society was corrupt, that a civilization had sullied itself. The same could be said of Africa where English observers, in their more reflective moments, were more likely to characterize slavery as a questionable trading practice of the less-than-honorable Portuguese rather than a fully rationalized domestic institution. When the English encountered people who willingly embraced an irrational, predatory system of slavery that reduced human beings to mere commodities, it reinforced an emerging exceptionalist worldview in which Englishness was buttressed by liberty while foreignness, strangeness, or corruption was indicted by institutional slavery.

It is also striking, considering the rapid development of the transatlantic slave trade and the emergence of scientific racism in subsequent decades, that early English impressions of slavery in Africa during this period were not especially distinctive in a comparative context. In the absence of any systematic English involvement in the transatlantic slave trade and as outsiders trying to break into a market largely controlled by the Portuguese, there were more reasons to embrace Africans as potential allies than to denigrate them outright and some logic to insisting that the English were not interested in the slave trade. To be sure, anti-black prejudice was on the rise in the Anglo-Atlantic world and the early stirrings of a racialized national consciousness was certainly in evidence even in the last half of the sixteenth century. But the pursuit of economic gain that underlay every English voyage to coastal West Africa played a larger role in conditioning the English to think and act in certain ways and helps explain why mariners might have been eager to point out the rather more positive qualities to be found in African societies and peoples. Interestingly, it was despite English activities in Africa rather than because of them that the English nation as a whole was increasingly inclined to associate African peoples with slavery. This occurred, however, because of circumstances in another part of the world: Spanish and Portuguese America, particularly the West Indies. In the Iberian Atlantic world of the early modern era, Englishmen thought of African peoples primarily as slaves, and English privateers, smugglers, and pirates—to the degree that it would further their mercenary aims—were perfectly content to engage them on that level.

CHAPTER 3

Imaginary Allies: Englishmen and Africans in Spain's Atlantic World

In conversation with the Englishman, I told him that England
must be good country as there were no slaves there; and he said to
me that it was true, they were all freemen in England; whereupon I
said that John Hawkins had been engaged in a slaving voyage, and
had brought the slaves here to New Spain, and I asked him, how he
accounted for this?

—Juan Gelofe, 1572[1]

As it made its way down the Atlantic seaboard in the direction of the Canary
Islands, the large English naval squadron must have been an impressive sight.
The year was 1595 and the 28 ships and roughly 2,500 men sailing under
the divided command of two aging knights—John Hawkins and Francis
Drake—represented England's first large-scale assault against Spain in six
years. But as impressive as it surely was to witness, it was a familiar scene.
English ships under the command of the nation's most renowned captains
routinely sallied forth to punish the Spanish and cripple their ability to continue prosecuting the now decade-old Anglo-Spanish War by plundering the
West Indies. The English were practiced pirates and privateers and had conducted similar expeditions throughout the previous decades, although they
typically did so with far fewer men and ships and with a greater commitment
to secrecy. Perhaps that would have been a good idea here, for this last great
privateering expedition of the sixteenth century would prove to be disastrous
in the end. The English would reap few rewards; Drake and Hawkins would

both perish; and many ships, soldiers, and sailors would never make it back to England.

The expedition began with a preliminary and fruitless assault on the Canary Islands in early October. With little to show for its efforts, the English fleet then headed across the Atlantic. During the initial planning stages, the English schemed to attack Panama, a familiar strategy by the 1590s, but Elizabeth was reluctant to commit the necessary resources and was worried about robbing the British Isles for an extended period of time of the ships that would defend the shores from another attempted Spanish invasion. Drake and Hawkins were therefore tasked with a less risky and less time-consuming mission: assaulting San Juan de Puerto Rico where, rumor had it, they might capture a crippled Spanish silver ship. But, as in the Canaries, the English once again failed to achieve their objective. Rather than return to England empty-handed, Drake (in sole command after the death of Hawkins off Puerto Rico in November) decided to try to salvage his reputation and do damage to Spain elsewhere. As a man who had faced adversity in the West Indies many times before, Drake was confident that he knew the solution to his present problem. Arriving off the northern coast of South America at Rio de la Hacha in December, Drake steeled himself and his men and determined to relive past glories and yet again embarrass the Spanish on their own turf. To do so, he realized, the English interlopers would need help from those people who had done so much in the past to help the northern Europeans amass wealth and undermine Spain's ability to defend its American territories. To snatch victory from the jaws of defeat, then, Drake went looking for his old friends, his African allies.[2]

Englishmen and Africans had been working together in the West Indies, sometimes willingly and sometimes not, for more than thirty years. Thousands of Englishmen sailing in hundreds of ships had passed through the Caribbean since mid-century, during which time they had repeatedly sought out Africans, free and enslaved, for the help they could provide as military allies, translators, intermediaries, and guides. When practicable, the English also took profitable advantage of Africans as hostages and slaves. African agents provided the English with valuable information about Spanish defenses, weak spots in the colonial armor, places where goods could be bought and sold, where ships sailed and provisions might be found, and how to exploit both the land and sea to their greatest advantage. Of course, most Englishmen knew and accepted that the vast majority of black-skinned people in the Americas were enslaved and were primarily of value in the region for their labor. When the English bought and sold Africans or took them hostage and ransomed them back to their owners, they became willing participants in (and endorsers of) the transatlantic slave system. But African peoples were more than simple objects of exchange in the global struggle for power among European nations. Numerous African peoples were actually free inhabitants of Spanish cities and armed for colonial defense. Other Africans, most notably *cimarrones* (cimarrons), were free by virtue of having run away or rebelled and could be found (though not easily) in the more remote regions of the Spanish Main and, especially, Panama. Africans were everywhere in Spain's Atlantic world and without them this massive expanse of land and water would have been incomprehensible and largely inaccessible to English merchants, mariners, and privateers. Not surprisingly, then, when Drake was lost in the waning months of 1595 he turned to Africans to lead his expeditionary force out of the morass.

After the English managed their first victory at Rio de la Hacha, the commander had little doubt about how to proceed. First, a member of Drake's personal entourage, Thomas Maynarde, reported that "we tooke many prisoners Spaniards & negroes, some slaves repairinge to us voluntarily." According to Governor Manso de Contreras, some of the "Negroes employed at the pearling station . . . gave Francis Drake information about my plans and where to find our people and your majesty's treasure." Once Drake gathered this intelligence, however, he almost immediately ransomed "the whole (except the slaves which voluntarily repayred unto us) . . . for 24000 peases." The English turned a tidy profit by selling many Africans back into slavery. At the same time, the English also left the region with scores of Africans who would augment the depleted English forces in their further depredations. Manso de Contreras claimed the English departed with "100 Negroes and Negresses from the pearl station, who for the most part joined him voluntarily."[3] When Drake and his men continued on to Nombre de Dios, in Panama, Drake expected to find more Spanish treasure and even more African assistance, this time in the form of the independent African bands that had so famously aided him in his exploits during the 1570s.

Through the waning days of 1595, English and Spanish officials were equally confident in the voluntary nature of the cooperative relationship between African peoples and the English. Drake's desire to get to Panama reflected his understanding, shared by Spanish authorities and repeatedly emphasized by Richard Hakluyt, that the "Negros Simerons [were] mortall enemies to the Spanyards."[4] English writers famously expressed sympathy for the plight of America's indigenous inhabitants and the atrocities they endured under the putatively cruel Spaniards, but only rarely were like lamentations recorded about the abuses Africans suffered under slavery. Nonetheless, in the 1590s John King, a charismatic preacher in Kent and future Bishop of London, working with what he had read in Girolamo Benzoni's *La Historia del Mondo Nuovo*, described "[t]he poore Nigrite their slave," who "after his toile the whole daie undergone, in steed of his meale at nighte, if he came short in any parcell of his taske enjoyned, they stripte of[f] all his cloathing, bounde him hande and foote, tied him crosse to a post," and then "beate him with wyre and whipcord, til his body distilled with gore bloud, they powred either molten pitch or scalding oile into his sores to supple them, washed him with pepper and salte, and so left him upon a boarde till he might recover himselfe againe." Predictably, King's intent was not to mourn the victim so much as it was to castigate the Spanish. As he recounted, after his tale of Spanish brutality, it was now much easier for him to understand why some Indians, "being accustomed to eate the flesh of man, would notwithstanding refraine the flesh of a Spaniarde, when they had caught one, fearing least such pestilent nutriment would breed some contagion within them."[5]

For Sir William Alexander a generation later, it was a matter of course that "to procure their libertie hating most what they feele for the present, and hoping for better by a change," enslaved Africans in Spanish America "will joyne with any strong enemy that landing there dare attempt the conquest of that Countrey." Few Englishmen dwelled on what motivated cimarrons and other Africans, beyond their suffering as slaves, and the depth of genuine English interest in the condition of Africans in the Americas is questionable. Most often, English observers argued that the Spanish brought the problem of slave resistance upon themselves. When the anonymous author of *The Drake Manuscript* put together his nearly 200 images of West Indian plants, animals, and human life (and drafted the brief captions) in the 1580s, he described Africans as slaves, but he also noted that the inhabitants of Nombre de Dios were "afraid to have the gold and silver transported by land from Panama . . . because of the runaway negro slaves who steal and plunder everything they find on the road belonging to the Spaniards. These runaway negroes form bands for fear to be surprised by the Spaniards." To Sir Richard Hawkins in 1593, cimarrons were "fugitive Negroes" who had rebelled or run away "for the bad intreatie which their Masters had given them [and] were then retyred into the mountaines and lived upon the spoyle of such Spaniards

Figure 3. "How the Negro Slaves Work and Look for Gold in the Mines of the Region called Veragua" [Panama]. From the *Histoire naturelle des Indes*, manuscript, ca. 1586, fol. 100r. The Pierpont Morgan Library, New York. MA 3900. Bequest of Clara S. Peck, 1983. Photographic credit: The Pierpont Morgan Library, New York.

as they could master." When Englishmen wrote about cimarrons in Spanish America, there was an undercurrent of sympathy for those who had rebelled from a system of slavery that had degenerated into "inhuman and barbarous cruel dealings."[6]

Whatever may have led the Africans to rise up against the Spanish, the English recognized that the rebels were potentially invaluable power brokers under the right circumstances. Unfortunately, what Drake and his men found after they landed in Nombre de Dios and proceeded to march overland to Panama in early 1596 was an even more complicated human terrain than they had anticipated. Some Africans stood ready to assist the English, including "twelve negroes . . . from Rio de la Hacha," "a mulatto cowherd named Amador, who went over to them, as their guide," and "a Negro of his majesty's at the Porto Belo works called Agustín" whom Spanish officials worried could also be an effective guide.[7] At the same time, the English were fiercely resisted by an even more impressive body of Africans whose collective attitude toward the English was far less accommodating than it had been in previous years. Whereas runaway Africans stood ready to assist Drake in his efforts during the 1570s, allies were much more difficult to come by during the desperate months when Drake was splashing about the West Indies looking to recapture the glory of his previous adventures. Now, it seemed, cimarrons would rather defend Spanish America from outside invaders. If only in part because of the efforts of Africans allied with the Spanish, the English retreated with little to show for their efforts.

This ultimately incidental moment in the larger history of Anglo-Atlantic colonialism is not typically given a great deal of attention by historians.[8] Early modern scholars interested in the intersection between Englishmen and Africans during the sixteenth century generally concentrate their collective gaze on John Hawkins's earlier dalliances in the transatlantic slave trade during the 1560s or Drake's intriguing alliance with cimarrons in Panama during the 1570s. But as the 1595 expedition reveals, Anglo-African encounters in Spain's Atlantic world were never especially straightforward and tended to be shaped by the pragmatic considerations of all parties. In the West Indies, of course, slavery mattered enormously. Yet, the role played by African peoples in the region was much more intricate and the English and Spanish both recognized the expertise, knowledge, and assistance of African individuals. In fact, as important as the slave trade would become in subsequent decades and as tantalizing as Anglo-cimarron cooperation appears in retrospect, English mariners seem to have interacted with African peoples more frequently in other arenas and through other mediums. Much more than we may appreciate, the success or failure of the English in an Atlantic world largely defined by the Spanish presence was contingent on how early English visitors viewed and used Africans and adapted themselves to a complex environment defined in large part by non-European actors.

Anglo-African encounters were also complicated by the ongoing and increasingly acidic Anglo-Spanish rivalry. Because of religious and national tensions, which boiled over into overt warfare after 1585, Englishmen in the Americas tended to think about human bondage as the likely plight of the unfortunates of any nation. Just as slavery framed the way Englishmen often thought about themselves as a nation or was invoked as a measure of the degeneracy of others, slavery provided a convenient explanatory framework for the African presence in the region. Even so, no simple correlation existed between Africans and slavery because other peoples—Europeans, Indians, and Moors—could also be found in bondage in Spain's and Portugal's American colonies. English seafarers rightly recognized that neither their whiteness nor their religion protected them from human bondage in the Americas and therefore worried a great deal about the likely possibility that they could be captured and enslaved should bad luck befall them on their sojourns. As we shall see later, by the latter decades of the sixteenth century, the capture and enslavement of Englishmen in the Mediterranean was becoming a more common problem and English West Indian privateers never doubted that a similar fate could befall them. English fears about their own susceptibility to captivity and bondage and the need for useful allies in the early modern Atlantic world made the Americas a distinctive arena for Anglo-African contact. Paradoxically, Englishmen in the West Indies relied heavily on the assistance, willing or otherwise, of African allies in the Americas even as they demonstrated their willingness to buy and sell the very same people and treat them as base commodities.

* * *

The Englishmen who encountered and subsequently wrote about Africans in the Americas were an unsavory lot. On the whole, they consisted of large numbers of smugglers and pirates whose actions in the West Indies would not be tolerated in and around the British isles.[9] But because of England's incipient colonial ambitions and its deteriorating relationship with Spain, maritime predation in the Americas was not only condoned but embraced. Even slave trading, something that would not become an integral part of English commercial activities in the Atlantic world until the second half of the seventeenth century, was pursued for a time during the 1560s. The sixteenth-century English slave trade imparted a dramatic, if unsurprising, message: Africans in the Americas were valuable commodities as slaves and the English—despite their self-professed abhorrence for human bondage—were eager to participate. It would be a mistake, however, to make too much of the sixteenth-century English slave trade. Of the more than one hundred English expeditions to the Caribbean between 1562 and 1603, only four were for the express purpose of profiting from the slave trade.[10] Even more, the records of these voyages suggest that there was only small interest in the captive Africans themselves. In the surviving accounts of Sir John Hawkins's three expeditions (1562, 1564, and 1567) and John Lovell's one voyage (1566), little information was recorded about the slave cargos, and the fate of the 1,300 transported Africans is difficult to determine with precision. If English mariners were uninterested in dwelling on the plight or characteristics of the Africans they bought and sold as slaves, readers at home were hardly clamoring for details either. The English were never shy about revealing their profound interest in the commodities that could be found in the Caribbean, sailing directions, and documenting their profound dislike for the Spanish. Slavery, or rather the English enslavement of other peoples, was a subject most early modern Englishmen would rather not talk about.[11]

Still, English sources drawn from the experiences of English pirates and privateers shed a great deal of light on Spanish America's African population, particularly the cimarrons. If the English slave trade is the most nefarious example of Anglo-African interchange in the early modern Atlantic, the coordinated activity and apparent friendship between English pirates and Panama's cimarrons during the 1570s is surely the most celebrated. During the course of at least thirteen separate voyages to the region between 1570 and 1577, cimarrons proved to be indispensable allies in English efforts to loot the Spanish possessions. Cimarrons were a continual source of anxiety to the local Spanish; in 1570, a minor official in the region informed the Spanish Crown that the "matter which, in this kingdom, most urgently demands remedial action is the problem of dispersing the *Cimarrones*, black outlaws in rebellion in its mountainous, unpopulated interior." According to this source, cimarrons were practiced thieves and murderers, but they also "carry off negroes sent out for fire-wood, and induce others to leave their owners, as they do every day." Spanish officials recognized that runaway slaves were serious power brokers and the desire of the formerly enslaved to exact revenge from those who had held them in bondage fed into their relationship with other Europeans who also hoped to see the Spanish come to some harm.[12]

The details of English interactions with the cimarrons are familiar. It was during Drake's third independent command to the Caribbean, beginning in 1572, that English privateers first established an alliance with cimarrons in Panama. In January of the following year, some twenty Englishmen and forty Africans combined their efforts in an assault on the highway between Nombre de Dios and Venta de Chagre. Whereas Spanish officials had once been mildly concerned about the separate activities of runaway slaves and foreign privateers, this new situation was utterly chilling. "The league between the English and the negroes is very detrimental to this kingdom," the Municipal Council of Panama concluded in February 1573, "because, being so thoroughly acquainted with the region and so expert in the bush, the negroes will show them the methods and means to accomplish any evil design they may wish to carry out and execute." For the English, this alliance would enable them to fleece the Spanish of their gold and silver, but rumors also circulated that the English marauders intended to attack certain cities and "deliver to them [the cimarrons] what Spanish inhabitants, men and women, it may have, to be their slaves."[13]

On the surface, English relations with cimarrons challenge the notion that Englishmen tended to view Africans either in a negative light or through the prism of slavery. To be sure, some imaginative observers envisaged revolutionary potential in the Anglo-cimarron alliance. Richard Hakluyt, after conferring with Drake on the subject, thought that Africans could be usefully employed in the effort to take over and establish a settlement at the Straits of Magellan. There, he suggested in 1580, they could "be planted by hundreds or thowsands" and "induced to live subject to the gentle government of the English." Based on his understanding of early modern climate theory, Hakluyt asserted that "the Symeron although borne in a hote region . . . has been bredde as a slave, in all toyle farre from delicacie" and would therefore be "able to endure the climate, and think himself a happy man when as by good provision he shal find himselfe plentifully fed, warmly clothed, and well lodged and by our nation made free from the tyrannous Spanyard, and quietly and courteously governed by our nation." Thus, in Hakluyt's mind, cimaroons could be transferred to another region and become the foundation for a permanent English settlement and the mechanism through which the English could "make subjecte to England all the golden mines of Peru and all the coste and tract of that firme of America upon the Sea of Sur. And work the like effect on the hither side of that Firme."[14] Hakluyt's imaginary cimarron transplants were not simply friends and allies, they were essential linchpins and agents of empire.

By the time it was written, however, Hakluyt's vision of an Anglo-African settlement was already outdated. No other expeditions had as much good fortune as Drake's first coordinated effort in 1573. John Oxenham's attempt to capitalize on the alliance in 1577 was as disastrous as his former commander's was profitable. Like his predecessor's, Oxenham's expedition was small—far fewer than a hundred men and only one ship in excess of a hundred tons. Oxenham established contact with the cimarrons soon after his arrival in Panama and proceeded to march inland. This time, local officials leaped into action. One force of Spaniards easily captured Oxenham's vessels while he was away with the body of his men and the cimarrons. The remaining Englishmen were either captured or rounded up in the ensuing months while the now-militarized Spaniards took the fight to the runaway slaves themselves. Oxenham was predictably angry and he was quick to blame the Africans whose support he had been denied. Before his execution, Oxenham reported that the English relationship with the cimarrons had soured and that "if at present the negroes meet any English in the bush or in their villages now, the English will have cause to fear greatly and will be in great danger, for . . . they did not wish the Spaniards to come in search of them."[15] Cimarron pragmatism seriously hampered future English prospects in the region.

One problem for the English was that their alliance with runaway slaves in Spanish America was largely a marriage of convenience. Cimarrons were valuable because they abetted England's (or, rather, Drake's) larcenous predilections and fueled imperial dreams (Hakluyt's).[16] Early modern Englishmen were neither interested in nor committed to eradicating the institution of slavery or assisting in the liberation of black peoples anywhere in the Atlantic world. Spanish officials in America, however, if only as a matter of self-preservation, were remarkably successful in diminishing the threat of an Anglo-African alliance because they were committed to a long-term resolution of the problems caused by runaway slaves. They reacted forcefully to the cimarron threat in 1577 by passing harsh legislation to try to curb the growth of extant runaway communities. Through the 1550s, Spanish laws concerning the African population in Mexico, which may have numbered more than

20,000 at the time, had typically followed Iberian precedents. Legislation provided for certain protections and immunities, guaranteed marital privileges and family solidarity, and articulated avenues by which individuals could become free. But none of these efforts diminished slave resistance. The escalating number of slave revolts after mid-century, increasing cooperation between Africans and Indians, as well as the coordinated efforts of interloping Europeans and cimarrons prompted more repressive legislation by the 1570s. Spanish officials drew up fugitive slave laws between 1571 and 1574 that established measures for better supervision and harsher penalties, including death. Other declarations were equally punitive. Viceroy Martín Enríquez declared in 1579 that any slave who "escaped from the service of his master and is found in the mountains, shall for the same be arrested and castrated."[17]

In addition, Spanish authorities organized and conducted military activities in Panama in an effort to subdue former slaves who demonstrated an inclination to work with the English. Generally known as the Vallano War, the military efforts of 1577–78 succeeded in destroying a number of rebel villages and either capturing or driving away hundreds of cimarrons. In January 1579, local Africans agreed to cease aiding foreign interlopers in exchange for semi-autonomy in two large towns, Santa Cruz la Real and Santiago del Principe. This peace, along with Oxenham's alienation of the cimarrons, soured further English relations. For this reason, when Drake returned to the region in 1596 with the intent of combining his forces with the independent Africans, he found that his former allies not only refused to assist him but actively opposed his efforts. Spanish reports indicate that upon Drake's arrival in the vicinity of Nombre de Dios, "the Negroes of Santiago del Principe would not allow the enemy to take water at the River Fator and killed some of them." This response surely disappointed Drake, but the Spanish were equally surprised with the response of the local African community. Miguel Ruiz Delduayen noted with obvious pleasure that "[t]he subjugated Negroes of both factions at Santiago del Principe and Santa Cruz la Real have rallied to his majesty's service with loyalty, hard work and energy, and the freed Negroes came to serve in this war under the banner of their captain Juan de Roales who is also one of them." Also, "[m]ore loyalty was found among the slaves than was expected, for it was their disloyalty which was feared here and which the enemy counted upon."[18]

Cimarrons may have been the first to recognize that English privateers were far from freedom fighters.[19] Englishmen valued Africans as the enemy of their enemy; they were not interested in the attributes, individually or collectively, of runaway Africans in the Americas. As privateers in search of gold and silver and as the tip of the sword in England's escalating conflict with Spain in the Atlantic world, English privateers did not have the luxury to be concerned with ethnography, international law, or the propriety of human bondage. It was sufficient to note that the cimarrons had "fled from the *Spaniards*, their Masters, by reason of their crueltie, and are since growne to a nation, under two Kings of their owne." In that light, runaway slaves could be conceptualized within the "Black Legend" framework laid down during the previous century. Africans were the victims of Spanish tyranny and of "incredible and more then barbarous and savage endeles cruelties." In this context, it was easy to conclude that Englishmen would be welcomed with open arms. Hakluyt even claimed that "Sir Fraunces Drake and somme other englishe are of so greate credite with the Symerons and with those that mayneteyne those frontier warres, that he mighte bringinge thither a fewe Capitaines and somme of our meaner souldiers late trayned in the base Contries with archers and lighte furniture &c bringe to passe that joyninge with those Inland people, kinge Phillippe mighte either be deprived of his governemente there, or at the leaste of the takinge of his yerely benefite of the mynes."[20] Ultimately, though, this sentiment was simply an aspirational declaration of English hopes and dreams for their own success in the Americas, not a critique of human bondage.

The perspective of other Englishmen in Spain's Atlantic world reinforces the idea that slavery was both commonplace and not especially controversial. Over the course of the sixteenth century, several hundred Englishmen spent some time as permanent or temporary residents in Spain and its American colonies. Well-placed Englishmen, particularly in the seaport towns of southwestern Europe, routinely witnessed African slaves rowing in the galleys or Venetian gondolas, serving as personal servants at royal and papal courts, or toiling among the laboring poor. English visitors to the court of Francis I may even have noticed, or heard rumors about, the young African woman with whom he shared a bed. Some Africans were placed on sale in Bordeaux in 1571, but they were ultimately released by the French government on the grounds that slavery did not exist in France. Slavery may have been rare enough in France for some people to believe that little piece of fiction, but there could be no doubt about slavery's legality on the Iberian Peninsula. A Flemish humanist, upon his arrival in Portugal in 1535, remarked that Moors and sub-Saharan Africans were present in such large numbers that "in Lisbon there are more men and women slaves than free Portuguese." Shocked, he declared that upon his arrival "in Évora I thought that I had come to some city of evil demons: everywhere there were so many blacks whom I so loathe that they may just be able to drive me away from here."[21] Increasingly, over the course of the fifteenth and sixteenth centuries, it was becoming difficult for European observers to ignore the fact that sub-Saharan Africans and their descendants were becoming an ever more important and ever more visible part of the population of southern Europe.

Englishmen were especially familiar with Iberian slavery because, in the wake of the Anglo-Spanish alliance during the 1490s, English merchants cultivated extensive trade networks in the coastal cities of the Iberian Peninsula, or those places where African slavery was most common. Robert Thorne, a wealthy London merchant-tailor and son of a Bristol merchant, resided in Spain during the 1520s. Upon his death in 1532, Thorne's inventory showed an enormous personal estate, including "a house and slaves in Sevyle [valued at] 94£." Ten years earlier, another English resident, Thomas Malliard, left four slaves to his Spanish mistress. Thorne and Malliard were among the small number of English merchants who not only lived in Seville but also were reputed to be active participants in the emerging Atlantic slave trade. Malliard may have left just a few slaves to his mistress, but executors identified fourteen slaves in his possession in the weeks before his death in 1522. Thorne also bought and sold slaves for profit; he and an associate sold thirteen slaves in 1531 to the Welsers, an Augsburg family of merchants and bankers. Like another Englishman, Thomas Bridges, who had bought and sold Africans during the 1510s in Seville, Malliard and Thorne demonstrate the early willingness of English merchants to adapt themselves to local circumstances and their eagerness to take advantage of local markets, including the market in slaves.[22]

Slavery was common in sixteenth-century Seville; notarial records indicate the presence of more than 5,000 slaves in the city between 1501 and 1525. A 1565 census recorded the presence of 6,327 slaves of a total population in excess of 85,000. A few of these individuals were Muslims and Canary Islanders, but most were sub-Saharan Africans. Indeed, throughout the sixteenth century, Africans routinely constituted anywhere from 5 to 10 percent of the population of Iberian coastal cities. This trade inevitably attracted the attention of local English merchants, like William Fowler of Radcliffe and others, who tried to benefit from the system however they could (which could be difficult because legal participation in the African slave trade required a special license). Nonetheless, during the early sixteenth century, English merchants possessed some influence. One group of English merchants received corporate privileges in San Lucar from the Duke of Medina Sidonia in 1517 and subsequently created the Andalusia Company in 1530.[23] Being English did not prevent certain individuals from benefiting from ill-gotten gains.

According to Richard Hakluyt, English merchants had also been involved with trade to the Canary Islands during the sixteenth century. Thomas Midnall and William Ballard took up residence in San Lucar and Andalucia, respectively, as early as 1526, from where they maintained a relationship with merchants in the Canary Islands, including the Englishman Thomas Nichols who composed a description of the islands and native peoples, the Guanches, which Hakluyt published in his collection. Even more significant were the "divers voyages to the Iles of the Canaries" conducted by John Hawkins during the mid-sixteenth century. According to Hakluyt, it was there that Hawkins, "by his good and upright dealing," gathered information about the West Indies from the local inhabitants and was assured "that Negros were very good marchandise in Hispaniola" and that they "might easily bee had uppon the coast of Guinea." When Hawkins made his first slave-trading voyage in 1562, he once again stopped at Teneriffe, "where he received friendly entertainment."[24]

Evidence of active English involvement in either slavery or the slave trade in the Spanish Empire is sparse, but the activities of these few individuals suggest that some influential Englishmen possessed exceptional knowledge and experience. Perhaps no one demonstrates the links between English and Spanish society during this era more than Roger Bodenham. Bodenham participated in several voyages into the Mediterranean in the 1550s and subsequently settled in Seville where he married a Spanish woman and started a family. As a merchant, Bodenham participated in the Barbary trade and transatlantic enterprises that involved slavery. The tables were turned when these risky ventures eventually landed Bodenham in the hands of Moorish privateers who sold him, along with nine other Christians, on the Cadiz slave market where he was fortuitously ransomed by a friend who just happened to recognize him in this moment of crisis. Bodenham did more than trade for his own personal profit, however; he also had important connections in the Elizabethan court, where he sent useful commercial and political information until he departed Spain in 1586.[25] As Bodenham's case demonstrates, there were important physical and intellectual connections between Spain's Atlantic world and that of the English.

The lesson that Africans could be bought, owned, and sold as slaves was therefore not lost on early modern Englishmen, decades before they were making much of an effort to profit from the practice. At the same time, few Englishmen could not have failed to notice that sub-Saharan Africans were neither the most despised group within the Iberian social order—that place was generally reserved for either Jews or Moriscos—nor were they necessarily always held in bondage.[26] Although Africans routinely found their way to Spain and Portugal as slaves, it was not difficult for slaves to become ex-slaves through manumission or self-purchase. The Catholic Church generally applauded manumission and Iberian society had a long tradition of incorporating diverse peoples into the larger social order.[27] The association between blackness and slavery, though palpable, was far from absolute on the Iberian Peninsula. As early as 1474, Ferdinand and Isabella appointed a man of African descent named Juan de Vallodolid, more popularly called "El conde negro," to be a judge and an official leader of Seville's African community. Freedmen also formed a religious brotherhood and operated a hospital to serve the African community in Seville. In 1472, a group of free Africans in Valencia received a license to form a religious brotherhood, which they named the *cofradía* of Nuestra Señora de Gracia. Skin color did not necessarily limit the ability of African peoples to coexist with Europeans and Moors as a free people on the peninsula.[28]

Not surprisingly, then, free Africans could be found throughout Spanish America, especially in the main urban centers and coastal enclaves. Africans had been present in America from the beginning of European colonization in the 1490s. By all accounts, African mariners sailed with Christopher Columbus in the 1490s and African soldiers aided Hernán Cortes and other *conquistadores* in their New World exploits. Many of the earliest African peoples in Spanish America were *ladinos*, or individuals who had already lived in the Iberian world for a number of years. Their numbers were small during the first half of the century; slave traders shipped perhaps 15,000 Africans to the Americas from Spain, the Atlantic islands, or Africa before 1550. During the remainder of the century, as African slavery became more routinized, slave traders transported another 40,000 slaves across the Atlantic. Increasingly, these new arrivals—*bozales* shipped to Spanish America directly from Africa—contributed to the Africanization of the local population. Enslaved Africans therefore lived and worked very visibly in the Americas during the sixteenth century, particularly in those places that interested English observers the most—the Caribbean islands, central Mexico, and the gold-mining region of northern South America.[29]

Perhaps even more surprising than the African presence in sixteenth-century Spanish America was the English presence that could be found there, particularly because Spanish imperial regulations discouraged the presence of foreigners and, especially, Protestants. Necessarily, many English merchants must have been Catholic and most were almost certainly closely connected with the Spanish trade itself. The ties that linked Englishmen throughout the nominal Spanish world are apparent through the case of Robert Tomson, who left England for Seville in 1555. Tomson lived an entire year in Seville, where he "repaired to one John Fields house an English Marchant, who had dwelt in the said city of Sivil 18. or 20. yeres." During this period, he also established ties with a group of English merchants, "servants of one Anthony Hickman and Edward Castelin," who resided in the Canary Islands. Hugh Typton, "an English marchant of great doing" in Seville also served Tomson's needs. When Tomson's fleet set sail from Cadiz in 1556, one of the ships departing for the New World was owned by John Sweeting and captained by his son-in-law Leonard Chilton. On board was yet another English merchant, originally from Exeter, named Ralph Sarre. And once Tomson arrived in New Spain, he found other countrymen and near neighbors he could rely on, including Thomas Blake, "a Scottishman borne [who] . . . had dwelt and bene married in [Mexico City] above twentie yeeres before I came." One Englishman, Thomas Tison, found his way to the West Indies as early as 1526, suggesting that Britons began arriving in the New World within just a few years of the Spanish and establishing loose footholds in the West Indies and on the mainland.[30]

Although the accounts of English merchants tended to focus more on trade possibilities and less on social relations, these men commented freely on Africans in the New World, usually in their mundane role as laborers. Tomson mentioned that the Spanish king owned "20. great and mightie Negroes" in San Juan de Ulua whose sole responsibility was to maintain an island in the harbor. John Chilton made note of the same island and reported that the king employed "about 150 negroes, who all the yeere long are occupied in carying of stones for building & other uses." In Cuba, Chilton remarked, "the Spanyards mainteine . . . many negroes to kil their cattell, and foster a great number of hogs." According to Henry Hawks, Spanish mines could not be operated without slave labor, and a "good owner of mines must have at the least an hundred slaves to cary and to stampe his metals." Africans were, to these English merchants who passed through the Spanish-American world, both instrumental and incidental to the social order. Their presence was necessary to augment native labor, yet their individual identity—culture, language, religion—was generally deemed unworthy of extended comment. There is little evidence to suggest that English residents and merchants sympathized with the plight of African slaves.[31]

Because most Englishmen in the West Indies were only able to relate their experiences from a precarious position as foreigners, interlopers, and even former captives themselves and because they were often motivated by their personal national interests—accessing American riches, promoting colonial enterprises, or even revenge—these early modern English renderings of African peoples in the Americas must be read carefully. It would be a mistake to suggest, for example, that general English attitudes toward Africans were either callous (based on the history of the slave trade) or benevolent (based on Anglo-cimarron cooperation) because these episodes are not particularly representative of broader English experiences at home and in Africa or the expressed viewpoints of typical Englishmen. Moreover, although historians have emphasized the Hawkins and Drake dramas and have attempted to divine some broader sociocultural implications, neither the slave trade nor English engagement with cimarrons provided the most common form of Anglo-African interchange in the early modern Atlantic world. As the observations of the handful of Englishmen who lived among free and enslaved Africans in the New World suggest, there was an array of English experiences with, and presumably attitudes toward, both African peoples and the institution of slavery during the latter part of the sixteenth century. A more careful look at the actions and experiences of English privateers during these decades makes this point even clearer.

*   *   *

Early encounters between Englishmen and Africans in the Atlantic world were even more frequent and mundane than the evidence reveals. Many African peoples, beyond the legendary cimarrons of Panama, were important allies and auxiliaries, and the success or failure of English maritime ventures during this age often hinged on the knowledge, expertise, and willing assistance of Africans. The relationship was not always beneficial to Africans; callous attitudes and a general disregard for Africans as human beings meant that they could just as easily wind up as cargo as serve among the crew. Nonetheless, as crewmen, concubines, guides, translators, hostages, and personal servants, African peoples were an increasingly ubiquitous feature of Elizabethan navies. And as English ships sailed with greater frequency throughout Spain's Atlantic world, the African presence on English ships became even more common.

Englishmen were most likely to interact with Africans on board their own ships and as auxiliaries in their armies than they were on land in Spanish America. Africans showed the English the way to wealth in the early modern Atlantic world. During Sir Francis Drake's stop in the Cape Verde Islands in 1585, on the outbound leg of his first grand privateering expedition to the West Indies, the English made plans to assault the city of Santiago. At least one observer found the town unimpressive and the inhabitants consisting of "some Spaniardes & some Portingalles who have Divers bond slaves bothe blacke men & women." In an effort to track down some valuables, Drake and his military commander, Christopher Carleill, marched 700 men to the inland town of Santo Domingo. At their head was "a *Nigro* to bee our guide which we brought owte of Inglande with us that dwelte before in this Ilande." Apparently, this individual had great incentive to serve the English, because "the generall promised this *Nigro* that if wee could take the Spaniarde that the *Nigro* before was slave unto, that then the Spaniarde shoulde bee slave unto the *Nigro*."[32] This vague indictment of the injustice of slavery and the bitterness of the formerly enslaved was rare, but clearly the English understood just how motivating the promise of retribution could be for former slaves regardless of who they were.

Drake's attack on the Cape Verde Islands failed to reap great profits, but it did provide a venue for the English to interact with Africans in the Atlantic setting. Significantly, the most important Africans may have been those the English carried with them for the express purpose of acting as guides. These were indispensable figures in many English expeditions to Africa, the Atlantic islands, and the Caribbean. Their knowledge of the landscape and, perhaps, desire to exact revenge on those who may have used them badly made them important auxiliaries. The first two Africans on board Sir Francis Drake's early voyage around the world, beginning in 1577, were already with the fleet when it departed Plymouth in November. Like other intermediaries, go-betweens, or "cultural brokers" in the Atlantic world, these men (who may have been picked up during Drake's earlier West Indian voyages) facilitated communication between Englishmen and Spaniards.[33] Drake also valued their input as guides and potential diplomats between English mariners and the cimarrons living near Panama. According to Spanish sources, Drake

acquired one individual in 1573 from among the runaway community in Vallano. This history aroused much speculation among Spanish officials, who
imagined that "under the protection of this negro, who must be a chieftain
amongst the negroes of that region, [Drake] could carry his booty, by land,
to the shore of the North Sea."[34]

Regardless of Spanish suspicions, the precise origin and identity of these
two men, who sailed with eighty-six Englishmen and three boys, is difficult
to determine. While on the west coast of South America, several Spaniards
who had been taken prisoner by Drake for a short period of time reported the
presence of two African men. Only one of these men, however, had actually
been with the fleet since the beginning. Soon after Drake rounded Cape
Horn, he went ashore at the island of Mocha, off the coast of Chile. During
a conflict with the natives, two of Drake's men were killed, including "Diego, a
black Moore, which was Drake's man." Diego died in November 1578, yet all
subsequent Spanish reports generally record the presence of two "negroes,"
only one of whom came from England. Thus, an official report to the Spanish Crown from Peru claimed that Drake left England with a Portuguese pilot and "one of the negroes whom he had taken from Vallano." But even this
simple fact could not be agreed upon. A royal licentiate from Guatemala
named Valverde wrote to Philip several months later in 1579 that he suspected
the "negro was not of those from Vallano but that he had been taken from a
ship near Panama." From a deposition recorded in Panama, it was reported
that Drake took "a negro who was said to be a Cimarron" from the ship of
Gregorio Alvarez, but that he "has also had with him, for the last six years, a
negro who used to belong to Captain Gonzalo de Palma." Juan Pascal, who
was deposed in 1580, also reported that Drake carried with him "two negroes.
One of the latter spoke Spanish, and also English, and all said that the Englishman had brought him from England. The other one also spoke Spanish,
and told witness so, and that he had been seized at sea."[35] When he had been
seized, and from where, is unclear.

In actuality, more than two or three Africans came aboard Drake's ships
during this expedition. From the time he reached South America, Drake
continually acquired a small number of Africans, some of whom were kept
for longer periods of time than others. Off the coast of Chile, Drake released
two Spanish prisoners, but he kept one, Nicholas Jorge, and an African slave.
He picked up another slave, along with three Spanish mariners, near Callao,
but this slave was set adrift with the Spaniards almost immediately thereafter. Several times during the voyage Drake abandoned Spaniards and slaves

rather than leave them ashore in order to prevent them from warning their countrymen about the English presence. Still, despite the constant food shortages that haunted all ships of the age, Drake continued to retain some African slaves. When he captured the ship of Benito Díaz Bravo, he kept the shipmaster and several African slaves because he expected they could provide him with useful information. In one notorious episode, Drake even tortured Díaz Bravo's nephew, Francisco Jácome, in an effort to discover the location of some treasure he learned about from the testimony of the Africans. Eventually Drake let the Spaniards go free, but he kept the slaves for a while longer.[36]

English mariners, like Drake, kept Africans aboard ship because they hoped to exploit them for their own advantage. Not only was "Drake's man" Diego a useful source of intelligence to Drake, he also "did us great service" in the construction of storehouses, "having a speciall skill in the speedy erection of such houses."[37] Africans were also useful to the English as intermediaries and messengers. As a people who, English authors occasionally argued, suffered under slavery in Spanish and Portuguese America, the English concluded that their messengers harbored little affinity for the Spanish and, if there was any foul play, the blow would be softened if danger fell on an African rather than on another Englishman. At the same time, their knowledge of the land and linguistic dexterity could not be underestimated. English interlopers were aware of the indispensable expertise of these go-betweens and understood how Africans facilitated their efforts to extract wealth from Spanish and Portuguese America. Thus, while the Earl of Cumberland's ships waited in the Rio de la Plata in 1586 with captives, the "Admirall sent a [captured] Negro ashore, with letters from the Portugals, that wee had prisoners aboord." In the Azores, ten years later, the same commander "sent a boat off with an old Portgull, and an African of Mozambique, who bearing a flagge of truce, should give the Ilanders to understand what his Lordships pleasure was."[38] Whether these intermediaries were entirely trustworthy or merely expendable, the English commander made good use of them.

Africans were not always deliberately sought after as crew members. When pressed by adverse circumstances, English ship captains were forced to fill out depleted crews with any and all available manpower during their Atlantic voyages. In October 1582, an Englishman off the coast of Guinea reported that "Ca[pt. William] Hawkins, Ca[pt. Nicholas] Parker & I went aboorde the portyngals to buy some of their slaves (for divers of o[ur] men were deadde). . . . We had 4 negroes, & there we had a boy w[hi]ch the vyce-ad. [Luke Ward] exchanged for a boy he had before."[39] High mortality rates compelled ship captains to make dramatic choices, including filling out the ranks with Africans. Given the option, though, many English ship captains chose to get rid of their Africans before returning to port, even if that meant selling them back into slavery. As early as 1566, George Fenner had five Africans on board, three of whom had originally served as hostages when the English ships attempted to establish a trading relationship on the coast of Guinea. As Fenner's fleet returned to England, they encountered a Portuguese vessel carrying sugar and cotton. Believing these goods to be more valuable commodities in England than the five Africans, "our Captaine and Marchants shewed them five Negroes that we had, and asked whether they would buy them, which they were very desirous to doe, and agreed to give for them 40 chests of sugar."[40] According to the deposition of Alonso de Ulloa de Toro, John Burgh's men seized more than a hundred African men and women in 1593, along with a quantity of pearls, after capturing two men "whom they tortured to find out where the pearl-fishers' camp was." Eventually, however, "they returned most of the negroes to their owners in exchange for some ransom." The ransoming of slaves back to their owners was common. James Langston chose this method during his 1593–94 raid on Santo Domingo, as had Drake during his attack on the island and in Cartagena nearly ten years earlier.[41] In 1600, Captain John Aday in the *Phoenix* captured a small bark off Barbados with more than a hundred African slaves bound for Cartagena. The English happily sold them for sixty ounces of pearls on the island of La Margarita.[42]

Clearly, Englishmen not only routinely held Africans against their will but also sometimes actively sought out Africans to buy and hold as slaves. In 1583, Diego Menéndez de Valdés wrote to the Spanish Crown from San Juan de Puerto Rico that "two negroes . . . were brought to me with the Englishman" who had been captured during a failed landing from a fleet under the command of William Hawkins. The Africans, he observed, "speak Spanish well and say they were captured in isla de Fuego although the Englishman says they bought them there." In their own defense, the Africans claimed to be "free men" but "while this is being looked into they . . . are working with the rest on the improvement of the fortress." Considering that the English had previously "asked the people on shore if they wanted to barter for women," it would seem that William Hawkins's fleet was actively looking to gain from selling Africans into slavery.[43]

But finding buyers for captured Africans was not always feasible and any potential future benefit of ransoming Africans back to their owners or selling

Figure 4. "Canoe for Pearl-Fishing." From the *Histoire naturelle des Indes*, manuscript, ca. 1586, fol. 57. The Pierpont Morgan Library, New York. MA 3900. Bequest of Clara S. Peck, 1983. Photographic credit: The Pierpont Morgan Library, New York.

them anew was often outweighed by the impracticality of having extra mouths to feed in the interim. Thus, on many occasions, English ship captains were content simply to put their African captives ashore rather than provision them during the Atlantic crossing. This option proved to be attractive to Christopher Newport in 1591 when his ships captured a Portuguese slaver loaded with 300 Africans bound for Cartagena. Newport took the slave ship to Puerto Rico where he "hoped to help us to some money for his Negros there," but the ship's merchant deceived the Englishmen and they were unable to sell the slaves. Thus, the Englishmen sailed some distance down the coast from the city of San Juan and "landed the Negros, and sunke the ship."[44] Abandoning Africans to their own fate ashore may have been callous, but it also ensured that Africans and Englishmen alike would have a better chance of surviving their Atlantic endeavors by fending off the threat of privation at sea and slavery ashore.

The record of Drake's circumnavigation also reveals that English ships picked up African women during their voyages. While sailing north along the western coast of Guatemala and Honduras, Drake captured the ship of Don Francisco de Zárate. In addition to looting the ship of its valuables, Drake took an African man and woman whom he found on board. The woman, called María, was thought to be "a proper negro wench," and may have been kept on board to satisfy the tawdry desires of crewmen during the long trans-Pacific voyage that lay ahead. After a voyage of more than two months, Drake's ships reached the islands of the western Pacific. By this time, the presence of the woman on board had either become problematic (she may have been a source of tension among the men or she may have become pregnant) or no longer necessary because other women would be encountered on Pacific Islands. An anonymous source clearly indicates that the decisive issue was pregnancy and that she was "gotten with child between the captaine and his men pirates." Whether he was more concerned about maintaining an infant or his reputation should his ship return to port with a mulatto child in tow, Drake decided to abandon María and two African men on Crab Island, just south of the Moluccas.[45]

Even more interesting, considering the options available to the English, is that many Africans returned to England from the Caribbean with English ships. John Lovell's largely unsuccessful slave-trading expedition of 1566–67 made landfall in Britain with a dozen or more unsold slaves from a cargo that originated in West Africa. When John Hawkins departed on his third slave-trading expedition in October 1567, a month after Lovell's return, Hawkins

reportedly took with him fifty Africans who had been part of the earlier expeditions. When he limped home from this voyage a year later, he still had a
dozen or so Africans with him.[46] An expedition led by William King in 1592
followed closely in the wake of Christopher Newport; in April, while off the
coast of Santo Domingo, he "tooke a shippe of an hundred tunnes come
from Guiny, laden with two hundred and seventy Negros." Once again, King
took the ship to Puerto Rico where, in addition to capturing another ship
loaded with wine, he "put the Negroes, except fifteene, all on land." The fifteen who returned with the ships to England would have constituted an ab-
normally large number. Typically, Africans arrived in England during the
sixteenth century in smaller groups of one to five. When Francis Drake returned to England from his 1572–73 expedition, he almost certainly had at
least two African men on board, including the previously noted "Diego a
Negro," who had provided valuable information about the military strength
of specific towns, the location of gold and silver, and the route most commonly traveled by Spanish treasure trains. The other was "a young Negrito of
three or foure yeeres old, which we brought away" from a Spanish ship, even
though they released five or six other African slaves "to seeke their Masters."[47]

Sporadic references to Africans in the British Isles can be found before
the mid-sixteenth century, but it was not until the late Elizabethan era that
Africans appeared more routinely in English society.[48] Little of any substance
is known about the African presence during the first three decades of Elizabeth's reign. In a fictitious dialogue published in 1559, the Norwich cosmog-
rapher William Cuningham crafted a conversation, partly concerning the
cause of dark skin, in which the student tells his teacher (in passing) that "I
have sene men of that colour, & we call them / Æthiopians."[49] Paul Baning,
a London alderman, claimed possession of three "blackamore maids" in 1568,
but it is not clear how he came by them or how they were employed. Edward
Stanley, Third Earl of Derby, may have employed or owned an African servant as early as 1569, although the records leave room for doubt.[50] Nicholas
Wichehalse of Barnstaple, however, certainly possessed an African servant or
slave who was referred to in his 1570 will as "Anthonye my negarre." Civil records from St. Andrew's Parish in Plymouth contain records of at least two
burials during the 1580s, including that of John Anthony, "a Neygar" in 1588
and "Bastien, *a Blackmoore of Mr.* Willm. Hawkins" four years earlier.[51] Taken
together, these faint traces of resident Africans in early Elizabethan England
suggest that although they lived there, they were likely most noteworthy for
their rarity.[52]

By the 1590s, however, Africans were easier to find in England and seem to have been especially visible in London and in several southwestern port communities.[53] From this period, English records contain occasional references to Africans being held or employed as household servants among the propertied classes. Lady Raleigh, wife of Sir Walter, and the Earl of Dorset were among those who possessed African servants or slaves. More striking, though, is the emergence of a class of Africans during the 1590s who fell into neither of these familiar categories. An assessment of "straungers" in the parish of Tower Ward records the presence of "Clare a Negra at Widdow Stokes . . . Maria a Negra at Olyver Skynnars . . . [Jesse?] a Negro at Mr Miltons . . . [and] Marea a Negra at Mr Woodes." Although it is not particularly surprising to discover impoverished Africans in England during a period when poverty and unemployment were rampant, it is striking that some Africans may have been thriving. One group of seemingly prosperous Africans built their own house in London in 1597 despite building regulations that militated against such efforts.[54]

Africans not only were living in England in the 1590s, but they also were gradually becoming a part of English society. The records of baptisms and burials during the late Elizabethan era are particularly suggestive of this development. Mary, an illegitimate "negro of John Whites" was baptized in Plymouth in 1594. Several Africans were baptized in Barnstaple in the years after 1596, following the baptism of "Grace, a neiger servante of Mr. Richard Dodderidge." In St. Andrew's Parish, Helene, the illegitimate daughter of "Cristian *the negro s[er]vant to* Richerd Sheere *the supposed father binge* Cuthbert Holman," was baptized in 1593. Another baptism occurred the following year, as did two more in 1596. In two of these cases, Devonshire officials recorded their suspicion that the illegitimate offspring were fathered by Portuguese men. More common are records indicating the death of Africans in Tudor and early Stuart England. By one account, two Africans died in Elizabethan England for every African boy or girl who was baptized. At least sixteen men, two women, and two children can be found in burial records for the fifty-year period prior to 1603. Typical of these is the case of a man who had been in the service of John Norris, a Barnstaple merchant. Richard Dodderidge was one of eight merchants named in "A Patent granted . . . for a trade to the river of Senega and Gambia in Guinea, 1588" and subsequently became mayor of Barnstaple in 1589. Thus, it is likely that the Devonshire Africans may have come directly from Africa sometime after 1591. Other Africans, however, were born in England.[55]

In exceptional cases, some Africans may even have married in England and begun the process of forming families. George Best, in his well-known *Discourse* of 1578, claimed to have "seene an Ethiopian as blacke as cole brought into England, who taking a faire English woman to wife, begat a sonne in all respects as blacke as the father was, although England were his native country, and an English woman his mother." Best's casual reference to this union, however, must be treated with caution. The larger aim of his *Discourse* was "to prove al partes of the world habitable" and therefore demonstrate that different human populations possessed certain essential qualities that could be passed through the generations. Best's often-cited case, then, could just as easily have been a creation of his imagination designed to buttress his larger argument as a record of a real marriage. The paucity of marriage records when parish registers contain both birth and death records is curious, though it might be explained by the relative youth of England's African population. If Best was indeed describing an actual circumstance rather than creating a situation to make a larger point, this example of integration and intermarriage was a remarkable (and certainly rare) phenomenon in Elizabethan England.[56]

Although the African population was small in early modern England, its significance outweighed the numbers because of the important role that Africa, Africans, and popular ideas about blackness played in the public sphere.[57] At one level, to refer to someone as black in Tudor and early Stuart England was to cast aspersions on his or her character. According to the *Oxford English Dictionary*, blackness suggested "deadly or dark purposes, malignant; pertaining to or involving death, deadly; baneful, disastrous, sinister" or something "[f]oul, iniquitous, atrocious, horribly wicked." It was no coincidence, then, that when Englishmen called up images of the diabolical or witchcraft, they might have visualized "an ouglie divell having hornes on his head, fier in his mouth, and a taile in his breech, eies like a bason, fanges like a dog, clawes like a beare, a skin like a Niger, and a voice roring like a lion, whereby we start and are afraid when we heare one crie Bough [Boo!]."[58] An image of a black figure with horns and a tail, engaged in some nefarious deed, was common in sixteenth- and seventeenth-century woodcuts. The anonymous author of the so-called *Drake Manuscript* included a similar image in watercolor accompanying a textual reference to Indians who were afraid to go out at night: "The Indians are much tormented at night of the Evil Spirit whom they call in their language 'Athoua.'"[59] Considering the ease with which these images circulated in contemporary society, it should not be surprising that the Elizabethan cult of whiteness and purity was promoted with such fervor during the last half of the sixteenth century.[60]

Although blackness could be associated with absolute evil, it was perhaps more common for English men and women to imagine black skin as merely an abnormal and a permanent stain. The Renaissance commonplace for futility—"To wash an Ethiop [or blackamoor] is to labor in vain"—was believed by some to be grounded in experience. According to *Biblioteca Eliotae* (1545), the proverb "grew out of one that boughte a Mooren, and thinking that the blacknesse of his skinne happened by the negligence of his first maister, he ceassed not to wasshe the Mooren continually with such things, as he thought would make him white."[61] This proverb was particularly widespread. Geffrey Whitney, in a work published in Leiden in 1586, included a plate featuring two light-skinned individuals attempting to wash a "blackamore," apparently unaware that "Nature is of powre . . . to keepe his former hue."[62] In a Spanish grammar published in 1599, Richard Percivale included the phrase *"Jurado ha el vaño de negro, no hazér blanco,"* or, as he translated it, "The bath of the blackmoore hath sworne not to whiten. That which is used in the bone will never out of the flesh." This truism was buttressed by the Christian Bible in Jeremiah 13:23: "Can the blacke More change his skin? or the leopard his spottes? *then* maie ye also do good, that are accustomed to do evill."[63]

The rhetoric of blackness, then, was not simply a way of casting aspersions on darker-skinned peoples, it was a popular and an effective way of emphasizing the whiteness, beauty, and virtue of Europeans in general and the English nation in particular.[64] On the Elizabethan stage, black skin proved to be a powerful visual device that numerous playwrights used to their advantage. As the Elizabethan writer George Whetstone put it, "[E]verie vertue is commended by his contrarie. A Diamond seemeth the fairer, for his foyle. Blacke best setteth foorth White: Good is most praysed in the reprehension of Evill: and Trueth [in] the hyest degree is renowned by the refelling of errour." And if it was in fact the case, as Shakespeare's Hamlet asserted, that "the purpose of playing . . . was and is, to hold, as 'twere, the mirror up to nature; to show virtue her own feature, scorn her image, and the very age and body of the time his form and pressure," then there were few ways of emphasizing the tension between good and evil as effective and obvious as the use of a dark-skinned character.[65] Thus, by virtue of their skin color alone, Africans could be exploited in a variety of ways not simply because there was a desire to denigrate them, or to justify some action taken against them (two of the hallmark characteristics of racial ideology), but because

L E A V E of with paine, the blackamore to ſkowre,
With waſhinge ofte, and wipinge more then due:
For thou ſhalt finde, that Nature is of powre,
Doe what thou canſte, to keepe his former hue:
Thoughe with a forke, wee Nature thruſte awaie,
Shee turnes againe, if wee withdrawe our hande:
And thoughe, wee ofte to conquer her aſſaie,
Yet all in vaine, ſhee turnes if ſtill wee ſtande:
　Then euermore, in what thou doeſt aſſaie,
　Let reaſon rule, and doe the thinges thou maie.

Eraſmus ex Luciano.
Abluis Æthiopem fru-
ſtra: quin deſinis arte?
Haud vnquâ efficies
vox ſit vt atra, dies.
Horat. 1. Epiſt. 10.
Naturam expellas fur-
ca tamen vſque re-
ſurret.

―――　　―――　*equuúq,*
Nunquam ex degeneri fiet generoſus aſello,
Et nunquam ex ſtolido cordatus fiet ab arte.

Anulus in pict.
poëſi.

H　　*Non*

Figure 5. Geffrey Whitney, *A Choice of Emblemes, and other devises, for the moste parte gathered out of sundrie writers, Englished and moralized* (Leiden, 1586), 57. By permission of the Folger Shakespeare Library.

their physical appearance helped contemporary moralizers instruct their audience.

The nature of the surviving evidence of African peoples in early modern England raises a number of questions that are difficult to answer with precision. Many Africans who lived in England were recent arrivals from the Iberian Atlantic world. Specifically, Africans in early modern England seem to have come either from or by way of the Americas rather than directly from Africa. The surviving ships of the fateful third slave-trading expedition of Sir John Hawkins in 1567, which left more than a hundred men behind after the defeat at San Juan de Ulua, returned to England with roughly a dozen Africans. Some of these men were certainly unsold Guinea slaves, but others may have been the survivors of a group of African freemen from England who had sailed with the expedition as interpreters or returned as hostages.[66] The practice of returning with Africans to serve as translators, hostages, or slaves would become increasingly common in subsequent years. Sir Francis Drake acquired three Africans from the Spanish off the coast of California during his circumnavigation and was carrying others who were captured with Indians and tools from the Spanish in the West Indies and taken to Roanoke Island in 1586. Ralph Lane, however, chose to leave the settlement and return to England with Drake and, presumably, the African slaves. Other English privateers, including Sir Walter Raleigh, also routinely employed Africans as crew members and carried captured African slaves off Spanish ships or out of Spanish or Portuguese colonies back to England.[67]

But there was a problem. If Englishmen were able to make full use of Africans in the Atlantic world, it was not always clear how Africans fit in England itself. At sea, Africans replaced lost crewmen, provided information, and generated revenue when they were ransomed back to their owners. At home, however, Africans created problems. In particular, they were seeping into England at a time when many people were bragging that their island's air was too pure for slavery. England was also suffering from high rates of unemployment, and the English were famously inclined to view outsiders with suspicion during this era. All of these things combined to make Africans an easy target for Elizabeth. Africans must have known that they were in a precarious situation in early modern England, but it is hard to say. Perhaps if he had lived longer than just a few months after his arrival in England in 1583, Bastien could have told us something about all of these issues. We know who brought him to England (William Hawkins), but we do not know if he came along willingly or if he was a slave. Considering the fact that he was part of an expedition that Spanish officials believed was engaged in illicit acts of kidnapping and slave trading, one suspects that Bastien did not expect his situation to improve among the English. When examined by a Spanish official, two Africans who had been aboard the same fleet as Bastien accused the English of taking them against their will and actively seeking out female slaves. Thus, we may not be able to perceive Bastien's thoughts or fully comprehend his standing in Tudor England, but it seems clear that some Africans understood that there was as much to fear from the English as there was from the Spanish. Perhaps the air in England was not so pure after all.[68]

Ultimately, the extant sources provide little indication of the precise fate of the Africans who happened to be on the ships the English encountered. One man who sailed with Captains Amias-Preston and George Sommers in 1595 recalled that they took "some few Spaniards and Negros their slaves with them" off a small island near Margarita, but he had nothing else to say about the matter. Similarly, Purchas's retelling of the voyage of the Earl of Cumberland in 1586 mentions the capture of "a small Portugall ship" in which they found "five and fortie Negroes." The following day they captured yet another ship, "in which were five and thirty Negro women," yet once again there is no indication about whether the Africans were kept on board, taken back to England, abandoned somewhere in the Caribbean, ransomed to their owners, or sold at another local market. All of these circumstances occurred during this era and each of them was feasible in the decades before the English established their own permanent American colony.[69]

*   *   *

Because English encounters with Africans might have been purposeful at times but could also have been both incidental and complicated by unique circumstances, it is difficult to use them to identify a singular English attitude or impression about either African peoples or the practice of slavery. Drake's 1585–86 expedition is particularly illustrative of this problem. In the Cape Verde Islands, for example, the English were clearly aware of the local African population, but their remarks on the subject could be quite cursory. Upon their arrival in Santiago, the English came across a hospital in which they found "abowt 20 sicke persons all *Nigros*, lyinge of verie fowle & fylthie Diseases." From this observation, the anonymous English scribe then moved on to comment on the bells the English pillaged from the attached church. There was nothing more to be said, apparently, about the diseased Africans. Their presence was neither alarming nor worthy of extensive consideration. If Drake's fleet had not subsequently suffered from a dangerous fleet-wide epidemic, the incident may not have even made it to print. Regardless, diseased Africans proved to be crucial to events as the expedition played out; a Spanish observer claimed that Drake's men "carried off 150 negroes and negresses."[70]

By the time the English fleet arrived in the West Indies less than a month later, the sickness that had made its first appearance in the Cape Verde Islands may have taken as many as 500 lives. Thus, before they could assault another fortified Spanish settlement, Drake's men rested and aired out the ships off the island of St. Christopher. Here the English spent Christmas, but soon afterward the fleet set sail for Hispaniola and the city of Santo Domingo. In one of the more famous events of the expedition, Drake launched a coordinated two-pronged attack, conducted on land by Christopher Carleill and at sea by Martin Frobisher. Predictably, Carleill's forces were opposed by a company of free African and mulatto musketeers, as they would be in subsequent engagements. That so many Africans were willing to defend Spain's grip on America surely disappointed Drake, but it was not remarkable in a larger Atlantic context. The English who sailed to the coast of West Africa commonly encountered indigenous peoples who also fought them off, often to defend the Portuguese or Dutch with whom they had closer relations.[71] Still, Drake's men took less than a day to beat back the Spanish and African forces and by the end of New Year's Day they held Santo Domingo. Not surprisingly, this effort was aided by an expert guide, though not an African. One day before the attack, Drake's fleet took a Spanish ship bound for Santo Domingo. On board they found "a woman *Nigro* with a boie & a Greeke." The Greek man turned out to be a pilot and guided the English landing the following day.[72]

English forces held onto Santo Domingo for more than a month while they awaited Spanish ransom payments and systematically destroyed the city. Once again, as with their attack on the Cape Verde Islands, the occupation of Spanish territory brought the English into repeated contact with Africans and other enslaved peoples in a variety of ways. Santo Domingo was the home of a manned galley. When Drake's fleet arrived, the galley's commander, Don Diego Osorio, positioned the ship so that her guns could be used against the English, but these proved to be of little consequence. The galley slaves, however, were an important element in the capture of the city, although not in the way the Spanish might have hoped. As the Audiencia of Santo Domingo reported to the Crown, the English eventually "took with them the galley-slaves from the galley, whose irons had been removed that they might help us. Later they rose against us and did more looting than the English." According to the author of "The *Primrose* Journal," this galley had "4 hundred slaves, Turkes, Moores, Nigros, Frenchemen & Greekes," which the English took with them when they left the city.[73]

The English also apparently acquired large numbers of both runaway and pilfered African slaves. And although it might be a bit generous to characterize these Englishmen as liberators, at least one Spanish source conceded that many "negroes belonging to private persons (who are the labourers of this country) went with them of their own free will." Other slaves took the opportunity to flee into the hills, choosing to carve out their own destiny rather than take a chance on the goodwill of Drake's forces. It was, of course, standard practice for English privateers to sail off with the slaves of Spanish settlers they looted in the Americas. The difference here was both a matter of scale and where the slaves ultimately ended up. Under normal circumstances, English raiders sailed in small fleets of two or three ships and therefore generally took only a small number of slaves. Drake's expeditionary force had more than twenty-five ships and the ranks were already seriously depleted by disease. There was plenty of room for additional cargo and probably a serious demand for more hands on deck. The English had done both things before and it appears as if they did so, yet again, in this instance.[74]

The English pirates continued to hold many Africans in slavery. On the one hand, the enslavement of Africans occurred when the English willingly ransomed slaves back to their legal owners. This behavior should hardly have been surprising, for one of the main avenues to wealth for Drake was to ransom anything the Spanish held dear and reap the rewards by threatening to relieve Spaniards of these valuables. In one case, Drake held a local official hostage for "four head of the best slaves I had," after which he "demanded a ransom for them. In like manner he carried off 50 slaves from this city." Pedro Martinez de Susuaga and other notables "ransomed slaves and things that were theirs," as well. Even when the Spanish elite were willing to pay a price for their slaves, the English were not always entirely willing to oblige. Don Luis de Guzman and Alonso de Tapia reported to the Spanish Crown that "most of the slaves . . . from the galleys went off with the English as did some of the negroes belonging to private owners. Although their masters were willing to ransom them the English would not give them up except when the slaves themselves desired to go." As noted earlier, during the 1595 voyage of Drake and Hawkins, the English captured a body of Spaniards and slaves off Rio de la Hacha. Some of the slaves and freedmen were apparently taken against their will, but English observers were quick to comment that many others ran away to the English voluntarily.[75]

Drake eventually agreed to a ransom of 25,000 ducats in exchange for the tattered remains of Santo Domingo, loaded up his ships with booty and former slaves, and sailed to Cartagena, where his forces easily took control of another important Spanish outpost. Here, slavery became an even bigger problem for the English. So many runaway and liberated Africans roamed the streets after the English occupation that Drake was forced to enact regulations regarding slave-holding. Because of infighting among the occupying forces, "it was sett downe that none under the degree of ansient [ensign] shulde keepe a Negro or other stranger." The ownership of slaves was a delicate issue for the English. Certainly, slaves were widely available after the sack of Santo Domingo and Cartagena. They symbolized power and prestige and English sailors, who otherwise were rather low creatures, craved the honorific value that the ownership of another human being imparted. Unfortunately, widespread greed and self-interest negatively affected Drake's ability to command. In addition to setting down regulations as to who could keep a former slave, "a general commandement [was] gyven for the well usage of Strangers, namely Frenchmen, Turkes & Negros." Because there were several hundred "strangers" that had been added to the expedition, the English commanders needed to make sure that peaceful conditions prevailed. In addition, not everyone taken from Santo Domingo or Cartagena continued to be slaves in the minds of the English. The continuation of slave status seems to have been reserved for Africans and some Indians.[76]

There has been some speculation that Drake's forces sought out the cimarrons in the hinterland of Hispaniola and may have hoped for their support at Cartagena. Even more, there is reason to believe that the fleet was bound for Panama at some point during the Caribbean voyage. The Spanish understood that "the Englishman brought much clothing with him for the negroes of Vallano and that when the corsair was on the isthmus he planned for this return." The same source also noted, however, that although "he had with him certain persons who were to put him into communications with the negroes . . . he very much regretted to hear that they were at peace with Spaniards." Based on Drake's earlier exploits, Spanish officials were always acutely concerned that Englishmen, or other Europeans, might try to rally the countryside against Spanish settlements. In fact, no evidence has been found in any English or Spanish documents that Drake tried to contact the cimarrons at any point during this expedition. The losses he suffered from disease and his inability to take the Caribbean port towns of Santo Domingo and Cartagena by complete surprise also put him in an awkward position. Thus, even if he had planned to contact the cimarrons in Panama, he abandoned that strategy in favor of beginning his return voyage.[77]

By the time Drake's expedition finally departed Cartagena in April, it was short on supplies, suffering from a large loss of life because of disease, and generally light on riches. The expedition did have, however, hundreds of liberated slaves that could still be useful and possibly add to the wealth of the voyage. Before it could continue, however, Drake's fleet stopped at the western end of Cuba where the English mariners gathered drinking water and firewood. After about a month in the area, the English armada sailed north to the Florida coast and arrived at the Spanish settlement of St. Augustine in late May. As he had at previous Spanish ports, Drake managed to take the town, which he proceeded to destroy during his subsequent occupation. He did not remain long; by early June, Drake's fleet was off the coast of North Carolina and soon he was in contact with the English commander of the settlement at Roanoke Island, Ralph Lane. Drake seemingly intended to re-supply the settlement until the relief ships arrived, but violent storms dispersed much of his fleet and Lane chose to abandon the colony. The English sailed from Roanoke in mid-June and were back in Portsmouth by the end of July. They arrived dispirited and generally short on funds, but the expedition had been an incredible moral victory for the English in their war with Spain. They may not have had much to show for their efforts in the form of gold and silver, but Drake's fleet had successfully attacked and severely damaged Santiago, in the Cape Verde Islands, Santo Domingo and Cartagena in the Caribbean, and St. Augustine on the Florida Coast.[78]

But what about the slaves? Although the English accounts are generally silent on the subject, throughout this final stage of the journey slavery continued to be an important issue. In particular, Drake's African slaves behaved in a manner that suggested the English commander was no benevolent liberator. According to Spanish depositions taken in Cuba, "three negroes . . . escaped from them (of those the English had seized in Santo Domingo) [and] said that the Englishman was going to Santa Elena to take that place." Others ran off during Drake's occupation of St. Augustine and similarly provided intelligence as to the destination and intent of the expedition. It was also these sources, along with several Spanish accounts, that provided the broadest outline as to the number of Africans and others who remained on Drake's ships. According to Diego Fernández de Quiñones, Pedro Menéndez Marguéz took the depositions of "three negroes who speak and remained behind [in Cuba] when the corsair left. They say he meant to leave all the negroes he had in a fort and settlement established at Jacan [Roanoke] by the English who went there a year ago. There he intended to leave the 250 Africans and all the small craft he had." Alonso Suarez de Toledo declared that Drake took "300 Indians from Cartagena, mostly women," in addition to "200 negroes, Turks, and Moors." Pedro Sanchez reported that Drake "carried off 150 negroes and negresses from Santo Domingo and Cape Verde—more from Santo Domingo."[79] Spanish sources would suggest that Drake's fleet was awash with Africans, Indians, and others who had formerly toiled for Spanish masters.

English sources are less clear on the subject of Drake's Africans. Whether English authors were simply reticent or circumstances have conspired against scholarly inquiry, it has proven difficult to determine the precise number and the ultimate fate of the Africans and Indians Drake held in June 1586. One of the most important English sources, "The *Leicester* Journal," falls silent with its final entry on March 15. "The *Primrose* Journal," which is generally the most informative about matters relating to English interaction with African people, records very little about Roanoke and nothing about any Africans after Drake's departure from Cartagena. The *Summarie and True Discourse* provides some useful information about Roanoke and the decision to abandon the colony, but its author recorded nothing about the several hundred Africans and Indians rumored to be with the fleet. In addition, none of the English settlers from Roanoke ever mentioned the presence of Africans on Drake's ships. Neither did they say anything about his intent to leave them with several hundred laborers. According to Ralph Lane's account, when Drake first arrived, he offered to supply the settlement with "victuals, munition and clothing, but also of barkes, prinnaces and boates." There was no mention, however, of Indian or African slaves.[80]

What, then, happened to the Africans on board the fleet? One possibility is, as several historians have suggested, that upon their departure from the North Carolina coast, the English ships simply disembarked the Africans in order to lighten their load. This scenario, however, seems unlikely, considering the commodity value of Africans, especially given how little gold, silver, or other valuables the expedition had collected. This supposition is based also on the assumption that Drake's fleet was badly overcrowded and the addition of 100 more Roanoke settlers meant that some people had to go. Unfortunately, this conclusion does not bear the burden of close scrutiny, either. By the time Drake's fleet reached Roanoke his ships were, if anything, undermanned, having lost more than 500 men, and perhaps close to 1,000, to sickness or to death in battle. Many Africans, who must have been dispersed throughout the fleet, were hard at work keeping the ships afloat when Drake's ships anchored off Roanoke Island. In fact, Drake was short enough on manpower that he was willing to part with the *Francis*, a 70-ton ship, as well as "two pinnesses, and foure small boats." Even after a storm dispersed the fleet, including the *Francis*, Drake offered to leave the *Barke Bonner*, a 170-ton ship.[81]

Another likelihood is that Drake took many if not all the Africans back to England with the fleet and disposed of them in London and various port cities. As previously noted, English ships that traveled to the Caribbean routinely returned to England with a number of Africans on board, even though the practice was becoming increasingly controversial in late Elizabethan England.[82] Although neither Drake nor Hawkins returned to England with the remnants of their 1595 expedition, at least ten Africans did return with the fleet. Considering this pattern of behavior over the course of thirty years, it should not seem remarkable that Drake would have felt perfectly comfortable returning to England with a cargo of Africans, many of whom may have been sold for profit or simply given away as gifts. That Drake returned from Roanoke with at least a few slaves is evidenced by the fact that Lady Raleigh, the wife of Sir Walter Raleigh, the sponsor of the Roanoke colony, possessed African servants during the late 1580s. Perhaps they were among those who returned to England with Drake in 1586. Also, it may be no coincidence that most of the compelling evidence for the presence of large numbers of Africans in England (many of whom seem to have Hispanic names) dates from after the mid-1580s.[83]

The story of the small but steady stream of Africans arriving from the Americas also sheds light on Elizabeth's supposed effort to eliminate the African population from the British Isles during the late 1590s. In 1596, England's Privy Council, at the request of Queen Elizabeth I, issued a directive ordering the removal of all Africans from England. "[T]here are lately divers blackamoors brought into this realme," the councilors observed with a hint of concern, "of which kinde of people there are already here too manie." The solution to this problem was simple enough—"those kinde of people should

be sent forth of the land." To that end the Privy Council licensed Edward
Banes and Casper van Senden to round up England's African men and
women and ship them elsewhere. Banes's task, it seems, was straightforward.
In an open letter to the Lord Mayor of London and the city's alderman, as
well as "all other Maiours, Sherfyes, &c.," Banes was directed "to take of
those Blackmoores that in this last voyage under Sir Thomas Baskervile, were
brought into this Realme to the nomber of Tenn" and transport them "out of
the Realme." Baskerville had been the commanding general of the land
forces on the recent English expedition to the West Indies under Drake and
Hawkins. When both eminences had unexpectedly died, he had the dubious
honor of commanding the fleet on its return voyage with little to show for its
efforts except, apparently, a handful of Africans.[84]

Casper van Senden's mission was more complicated, having been generated by a unique business opportunity the Lubeck merchant presented to the
Crown. Apparently on his own initiative, Van Senden "procure[d] 89 of her
Majesties subjectes that were detayned prisoners in Spaine and Portugall . . .
and brought them hither in this Realme at his owne cost and charges." Seeing
an opportunity to profit from the expanding transatlantic market for enslaved Africans, Van Senden only asked in return for a "lycense to take up so
many Blackamoores here in this Realme and to transport them into Spaine
and Portugall" where, presumably, he could sell them as slaves. As far as
Elizabeth was concerned, the "reasonablenes" of the proposition was undeni-
able. "[I]n regard of the charitable affection" Van Senden had shown in redeeming "our contrymen that were there in great misery and thraldom and
to bring them home to their native contry," Elizabeth agreed to the bargain.
After all, her Privy Council averred, "those kind of people may be well spared
in this Realme." The enterprising van Senden was therefore granted the authority to gather eighty-nine people of African descent, and local officials
were required "to aide and assist him to take up such Blackamores as he shall
find within this Realme with the consent of their Masters who we doubt not
considering her Majesty's good pleasure to have those kindes of people sent
out of the lande & the good deserving of the stranger towardes her Majesty's
subjectes, and that they shall doe charitable and like Christians . . . yilde
those in their possession to him."[85]

What seems like a simple business proposition was, in fact, exceedingly
difficult to expedite in practice. Van Senden complained in 1600, in a letter
to the queen, that English masters would not voluntarily part with their Af-

rican possessions. In the meantime, van Senden had incurred even greater debts by procuring the release of another two hundred Englishmen, leading him to petition the queen "for [another] license to take up and carry into Spain and Portugal all blackamoors he shall find, without interruption of their masters or others." Thus, in January 1601, Elizabeth issued a royal proclamation expressing her discontent with the "great number of Negroes and blackamoors which . . . are carried into this realm since the troubles between her highness and the King of Spain; who are fostered and powered here, to the great annoyance of her own liege people that which co[vet?] the relief which these people consume." Elizabeth therefore issued a "special commandment that the said kind of people shall be with all speed avoided and discharged out of this her majesty's realms." In this more forceful declaration, Elizabeth added that "if there shall be any person or persons which be possessed of any such blackamoors that refuse to deliver them in sort aforesaid, then we require you to call them before you and to advise and persuade them by all good means to satisfy her majesty's pleasure therein." If they remained obstinate, Elizabeth licensed van Senden "to certify their names to us, to the end her majesty may take such further course therein as it shall seem best in her princely wisdom."[86]

In the long run and despite the endorsement of the English government, Casper van Senden's private slave trade was foiled by Englishmen who cherished the liberty to do what they pleased with their own property, even when that liberty meant the privilege of holding another human being in slavery. As with the unwillingness of Tudor monarchs to pass a sweeping manumission act earlier in the sixteenth century, which would have freed all of England's villeins, because of reservations about personal property rights, Elizabeth also could not explicitly order her subjects to part with their African possessions. The forcefulness of the language in the 1601 royal proclamation, however, suggests that the willingness to expel Africans from England was more than a simple matter of compensating van Senden for redeeming captive Englishmen out of bondage. Scholars have often taken this episode as evidence of the callousness with which the English were willing to treat African peoples and, perhaps, an early indication of anti-black prejudice, racism even, in Tudor England.[87] Certainly the willingness of the English government to pay for the redemption of English captive slaves by selling Africans (back?) into slavery would suggest disregard for the lives and liberties of African peoples. Why, however, did Elizabeth and her ministers claim that this enterprise was not merely necessary but desirable? In 1596, the Privy Council claimed that "those kinde of people may be well spared in this Realme being so populous and nombers of hable persons the subjects of the land and Christian people that perishe for want of service, whereby through their labor they might be mayntained." Perhaps recognizing the limitations of this particular argument—the transportation of a few hundred Africans would hardly seem to have energized the domestic labor market—the 1601 measure reiterated that the English were living in "hard times of dearth," but it added "that the most of them [the Africans] are infidels having no understanding of Christ or his Gospel." Did Elizabeth believe an appeal to her subjects' native prejudices would bear more fruit?[88]

Africans may have numbered only in the hundreds in early modern England, but interest in African peoples, as both human subjects and physical objects, permeated the Tudor world.[89] This interest was enabled, in large part, by the increasingly vigorous activities of English mariners throughout the Atlantic world and their frequent encounters with African peoples in the Americas. Africans were an important part of Spain's American colonies, primarily as slaves but also as free members of society. Africans were therefore visible to the English quite often as defenders of the status quo, particularly when they took up arms for colonial defense. Englishmen, however, often had Africans on their side as well. When they had the opportunity, Englishmen employed Africans as their personal colonial agents. Africans toiled, translated, guided, served as combatants (for the English, Spanish, and themselves), and sometimes simply changed hands when hostage-takers accepted payoffs for the return of these human commodities to their Spanish owners. English mariners needed African assistance and they were willing to place themselves at the mercy of African men and women in order to achieve their goals. Whether the vast majority of Africans were enslaved in the Americas was of little consequence to Elizabethan pirates and privateers. But in the absence of other alternatives, Africans were generally the first to be ransomed, set adrift, sacrificed, traded, or resold to ensure that the larger goals of England's maritime enterprises were achieved. From the English point of view, Africans were indispensable. They were also disposable, as Drake's activities and Elizabeth's pronouncements make clear. As a result, the lives of Africans who found their way on board English ships were as precarious as they were on the Spanish American mainland.

*   *   *

Anglo-African encounters in the Americas were shaped primarily by slavery, but neither the institution itself nor Africans as a people were understood in simple terms in the early modern era. Englishmen often claimed that they hated slavery, but English mariners were more than willing to participate in the emerging Atlantic slave system to the degree that they stood to benefit materially from doing so. If their behavior in Spain's Atlantic world is an accurate indication, many Englishmen accepted both the legality and propriety of slavery. They might express sympathy for Indians or Africans, but that was more likely to be a product of their hatred for the Spanish than it was for any real fondness they might possess for non-European peoples. With regard to the cimarrons, Spanish malfeasance rather than any inherent objection to slavery explained why so many runaway Africans seemed to be living in independent communities. The supposed cruelty of the Spaniards, not the injustice of slavery, also explained to the English why African peoples might even be willing to assist the English (or any other non-Spanish European, for that matter) should they muster the courage to mount an invasion. Indeed, if the English could avoid the Spanish mistake of governing the Indies by terror, there was no reason why they might not themselves continue profiting from the manifold benefits of African slavery.

Drake, Hawkins, and other Englishmen recognized early on that African peoples in the western Atlantic world were extraordinarily valuable resources. To a greater degree than other peoples of the Atlantic littoral, Europeans perceived Africans in the Americas to be rootless, mobile, merchantable, and subservient. Sixteenth-century Englishmen therefore accepted without hesitation, and scarcely more reflection, that the primary explanation for the presence of African peoples in Spanish and Portuguese America was slavery. The English saw Africans diving for pearls, laboring on land, and working in an array of seafaring enterprises. That seemed to be their primary function in the Americas and the English did not hesitate to emulate the Spanish by selling slaves when they could, trading captured slaves for other valuable commodities, or simply holding them ransom until their owners repurchased their laborers. When none of these options proved viable, English ship captains might simply abandon Africans to their own devices at the nearest shore, regardless of conditions or lack of supplies. Most English seamen were nothing if not pragmatic and they therefore contented themselves to use Africans as slaves or treat them as disposable commodities.

Yet, the role of African peoples in the colonial world was even more complicated. Circumstances that created opportunities for the English to treat

Africans as slaves could just as easily dictate that they work side-by-side with Africans as allies. Whether on land or at sea, Englishmen often capitalized on the expertise of Africans as guides, translators, and messengers. Englishmen also employed Africans on board their ships as crew members. Some Englishmen, like Drake, even forged military alliances with cimarrons, whose hatred for the Spanish (so the English imagined) made them ideal partners. Slavery may have been the lens through which most Englishmen saw African peoples in the Atlantic world, but that did not prohibit the English from recognizing that African peoples could play other, equally valuable roles. Slavery was normative for African peoples in the Americas, but freedom was also possible. This important lesson would not be lost on future generations of entrepreneurial English men and women when they came to the Americas not to plunder but to settle.

CHAPTER 4

Englishmen Enslaved: The Specter of Slavery in the Mediterranean and Beyond

Anthony up was tane by an English Runagade,
With whom he did remain at the Sea-roving trade:
I'th nature of a Slave he did i'th Galley row;
Thus he his life did save but Constance did not know:
still she cries Anthony, *my bonny* Anthony.[1]

Vincent Jukes was born in Shropshire, England, during the second decade of the reign of King James I. As a young man of insignificant means, he was bound out as an apprentice for two years before he went to sea as a ship's cook. In 1636, on only his second voyage, he and his mates were "set upon by Turkish pirats." After "a dangerous fight, wherein seven were slaine and about twenty more wounded and maimed," Jukes and more than thirty other English mariners "were carried away to *Argier*, where . . . they were sold for slaves in the Market place." As Jukes would later tell the story, he was actually one of the lucky few: "It is a custome there," he noted, "that their King have his choice of every eighth person to bee sold," and that proved to be his fate. Many English slaves ended up in more treacherous situations. William Gouge, who retold the tale of Vincent Jukes during his sermon on the subject of apostasy, claimed that most of the captured English mariners were dead by 1639, while four had been ransomed out of bondage, "and seven there still abide in slaverie." Jukes spent only two months as a royal slave before he was "sold to a *Negro*" who "used him most cruelly" and abused the young man daily until he abjured his faith, allowed himself to be circumcised, and in all ways

"conforme[d] himselfe to the *Turkish* rites, and attire." The African soon resold Jukes, this time to a Greek master, who placed him on board a Turkish
pirate ship. Jukes recognized at once that this new situation created an unusual opportunity. Once at sea, Jukes and three other men—"two *English*
Christians and a *Flemming* Circumcised as himselfe"—seized control of the
ship, "freeing themselves from slavery," and sailed to Spain. Jukes then set
out for home, seeking forgiveness.[2]

If Jukes expected a joyful welcome, he was certainly disappointed. Nobody doubted that Jukes had suffered physical abuse and had been humiliated by his enslavement, especially "when he was under the harsh and hard
handling of the cruell *Negro*." But Gouge was also forced to concede that
Jukes erred mightily in seeking relief from his sufferings by turning his back
on his Christian faith. "Is the rage of man," Gouge wondered aloud, "more to
be feared then the wrath of God? [C]haines of iron more then the bonds of
the law? Bondage under Turkes more then slavery under Satan, whose worke
which he enjoynes is villany; whose wages, which he gives is damnation?"
Surely not. But of the "many thousands surprized by Turks as he was,"
Gouge was more inclined in this instance to celebrate the remarkable willingness of Jukes to confess that he had erred when he had sought relief
through conversion. Even more, Jukes provided Gouge with an opportunity
to remind his listeners to "have pittie on those that are in bondage under
adversaries, and persecutors of the said faith; on [s]uch in particular as are, as
this *Penitent* not long since was, taken captive by Turkes." Jukes was a living
and visible reminder of the tragedy endured by thousands of Englishmen in
the Mediterranean world whose bodies stood in need of redemption "from
slavery" and whose souls needed to be shielded "from Apostacy."[3]

Gouge made the story of Vincent Jukes meaningful for English audiences by characterizing it in spiritual terms. Jukes endured real physical misery, but Gouge was more interested in the notorious problem of Christian
English mariners choosing to embrace Islam in an effort to rescue themselves. But the story of Englishmen enslaved in foreign lands was also becoming all too familiar. Slavery, as far as English commentators were concerned,
was on the rise in the early seventeenth century. William Davies, a London
barber-surgeon and former slave himself in the Mediterranean galleys, urged
his countrymen in 1614 to keep in mind just how fortunate they were when
he asked, "What English heart (I say) duly pondering these things . . . can
otherwise choose but falling downe on his bended knees, yeeld God immor-
tall and innumerable thanks and prayse-giving . . . for preserving him so

long from so many miseries and wretched thraldomes, whereunto most Nations of the Earth are subject?" Samuel Purchas echoed this sentiment in the 1620s when he claimed, somewhat misleadingly, that God's providence had "denied Learning to those Barbarians, and skill or care of remote Navigations." Otherwise, he argued, the "barbarous Empires" of the Mediterranean "might infest the World" with "their Christian Slaves and unchristian Pirats, whereof they make use against us." The infestation of slavery in the Mediterranean world was a compelling reminder that the absence of human bondage in England was an aberration from larger historical patterns and contemporary global realities. And there was no guarantee that England's good fortune would last forever.[4]

Englishmen subscribed to a body of assumptions concerning the significance and legitimacy of human bondage and they did not need to travel abroad to know what slavery meant. At the same time, most literate Englishmen were fully aware that, compared to what they might find lurking uncomfortably below the self-congratulatory veneer that covered up the unfreedoms of their own world, slavery was a vicious and pervasive presence beyond their shores. If slavery could be found hovering about the margins of early modern English society, few people doubted that the real problem with slavery was that it effectively blanketed much of the known world and it did so under God's purveyance. Some scholars were uncertain about whether slavery was part of God's plan, but it was hard to ignore the fact that it had certainly flourished throughout history. Even those people whom God had blessed with greatness in the past were not exempt from lapsing into a state of "extreame bondage" at a later time. With a great appreciation for the vicissitudes of time that only God could comprehend, Davies therefore warned his countrymen that if the Jews, "being a Nation [God] had once selected himselfe from all the Nations of the earth," and the Greeks, who were once the "Monarches of the Earth," could lapse into a condition of "extreame thraldome and punishment," there certainly was no guarantee that a vain and unrepentant English nation might not suffer the same fate in the future.[5]

Englishmen could not comprehend either their secular or sacred history without reference to human bondage and it was equally difficult to make sense of the contemporary world at large without confronting slavery either. What it meant to be English in the early modern world—temporally and spatially—was intrinsically connected to slavery. For the most part, the links between slavery and Englishness were veiled by the passage of time or, in the case of various forms of domestic bondage, increasingly thought of as either anachronistic or the deserved fate of those whose own actions disqualified them from the initial benefit of having been freeborn in England. Slavery might also be viewed as the unfortunate condition of countless African peoples in the Atlantic world, regardless of whether the fate was deserved. But it was also clear that slavery was an escalating problem that struck at the heart of England itself: the capture and enslavement of English men (and a few women) in foreign lands, especially the Mediterranean. By the late sixteenth century, the capture, transportation, and bondage of African peoples had shaped English conceptions of normative slavery throughout the Atlantic world. Yet, and despite the efforts of English nationalists to define their country against the institution of slavery, the more pressing concern and terrifying reality at this time was that Englishmen, too, were being turned into slaves in shockingly large numbers.

The capture and enslavement of English mariners in the Mediterranean became an increasingly common problem and familiar theme in English publications beginning in the last decades of the sixteenth century.[6] As the story of Vincent Jukes indicates, it was not at all unusual for English mariners to be waylaid in the Mediterranean during the course of their travels and slavery was a predictable outcome for the survivors. By the seventeenth century, thousands of Englishmen would suffer a similar fate and only a small number would find their way back to England, either as a product of their own ingenuity and heroic actions or simply because they were lucky enough to be ransomed out of bondage. It was a distinguishing characteristic of Mediterranean slavery that there were established avenues for redemption, largely because North African pirates and their sponsors routinely took captives for the express purpose of generating revenue from ransoms Christians willingly paid to buy their coreligionists' freedom. But the possibility that captive slaves might be freed in no way diminished slavery's impact on the individual and it did little to lessen the sense that Europe, including England, was at the mercy of slave traders.[7] Certainly, Mediterranean slavery was a form of institutionalized hostage-taking and few in Europe, not least the English, were willing to condone the practice. Captive-taking offended English sensibilities, but the truly horrifying prospect was slavery itself. Enslavement was a vicious assault on the character and identity of the unfortunate victim; many victims were England's fathers, brothers, and sons. The ease with which an Englishman could be turned into a slave was a devastating contrast to the native liberties and freedoms English writers were otherwise so inclined to celebrate. And because it was a form of slavery they experienced firsthand, because it was so personal, nothing shaped the way most English men and women thought about slavery in the early modern era as much as the enslavement of Englishmen in foreign lands, especially in the Mediterranean world.[8]

*   *   *

English mariners were relatively new arrivals in the Mediterranean during the sixteenth century. Beginning in 1511, ships out of London, Southampton, and Bristol began sailing in larger numbers down the Atlantic seaboard and through the Strait of Gibraltar with their cargoes of tin, lead, salted fish, and woolen cloth. The potential profits in Persian silks, Turkish carpets and cloths, wines and currants, and other exotic commodities brought Englishmen to this most ancient, diverse, and contested part of their known world. During the 1530s, Turkish sea power and heightened competition from other nations effectively shut English merchants out of the region. For a short time, English merchandise continued to flow into the Mediterranean world via overland trade networks, in no small part as a result of the efforts of people like Anthony Jenkinson who identified the best inland routes. But in the last third of the sixteenth century, English ships once again entered the Mediterranean in significant numbers; by the turn of the century, the Levant Company alone had more than thirty ships and several thousand seamen working in the region. With increased activity and larger numbers, however, came increased dangers as English ship captains, mariners, and merchants came into more regular contact with piracy, Turkish maritime power, and slavery.[9]

Although real slavery threatened few Englishmen at home in the early modern era, the same could not be said about the Mediterranean world. Writing specifically about Algiers, Samuel Purchas comfortably described the region as "the Throne of Pyracie, the Sinke of Trade and Stinke of Slavery; the Cage of uncleane Birds, of Prey, the Habitation of Sea-Devils, the Receptacle of Renagadoes to God, and Traytors to their Countrey." Other Englishmen concurred, noting casually that the Mediterranean world was rife with a number of forms of human depravity. Nicholas Nicolay's 1551 account of Algiers described it as being inhabited by a people "given all to Whoredom, Sodometrie, Theft, and all other detestable vices." Algerians also tended to bring large numbers of "poor Christians" to the city, "which they sell unto the Moores, and other Merchants of Barbarie for slaves."[10] English merchants and sailors were therefore well aware of the risks they faced by sailing into foreign waters and it was hardly surprising that many Englishmen fell into the hands of the feared Algerian pirates and others who routinely incorporated Britons into the same slave system that accommodated so many other Europeans.[11] The numbers, however, were bracing. During the seventeenth and eighteenth centuries, tens of thousands of Englishmen were captured, enslaved, and chained to the oars of Mediterranean galleys.[12] A quick death was a common fate, but thousands found themselves bound in chains for many years. Yet, some Englishmen did escape, or were redeemed, and returned to their native land where they became vehicles for the transmission of detailed information about the plight of those they left behind. Thus, despite the varieties of human bondage that could be found throughout the world and all of the information available in written texts, and regardless of early English encounters with Africa and African peoples in the Atlantic world, the most reliable—or, at least, consistent—information about the nature and meaning of slavery in the early modern era came from the experiences of former English slaves.

There were many ways to learn about slavery in the Mediterranean region. Contemporary news reports, which relied primarily on private letters for information, appeared with increasing frequency during the early decades of the seventeenth century. In one account from 1622, the English editor reported on the recent success of the Dutch ambassador to Algiers who had "gotten libertie for divers of the Countrimen, whom the Pyrates of *Algier* had taken at Sea, and made Galley-slaves of." The same issue also contained an abstract of a letter from Rome reporting that Turkish pirates had recently captured a ship from New Spain and that the "200. men which were found aboard her, were all made slaves."[13] But as interesting and predictable as these kinds of reports may have been, firsthand accounts of piracy and privateering in the Mediterranean world, as well as narrative recollections concerning the ancient conflicts between Islam and Christendom, made for even more lurid reading. Exotic tales, fanciful renderings, horrific episodes, and dramatic exploits found a receptive audience in early modern England as sailors and merchants spread their horror stories by word of mouth and publishers issued a steady stream of slave narratives. Like the slave narratives of a later time and place, the English slave narrative conformed to a fairly reliable pattern, dramatizing for the literate English public the nature of the capture, the process of being sold, the conditions of enslavement, the types of work performed, and the recovery of English freedom. Throughout these narratives, religion predictably served as a central point of contention, whether between Christians and Muslims or Protestants and Catholics, as enslaved Englishmen struggled to maintain some sense of their original, freeborn condition within their newly acquired status as wretched slaves.

Many narratives appeared during the late seventeenth and through the eighteenth centuries, but the English reading public already had more than a dozen separate accounts of their enslaved countrymen by the mid-seventeenth century.[14] Many slave narratives appeared in the collections issued in multiple editions by Richard Hakluyt and Samuel Purchas, but several others were published independently.[15] Typically these works followed a standardized pattern that began with innocent Englishmen exercising their self-professed prerogative to trade in the Mediterranean. At some point, however, freeborn Englishmen lost their liberties and became slaves, either as a result of a violent encounter with an overwhelming force of Turkish or Algerian pirates or simply because of some misfortune, such as shipwreck or subterfuge. Richard Hakluyt retold one such tale: In 1563, an English ship out of Portsmouth, bound for Seville, encountered a fleet of eight Turkish galleys. Refusing to surrender and despite long odds, the English sailors said a prayer and prepared for battle. In a typical gesture of bravado, the men took up their swords and held them up in defiance as other Englishmen let loose a volley of arrows while the gunner, John Fox, fired his weapons. In the end, "the Englishmen shewed themselves men in deed," especially the boatswain, who "fared amongst the Turkes like a wood Lion" until he was fatally wounded. With his last breath, however, he bid his shipmates farewell and encouraged them "to winne praise by death, rather than to live captives in misery and shame."[16] But, it would not be.

The bloody fight at sea against infidel pirates who overmatched the English by virtue of their raw numbers—not bravery—was a staple feature of English slave narratives. That firepower sometimes trumped valor was a particular point of emphasis when Edward Webbe claimed in 1610 that his ship of sixty men resisted fifty Turkish galleys for two full days before the death of most of his shipmates and a lull in the wind gave their attackers the advantage. Most Englishmen accepted the existence of slavery, but stories like Webbe's helped document how misfortune and injustice could conspire against the innocent. English bravery in the face of death or enslavement was therefore both an expression of their native character and outrage at their looming subjugation. In an exemplary account from the seventeenth century, an English merchant taken by Algerians reported that the fight was "furious and bloody on both sides for four hours: Our men behaved themselves gallantly; neither

Death nor Wounds could force them from their Charge and Posts. Some when their Limbs were all bruised, their Bones shattered, and their Bodies torn with Splinters, did obstinately continue to handle and manage the Guns."[17] The suggestion that Englishmen and Christians would triumph in a fair fight was also implied in the story of the capture of Thomas Sanders and the crew of the *Jesus* in 1584. Turkish gunners proved incapable of striking the English ship in this account, so they offered freedom as a reward to any Christian captive who could either sink the English ship or cause it to surrender. A Spaniard named Sebastian took the offer and quickly disabled the *Jesus*, but for all his assistance he was sent back to prison "whereby may appeare the regard that the Turke or infidell hath of his worde." Ultimately, the damage done to the ship compelled the crew to come ashore where they were "cheined foure & foure, to a hundred waight of yron."[18]

Although the treachery of pirates (and the duplicity of a Spaniard) helped explain how many Englishmen ended up as slaves, other Englishmen were simply unlucky. In 1593, the crew of the *Tobie* found itself shipwrecked on the Barbary Coast. When the crew members came upon some of the local inhabitants and begged for assistance, they were taken captive, robbed, and used "like their slaves." John Smith, who would become more famous for his exploits in Virginia, cut his teeth in the early years of the seventeenth century on the continent fighting against the Ottomans. When Christian forces were overwhelmed in the Battle of Rottenton, where many men "left there their martyred bodies, in testimonie of their Martial minds," John Smith was among the survivors. After the battle, some looters came across a prone Smith and judged by "his Armour and habit, that his ransome might be better to them then his death." An incapacitated and unfortunate Smith was therefore dragged eastward where he and countless others were "sold like beasts."[19]

Englishmen, in the stories they told, did not become slaves because of their own actions and certainly did not deserve the fate. They were not at war with Islam and were not engaged in illicit activities, at least by their own measure of things. They were surprised at sea, tricked by scoundrels, or just in the wrong place at the wrong time. The accidental, or criminal, nature of English enslavement buttressed the conventional wisdom that Englishmen were, in a pure state of nature, free. Perhaps, at home, there were things individual Englishmen could do that would result in their being reduced to a state of bondage by their own rulers, but that was different. Domestic slavery was justified in theory because it was earned by individuals engaged in

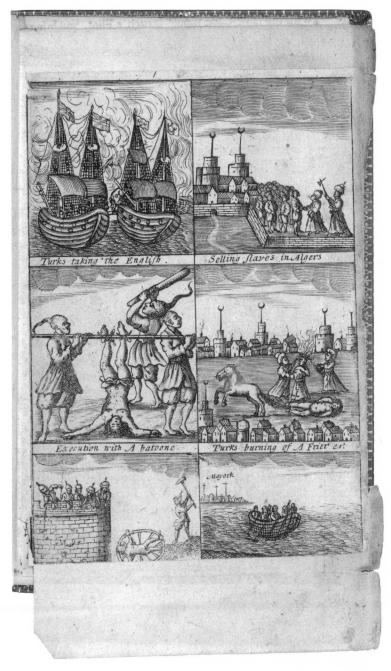

Figure 6. William Okeley, *Eben-ezer: or, A small monument of great mercy, appearing in the miraculous deliverance of William Okeley, Williams Adams, John Anthony, John Jephs, John—carpenter, from the miserable slavery of Algiers . . .* (London, 1684), frontispiece. By permission of the Folger Shakespeare Library.

Figure 7. John Smith, *The true travels, adventures, and observations of Captaine John Smith, in Europe, Asia, Affrica, and America, from anno Domini 1593 to 1629 . . .* (London, 1630), foldout image before p. 1. By permission of the Folger Shakespeare Library.

criminal activities and further legitimated because the institution itself was purposeful. Slavery in England was both punitive and an opportunity to rehabilitate the enslaved. The English did not make people slaves; some Englishmen forfeited their natural liberty as a result of their poor choices. And slavery did not exist for any other reason than to punish individuals—not to get work done—and, ideally, funnel them back to freedom. Slavery was far from arbitrary. It was a mechanism to reclaim wayward Englishmen from their scurrilous lives and, in its most idealized expression, make England better by making better Englishmen. None of this, however, was in evidence in the Mediterranean.

After capture, Englishmen needed to be transformed into brutes. However Englishmen became slaves, English authors (former slaves or otherwise) reported that all newly captured individuals went through a similar process that involved practical and symbolic assertions of mastery on the part of the captors. Whatever the slaves' national origin, the "first villany and indignitie that was done unto them, was the shaving off of all the hayre both head and beard." Soon after Thomas Sanders and the crew of the *Jesus* were condemned as "slaves perpetually unto the great Turke" in 1584, they were "forceably and most violently shaven, head and beard." John Smith described his slavery in relatively innocuous terms until the moment when his captors "shave[d] his head and beard as bare as his hand." The shorn head of the slaves was a common feature of most early modern slave societies and the Mediterranean world was no different in this regard. In the case of Mediterranean galleys, the act tended to be partly associated with hygiene, but shaving a newly enslaved individual's head was also highly symbolic. As Anthony Munday informed his readers, shaving Englishmen's heads robbed "them of those ornaments which all Christians make much of, because they best become them." Likewise, by taking a man's hair, captors began the symbolic process of stripping the individual of his manliness and freedom. As George Sandys reported, Turks wore "their Beards . . . at full length, the marke of their affected gravietie, and toke of freedome, (for slaves have theirs shaven) insomuch that they will scoffe at such Christians as cut, or naturally want them, as if suffering themselves to be abused against nature."[20]

In addition to their hair, slaves were also deprived of their clothing and personal possessions. Like the shipwrecked crewmen from the *Tobie* noted earlier, Muslim masters stripped the newly captured slaves naked as part of the search for hidden valuables, but the stripping and reclothing of new bondmen was also a way to break the man and make the slave. Richard Hakluyt retold the popular story of John Fox late in the sixteenth century, detailing that no sooner were the Christian captives sent to the galleys than "their garments were pulled over their eares, and torne from their backes, and they set to the oares." Others simply went naked, "onely a short linnen paire of breeches to cover their privities." William Davies, who spent nearly nine years as a slave in the galleys of the Duke of Florence, reported in similar terms that, upon his capture, every man was stripped naked and placed in irons in the galleys and after they had been shaven "every man had given him a red coate, and a red cap, telling us that the Duke had made us all slaves, to our great woe and griefe."[21]

But being shaved and forced to go naked by those who would oppress them only served to introduce Englishmen to the hardships of North African slavery. Things got much worse. By the early decades of the seventeenth century, it was already common currency among the English that there was "no calamitie [that could] befall a man in this life which hath the least parallel to this of Captivitie." Being held against one's will for arbitrary reasons was the very definition of unfreedom in the English world, but the fate of individual Christian slaves varied greatly depending on the circumstances of capture, national origin, social status, and skills. Individuals seized in military encounters typically became state property and were regularly consigned to the galleys, sent to work in the mines, or condemned to labor on arduous construction projects. In contrast, Christians captured by private corsairs were the captain's property. In Samuel Purchas's account of John Rawlins, English prisoners in Algiers experienced much the same thing as Vincent Jukes would later describe when they appeared before the local Bashaw, or ranking Ottoman official, who took one of every eight as a fee for himself. The remaining captives were subsequently sold at the local slave market, "whereat if either there were repining, or any drawing back, then certaine Moores and Officers attended either to beate you forward, or thrust you into the sides with Goades [because] this was the manner of the selling of Slaves."[22] Resistance meant only further suffering.

By all accounts, the public sale of captive-slaves in the marketplace was a degrading and dehumanizing experience that epitomized the transition from freedom to bondage. The men were taken "like dogs" to the market, and "whereas men sell Hacknies in England, we were tossed up and down to see who would give most for us." Another slave reported that prospective buyers examined his hands to see if they were "hard and brawny by working, and they caus'd me to open my mouth to see whether my teeth were able to overcome Bisket in the Galleys." George Sandys reported that women suffered even greater indignities at the weekly market because buyers typically sought "assurance (if so she be said to be) of her virginitie." Even the men, though, suffered brutalities at market, according to J. B. Gramaye in 1619, where "you may see them goe up and downe naked, and with whips compelled to runne and leape, for augmenting the price." In the simplest terms, slaves were "bought and sold, as Beasts and Cattle are; they being viewed and reviewed, and felt all about their Limmes and Bodies, as if they were so many Horses." The physical examination of captives and their sale at the slave market never ceased to be compared to the way Englishmen sold draft animals in England.[23]

After the newly acquired English slaves were sold, their housing conditions, work, and treatment depended entirely on the master. A Christian slave might find himself in relatively benign surroundings in a private household where he could live in a manner similar to that of the free family members. A slave might also continue to be locked up in a private bath house or be consigned to accommodations that amounted to no more than "the bare boords, with a very simple cape to cover us" or, possibly, merely "cold earth." Many slaves were sent to the galleys, "chained three and three to an oare," where, the survivors would later lament, they were subjected to harsh, inhuman treatment. The galley slave was the very emblem of slavery and his plight evoked nothing less than a sense of horror among those who contemplated it. According to one former slave, while they rowed the boatswain and his mate hovered above "eche of them a bulls pissell dried in their hands, and when their divelish choller rose, they would strike the Christians for no cause." No slave narrative would have been complete without a detailed lamentation on the fate of the miserable galley slave who was "at the pleasure of the prowd and dogged Turke for the least fault, nay for none at all, but onely to feed his humor, to receive a hundred bastinadoes on the rim of the bellie with a bulls dried peezle, at one time, and within a day after two hundred stripes on the backe." Those "employed in Gallies and Ships . . . were kept with chaynes, stripes, a little moldy Bisket and stinking water."[24]

Life as a galley slave was therefore predictably short. Even in moments of peace the slaves remained at their oars, "cruelly manacled in such sort, that we could not put our handes the length of one foote asunder the one from the other, and every night they searched our chaines three times, to see if they were fast rivited." Francis Knight bemoaned that all things conspired against the pitiful slaves who "for want of sleepe are in continuall extasies." In lurid detail, Knight remembered the state of slaves at oares: "the scorching heate now penetrates their braines, their flesh is burned off their backes, which anon they are as much pinched with cold: strong fetters are their neerest consorts from which they are never exempted, unless for equal miseries." When they "come on shore," J. B. Gramaye noted, they were "chained in rowes, laid up in prisons, sleeping on the ground, called onely Dogs." At sea, Knight remembered, "their repose, when they have any, is sitting, their pillow the banke upright, and that bubble, not having so much roome as to stretch their legges, their sleepe when they have any is an houre in twelve, and that at night, when one holfe Roaes and the other slumbers."[25] Food and water were also often difficult for slaves to come by, especially at sea. Thomas Sanders and others reported that the diet was sparse and rarely consisted of more than a little bread and "stinking water." The limited cargo space of the Mediterranean galley and the problem of obtaining fresh water often resulted in the death of galley slaves from thirst. Knight recalled that galley slaves would "pawne their soules" for a drop of water and were often "constrained to drink of the Salt Oceans." In one instance in 1579, thirty-two oarsmen in one vessel died of thirst.[26]

Although English authors repeatedly characterized galley slavery as the worst fate that could befall a captive, there were few guarantees that labors on shore would be much kinder. Galley oarsmen typically spent their winters on land, where they might be required to work on construction projects or any number of possible manual tasks. After a stint in the galleys, Sanders returned to Tripoli only to be put to the task of hewing stones at the construction of a religious site while his companions hauled boulders and dirt. His labors, and the labors of other Christian slaves, were doubly complicated by the iron collar he was forced to wear around his neck. But slavery on land was generally better than in the galleys because food and water were more readily available and rest at night more regular. Likewise, although they were required to perform a number of debilitating tasks, slaves served in a wider variety of roles on land, some of which were not particularly labor intensive. Slaves who had special skills were especially fortunate. John Fox found some relief "being somewhat skillful in the craft of a Barbour, by reason thereof made great shift in helping his fare now and then with a good meale." Another Englishman, a merchant by trade, avoided back-breaking labor by convincing an Algerian sultan that he could cook.[27]

If hard work and a poor diet were not enough to highlight the miseries of human bondage, some authors elaborated on the seemingly random physical punishments suffered by English and other Christian slaves. In a 1595 account, possible tortures included being "tied hand & foote, and laide on the ground, with a stone of almost insupportable waight on their backes. Others are put in the galleys, where they be galled in deed and used most doggedly." Others endured more intricate tortures. Captors placed some slaves "on their backes, and let a long rag of cipres or fine linnen dipped in pickle or salt water, sinke by little and litle into their throats, till it reach downe to their stomackes, and then they plucke it out againe, and so put the poore Christians to un-speakable paine and torment." Gramaye claimed that for "a small fault" a Christian "is burned alive, or stamped in the earth as in a Mortar, or gaunched (throwne from the wall on a hooke) or crucified, or flayed alive." Worse, he added, "to the execution of which tortures they take up any Christian they meet, to make them their brethrens tormentors."[28] Although slavery amounted to a lamentable fate and an increasingly familiar reality, the physical suffer-ings exacted on English bodies were horrifying and nearly incomprehensible.

Whatever physical hardships captive slaves may have endured, the most pointed moment in the majority of the narratives occurred when the enslaved Englishman was compelled to "turn Turk."[29] For many people in England, the enslavement of their countrymen was tragic, but it paled in comparison to the apostasy of Christians who voluntarily converted to the Muslim faith. Royal proclamations designed to raise revenue to redeem captive slaves out of bondage retold many of the same tales of woe and suffering, but special space was often reserved for the shocking pronouncement that "most of the youth-fuller sort are of late forced and compelled by intolerable and insufferable punishments and torments, to deny their Saviour, and turne to the Mahu-metan Religion." The minister Charles Fitz-Geffrey could not contain his sense of profound disgust when he stood before an audience in Plymouth in 1636, particularly when he reported that conversion also included "the abomnable *circumcision* in their flesh."[30] The embrace of Islam by English Christians, forced or otherwise, was certainly a spiritual matter of great sig-nificance to religious leaders, but the actual process by which the conversion was achieved was also rife with symbolism and undeniably theatrical.

Certainly, those who witnessed the conversion process were genuinely fascinated. John Rawlins claimed that Muslim converts were generated by taking Christians and laying them "on their naked backes or bellies, beating them so long, till they bleed at the nose and mouth; and if yet they continue constant, then they strike the teeth out of their heads, pinch them by their tongues, and use many other sorts of torture to convert them." Rawlins added that "many times they lay them their whole length in the ground like

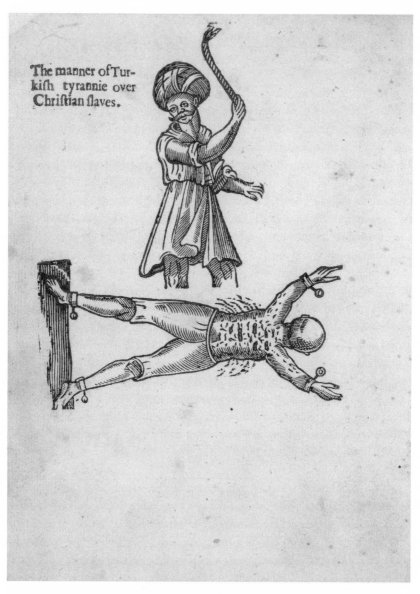

The manner of Tur-
kiſh tyrannie over
Chriſtian ſlaves.

Figure 8. Francis Knight, *A relation of seaven yeares slaverie under the Turkes of Argeire, suffered by an English captive merchant* . . . (London, 1640), frontispiece. By permission of the Folger Shakespeare Library.

a grave, and so cover them with boords, threatening to starve them, if they will not turne; and so many even for feare of torment and death, make their tongues betray their hearts to a most fearefull wickednesse, and so are circumcised with new names." Once they were broken, William Davies recounted, they were then placed on a horse facing backward with a bow and arrow, "then the picture of Christ is carried before him with feet upwards, at the which he drawes his Bow with the Arrow therein, and thus he rideth to the place of his Circumcision." Along the way, the convert would curse "his father that begate him, and his mother that bore hym, his Country, and all his kindred: then comming to the place of Circumcision, he is Circumcised, receiving a name, & denying his Christian name, so that ever after he is called *Runagado*, that is, a Christian denying Christ and turned Turke: of which sort there are more in Turkie and Barbary then of natural Turkes."[31]

Galley slavery in the Mediterranean and the forced conversion of former Christians combined to produce the clearest image contemporary Englishmen could find of a world turned upside down, or a hell on earth. But it was also fruitful material for commentators bent on reminding their readers of their dependent relationship to God, the ongoing struggle with Satan, and the inextricable link between sin and redemption. Thus, Samuel Purchas intoned that "the Devill hath sent the Moores with damnable Mahumetisme in their merchandizing quite thorow the East, to pervert so many Nations with thraldome of their states and persons." Finding oneself in bondage in the Mediterranean, in other words, was somewhat predictable, but as much as Purchas might sympathize with the suffering of slaves and detest Islam, he and other English clergymen generally chose to use the physical suffering and profound humiliation of their countrymen to remind readers and audiences that Christians "are not their owne" to begin with, "they are bought with a price (the greatest of prices, the blood of God) they are gained by conquest." Nothing could be done in this world to break the bond between Christ and his flock, so "hee that denieth himself and his owne will, puts off the chaines of his bondage, the slavery to innumberable tyrants, impious lusts, and is thus a free man indeede."[32] As a consequence, those who gave in, Edward Kellet told one English renegade who hoped to find his way back into the Christian community, had sinned more "than the sinne of *Caine* . . . or of the Jewes, which murthered Christ." Another minister, Henry Byam, lamented the "intolerable servitude" of Christian captives, but he concluded that anyone who sailed into the Mediterranean should have been aware of the danger from "[t]hat *African* monster, to which so many poore soules have been made a prey; The Turke, (which God forbid) may bring you under his Lee."[33] In this version of things, the torments endured by English slaves were but an opportunity to revel in God's glory and celebrate their real freedom.[34] Those who endured in their suffering and, perhaps, died in the process, were the great victors.

The theatricality of piracy, slavery, and forced conversion were all evinced in royal proclamations and sermons, but a number of genuine theatrical productions made full use of these themes during the late Tudor and early Stuart eras as well. Literary scholars have demonstrated the emergence of a popular fascination with historical events that concerned the conflict between Islam and Christendom and often featured infamous English characters like the celebrated, martyred English captain Thomas Stukely and the reviled English renegade pirate John Ward. George Peele, in *The Battle of Alcazar* (1591), and Robert Daborne, in *A Christian Turned Turk* (1612), took these historical figures and turned them into dramatic opportunities to reflect on the meaning of English national identity and the many threats faced by freeborn Englishmen in an increasingly complicated Mediterranean world. Other works, like Philip Massinger's *The Renegado* (1624) were less concerned with specific individuals and historical events and more focused on dramatizing what appeared to be, in the words of Giles Fletcher in *The Policie of the Turkish Empire* (1597), the Muslim desire to do "nothing more then . . . drawe both Christians and other to embrace their religion and to turn Turke."[35] A trip to the theater, as much as royal proclamations and weekly sermons, reinforced the idea that the Mediterranean world was not merely an arena for economic exchange and international competition, it was a forum where the national and spiritual integrity of the English nation was threatened by the forces of Islam.

Predictably, Englishmen did not view Muslim conversion efforts, including ritual circumcision, in the same light as the European desire to indoctrinate others into the Christian faith. Englishmen ridiculed the Muslim rite, though, not simply because they were offended by the religious sensibilities of Islam. There was also a widespread notion that North African peoples were sexual deviants. Francis Knight claimed that "they are said to commit Sodomie with all creatures, and tollerate all vices." James Wadsworth related that, after his ship was taken by the Moors in 1622, many of the men were stored in the prow. One night, "two *Moores* came down unto us, and secretly selecting two of the youngest and fairest amongst us, abused their bodies with insatiable lust, and on the next morning they stripping themselves starke naked, and powring out water one upon the others head, supposed by this washing they were cleansed from their new acted sinne." Another English merchant reiterated the lechery of the Muslim world when he recounted his good fortune in being selected by the local ruler in Algiers after his capture, allowing him to avoid a sentence in the galleys. Among the ruler's selections, however, was "a pretty *German* Boy of a ruddy Countenance." Because local rulers tended to select those individuals who held out the promise of a high ransom, the Englishman wondered about the choice of a German youth. He could only conclude that "the old man was a greater Lover of his Pleasures than of Money, and therefore he pitcht upon him as one whom might procure unto him some in his old Age." This episode was sadly predictable to the Englishman who believed that "a strange Fancy possesses the minds of all Southern People; they burn with an unnatural Fire, which consumed *Sodom* and *Gomorrah*."[36]

To this point in the typical English slave narrative, it was impossible to escape the impression that slavery was brutal and dehumanizing and meant that the enslaved would endure torturous labors, be exposed to sexual violence, and quite likely die.[37] And because the actual victims in many of the tales printed after the late sixteenth century were fellow Englishmen, the possible implications were more profound.[38] Slavery threatened the English nation's ability to protect its material interests, lent the lie to assertions of the inherent freedom enjoyed by the English, and raised questions about the ability of English merchants and mariners to extend the economic and geopolitical interests of their homeland beyond the British Isles. The menace of slavery, then, prompted the Tudor government, first, and then the Stuart to begin what amounted to an annual effort to secure the freedom of Englishmen. One avenue to diminish the potential for Englishmen to fall into a state of bondage involved diplomacy, including the conclusion of treaties of amity with several of the ruling powers of North Africa. Much to the dismay of other Christian nations, which were in perpetual conflict with their southern foes, England even reached a trade agreement with the Ottoman Turks in 1580. As a part of this thirty-five point agreement, the "great Turk" agreed to release, or seek the release, of any English slaves found in his dominions. Subsequently, England concluded a similar treaty with Morocco in an effort to ensure that Mediterranean trade would remain safe for English merchants and sailors. As a continuing measure of good faith, the English government even went to some lengths to return the "100 Turkes brought by Sir Francis Drake out of the West Indyes (where they served as slaves in the Spanish Galleyes)" to their homeland. This benevolent gesture, it was hoped, might also lead to "the release of some of the captives of the English nation there."[39]

Were it merely the experience of several thousand Englishmen or simply the publication of a relatively small number of slave narratives and sporadic government action, the experience of English slaves might not have contributed as much to the broader English understanding of slavery as the image of the enslaved African or the influence of biblical and classical sources. But the plight of English slaves in the Mediterranean world was arguably much more well-known and a much more emotional subject for the mass of English society because it was effectively broadcast throughout the land. For example, where treaties and other high-level international affairs failed to settle the issue of Englishmen held in bondage, the English public was called on to provide the funds to pay the ransoms demanded by the Barbary States. At least as early as 1567, Elizabeth's government received requests for licenses to collect ransom funds to redeem Englishmen from Algiers. In the last two decades of the sixteenth century, frequent collections were recorded at the parish level for the redemption of Englishmen and others who had been "kept bond and thrall in most cruell slaverie and Bondage" in the Mediterranean.[40] As it turned out, the most effective way to convince Englishmen to empty their coffers was to tell the story.

By the 1580s, the Elizabethan Privy Council routinely suggested that charitable funds that might otherwise be devoted to relieving distressed English men and women at home be diverted instead to the cause of redeeming Englishmen out of slavery. In a typical entry, the Council ordered the Bishop of London in 1582 "to geve order unto the preachers at the Spittal in their Sermons these Easter Holy Daies . . . to move the people for their charitable donation" to redeem "their countrymen from thraldom and miserie." General declarations along these lines were the norm, but occasionally the Privy Council was more specific, as when it specified that "Thomas Lowe, gentleman . . . deserved [to be reimbursed] for his great paynes taken in redeming of divers poore captives out of Barbary." The Council therefore requested the lord mayor and aldermen of London "to take some course that he may receive some good receite by the collections which are accostomed to be made at the spittle sermons . . . at Easter for occasyons and neccessities of this kynde, that his good endevors in performance of so good a worke may not turne to his ruyne and others be discouraged by his example to undertake the lyke."[41]

It was a mark in his favor that Thomas Lowe had sought to liberate his fellow Englishmen, but English slavery was escalating so rapidly by the late sixteenth century that it would take the combined efforts of the English government and the English public to resolve this problem.

The normalization of the practice of using public charities to redeem Englishmen out of slavery reveals how thoroughly the information contained in slave narratives was disseminated throughout society. The ransom collector, it has been argued, was a common figure in the English countryside, as were "thousands of destitute wives and dependents [who] repeatedly took to the streets with petitions on behalf of their captured kinsmen," especially after the 1620s.[42] Like the licenses issued during the Tudor era, Stuart royal proclamations were typically issued for the benefit of one or two specific individuals. In early 1624, the king authorized collections in London in several nearby shires to assist Amy Lynsteed and Joane Morse. William Lynsteed's ship had been taken "by those miscreant Sea-robbers the Turkes" and he had lost his life and his family's fortune in the process. Robert Morse, in a separate incident the following year, lost his fortune and "his liberty" when he was "carryed to *Argier*, where he is deteyned a Captive in great slavery and misery among those inhumane Creatures; from which place of Bondage" he could not be recovered without sufficient funds to pay his ransom. Along with the poverty of the two women and the suffering of their children, the abominations of "those unmercifull Pagans" reminded an English public that had heard it all before that death and slavery were looming possibilities for all.[43]

Perhaps the most systematic expression of the relationship between public charity, redemption, and ideas of slavery occurred at the annual Easter-week sermons preached at the Hospital of St. Mary Without Bishopsgate, or St. Mary Spital. Once one of the five main hospitals in London, by the late sixteenth century St. Mary Spital had ceased to care for the sick but continued to be famous for the sermons that took place on special occasions in the churchyard. These were elaborate and well-attended affairs. As John Stow recounted in his *Survey of London*, "the Maior, with his brethren the Aldermen were accustomed to bee present . . . in their Scarlets at the Spittle in the Holidayes." There the local dignitaries, including the Bishop of London "and other Prelates," heard "some especiall learned man . . . preach on the forenoones at the sayde Spittle, to perswade the Article of Christs resurrection." The Easter sermons continued to be well-attended affairs later in the century and the connection with slavery persisted. The famous diarist Samuel Pepys attended in 1662, noting what a "fine sight of charity it is," before he and his wife went to the theater to see *The Bondman*, which "we had seen . . . so often, yet I never liked it better than today."[44] Seemingly, for nearly a century by this time, the desperate plight of English slaves in the Mediterranean was memorialized and even performed on an annual basis for audiences of captivated English men and women at home.

Though it dates from a slightly later era, Pepys's *Diary* is a reminder that information about the enslavement of Englishmen could wend its way throughout English society, often through casual conversation. In February 1661, Pepys recounted that he "met with sea-commanders: and among others, Captain Cuttle, and Curtis and Mootham; and I went to the Fleece tavern to drink and there we spent till 4 a-clock telling stories of Algier and the manner of the life of slaves there." This conversation proved to be especially compelling because Mootham and Mr. Dawes, who was also in attendance, "have both been slaves there." Mootham and Dawes shared with their friends stories about how "they eat nothing but bread and water" and how "they are beat upon the soles of their feet and bellies at the Liberty of their *Padron*. How they are all at night called into their master's Bagnard [bath house]." Not every one of these conversations had the benefit of a renowned diarist to record the details for posterity, but they had been occurring in any number of taverns on any number of occasions for a long time. Former English slaves were not hard to come by.[45]

Regardless of these efforts, the capture and enslavement of Englishmen in the Mediterranean would only increase during the seventeenth century, leaving the Stuart government no choice but to try to raise funds to rescue captive Englishmen from their slavery. And the funds that were either promised or raised for this effort were rather remarkable. Edward Eastman, apparently working on his own, collected more than £820 in 1618 "by virtue of the King's patent, for the redeeming of Englishmen." A year later, the London merchants promised to contribute £40,000 toward an expedition to destroy the pirates of Algiers and Tunis, something that would be attempted in 1620 (and again in 1637) to little effect. In 1624, Devonshire representatives consented to disburse £137 to redeem twenty individuals "of these western parts," which they hoped would be repaid "with interest, out of the money collected for that purpose, by virtue of the King's Letters Patent." And in this same spirit, Captain Thomas King, "Admiral of the Narrow Seas," petitioned the king "for permission to take out two ships at his own charge to Sally, to revenge the seizure there of his factor and goods."[46] By the 1620s, individuals and discrete groups within England were prepared to devote significant resources to resolving the festering problems of piracy and slavery in the Mediterranean world.

Occasionally, however, even more sweeping efforts were called for, as in 1624 when James I took notice of the case of "fifteen hundred of our loving Subjects, English men, remaining in miserable servitude and subjection in *Argier, Tunis, Sally*, [and] *Tituane*." Turkish pirates had surprised 150 English ships at sea and had taken the men into "miserable slavery" where they were "sold from party to party, and kept in chaines of Iron, their food, bread and water to their extreme grief." In addition to physical sufferings, many Christians were also "forced and compelled by intollerable and insufferable punishments and torments, to deny their Saviour, and turne to the Mahumetan Religion, and to deny their King and Country." To address these issues, Parliament ordered ministers throughout the realm "to stirre up the charity of their Parishioners" in order to raise the necessary funds to rescue their countrymen, who were compelled to labor "in a bestiall manner like horses, for to get some foode to preserve their wretched lives, with infinite miseries." Members of Parliament took the symbolic lead when "each peer gave 40s. [and] each member of lower rank 20s." to the effort. Although it occurred in a different context, it was in this spirit that the aforementioned Charles Fitz-Geffrey dutifully reminded his audience in 1636 that, although their brethren were suffering from backbreaking labor and senseless beatings, the "want of liberty is sufficient to make up misery." With great flourish, Fitz-Geffrey castigated Turks who sunk so low as to "make marchandize of *men*," which resulted in Englishmen being "sold in markets like beasts, by creatures more brutish than beasts, stigmatized, branded when they are bought by circumcised *monsters, miscreant Mahumetans*."[47]

What is perhaps most remarkable about Fitz-Geffrey's sermon, as well as the others that became common after the 1620s, is not that it used metaphors of slavery and captivity—*that* happened routinely in Tudor and Stuart England—but that the imagery used in the speech repeated the language and metaphors of published slave narratives almost verbatim. Sermons and royal proclamations, precisely the kinds of materials that many Englishmen would have been able to hear or read in public forums, were laced with the vivid stereotypes and impassioned vitriol that emanated from the experience of fellow Englishmen, at least as they were related in English narratives. Thus, Fitz-Geffrey did not limit his lament to the fact that English slaves lacked personal liberty, which was "sufficient to make up misery," but he asserted that his countrymen suffered "hunger, nakednesse, and blowes" at the hands of "*miscreants.*" Human bondage, Fitz-Geffrey recognized, was not the same in every place and in every circumstance, for "bondage is the more grievous by how much the baser they are to whom a man is in bondage." In that regard, Vincent Jukes's enslavement was cast in stark terms by William Gouge in 1638 when he told his audience that their countryman had been "sold to a *Negro* [who] used him most cruelly."[48] When private and public sources dwelled on notions that enslavement involving extreme brutality, dehumanization, sexual degeneracy, and unfathomable misery, the experience of slavery was made meaningful to a large swath of the English public.

*   *   *

Slavery's imminence conditioned the way English merchants and mariners approached the early modern Mediterranean world, but the crossroads of Christianity and Islam was not the only place where English lives and liberties were imperiled. Capture and enslavement were twin fates that could befall Englishmen anywhere. And, perhaps unsurprisingly, as a result of the publication and dissemination of so much information about the plight of English slaves, English writers invoked the language of slavery in other places where the precise condition of their forlorn countrymen was unclear. Beginning in the late sixteenth century, English voyagers worried about the loss of their lives, fortunes, and especially their personal freedom regardless of their destination. The language of slavery was largely crafted in the context of English experiences in the Mediterranean, but the experience could be endured any place where English merchants and mariners were unfortunate enough to be seized by forces that had little regard for the often-celebrated English liberties. For the English government, too, this threat could scarcely be ignored, as England's economic livelihood would be difficult to ensure if the well-being of English adventurers could not be guaranteed.

Queen Elizabeth was particularly interested in protecting her subjects from captivity and slavery and actively sought the release of English slaves during her long reign. The most famous examples of her efforts date from the early 1580s when William Harborne, an agent for the Levant Company who then became English ambassador, completed an agreement with the Ottomans to facilitate English trade in the region. The Ottomans were keenly interested in acquiring English commodities that could enhance their growing power in the region, not least among these were gunpowder and ships. English merchants, too, saw similar advantages in forging a relationship, but

they were worried about difficulties arising from Venetian and French competition and the lack of any guarantee that the Ottoman Turks or anyone else
would respect the personal safety of English merchants. Predictably, as English ships and mariners became increasingly common in the Mediterranean,
escalating numbers of Englishmen were being taken captive and enslaved
in the region. Elizabeth therefore signaled her willingness to reach a trade
agreement with the Turks in 1579 but urged the Ottoman sultan "to intreat
and use mediation on the behalf of certaine of our subjects, who are deteined
as slaves and captives in your Gallies." Because, she asserted, "they are fallen
into that misery, not by any offence of theirs," future Ottoman-English relations hinged on guaranteeing the security of English merchants and the
freedom of English slaves. The sultan agreed and, in 1580, promulgated that
"if any slave shall be found to be Englishman, and their Consull shall sue for
his libertie," he will "be discharged and restored to the Englishmen." Moreover, if "any pirats or other free governours of ships trading the Sea shall take
any Englishman, and shall make sale of him," the sultan promised that the
case would be examined and the English slave released. In all ways, the agreement promised greater protection for English merchants and sailors than
they were likely to find any place else in the world.[49]

Pirates and Muslim princes were hardly the only ones to prey on English
mariners. Elizabeth devoted even more attention during the 1560s to the redemption of English slaves held in France and Spain. Sir Nicholas Throck-
morton, who had previously served as Elizabeth's first ambassador to France,
warned her in 1564 that a great number of English captives were languishing
in that country's galleys and a steady stream of reports filtered back to England concerning the plight of Englishmen condemned to the oars. In response, Elizabeth instructed her new ambassador, Sir Thomas Smith, to see
"that her subjects . . . be delivered from the galleys, where they are cruelly
used." At the same time, Sir Thomas Challoner, Elizabeth's first ambassador
to Spain, found himself wrapped up in a frustrating effort to liberate English
slaves on the Iberian Peninsula. In one case, Challoner petitioned King
Philip in 1564 to relieve 240 English sailors from "perpetual slavery in the
galleys."[50] France and Spain were generally unsympathetic toward official
English protests and claimed that the Englishmen were guilty, at best, of illicit trading or, worse, piracy. The English sailors held captive in Spain were
specifically accused of attacking a French ship in a Spanish port. Regardless
of these criminal offenses, the efforts of the English government to redeem its
countrymen sometimes bore fruit. In 1568, after months of letter writing,

petitioning, and protesting about English galley slaves in Marseilles (who were bound "in chains[,] fed with hard bread and water [and] beaten every day with cords"), the king of France ordered one of his men "to search out and set at liberty such Englishmen as still remain in the galleys at Marseilles."[51]

Problems with Spain, however, persisted throughout the rest of the century. In 1576, the English ambassador to Spain, John Smith, issued a memorandum to Philip II on behalf of his queen. Smith addressed a variety of issues, but he also specifically requested the liberation of eight Englishmen "condemned to the galleys and perpetual imprisonment by the Holy Office in Seville." By the late sixteenth century, the imprisonment or enslavement of Englishmen in Catholic Spain was becoming more common. As part of its comprehensive effort to prevent religious heresy, the Spanish government had placed harbors under control of the Holy Office. Subsequently, stories began circulating in England that Protestant English sailors could be thrown into dungeons, tortured, starved, condemned to the galleys, or even burned at the stake merely for owning an English Bible. To try to resolve this troublesome issue, Elizabeth urged Bernardino de Mendoza, Spain's ambassador to England, to press Philip for the release of her English subjects. Mendoza dutifully informed Philip that he should at least look into the cases of two men, Edward Taylor and Robert Williams, because "all London is speaking to me about them." Thomas Cely, a Bristol merchant living in Andalusia, put the English perspective on this subject bluntly in 1579 when he wrote to Elizabeth's closest advisor, Lord Burghley, that it was a pity how a "true subject doing his Prince's command" might "lose all his goods, and be tormented, and made a slave for seven years, three in close prison and four in the galleys."[52]

The timing of these efforts in Spain was hardly coincidental. As dangerous as continental Europe might be for a few unfortunate souls, the chances of falling into a state of slavery were even greater in the wider Atlantic world. Englishmen could easily run afoul of Spanish justice in the Americas, largely as a result of their involvement in piracy, smuggling, and outright warfare. Throughout the last half of the sixteenth century, privateers under the command of John Hawkins, Drake, and others ventured into the Spanish West Indies in search of personal gain by despoiling the locals. Under the best of circumstances, English interlopers turned a tidy profit and lent the lie to the myth of Spanish hegemony in the Americas. Under the worst of circumstances, however, scores of English ships were sent to the bottom of the sea, thousands of English mariners lost their lives, and an unknown number of others were captured and forced to labor in bondage, side-by-side with Indians and Africans. One event, in particular, generated nearly a hundred candidates for galley slavery in the Spanish Atlantic world—John Hawkins's failed third slave-trading voyage of 1567–68.

Richard Hakluyt dramatized all of these hazards through the story of Miles Philips, an English youth who set sail in 1567 as Hawkins's page when the English knight embarked on his third and final slave-trading voyage. Like Robert Tomson, Henry Hawks, and the other English observers with firsthand experience in Spain's Atlantic world, Philips was ultimately well-placed to supply additional information about the depth and breadth of human bondage as it was practiced in the sixteenth century. He did so, however, from a slightly different perspective. When Hawkins barely escaped San Juan de Ulua with the battered remnants of his fleet in late 1568, he found himself with too few ships and too many men to provision during the return voyage across the Atlantic. As a result, Hawkins abandoned Philips and more than a hundred other men some distance north of Veracruz near the modern-day city of Tampico.[53] Once ashore, the abandoned Englishmen endured great hardships that, when retold by Hakluyt, echoed the drama of captivity and enslavement performed by unlucky Englishmen in the Mediterranean. But the tale of Miles Philips also reminded readers that Englishmen, Africans, and Indians had much in common, if only because they were bound together by the likelihood of suffering from Iberian rapacity in Africa and the Americas.[54]

As Philips told the story to Richard Hakluyt, some twenty years after it happened, within a day or two of straggling ashore they were "assaulted by the Indians, a warlike kind of people, which are in a maner as Canibals." The Indians, or "Chichimici" as Hakluyt recorded their name, were "very ougly and terrible to beholde," but they had also bene "very cruelly handled" by the Spanish, from whom "there is no mercy." Like the accounts of other Englishmen in Africa and the Americas, Philips claimed that they were initially met with violence because the natives assumed the newcomers were their Spanish oppressors. Eight Englishmen died in the attack, but once the English were able to convince the Indians that "we were not their enemies the Spaniards, they had compassion on us," although many of the English survivors "they did strip starke naked." Breaking into several smaller companies, the English traveled north and west in search of refuge even as they were continuously harassed by random Indian attacks and even more troublesome plagues of mosquitoes, both of which were made more difficult to endure because of "our naked bodies."[55] Nakedness itself proved to be both a source of confusion and an explanation for English weakness as the men were eventually forced to surrender themselves to a small band of Spanish soldiers who initially mistook them for "the Chichimeci."[56]

Initially, the Spanish took Philips and the other captive Englishmen on a lengthy overland journey to Mexico City where they subsequently gave the wayward Protestants a chance to recover their strength. Within a few months, however, Spanish officials condemned the men to the workhouses, or *obrajes*, "into which place divers Indians are sold for slaves, some for ten yeeres, and some for twelve." This turn of events horrified Philips, who claimed (in the now familiar refrain) that the Englishmen would "rather be put to death" than "bee used as slaves." But, to his surprise, "we were not put to any labour, but were very straitly kept, & almost famished" over the course of several months. After a failed attempt at escape, Philips and about a hundred other Englishmen found themselves in Mexico City where the gentlemen took them "for their servants or slaves." In this context, slavery meant waiting upon their masters as body servants, a task that would have otherwise been performed by Indians and "Negroes which be their slaves during their life."[57] For the next year or so, it looked as if the English were fated to spend the remainder of their days in bondage.

As it turned out, most of the Englishmen fared much better than Indian or African slaves whose lives were often defined by abject labor. Some men continued to serve as the personal servants of wealthy Spanish gentlemen in Mexico City. John Lee, whose father had been killed at San Juan de Ulua, worked for a time as a hosier. John Martin, an Irishman, somehow made it to Guatemala where he earned a living as a barber surgeon. Others, however, were sent to the silver mines at Zacatecas, but even in those unpleasant surroundings the Englishmen typically served as "overseers of the Negroes and Indians that labored there." Moreover, Philips recounted, "[M]any of us became very rich" because they were accorded wages. They also found that the Indians and Africans under their command routinely gave them silver on the side, perhaps as a reward for being kind overseers (as Philips assumed) or simply to ingratiate themselves with the men who were best positioned to ameliorate their condition.[58] Initially, then, a number of Englishmen found themselves in a state of bondage, but it was a life not without certain comforts. From what they may have known about the varieties of slavery in other parts of the world, particularly in the Muslim world, slavery equaled captivity, but it was not always physically grueling.

Philips hinted that there were worse things to come when he noted, almost in passing, that a few English gentlemen were sent to Spain, where "many of them died with the cruell handling of the Spaniards in the Inquisition house." The Inquisition, even more so than the capriciousness of secular authorities, haunted the English in the Iberian world after midcentury, to the degree that Philips could claim that life as a slave in Mexico was preferable to being brought before the Holy Office anywhere in the world. Since the 1550s, a few unfortunate English merchants and sailors had been arrested, examined, or even tried for heresy by the Inquisition. English merchants in the Canary Islands, for example, came under increasing scrutiny upon Elizabeth's ascension to the throne in 1558. Robert Tomson, the English merchant who traveled to Mexico in 1556, was arrested in 1559 for saying "many things against our Holy Catholic faith, which are those preached by the Lutheran sect." His sentence, handed down early the following year, was typical. Tomson was forced to endure public humiliation, wear a special robe called a San Benito for two years, and suffer imprisonment for a full year.[59] Even so, Tomson's fate was relatively mild compared to what would follow because the Inquisition operated on a somewhat informal basis in Mexico during this period. All that changed in 1571, however, when the Spanish Inquisition was formalized in Mexico. From that date forward, the situation of the English slaves in Mexico worsened considerably.[60]

Traces of the horror evoked by the forced conversion of Christian slaves in the Mediterranean can be detected in Philips's plaintive complaints about the sufferings of Englishmen at the hands of the Mexican Inquisition. Beginning in 1572, the Spanish began rounding up many of the men who were scattered about New Spain. Although the Englishmen had been ashore for about four years by this point, it was only with the Inquisition that they were imprisoned, in some cases for more than a year, and sentenced as "English heritikes." Many of the men were subjected to repeated questioning and torture as church officials sought to weed out any traces of Protestantism. Despite their protestations that "we came into those countreys by force of weather, & against our wils, and that never in all our lives we had either spoken or done any thing contrary to their lawes," Philips recalled, "we were al rackt, and some enforced to utter that against themselves, which afterward cost them their lives." At an appointed date, the men were then reclothed in "fooles coats," or long yellow gowns with red crosses, and marched to the market square to receive judgment.[61]

Considering the times and despite the religious context, the sentences were unsurprising: whipping, galley slavery, or death (and quite often all three in rapid succession). On Good Friday in 1574, "[W]e were all brought into a court of the Inquisitors pallace, where we found a horse in a readinesse for every one of our men which were condemned to have stripes"—60 men in all, according to Philips. The men were ceremoniously stripped naked from the waist up, had a rope tied around their necks, placed on horseback, and paraded through town "as a spectacle for all the people to behold." With criers shouting, "Behold these English dogs, Lutherans, enemies to God," their Spanish tormentors whipped the Englishmen through the city until they returned "with their backs all gore blood, and swollen with great bumps." The physical suffering endured by the Englishmen was severe, but it was consistent with the kinds of punishment handed down by the Inquisition to Indians, "crypto-Jews," and others convicted of blasphemy or heresy. And things could have been much worse. Three men who had sailed with Hawkins— George Rively, Peter Momfrie, and John Martin—were "burnt to ashes" in 1574 and 1575 for their supposedly heretical crimes. Martin's downfall was particularly sudden. The offending Irishman had a wife and child and a successful business when he was arrested in the summer of 1574. Regardless, he was dragged back to Mexico City from his home in Guatemala, sentenced, strangled, and burnt at the stake.[62]

After being ritually tortured and humiliated, the Englishmen returned to prison until more than fifty of them "were sent into Spaine to the gallies, there to receive the rest of their martirdome." Philips's choice of words here was no accident. Neither he nor anyone else seriously expected galley slaves to survive a six-year sentence, much less eight or ten (which many of the men were expected to endure). The prospect of galley slavery in the Spanish Atlantic world was as horrifying as it was in the Mediterranean. So many Englishmen suffered this fate that it not only prompted the English government to try to liberate English galley slaves during this era but also prompted English sailors to worry aloud about the prospect. When John Noble was captured with his twenty-eight men off Nombre de Dios in 1574, "[t]hey were all killed, excepting two boys who were condemned to the galleys for life." In the mid-1580s, when Hawkins took his large force into the West Indies, several Spanish prisoners reported to the author of "The *Primrose* Journal" that, after they had routed the English, "wee should all die but [20] of the beste & they shoulde bee made gallie slaves." When the English ship *Help* was captured off Havana in 1596, the surviving crew members were either put into the galleys or sent to Spain for punishment. The threat of being enslaved by the Spanish was very real, not least because this is exactly what happened to so many of the survivors from Hawkins's ill-fated slave-trading expedition when they went before the Inquisition in the 1570s.[63]

Interestingly, galley slavery could be turned to certain advantages. Drake's 1585–86 voyage created an opportunity for the English to try to gain certain diplomatic concessions.[64] Scores, if not hundreds, of liberated galley slaves were taken during the course of this voyage. Although there was no mention of any of them being English, there were Germans, French, Turks, North African Moors, Spanish convicts, and Africans. When the fleet returned to England in 1586, the Privy Council directed the merchants trading into Turkey to take charge of the Muslim slaves and to return them to their homeland in the hope that "they maie drawe on greater favor and liberties unto them selves then they yet enjoye." How many men may have been involved in this remarkable eastward-flowing transatlantic liberation scheme is difficult to ascertain. The author of "The *Primrose* Journal" recorded only that "manie Turkes, Frenchmen, *Nigros, Moores, Greekes* & Spaniards went with us from This towne [Cartagena]." Alonso Suarez de Toledo reported to the Crown that Drake took "200 negroes, Turks and Moors" from Cartagena, "though they are not useful in his country." Pedro Sanchez claimed that Drake "carried off the Moors from the galleys at Cartagena and at Santo Domingo, about 200." These, Sanchez believed, "he promised to send to their own country." Drake may have done just that, for upon his return the Privy Council ordered the return of the "100 Turkes brought by Sir Francis Drake out of the West Indies." Ultimately, however, when Richard Hakluyt recorded the voyage of Laurance Aldersey to Egypt in 1586, he only noted that he carried 20 Turkes "which were to goe to Constantinople, being redeemed out of captivitie, by Sir Francis Drake in the West Indies." Clearly the English government recognized a rare opportunity to leverage its beneficence as part of its larger strategy to diminish the likelihood of Englishmen being captured and enslaved in the Mediterranean World.[65]

Captivity and slavery also made it easier for people like Miles Philips to understand the plight of Africans and Indians in the Americas. Philips "was appointed to be an overseer of Indian workmen" whom he "found to be a courteous and loving kind of people" who "hate and abhorre the Spaniardes" because of the "horrible cruelties" the Indians had endured and because the Spanish kept them "in such subjection and servitude." This experience led Philips to conclude, like Hakluyt, that the Indians "and the Negros doe daily lie in waite to practice their deliverance out of that thraldome and bondage."[66] Much as the captivity and enslavement of Englishmen was to be lamented, then, the practice made it easier to understand the plight of other people who found themselves in similar circumstances. In the Americas, slavery bound Englishmen, Indians, and Africans together by virtue of their shared sufferings and promoted the idea that they had at least one important thing in common—they all hated the Spanish. However, captivity helped some Englishmen form even more enduring bonds. While he was held by the Portuguese in Bahia, Peter Carder worked with his "friends Negros and Savages in their planting of ginger." Philips reported that "David Alexander & Robert Cooke returned to serve the Inquisitor," after their terms of service expired, "who shortly after maried them both to two of his Negro women." John Storie, another former captive, also married a black woman.[67] Misery was but part of the story. Some Englishmen clearly made friends (even if only by convenience) and formed more permanent interpersonal relationships grounded in a sense of camaraderie or, perhaps, genuine affection.

None of this, however, softened the blow, and Philips determined—like other English captives and slaves throughout the Atlantic world—that his best option was to try to escape. He could have married and accepted his lot in life, he later wrote, but he "had alwayes a longing and desire [to return] to this my native country." Philips thought he might have a chance when he was sent to Acapulco when rumors began to circulate that an English fleet under the command of Sir Francis Drake was plundering the Pacific Coast. "I hoped," he remembered, "that if we met with master Drake, we should all be taken, so that then I should have beene freed." Unfortunately, it was not to be. Philips soon after tried to sneak aboard a ship in San Juan de Ulua, disguised as a soldier, but he was arrested and thrown in jail. He schemed to get a file and tried to work the irons off his legs, only to be placed in a new set of shackles before he could finish the job. On the wagon ride from the coast back to Mexico City, where he would likely face the Inquisition once again, Philips finally got his hands out of his manacles, "filed off my boltes," and snuck off into the darkness "freed from my mine yrons all saving the collar that was about my necke, and so got my libertie the second time." Some nearby Indians provided Philips with refuge and release from his collar. He later made his way to Guatemala, where he found his way aboard a ship by claiming to be "borne in Granado." After torturous delays in Havana, Seville, and Majorca, Philips finally found a sympathetic countryman and snuck aboard an English ship. By February 1583, "after 16. yeeres absence, having sustained many and sundry great troubles and miseries," Philips was home.[68] There, like so many others at the time, he was finally at liberty to tell the story of slavery in the Atlantic world.

*   *   *

During the middle decades of the seventeenth century—well after the English nation had established its own American colonies—pamphlet writers and colonial promoters continued to insist that their countrymen were being enslaved by the Spanish. Despite England's ongoing efforts to maintain peaceful relations, writers argued, Spain had engaged in "a continual state of open War and hostility; at the first most unjustly begun by them, and ever since in the like sort continued and prosecuted, contrary to the Common Right and Law of Nations."[69] Nearly a century after Miles Philips was made a slave and just a few decades after Vincent Jukes came home begging for forgiveness, Richard Blome argued that the Spanish "would never contract a Peace with the *English* in *America*." The Spanish had regularly taken English ships and had even "Sacked *St. Christophers, Mevis* [sic], *Providence, S[anta] Cruz,* and *Tortugas,* murthering and carrying away most of the *Inhabitants* into slavery." Moreover, "Their barbarous cruelty" extended to the practice of "compelling our Merchants, and others which they have took prisoners, to turn their Religion." That, in and of itself, "doth sufficiently justify any attempt or mischief we can do against them, either in seizing on their Ships, or the landing on their Countreys."[70] Because the Spanish had "continually invaded, in an hostile maner, Our Collonies, slain Our Countreymen, taken Our Ships and Goods, destroyed Our Plantations, made Our People Prisoners and Slaves," it was asserted, "the honour of the Nation would lie rotting [if] they should any longer suffer themselves to be used, or rather abused in this manner."[71] But to anyone who had been paying attention over the course of the preceding decades, none of these accusations would have been the least bit surprising. Slavery was the price of doing business in contested territories.

It proved to be rather easy for the inhabitants of the British Isles to learn about the miseries endured by the enslaved. Former slaves, whether freed by their own audacity or liberated through the charity of others, were an increasingly common sight in early modern England. It is difficult to say with precision just how many Englishmen experienced slavery firsthand in the Mediterranean world or in other parts of the Atlantic. Certainly, English slaves numbered in the thousands at the intersection of Islam and Christianity and likely in the hundreds where Protestantism met Catholicism. As a result, the horrors of slavery, as detailed after the fact by the few survivors, were becoming ever more familiar. Whether in print or from the pulpit, whether on stage or in song, whether the alms collector came calling or simply because of a random encounter in a dockyard tavern, slavery confronted and challenged English society in the late sixteenth and early seventeenth centuries.[72] Written accounts detailing the experience of slavery heroicized several particularly well-known individuals, but they also ennobled the English nation as a whole as writers constructed an image of their countrymen as freeborn and liberty-loving people. Sermons, royal proclamations, and public collections extended the reach of the rhetorical boasts of English patriots to the eyes and ears of the mass of society. Englishmen did not have to be literate or even particularly worldly in order to encounter the prevalence of slavery in the world around them. Former slaves lived right next door.

Their rejection of slavery made the English people special, civil, and humane, or so they would have everyone believe when they contrasted themselves with the inhabitants of other parts of the world. Viewed from England, and without shading the facts too much, it was certainly possible to argue that the English were different, in part because they did not take and hold other people in slavery. This self-congratulatory tale of a people's collective antipathy for human bondage, however, would be sorely tested during the seventeenth century as the English established new societies in the Americas. There, unlike at home, they would be living side-by-side with Indians and Africans. There, unlike at home, they would be forced to figure out who should be entitled to the benefits of English liberties and freedoms and who should not. The demands of maintaining order, guaranteeing security, and turning a profit would mean that Englishmen in the Americas would have to determine whether there was a place for slavery in a world that was theoretically "English." Their response to this problem varied, depending on the circumstances and whether a potential slave happened to be of European, African, or American descent. And those distinctions would prove to be crucial. Simply put, slavery would play a more important role in the English colonies than perhaps anyone would have cared to acknowledge.

CHAPTER 5

"As Cheap as Those Negroes"?:
Transplanting Slavery in Anglo-America

Scapethrift: *And is it a pleasant countrie withall?*
Seagull: *As ever the Sunne shind on: termperate and ful of all sorts of excellent viands; . . . And then you shall live freely there, without sargeants, or courtiers, or lawyers, or intelligencers. . . . You may be an alderman there, and never be a scavinger; you may be any other officer, and never be a slave."*[1]

When three English ships unloaded their band of more than a hundred settlers at Jamestown in the spring of 1607, few people involved in the enterprise were thinking about either slavery or Africans. The planting of a Chesapeake settlement was part of a larger English colonial endeavor famously articulated in Richard Hakluyt's "Discourse of Western Planting" a quarter century before. To some, the new plantation was a visible sign of God's providence. Many others characterized the venture in base economic terms. Regardless, there were obvious parallels in people's minds—investors and colonial promoters particularly liked to invoke the historical greatness of the Roman Empire and the burgeoning wealth and power of the Iberian nations. But the English were not simply conscious imitators; many intellectuals envisaged their overseas activities as missionary projects that could save the indigenous inhabitants of North America from both their own inherent savagery and the cruelty of the Spanish. Fundamentally, however, people—whether English, Indian, or African—were an ancillary concern in the establishment of English colonies. English colonial promoters and investors were primarily interested in the profits that could be extracted from the land, the ability of that land to sustain settlements where religious and economic freedoms could develop unhindered, and the potential for national greatness compared to that of other European nations.[2]

Nonetheless, English settlements were necessarily filled with human beings, and the nature and condition of the inhabitants of England's American colonies were central to determining their success or failure. English settlers, nearby Indians, and newly arrived Africans proved to be a constant source of tension for colonial officials both at home and abroad in subsequent decades. Between 1607 and 1660, English colonists in the Chesapeake, Bermuda, New England, Barbados, and other West Indian islands, seemed to undermine as much as they contributed to efforts to turn overseas ventures into stable, profitable, yet still essentially *English* ventures. In each colony, an effort was made to replicate England, either as the settlers and organizers believed it to exist or, in some cases, as they believed it had once existed in some idyllic (if perhaps wholly imagined) past. Few things mattered more in English society than order. Individuals presumably knew their place, recognized the natural capacities of their social betters, and unquestioningly accepted the proposition that all men were not created equal. Some people were meant to rule, others to serve. In an English context, this sentiment could mean that human beings who refused to live up to society's standards could and should be subjected to harsh punishment or some kind of potentially slavish rehabilitative program. Although it was rare and controversial, slavery was indeed among the several options available during the late Tudor and early Stuart era. English leaders in the Americas inhabited a world where slavery was recognized as an appropriate punitive or correctional device that could redeem wayward Englishmen from criminal, sinful, or simply slothful ways.

Slavery appeared early on in the Anglo-Atlantic world, but it did so in ways that have often been overlooked by historians. First, much as it had been in a domestic English setting, colonial officials in the American colonies continued to imagine that slavery was an appropriate and potentially useful way of dealing with recalcitrant individuals. Although the literature is not extensive on this point, a few historians have sympathized with the lowliest early English colonists, comparing the plight of English indentured servants and convict laborers with slaves.[3] Government officials, particularly in Virginia, threatened English colonists with slavery for a number of offenses and English colonial courts repeatedly sentenced English men and women to be slaves to punish them and, sometimes, to reform their behavior. Ironically, the use of slavery among the English inhabitants of new American settlements was designed not simply to instill order but was part of the broader effort to maintain some semblance of living in an English community. In other words, slavery paradoxically was used to preserve English society and culture. Not surprisingly, however, voices were raised in opposition by people who argued that condemning English men and women to slavery, or simply treating English men and women in a slavish fashion, could not be tolerated. Indeed, they argued, any pretense of slavery undermined all efforts, real or imagined, to transplant English society into American soil.

, Second, slavery shaped early Anglo-Indian relations in important ways, just as it did in other parts of the Americas where the Portuguese, Spanish, and French encountered large indigenous populations. We have already seen how Englishmen encountered human bondage during the late sixteenth and early seventeenth centuries in a variety of contexts. Because there was no single model of slavery, Englishmen tended to think about human bondage circumstantially rather than as a consistent or uniform phenomena. They understood, for example, that African peoples were likely slaves throughout the broader Atlantic world because of labor demands and extractive economic practices. But firsthand experience taught many other Englishmen that they, too, could be enslaved as a result of piracy, religious strife in the Mediterranean, or plain bad luck. Indian slavery was yet another matter. English colonial promoters and many Anglo-Americans liked to imagine that they would be able to cultivate a working relationship with the natives and even suggested, in their more optimistic moments, that Indians would come to see in England a culture and civilization worth emulating.[4] Enslaving Indians in this context was not especially desirable. When it happened, then, it was quite often a cultural or geopolitical construction that emerged as a result of negotiations between Europeans and indigenous peoples, rulers and ruled, and men and women trying to make sense of each other and articulate new societies in the Americas. Certainly, some colonial Americans viewed Indians as potentially useful laborers, but Indian slavery was initially a normative institution with its own parameters that was quite unlike the chattel slavery practiced by Europeans in other contexts.[5]

Anglo-Americans transplanted slavery in early America because they lived in a world where slavery was difficult to avoid. When it appeared, however, it was often in the context of contentious debates concerned with how Anglo-Americans could make their rough-hewn outposts more English. Unlike the increasingly popular use of Africans as slaves, English officials neither

enslaved their own nor enslaved Indians because they were looking for laborers. Rather, English men and women and Indians were made slaves for failing
to live up to the expectations of colonial officials bent on preserving order
and English rule in the Americas. Colonial leaders also hoped that enslavement would maintain a sense of Englishness among the European colonists
and facilitate the transformation of Indians into English subjects. Early
modern Englishmen believed that human bondage was a rational, purposeful, and conceptually legitimate institution. Yet, they also accepted that
slavery should only be applied under certain specific circumstances to certain
specific groups of people in order to achieve measurable, individualistic results. Whether slavery was just, even if it was controversial, was less of a
problem than determining when and where and upon whom it could be justifiably imposed. That English men and women and Indians were deemed
candidates for bondage, then, not only reveals a great deal about how early
modern Anglo-Americans thought about themselves in relation to other human populations, it also highlights some of the varieties of slavery practiced
in early America before slavery became a race-based labor system.

*   *   *

If early seventeenth-century colonial promoters were to be believed, transatlantic enterprises promised great rewards for England and an even greater
boon for those men and women lucky enough to be destined, in the words of
Michael Drayton, for "Earth's only paradise."[6] Much to the chagrin of the
promoters, however, a large number of people seemed to be willing to cast
aspersions on the fledgling settlements. Critics bemoaned conditions in the
colonies with graphic depictions of harsh climates, poor Indian relations,
poverty, disease, and tenuous food supplies. Perhaps most troubling for colonial sponsors of the labor-starved American plantations was the popular recognition that life as a servant in the colonies was not simply unpleasant, it
could be inhumane, life threatening, and slavish. As the former indentured
servant and colonial promoter George Alsop revealed in 1666, the "clapper-
mouth jaws of the vulgar in England" seemed to believe that "those which
are transported over thither, are sold in open Market for Slaves, and draw
Carts like Horses." George Gardyner wrote in 1651, "[W]e are upbraided by
all other Nations that know that trade for selling our own Countrymen for
the Commodities of those places." Perhaps even more startlingly, Gardyner
added that he had been told "that we English were worse than the Turks, for

that they sold strangers onely, and we sold our own Countreymen." Englishmen might get themselves hanged for "selling or taking away an Indian that worshipeth the Devil," while at the same time they "allow[ed] others, and will themselves buy of their own Nation, which have most barbarously been stolne out of their Country."[7]

The idea that slavery was neither absent nor inconsequential in early America had some basis in reality. Numerous reports—issued by "base and idle lubbers . . . that are ever opposite to all good publicke workes," according to the Virginia Company of London—declared that thousands of settlers had perished in just a few short years, and many more were suffering, in the early Chesapeake. In the aftermath of the Powhatan Uprising in March 1622, which resulted in the deaths of 347 English men, women, and children, Richard Frethorne wrote home complaining of the want of food and clothing and the specter of death that hung like a black cloud over the colony. Frethorne begged to be "freed out of this Egipt," informing his parents that his situation was no better than that of armless beggars back in England. "[A]s your Child," he entreated his father, "release me from this bondage." Frethorne was not alone in his misery. Thomas Best wrote home in the spring of 1623 to complain that his master "Atkins hath sold me . . . like a damnd slave." A year later, Jane Dickenson lamented that Dr. Potts threatened to make her serve him "the uttermost day" in a fashion akin to "her slavery with the Indians" unless she procured 150 pounds of tobacco. In the minds of disgruntled servants, any protection their native Englishness might have offered them was of little value in the New World.[8]

That slavery existed in early America was further encouraged by the disputes among some members of the Virginia Company. John Bargrave, an adventurer and merchant who opposed existing limitations on free trade, submitted a petition to the Privy Council in 1622 accusing the former secretary, Sir Thomas Smith, of having "contrary to the patent and royal instructions caused a certain book to be printed of tyrannical government in Virginia, whereby many lost their lives, and were brought into slavery." Less than a year later, the Privy Council received another communication endorsed by the governor, Council, and Assembly in Virginia in response to the publication of Nathaniel Butler's unflattering *Unmasking of Virginia*. Butler, a protégé of the Earl of Warwick and the former governor of Bermuda (1619–22), accused colonial officials of mismanagement and held them responsible for the extraordinary loss of life suffered in the colony. According to Company officials, however, high mortality rates were a legacy of the "Egyptian slavery and Scythian cruelty exercised upon them by the laws written in blood" during Smith's government. It was with great pleasure, then, that Governor Francis Wyatt was able to assure London officials in 1624 that "their slavery from that time has been converted into freedom."⁹ Or so they claimed.

John Bargrave, Nathaniel Butler, and other colonial officials who used the language of slavery did not do so lightly or without cause. Slavery had enormous rhetorical value in the Anglo-Atlantic world, but there was also evidence that it had practical applications that mirrored the recommendations issued by Englishmen in England. The claim that Anglo-Americans practiced slavery among themselves therefore could not be easily dismissed. For example, much of Sir Thomas Smith's tenure as secretary of the Virginia Company had in fact coincided with the implementation of martial law after its introduction by Sir Thomas Dale, who had arrived as Governor Lord de la Warr's deputy in 1611. The *Laws Divine, Morall and Martiall*, or Dale's Laws, prescribed a strict work regimen for malingering colonists and laid out severe punishments, including death and slavery, for a number of possible offenses. Several planters claimed, after the downfall of Smith and the emergence of Sir Edwin Sandys as secretary, that upon Dale's arrival in Virginia he had "oppressed the whole company with such extraordinary labors by daye and watchinge by night, as maye seeme incredible to the eares of any who had not the experimentall thereof." The list of abuses has left an indelible stain on Dale's name in Virginia lore. It was reported that "for stealinge to satisfie their hunger [some men] were hanged, one chained to a tree till he starved to death." Others who attempted to escape into the forest or back to England "were shott to death, [or] hanged and broken upon the wheele." Still others were whipped and compelled to work "as slaves in irons for terme of yeeres." Not surprisingly, considering the broader context of the Anglo-Atlantic world, criminals in Virginia were even threatened with galley slavery.¹⁰

Slavery was a legitimate part of early Anglo-American penal law, but it was a threat typically directed at individuals who behaved in a manner that undermined the common good. Governor Samuel Argall determined in 1617 that individuals found guilty of price gouging could be punished with "3 years Slavery to the Colony." In 1618, Virginia leaders threatened colonists who failed to attend church with punishments that could include laying "neck & heels on the Corps du Guard" and then serving as "a slave [y]e week following." A second offense would lead to a month as a slave and a third, "a year & a day." The same month the governor determined that slavery would also be a fit punishment for individuals who failed to set aside at least two

acres of their land to plant corn or, potentially worse, for wasting scarce resources by shooting back even "in defence of himself against Enemies till a
new supply of ammunition comes in."[11] These measures partly indicate the
desperation of colonial officials who were trying to bring order to the English
frontier. At the same time, there is little indication that slavery as a form of
punishment, and as something that might teach people a lesson, was particularly remarkable or especially problematic.

Virginia was unexceptional in its willingness to threaten slavery, although in other places the violations were arguably more recognizably criminal. A Bermudian court sentenced Nicholas Gabriel to be "a slave unto the
colony" for slandering the governor.[12] When officials in Massachusetts condemned eight men and one woman to slavery for assault, rape, and theft between 1638 and 1642, they too were falling back on a conception of human
bondage deeply rooted in English legal culture. Thus, William Andrews was
"censured to bee severely whiped, & delivered up as a slave" for having "made
assault upon his m[aster], Henry Coggan." It was hoped that slavery would,
in effect, serve to reform Andrews's behavior and in this case it appears the
Boston court was satisfied with the results. In September 1639, less than a year
after his original sentence, William Andrews, "who was formerly com[m]itted
to slavery for his ill & insolent carriage," was "released (upon his good carriage) from his slavery, & put to Mr Endecott." Having mended his behavior,
Andrews ceased to be a slave and, instead, became a common servant.[13]

Colonial elites determined that slavery was an appropriate device to rein
in Englishmen who acted unlawfully or behaved in a manner that undermined the safety and stability of separate colonial ventures. The use of human
bondage as a means of punishing English settlers in the Americas and as a
way of reforming their behavior was consistent with early modern English
attitudes about slavery.[14] Debating the issue in Parliament in 1621, one member
suggested that criminals who were "adjudged to die for smale faultes" might
"be saved and Condemned as Slaves during lief and be used as in other Cuntreys unto anie Publique workes." If, after several years, "they become newe
men, and Demeane themselves well," their master could "release them of
theire bondage and Slaverie, into theire former libertie and fredome, never
after to be taxed or twitted in the teeth either with theire bondadge or with
theire Crimes for which they weare soe punished." Special attention was also
given to those who might run away "or doe anie violent Acte against the
Master of the Worke, their Captain or Keeper or anie other." In that case,
prisoners would "never have their libertie but contynue Slaves all their lief

time, without release or Redempcion."[15] Dale's Laws, in particular, also resembled the Tudor government's efforts at social control and the desire of the
ruling elite to quell vagrancy and idleness. These laws were also almost certainly part of the tradition of *conciliar* justice used in Ireland and the English
marchlands, a legal tradition rooted in the effort to preserve order and security in potentially hostile surroundings.[16] But the continuing references
to slavery as a useful tool, at home and abroad, suggests that the enslavement
of freeborn English men and women continued to be a viable possibility to
those tasked with maintaining order even as it was routinely abjured by tri-
umphant nationalists.

No matter its purpose or theoretical legitimacy, domestic slavery could
easily engender ill will among colonists and voices were raised in protest
when it appeared that colonial officials were abrogating the rights of freeborn
English men and women. That labor contracts could be annulled or individuals might be treated in an exceedingly harsh fashion were genuine concerns,
even if the fear of such things did not necessarily require people to invoke the
language of slavery. But slavery terrified Englishmen and the fear of bondage
was a grammar that united Anglo-Americans across time and space with
their countrymen. The choice of words was no accident, then, when inhabitants in Bermuda issued a list of grievances in 1622 expressing their worry that
orphans were "kept here in litle better Condition than Slaves." Similarly,
Bermudians knew they stood a good chance of getting a response when they
expressed their concern that Nicholas Gabriel had not been executed for his
particular offence (as might be expected) but had instead been condemned
"to remaine a slave to the Colony."[17] Slavery might have been impermanent,
but it was an absolute and abject condition against which Englishmen were
used to measuring themselves. It was as much a positive declaration of their
Englishness as anything else, then, when the Massachusetts Bay Colony included in its *Body of Liberties* in 1641, that "there shall never be any bond-
slavery, villenage or captivitie amongst us."[18] Few things were as definitively
English in the early modern era as the rejection of slavery.

When English men and women complained that they were being treated
like slaves, they were able to do so because of a shared historical experience in
early modern England. The linguistic evidence alone indicates that slavery was
both recognizable and meaningful across a broad stratum of society during the
initial decades of American settlement; however, it is also clear that slavery
implied something different to early Anglo-Americans than the system of
bondage that would manifest itself in a later era.[19] And regardless of the first-

hand experiences of thousands of English travelers, merchants, and mariners in the early modern Atlantic world, few people in England were intimately familiar with the emerging race-based plantation system that would ultimately reconfigure the social meaning of slavery throughout the Atlantic world. Furthermore, even if the Bible, some abstract appreciation of the history of slavery in England, or even the legacy of Roman law shaped the way English men and women thought about slavery during this period, the subject of slavery may have been even more complicated in Anglo-America than it had been in Tudor and early Stuart England.

Accusations of slavery, in one form or another, were tossed about with astounding frequency and for a variety of circumstances during the 1640s and 1650s. A number of publications dealt with the familiar subject of Englishmen held in bondage in the Mediterranean, such as Francis Knight's previously discussed *A Relation of Seaven Yeares Slaverie* (1640) and the brief *Newes from Sally* (1642), which recounted the rescue of four Englishmen from the "slavery of the Turkes."[20] Writers and publishers also increasingly invoked the language of slavery in the political controversies of the day, particularly in the late 1640s when pamphlets accusing the Stuart government of seeking to reduce the commons of England to a state of slavery reached their peak, and during the late 1650s when similarly acrid diatribes accusing the Lord Protector Oliver Cromwell of doing much the same thing to his foes became equally commonplace.[21] Slavery also had metaphorical resonance in religious circles during the mid-seventeenth century.[22] Even mundane matters, such as debt and false imprisonment, were deemed worthy of characterizing in the language of slavery, as in the 1648 case of "all the poor afflicted and miserable, inslaved and immured Prisoners for Debt, Contempts, and other trivial matters" who issued a public declaration asserting that their plight was not merely unjust, it was a "slavish Innovation" that threatened to undermine the liberty of all free Englishmen.[23] As the rabble-rousing English Leveller John Lilburne argued in his *Liberty Vindicated against Slavery*, however, even seemingly trivial matters were significant because "the present inslaved condition of this Nation" revealed that "the Law of England" is "now turned into a shadow."[24]

In the colonies, there were different issues. The ease with which Englishmen were able to use slavery to condemn practices that some people might consider to be inconsistent with English laws and traditions also informed the rising tide of complaints against abuses in the servant trade. The supply of servants to the increasingly labor-hungry American plantations was a critical problem in mid-seventeenth-century England. In theory, indentured servants were willing emigrants who signed contracts to labor for another person for a period of several years in exchange for transatlantic passage and the promise of eventually achieving free status in one of the English colonies. Servants who arrived without a contract were routinely subjected to the so-called "custom of the country," which in Virginia meant a term of service of four to six years, depending on their age at arrival. This method of supplying the colonies with necessary laborers proved to be so popular that most of the English men and women who appeared in the Chesapeake during the seventeenth century (and West Indian colonies between 1630 and 1660) arrived as indentured servants.[25] Indentured servants were the backbone of the early American colonies during the settlement era and indentured servitude was the definitive way of getting work done in many of the southern mainland colonies and West Indies for several generations.

Indentured servitude, however, was not without complications and, as an institution, was open to criticism that it was nothing more than a species of slavery. William Bullock, a colonial promoter and the author of *Virginia Impartially Examined* (1649), observed that "it hath beene a constant report amongst the ordinarie sort of people, That all those servants who are sent to *Virginia*, are sold as slaves." The truth, he continued, was "that the Merchants who send servants, and have no Plantations of their owne, doe onely transferre their Time over to others" and "servants serve no longer then the time they themselves agreed for in *England*." As this was "an ordinarie course," so it was in the colonies.[26] Indeed, indentured servitude was structurally grounded in traditional English forms of apprenticeship or the use of annual labor contracts in agricultural districts which limited the ability of laborers to move about freely while they were under the legal control of another person. In the colonies, however, servitude developed into something harsher after the 1620s in response to local conditions, including both the demand for labor and the need of masters to control their workers for an extended period of time.[27] Servitude certainly entailed a temporary loss of liberty in England, but it was also a contractual relationship that limited the power of the master over the servant. Even more, servitude was often viewed as an opportunity for youthful Englishmen rather than a measure of last resort because it was an essential training ground for future practitioners of various skilled trades. Indentured servitude in the colonies could therefore be compared with English practices in general, but the specifics of this new American institution looked suspiciously different.

When critics of indentured servitude compared it to slavery, they did so for a variety of reasons. First, it is worth recalling that there were domestic institutions—like villeinage—that were open to criticism because they possessed characteristics that detractors could legitimately assert were slave-like. The fact that villeinage was a largely arbitrary, unfree status passed down through the generations, was becoming problematic because of the emerging English sense of themselves as freeborn. Villeinage, in other words, was a social status foisted on people against their will. A similar argument was often made about indentured servitude. Most indentured servants entered into the condition willingly, but because England also routinely unloaded masses of rogues, vagabonds, convict laborers, and political prisoners on the colonies— all of whom could legitimately claim to have been transported against their will—it could be argued that servitude in the colonies was frequently involuntary. There was also the question of deceit. In the preface to the published version of a sermon he preached at Westminster Abbey in 1685, Morgan Godwyn decried what he characterized as the common practice of "trapanning and spiriting Men out of *England*, with sugar Promises of large kindness to be exhibited to them at their arrival in those Parts: whilst at the very instant they intend nothing else but to expose them to sale, and to make *Slaves* of them, at least for some term of Years."[28] Thus, even when indentured servants willingly contracted themselves, there was still a chance that they might find themselves in slave-like conditions.

As Godwyn's accusation indicates, whether indentured servitude was an involuntary condition was also debated during the seventeenth century in the light of the practice of kidnapping, or spiriting. English precedents provided legal cover for what was a highly exploitative system that seemingly operated as much to replicate the advantages of chattel slavery as it did to facilitate immigration or sustain the emerging and still quite precarious English settlements. Indentured servitude was particularly open to abuse at the point of acquisition. Ideally, servants were volunteers whose temporary status was delineated by the specific terms set out in a written contract. But many young men and women, and not a few children, were preyed upon by "divers lewd persons" and found themselves sold into servitude either against their will or under false pretenses.[29] In July 1660, the Privy Council was forced to confront the problem of children and others being "inticed away, taken upp, and kept . . . against their Wills, by Merchants, Planters, Commanders of Shipps, and Seamen." Endeavoring "to make Sale and Merchandise" of freeborn Englishmen was "[a] thinge so barbarous and inhumane, that Nature itself, much more Christians, cannot but abhorre." The image of children and servants being "so deceived and inticed away Cryinge and Mourninge for Redemption from their Slavery" was too much to bear.[30]

The concern over treating English men, women, and children as disposable commodities prompted Parliament to take a stand. On April 11, 1662, Parliament ordered that the committee that was tasked with the question of the "stealing of children and servants . . . do also take into their considerations what persons (who have been taken in arms, or otherwise seized, and taken into custody, for their service and loyalty to his Majesty, or his royal father) have been transported into and enslaved in any plantations, or parts beyond the seas." Those individuals who "have been instruments in their transporting and enslaving" were also sought out so that they could be questioned. Parliament had good reason to attack this problem, having received in recent years a number of complaints from individuals claiming to have been transported against their will and sold into slavery in the Americas. In 1660, for example, John Baker petitioned Parliament, claiming that "by the cruell contrivance of his sister" he was sent to Virginia when he was but eleven or twelve years of age. There, "hee served as a slave and endured greate hardshipp by thespace of nyne yeares."[31] Stories such as Baker's troubled the members of Parliament throughout the 1660s. The notion that the servant trade was rife with abuses ultimately forced Parliament to pass bills in 1670 and 1671 "to prevent stealing and transporting Children, and other Persons."[32]

Second, critics characterized indentured servitude as slave-like because servants could be bought and sold. Indentured servants were property, but the idea that human beings could be bought and sold as mere commodities was a disquieting notion in an Atlantic world where Englishmen prided themselves—as Richard Jobson noted in the context of Africa in the 1620s—on their unwillingness to make merchandise of men. That human beings could be bought and sold like chattel horrified many Englishmen, but two Virginia luminaries did not shy away from accusing Anglo-Americans from crossing that line. In 1618, John Rolfe observed that "there have beene many complaints against the Governors, Captaines, and Officers in Virginia, for buying and selling men and bois." Such a practice, he noted, "was held in England a thing most intolerable."[33] John Smith, writing six years later about the deficiencies of the government in Virginia, accused "the old Planters" of such "pride, covetousnesse, extortion and oppression" that they would sell "even men, women and children for who will give most." "God forbid," he continued, "that the masters there should not have the same privilege over their servants as here, but to sell him or her for forty, fifty, or threescore pounds, whom the Company hath sent over for eight or ten pounds at the most" was "odious."[34] Rolfe and Smith thus represented a popular opinion that servitude in the Americas was problematic not because it entailed service or labor, but because it was conducted as a for-profit enterprise by scurrilous individuals.

Third, the argument that indentured servitude was slave-like was made most easily by virtue of the common perception that servants were treated exceptionally harshly, something that brought to mind the human sufferings endured by fellow Englishmen in other parts of the world, not least in the Mediterranean, where physical abuse was one of the hallmarks of slavery. Richard Ligon, who arrived in Barbados in 1647, claimed that, compared to African slaves, "servants have the worser lives, for they are put to very hard labour, ill lodging, and their dyet very sleight." The possibility always existed, of course, for servants to be treated well because there were kind masters. "But if the Masters be cruel," Ligon noted, "the Servants have very wearisome and miserable lives." Recalling one episode in particular, he claimed to "have seen an Overseer beat a servant with a cane about the head, till the blood has followed, for a fault that is not worth the speaking of." Less than the actual physical violence, Ligon was dismayed because he "did not think one Christian could have done [such a thing] to another." Predictably, because of "the intolerable burdens they labour'd under," Ligon reported that there were "some amongst them, whose spirits were not able to endure such slavery," which led them "to break through it, or dye in the act."[35] Barbadian planters heard of the planned rebellion before it could be set in motion, but the willingness of servants to risk their lives to free themselves from their bondage is a fair indication of the measures numerous individuals were willing to take.[36]

Because it was open to criticism as just another form of slavery, servitude occasionally created as many problems as it solved for the English in places like early Barbados.[37] The West Indies were hotly contested terrain in the mid-seventeenth century, something that contributed to its inhabitants' sense that life was precarious even under the best of circumstances in the region. Liberty, too, was imperiled as a result of frequent conflicts among the Spanish, French, and English. During the 1640s and 1650s, then, many Englishmen were quick to conclude that slavery was particularly problematic at the crossroads of the Old World and the New, at the intersection of Protestantism and Catholicism, where competing European powers struggled to assert their mastery over new lands and old enemies.[38] Considering the historical patterns that had been established over the course of the preceding century, nothing was especially surprising in these developments. But sometimes voices were raised in protest, claiming that much of the violence being done to Englishmen was being perpetrated by their own countrymen. Being English was supposed to offer certain guarantees, but some Anglo-Americans clearly believed that their national identity provided little security and, in particular, apparently offered them no protection from slavery.

In one instance from the 1650s, Parliament received two petitions from Barbados authored by men who had been sent to the island as laborers as punishment after the Salisbury rising of 1654. Marcellus Rivers, Oxenbridge Foyle, and Rowland Thomas complained that they and seventy other Englishmen had been sold as "goods and chattels" in Barbados and continued to be "bought and sold still from one planter to another, or attached as horses and beasts for the debts of their masters."[39] The petitions, which claimed that "freeborn people of this nation" were "now in slavery," prompted Parliament to conduct an abortive debate about slavery. Because the petitions had been introduced through irregular channels, however, many members of Parliament ignored the content of the complaints and simply expressed their conviction that the documents were a Cavalier ploy "to set you [the members of Parliament] at division." Other members were directly implicated either by name or as property holders in Barbados and other American colonies. Martin Noel of Staffordshire noted that he traded in those parts and to the best of his knowledge the work was indeed hard, "but none are sent without their consent" and those who went "were civilly used, and had horses to ride on." Besides, Noel added, they were commonly contracted for five years and did not work as hard as the petition claimed because "the work is mostly carried on by the Negroes." Captain Hatsell, who petitioners also singled out, confirmed that he had indeed been present at Plymouth when the men were dispatched, but according to his recollection he "never saw any go with more cheerfulness." Secretary of State John Thurloe took such offense at being accused of selling an Englishman "as a slave to Barbados" that he reintroduced the subject five days after the original debate subsided in order to produce further evidence to clear his name. For Thurloe, his reputation was at stake and he resented whisperings that he "could enslave, and had enslaved, the people of England, at his pleasure."[40]

The protestations of Noel, Hatsell, and Thurloe reveal that these men wanted to distance themselves as much as possible from any taint of English slavery, but they did not address some of the central complaints of the petitioners or allay the concerns of other members of Parliament. Indeed, the petitioners failed to comment extensively on either the nature or oppressions of their work in Barbados. They made some passing references to "grinding at the Mills attending the Fornaces, or digging in this scorching Island," but they said little else in that regard. As these Englishmen understood, forced labor was not the mark of slavery in early modern England and certainly was not generally regarded as unjust. Thus, the focus of the petitions was on other matters: They were the victims of a pernicious "man-stealing trade," having been apprehended without cause "as they travelled upon their lawful occasions," and never "so much as tryed or examined." After having been held as prisoners for a year, they were transported across the ocean on ships that provided "every vitious servant which *Bridewell* and *Newgate* had vomited" while they "were forced to ly on the bare boards." Once they arrived in the "heathenish *Indies*," they were "sold in the publick market, as beasts," becoming "to all intents and purposes, like those our fellow-creatures that have no understanding, being bought and sold still, from master to master, or attacht as their goods." Thus, having "never made any contract with them," they had no indication "whether ever or never the tearm of our slavery shall end." With a subtle understanding of what made slavery meaningful to early modern Englishmen, the petitioners added that not even "the cruell Turks" would "sell and enslave these of their own Countrey and Religion, much lesse the Innocent." To be brutalized by "their (more then *Egyptian*) Taskmasters," by "these unchristian Janisaries," was beyond comprehension to the petitioners. There was, therefore, no "more charitable Office, then to endeavour the Redemption of the Innocent Slaves at *Barbados*, and the prevention of the further slavery of *England*." The case of the Englishmen transported to Barbados against their will centered on this point: "Our case, is but your Touchstone, by which you may discover whether *English*, be Slaves or Freemen." Their plight was England's plight: "If this be allowed, an easie understanding will quickly find, what must necessarily become, of all the (formerly free) People of England."[41]

Strikingly, the petitioners made no mention of African slaves. Their references were wholly English and the petition reads as if it could have been written as easily in the 1580s as in the 1650s. Too, the responses of the members of Parliament to both the petition and the defensive rebuttals of Noel, Hatsell, and Thurloe suggest that the case was not necessarily understood in terms related to the emerging transatlantic plantation complex. Sir Henry Vane, for one, did not believe this "Cavalierish business" but considered the matter well worth discussing because it "concerns the liberty of the free-born people of England." The idea that English subjects could be used in a "barbarous manner" and be "sold there for 100*l*" was reprehensible to Vane. Major Beake concluded that "slavery is slavery" and petitions that carried such grave accusations should be considered regardless of how they were introduced. Hugh Boscawen of Cornwall raised a biblical concern when he noted that he was as much against any purported Cavalier plot as anyone else, "but you have Paul's case before you. A Roman ought not to be beaten. We are miserable slaves, if we may not have this liberty secured to us." Historically, of course, English nationalists had always claimed as much. In the light of rhetoric of the English Civil War and Commonwealth-era politics, English civil liberties were guarded even more jealously. But in the context of an Atlantic world characterized by starkly divergent conditions of freedom and bondage, many people were inclined to believe that an Englishman's rights were not "beyond the line" and needed to be defended with vigor. By the middle of the seventeenth century, the members of Parliament already understood what Rivers, Foyle, Thomas, and others chose not to invoke: If Englishmen lost the right to a trial or to petition Parliament, "our lives will be as cheap as those negroes. They look upon them as their goods, horses, &c., and rack them only to make their time out of them, and cherish them to perform their work." For that reason, perhaps above all others, Boscawen "would have [Parliament] consider the trade of buying and selling men."[42]

Boscawen's language here is revealing, for although the petitioners were not thinking about African peoples in the Atlantic world, the responses of the members of Parliament were somewhat different. Noel's defense and Boscawen's critique reveal a concerted effort to preserve the sanctity of Englishness by ensuring that there were some important differences between the rights of Englishmen, regardless of where they might live, and the plight of "those negroes" who could be found in increasing numbers in the Anglo-American colonies. This concern is evidenced from a second case that occurred during the 1650s in Bermuda when four men—Henry Gaunt, John Cowper (or Cooper), John Saunders, and John Braum—were each sentenced "to be a slave of the colony" for periods ranging from one to three years. On the surface, these punishments were unremarkable; dozens of English men and women had been sentenced to penal slavery in colonial America during the preceding decades. Yet, these men's crimes were different and further complicated by an emerging sense of racial exclusivity that was becoming common throughout Anglo-America. Henry Gaunt was convicted of "incontinence with the daughter of Capt. Forster & an Indian of Mr. Wilkinson." The other men were similarly convicted of incontinence (or fornication) but this time with black women. The women, presumably slaves, were whipped for their indiscretions. The men were sentenced to slavery (although for relatively short terms). Whether it was because they violated the property rights of the owners of the enslaved women or because they offended the broader community's sense that Englishmen and Africans should not engage in intimate relations (or both), they were dealt with in the harshest terms available to English judges: They were to be slaves.[43]

Put another way, the four Englishmen were not simply incarcerated, they were transformed into slaves in a world in which "slavishness" was increasingly associated with decidedly non-English physical characteristics. On the one hand, there was still some acceptance for the idea that slavery might be a useful remedy for English offenders. On the other hand, what the practical application might mean was becoming more complicated. Governor Sir John Heydon, who arrived on the island in 1669, met this problem head on when he ordered, in 1672, that "whatsoever marries one of ye Company Negroes shall become a Colonie Slave and their posterltye likewise." By this late date, however, Anglo-Americans could no longer easily tolerate the prospect of Englishmen being condemned to slavery, much less a condition that was perpetual and inheritable. When Thomas Wood fathered a child with the Company's mulatto slave, Ann Simons, he expressed his intention to marry the woman "to prevent their living in sin." Against the spirit of his own directive, Governor Heydon accepted £20 from Wood and freed Simons rather enforce his own decree.[44]

Slavery was an emerging problem during the second half of the seventeenth century but not just as a labor system in need of defining. If it was true, as the well-traveled Anglican minister Morgan Godwyn would later note in 1680, that "[t]hese two words, *Negro* and *Slave*" had "by Custom grown Homogenous and Convertible; even as *Negro* and *Christian, Englishman* and *Heathen*, are by the like corrupt Custom and Partiality made *Opposites*," then it was nearly unthinkable by the second half of the seventeenth century for colonial officials to try to use the logic of a system of slavery imperfectly transplanted from an older time and another place where considerations of labor and identity had little to do with human bondage.[45] Reflecting on the case of the Barbadian petitioners, Sir John Lenthall expressed his fervent hope that it was not "the effect of our war to make merchandize of men," especially as these were Englishmen. Englishmen were "the freest people in the world" and even the possibility that they could be "put to such hardships, to heats and colds, and converse with horse" was an unconscionable affront to their rights as Englishmen. Even more, Lenthall added, "[W]e know not what may become of us if we" turn a blind eye.[46] If one Englishman could make his fellow countryman a slave, no matter his crime, then what did it mean to be English?

Ultimately, the problem with indentured servitude in the Americas was that, although there were English touchstones that could help rationalize the practice in the Americas, there were no hard-and-fast English precedents. Indentured servitude or, more crudely put, bound white labor *for labor's sake* was an innovation of the early seventeenth century. Certainly Englishmen understood service, labor, apprenticeship, punishment, and unfreedom, but indentured servitude (with its emphasis on long-distance transportation, multiyear contracts, unskilled labor, and potentially forced transportation) was unfamiliar. Not surprisingly, then, when early modern Englishmen and Anglo-Americans looked around for contemporary parallels, many people's minds alighted on slavery (something that was frighteningly familiar). Although there did not exist a single, monolithic understanding of slavery in early modern England, the Englishmen who found themselves in the Anglo-Atlantic world certainly had firmer ideas about slavery than they did indentured servitude. They knew why it existed and where it predominated. They knew why people became slaves, justly or unjustly. And they could list a whole catalog of miseries in their effort to describe what made it so terrible. Unfortunately, at least for early colonial promoters, there was a great deal about indentured servitude that resembled these early English conceptions of slavery.

*   *   *

Although English colonists could argue that slavery was antithetical to Englishness in the Americas, there was much less certainty about whether Indians were legitimate candidates. Certainly, the authors of early promotional literature did not shy away from the idea that Indians were either naturally slavish or lived in societies that were bound together by relationships premised on human bondage. Richard Hakluyt translated and published a Portuguese narrative in 1609 in an effort to stir up interest in Virginia by comparing it to Florida, "her next neighbour," as the title page emphasized.[47] Throughout, readers encountered numerous passing references to slaves and slavery that highlighted many of the same themes that appeared in contemporary written accounts of other parts of the world. But while this and other works coming out of the Iberian world clearly implied that slavery was common in the North American southeast, most English authors wrote about the subject of Indian slavery in metaphorical terms. Alexander Whitaker made almost casual reference to the indigenous inhabitants of Virginia as "these naked slaves of the divell" in his effort to generate a sense of compassion for Indians in early Stuart England. "[W]e all have *Adam* for our common parent," he observed in the same spirit of monogenesis that shaped writings about all the peoples of the world in the early seventeenth century, which meant that all human beings were effectively the same: "the servants of sinne, and slaves of the divell."[48]

The physical enslavement of Indians by Englishmen was another matter. By the time the English got around to the business of establishing permanent settlements in the Americas, Indians had long been a part of the emerging Atlantic slave system that was premised on the need for laborers. Not surprisingly, some English colonists willingly followed in the footsteps of their predecessors by taking and holding indigenous peoples against their will for a variety of reasons, including, on occasion, because they needed laborers. But finding Indian slaves scattered throughout the early colonies in small numbers does not reveal much about the nature or intent of Indian slavery in the early seventeenth century. In fact, Indian slavery differed a great deal from the enslavement of African peoples because English colonial promoters and many Anglo-American colonists did not think about the natives primarily as laborers. Anglo-American officials were much more likely to subject Indians to slavery because of their effort to create ordered societies in the new world. In this regard, the problem of Indian slavery was closely related to the problems created by the perception that Englishmen might be reduced to a state of slavery in the New World. Englishmen and Indians alike, in other words, might both become slaves but only when they did something to deserve it and usually because colonial leaders believed that slavery might actually redeem the individual and stabilize colonial society. From a theoretical point of view, Indian and English slavery were close cousins.

The justice of English colonialism was partly an abstract noble ideal, but it was also meaningful to commentators who wished to set their nation's Atlantic enterprises apart from those of other Europeans, especially the Spanish. On some matters, of course, Anglo-Americans made little effort to depart from Spanish or Portuguese precedents; English colonists emulated their forebears in the Americas by absorbing Africans into their midst as slaves. When it came to Indians, however, Englishmen asked themselves challenging questions that effectively forestalled the exploitation of indigenous peoples as laborers for several generations. If, eventually, Anglo-Americans would hunt down or trade for Indian slaves, hold them in bondage without concern, and otherwise roll them into the general population of enslaved peoples in order to satisfy the appetites of labor-hungry planters, the story was somewhat different initially.[49] How the English behaved with regard to the natives was a measure of the character of the English people as a whole and an important indicator of just how different the English were from the Spanish. If the English cared about their reputation, much less hoped to attract investors and additional colonists, then Indian slavery was a complicated proposition.

Few people in England during the late sixteenth century were troubled by the idea of captive or enslaved Indians. Much like African peoples, American Indians from both North and South America appeared in England in small numbers as a by-product of English exploration and privateering expeditions, particularly during the last three decades of the sixteenth century.[50] Martin Frobisher brought four Inuit Indian captives to England in the 1570s where they became the objects of much curiosity despite their relatively quick deaths. English merchants, privateers, and pirates brought even more Indians home from other parts of the Americas during the 1580s and 1590s, continuing the early tradition of bringing back people as physical specimens, objects of curiosity for a curious English public, and perhaps even agents for future trading or colonizing endeavors. Indians fascinated for a number of reasons. Their apparent physical differences occasioned considerable debate about whether they were truly a distinctive human population or simply a product of their environment and upbringing. Others, like Sir Walter Raleigh and investors in the Virginia Company of London, were more interested in using indigenous peoples as guides, translators, diplomats, or, more generally, agents of cultural convergence between the English and the American Indians. But a few entrepreneurial souls saw in Indians an opportunity to turn a profit. In the most famous early example, Captain Thomas Hunt kidnapped twenty-four Indians in 1614, including a young man known as Squanto, and sold them into slavery in Spain. His commercial endeavor seems to have been frowned upon by his contemporaries, but it was nonetheless common practice among European interlopers looking for advantages in the early modern Atlantic world.[51]

Once the English began thinking about establishing a colonial presence in the Americas, however, a broader English constituency was more likely to frown upon indiscriminant kidnapping and slave trading. English colonial promoters simply could not justify New World settlements without considering America's native peoples. In regions that appeared lightly populated, colonization was typically justified, if at all, on the basis of the Roman Law argument of *res nullius*, which established that unoccupied or empty lands fell to those who first occupied them and put them to some productive use. In regions that were clearly populated by Indians, including most of North America, English officials often used a modified *res nullius* argument, which emphasized that, while Indians may live there, they "inclose noe land neither have any setled habitation nor any tame cattle to improve the land by, & soe have noe other but a naturall right to those countries." The idea that the indigenous peoples had, at best, simply failed to develop the land they inhabited at the time they were encountered by the English or, at worst, were lazy and profligate, appeared in promotional literature regularly. If anyone was squeamish about the validity of these assertions, it was also possible to justify colonization by emphasizing that "we shall come in with the good leave of the Natives" or, conversely, by suggesting that the inhabitants of coastal North America were not natives at all, but migrants and therefore could lay no claim to the land based in natural law. Rarely did the English justify their actions in the New World on the basis of conquest, just or otherwise.[52]

With regard to the possible enslavement of Indians, the rhetoric of colonial promotion demanded that indigenous peoples could not be treated either indiscriminately or arbitrarily by English settlers. Indeed, sixteenth- and seventeenth-century colonial promoters liked to imagine that English settlers would be welcomed by the indigenous inhabitants of the Americas with open arms, even as liberators "from their [Spanish] devourers." English authors routinely claimed that overseas settlement would stem the tide of Spanish global expansion and efforts to establish a "universal monarchy" by taking up the cause of "their Brethren, the sons of Adam, from such hellish servitude and oppression."[53] This framework had served English colonial promoters like Richard Hakluyt well at the end of the sixteenth century and would continue to be useful for generations to come. As late as the mid-seventeenth century, Edmund Hickeringill, a clergyman who had spent time in Jamaica, described the Spanish in the harshest terms possible when he noted that "our mother Earth doth indifferently *prostrate* her womb to the common embraces of any *Ravisher*, that hath Arms strong enough to secure him, in the Rape; the only *Patent* that the *Spaniard* can show for his *Indie*-Mines." The Spanish, in other words, "can shew no *Bill of Sale* but his *Sword*." Therefore,

Cromwell's "Western Design" was imagined in 1655 as a worthy and noble enterprise if only because it would exact "just Revenge of so much . . . Indian blood, so unjustly, so unhumanely, and so cruelly spilt by the Spaniards in those parts." With a somewhat self-serving sense of providential design, English authors liked to believe that "God will have an accompt of the Innocent Blood of so many Millions of Indians, so barbarously Butchered by the Spaniards, and of the wrong and Injustice that hath been done unto them."[54]

The assertion that the Spanish were the real savages in the Americas was low-hanging fruit for English propagandists. To be sure, there was no shortage of commentators in the mold of Richard Eden during the 1550s willing to defend the Spanish. In response to those who might claim that the Spanish "possesse and inhabyte theyr [Indians'] regions and use theym as bondemen and tributaries, where before they were free," Eden declared that the Spanish were actually the "mynisters of grace and libertie" whom "god hath ordeyned to be a lyght to the gentyles, to open the eyes of the blynde, and to delyver the bounde owt of pryson and captivitie." Eden claimed that the "Spanyardes have shewed a good example to all Chrystian nations to folowe." Thus, while Richard Hakluyt would later goad the English government into sponsoring overseas settlement to counteract Spain's actions, Eden proposed a plan of conscious imitation. "[T]here yet remayneth an other portion of that mayne lande reachyng toward the northeast," Eden suggestively noted, with "manye fayre and frutefull regions," that lay open for English colonization.[55] As late as 1616, Captain John Smith could declare that "[i]t would bee an historie of a large volume, to recite the adventures of the *Spanyards*, and *Portugals*, their affronts, and defeats, their dangers and miseries; which with such incomparable honour and constant resolution, so farre beyond beleefe, they have attempted and indured in their discoveries and plantations, as may well condemne us, of too much imbecillitie, sloth and negligence."[56] To some, it would be wise to follow the Spanish lead.

But anti-Spanish sentiment that espoused sympathy for Indians was even more common during the early years of colonial settlement. In some extreme cases, English writers not only criticized how the Spanish conducted themselves, they also cast aspersions on the Spanish character and engaged in what can only be described as a form of proto-racial stereotyping. In the light of the decade-old Anglo-Spanish War, it was easy for Sir Walter Raleigh to comment in 1595 in his *Discoverie of Guiana* that the indigenous inhabitants of South America were initially reticent to treat with the English because they confused Raleigh's men with the Spanish. Raleigh accused the Spanish

of the most pernicious carnal crimes when he claimed that the Spanish kidnapped Indian women "and used them for the satisfying of their own lusts."
Unlike Englishmen who, Raleigh claimed, "by violence or otherwise, [never]
knew any of their women," the Spanish behaved in a lascivious manner that
revealed their essential nature.[57] Subsequent references to the "numerous mul-
titudes of a mixt generation, which [the Spanish] beget in Negroes and Indian
Women" were more benign, but they furthered the impression that the Spanish were "a confuse [sic] and beastly conceipt . . . mixed with the Goths and
Vandals [and] mingled with the Mores." By accusing the Spanish of doing
violence toward the natives and by mixing freely with non-European peoples,
English writers perpetuated the idea that the Spanish lacked propriety, integrity, and purity.[58] Just as the English claimed that the Portuguese posed the
greatest threat to their liberties on the coast of Africa, they set the Spanish up
as the most dangerous element in the Americas.

Others engaged in less comprehensive denunciations. The colonial promoter Richard Eburne offered some praise of Spanish efforts in 1624 when he
noted that "the *Spaniard* hath reasonably civilized" Indians, but he also observed that they might have been even more successful had they "not so
much tyrannized" native peoples. From an English perspective, barbarity
was more easily associated with the Spanish in America than with the New
World's indigenous inhabitants. This theme was picked up by other English
authors. Samuel Purchas, in the process of recounting the misadventures of
Hawkins's third slave-trading voyage, claimed that the abandonment of more
than a hundred Englishmen in America meant that they had been left "to the
mercy of cruell elements, crueller Savages, [and] cruellest Spaniards." William
Castell petitioned Parliament in 1641 on behalf of more than seventy English
divines to encourage a more comprehensive effort to propagate the gospel
among the Indians. To that end, the Northhamptonshire parson chided the
Spanish for their record of "unchristian behaviour, especially their monstrous
cruelties," which "caused the Infidels to detest the name of Christ."[59]

The assumption that English colonialism would amount to a kind of
stewardship and lead to the creation of an inclusive community—not a conquest that would lead to Indian destruction or removal—was a predictable
outgrowth of anti-Spanish rhetoric. It was also evidence of the powerful
influence of natural philosophy and the search for a noble history. Englishmen wrote about the American environment not simply because they
wanted to describe it as a pleasant place to live, but because they wanted to
allay fears about what might happen to English bodies. As everyone knew,

the "Temperature of the Climate, the goodnesse of the Aire, and the fatnesse of the Soile," were prime considerations in "every Countrey to bee inhabited." In the case of America, Robert Johnson emphasized that "the ayre and clymate [are] most sweete and wholesome, . . . and very agreeable to our Natures." In 1612, in yet another publication designed to encourage settlement, Johnson reminded readers that "the soile and climate is so apt and fit for industrious mindes" to plant "pretious" goods and conduct trade in such a fashion that "no Countrie under heaven can goe beyond it."[60] Four years later but with an eye toward more northern climes, Captain John Smith lauded the "moderate temper of the ayre," of New England, which proved that it was "a most excellent place, both for health and fertility." Thomas Morton, who like Smith had spent considerable time in the New World, was even more direct in the opening lines of his *New English Canaan*, when he declared without reservation that "[t]he wise Creator of the universall Globe, hath placed a golden meane betwixt two extremes: I meane the temperate Zones, betwixt hote and cold; and every Creature, that participates of Heavens blessings, with in the Compasse of that golden meane, is made most apt and fit, for man to use, who likewise by that wisedome is ordained to be the Lord of all."[61]

Celebration of the American climate was the operative premise from which English colonial promoters similarly praised Indians' physical constitution. Just as there was a necessary correlation between English bodies and the environment of the British Isles, English writers routinely noted the "perfect constitution" of the indigenous inhabitants of North America. Indians were, to Bartholomew Gosnold in 1602, "strong and well proportioned." James Rosier, who sailed with Gosnold on his New England voyage, wrote to Sir Walter Raleigh that the natives were "of a perfect constitution of body, active strong, healthfull, and very witty." This combination of strength and wit—classically contradictory qualities that English nationalists had only recently managed to reconceptualize to describe themselves—must have been encouraging. It was even more promising that this laudatory impression of natives continued to hold favor in Virginia in the initial settlement years. William Strachey, writing from the colony sometime after 1612, described Indians as "nothing so unsightly as the Moores; they are generally tall of stature, and streight, of comely proportion, and the women have handsome lymbes, slender armes, and pretty hands." Although most Englishmen possessed genuine concerns about religious practices, living arrangements, the sexual division of labor, dress (or lack thereof), and other cultural attributes,

they repeatedly characterized Indians as exceedingly fine physical specimens.[62]

Mythic history also informed the way Englishmen wrote and thought
about Indians. History also proved to be a useful guide to those people who
were interested in drawing parallels between the English past and Indian
present in order to emphasize the fundamental similarities between natives
and newcomers. The 1590 edition of Thomas Harriot's *Briefe and True Report
of the New Found Land of Virginia*, with engravings by Theodor de Bry, famously included images of several Picts as a way of suggesting how the ancient "Inhabitants of the great Bretannie have bin in times past as savage as
those of Virginia." Richard Eburne added that the conversion of American
Indians would not only be similar to the introduction of Christianity in Britain, it should be easier than "the Conversion of our Ancestors and predecessors in this land, a people as rude and untractable, at the least that way, as
these now." Eburne imagined that some awareness of the history of ancient
Britons—"for wee are also their Off-spring"—would prompt the English "not
to despise even such poore and barbarous people, but pitty them, and hope,
that as wee are become now, by Gods unspeakable mercy to us-ward, to a
farre better condition, so in time may they." Civil societies, in other words,
required cultivation or, sometimes, violent assistance from outside forces. As
Eburne observed, "Were not wee our selves made and not borne civill in our
Progenitors dayes?" Indeed, King James I rationalized English overseas settlement partly on the grounds that Indians were "slavish" and "beastly" and
in need of good government and godly religion.[63]

English writers were so intent on establishing the basic similarity between themselves and Indians that they took care to note that indigenous
peoples were, like Britons, naturally white. Robert Fabian, who had sailed
with John Cabot during the 1490s, was among the first Englishmen to comment on the physical appearance of Indians. Fabian reported that Cabot had
returned to England from his Newfoundland voyage with three natives who
were "clothed in beasts skins, & did eate raw flesh, and spake such speach
that no man could understand them, and in their demeanour like to bruite
beastes." After living among the English for two years, however, Fabian "saw
two apparelled after the maner of Englishmen in Westmenster pallace, which
that time I could not discerne from Englishmen." Considering the tendency
of sixteenth-century English observers to describe Indians as tawny, olive,
swarthy, or brown in color, this observation might seem odd were it not for

the fact that the skin tone of the indigenous inhabitants of the Americas was not necessarily imagined to be fixed. Indians, therefore, could be characterized as "inclined to a swart, tawnie, or Chestnut colour," but the more important point was that such appearances were "not by nature but accidently." Both John Smith and Thomas Morton claimed that Indian children emerged from their mother's wombs "of complexion white as our nation, but their mothers in their infancy make a bath of Wallnut leaves, huskes of Walnuts, and such things as will staine their skinne for ever, wherein they dip and washe them to make them tawny." William Strachey concurred, attributing color to the effect of the sun as well as a combination of "arsenick stone," "red tempered oyntments," and the "juyce of certaine scrused rootes," which they applied to ward off mosquitoes and other biting insects and because they believed "the best beauty [was] to be neerest such a kynd of murrey as a sodden quince."[64]

Natural philosophy, history, and promotional necessity therefore combined to encourage a discourse of similitude in which early modern Englishmen and the indigenous peoples of the Americas were related to each other in essential ways while the Spanish were set apart as different.[65] Of course, the English and Spanish were quite alike in many ways, but the Spanish had treated the "Indians as Barbar's, and thereby Naturally slaves," according to one writer in 1606. Anglo-Indian relations would be different. Thus, both Sir Thomas Gates in 1609 and Sir Thomas West, Lord De la Warr, in 1610, were instructed by the Virginia Company of London to "indeavor the conv[er]sion of the natives and savages to the knowledge and worship of the true god," which could best be achieved by taking "some of theire Children to be brought up in o[ur] language and mann[er]s." John Rolfe's assertion in 1617 (soon after the death of his wife Rebecca, otherwise known as Pocahontas) that the Indians were "very loving, and willing to parte w[ith] their children" may not have been a wholly accurate characterization of the situation, but it does suggest that the English preferred to believe that their presence in America was inoffensive to the indigenous inhabitants.[66]

*   *   *

It was the subject of slavery, however, that provided some of the most compelling possibilities for linking the historical experience of Englishmen and Indians in their combined opposition to the Spanish in the Atlantic world.[67] English condemnations of the Spanish character were augmented by the accusation that Indians and Englishmen were bound together by their shared vulnerability to Spanish rapacity and possible enslavement. Even if Indians were treated harshly by English settlers during the early modern era, the historical and ideological context of early colonial settlement often sheltered natives from outright enslavement. At the very least, Anglo-Spanish relations made the prospect of Indian slavery even more complicated than the possibility that other groups, like Africans, might be held in bondage. For if Indians were truly like the English, it was an affront to conceptualize them as natural slaves or to ignore the unjust circumstances that led to their enslavement. Yet, just as there was room to maneuver when it came to the possible enslavement of Englishmen, primarily when putative slaves behaved in a manner that legitimized their subsequent enslavement, so too could Indians be enslaved without contradiction when they brought the condition upon themselves or when slavery might even be imagined to be productive of some larger good. The subject of Indian slavery demanded careful consideration.

If colonial promoters and early leaders are to be believed, Anglo-American colonists had little interest in exploiting Indians for their labor. The English and natives were not always on friendly terms, of course, but even in the aftermath of violent episodes English governors routinely tried to protect Indians. Virginia, for example, suffered two violent periods of warfare during the 1620s and 1640s, but colonial leaders still passed laws in the aftermath of these conflicts to ensure that the remaining Indians were not treated as cheap commodities.[68] In 1656, the colony's governing elite declared that if any "Indians shall bring in any children" then "wee will not use them as slaves, but . . . bring them up in Christianity, civillity and the knowledge of necessary trades." Five years later, colonial legislators declared that if any traders brought in "Indians as servants," they could not "sell them for slaves nor for any longer time than the English of the like ages should serve." Only after the onset of Bacon's Rebellion in 1676 would lawmakers avow "that all Indians taken in warr [would] be held and accounted slaves dureing life." Even when officials attempted to dissuade colonists, Anglo-Virginians openly asserted their right in the years after Bacon's Rebellion to "reteyne and keepe all such Indian slaves or other Indian goods as they either have taken or hereafter shall take their owne proper use for their better encouragement to such service."[69] Early modern Englishmen accepted that captured Indians could be held, or sold, as slaves in a time of war but during the first half of the century, especially during times of peace, colonial leaders preferred to emphasize that Indians should be treated no differently than the English.

What helped Indians the most was the loosely framed notion, often articulated by colonial promoters, that the Indian peoples were, or should be, part of an inclusive (though fundamentally *English*) community. Moreover, they claimed that the establishment of English colonies in the Americas would benefit Indians to the degree that it would insulate them from the Spanish and connect them in a more concrete fashion with their English brethren. In 1610, the Virginia Company expressed its unwillingness to take and use Indians as slaves as part of an explicit critique of Spanish colonialism. "To preach the gospel to a nation conquered; and to set their souls at liberty when we have brought their bodies to slavery" seemed to these English officials somewhat disingenuous. "[I]t may be a matter sacred to the preachers," they continued, "but I know not how justifiable in the rulers, who for mere ambition do set upon it the gloss of religion. Let the divines of Salamanca discuss that question how the possessors of the West Indies first destroyed then instructed."[70] As late as 1672, while justifying the English conquest of Jamaica, the English editor and publisher Richard Blome noted that "*Indians*, who are the natural proprietors of *America*, do abominate and hate the *Spaniards* for their cruelty and avarice; and upon every occasion will shew their willingness to give themselves and their Countreys, freely into the power and protection of the *English*." Of course, very few Indians remained alive in Jamaica at this late date. Nonetheless, "[w]e, as avengers of those peoples bloud and wrongs," another author maintained, "should have had a better Title to their Countries then their oppressors, and murtherers."[71] Ironically, this unique perspective encouraged the idea that Indians *could* be enslaved but, unlike Africans, only for reasons that might be applied to the English themselves or to the inhabitants of other recognized nations. Because colonial promoters initially emphasized the fundamental similarity between English and Indian peoples in order to promote and encourage overseas settlement and defray concerns about what might happen to English bodies in the New World, Anglo-Americans allowed the idea to develop that natives might be justifiably enslaved. Moreover, it was even imagined in some circles that there might be a purpose for Indian slavery that could be punitive, but it might also be redemptive, and it might have nothing to do with labor (or, at least, production). Whatever the case, the key point was that Indian slavery required justification.

Predictably, the idealistic musings of colonial promoters did not always find fertile soil in the New World, where the exigencies of survival trumped all other concerns. Thus, widespread animosity toward natives was routinely displayed in the wake of violent conflicts between English colonists and Indians. In Virginia, the events of early 1622 are instructive and reveal the tension between the high ideals of Anglo-American colonialism and the pressure of escalating anti-Indian sentiment.[72] Fed up with the steadily growing demands English colonialism placed on their resources, Opechancanough and members of the Powhatan Confederacy launched a devastating coordinated attack on the morning of March 22 (Good Friday). In that attack, 347 English colonists were killed, as were some of the efforts of colonial promoters to cultivate an optimistic image of the indigenous peoples in the region. A bitter Edward Waterhouse asserted that the actions of "that perfidious and inhumane people" revealed at last their true nature and that the English would take the battle to those "naked, tanned, deformed Savages" and exact revenge by "force, by surprize, by famine in burning their Corne, by destroying their Boats, Canoes, and Houses." As the Spanish had done before them, the English imagined they could finally set their colony on the right path "by pursuing and chasing them with our horses, and blood-Hounds to draw after them, and Mastives to seaze them." This proposal agreed with the sentiments of the Virginia Council, which ordered the colonists "to roote out from being any longer a people, so cursed a nation, ungratefull to all benefitts, and uncapable of all goodnesse." As a reward for service, colonists could expect to acquire "men for slaves" from among the defeated natives.[73]

The dramatic outbreak of violence in 1622 prompted frustrated Englishmen in Virginia to rethink their idealistic musings about shielding Indians from bondage.[74] Accepting, as they did, that prisoners of war could legitimately be held as slaves, some Englishmen could comfortably conclude that Powhatan Indians had effectively made themselves candidates for bondage by their own actions. Indians, according to Waterhouse, "may now most justly be compelled to servitude and drudgery" in Virginia, including the "inferiour workes of digging in the mynes" or being "sent for the service of the *Sommer Islands*." John Martin wrote that the Indians were "fitt to rowe in Gallies & friggetts and many other pregnant uses too tedious to sett downe." In the midst of recounting his misery as an indentured servant in post-1622 Virginia, Richard Frethorne paused to note that "wee live in feare" of the natives, "yet wee have had a Combate with them . . . and wee took two alive and make slaves of them."[75] Because Indians had risen up—unjustly in the minds of the English—they created the circumstances that encouraged Anglo-Americans to reduce the natives to a state of bondage. Indians had brought it upon themselves and the English could only respond as other Europeans would have responded in similar circumstances.

More acid-tongued Englishmen, however, were quick to note that the events of March 1622 were important because they revealed that Indians were not at all like the English and could never be truly incorporated into the Christian, much less the English, social order. Exceptionally angry yet prescient English authors recast Indians as an irreconcilably different human population. More conciliatory voices, like that of the Virginia Company of London in August 1622, hoped that colonists would remember "who we are, rather then what they have been," and advised that "the younger people of both Sexes, whose bodies may, by labor and service become profitable, and their mindes not overgrowne w[ith] evill Customes, be reduced to civilitie, and afterwardes to Christianitie." That, after all, was the purpose of slavery. But others were eager to suggest that Indians should be treated with impunity: "[T]hat bloudy Massacre . . . requires that servile natures be servily used," Samuel Purchas claimed in 1625, and "that future dangers be prevented by the extirpation of the most dangerous, and commodities also raised out of the servileness and serviceablenesse of the rest." Clearly, John Morton asserted, recent events had demonstrated that "natives are apter for worke then yet o[ur] English are."[76] Basing slavery on some general sense of innate differences or attempting to justify it by suggesting that it might prevent future difficulties were novel ideas in English America in the 1620s. Strikingly, English authors did not deploy this new logic of slavery in reference to the African peoples they had routinely encountered as slaves in the early modern Atlantic world. But they began to rethink the logic of Indian slavery because the indigenous inhabitants of the Americas refused to behave like the fanciful Indians English colonial promoters invented in order to encourage migration, attract investors, and justify the actions of the English nation in a way that made the English look more like the liberators they hoped to be rather than the invaders they really were.[77]

By May 1623, the Virginia Company of London had taken a giant step away from its avowed intention of "converting . . . the Infidells," something that would have disqualified Indians as candidates for outright enslavement, by declaring that "itt was an attempt impossible they being descended of ye cursed race of Cham." As Waterhouse put it in 1622, in his account of the efforts of George Thorpe to "earnestly affect their conversion" only to have "this Viperous brood" murder him "out of devillish malice," the "sinnes of these wicked Infidels, have made them unworthy of enjoying him, and the eternal good that he most zealously always intended to them."[78] The idea that Indians were damned and that English efforts at conversion or inclusion of any kind were foolhardy appeared in other places as well. If the author of *The Planters Plea* (1630) is to be believed, the real problem was that "some conceive the Inhabitants of *New-England* to be *Chams* posterity, and consequently shut out from grace by *Noahs* curse."[79] The suggestion that the indigenous inhabitants of America may have constituted a separate race, in the modern sense of the term, was not embraced by many people in the seventeenth century. Nonetheless, the willingness of Anglo-Americans to posit new theories, especially ones that offered essentialist rather than circumstantial explanations for the differences between the natives and newcomers, allowed alternate justifications for Indian slavery to come to the fore and contributed to the racialization of Indian identity.[80]

As the passing observation from the author of *The Planters Plea* should indicate, the ideological challenge of Indian slavery was also in evidence in early New England. Puritan settlers generally made little effort to convert Indians before the 1640s.[81] Considering the tendency of many early Puritans to construct their new settlements as Calvinist enclaves, it should not be surprising that few people in early New England seemed to worry about the propriety of Indian slavery. John Smith did sound a regretful tone in the 1620s when he recalled that Thomas Hunt had "abused the Salvages . . . and betrayed twenty seaven of these poore innocent soules, which he sould in Spaine for slaves."[82] Colonial leaders did endeavor to ensure that Indians were neither preyed upon nor enslaved by Anglo-Americans. Soon after their arrival in Massachusetts Bay, for example, local officials ordered that "whatever p[er]son hath received any Indian into their Famylie as a serv[ant] shall discharge themselves of them" within a year unless he was granted a "license from the Court." This measure was desirable, in part, to prevent "the hurt that may follow through o[ur] much familiaritie w[ith] the Indians."[83] Ultimately, though, abstract ideas about Indian slavery were put to the test in the wake of the Pequot War. English forces took hundreds of captives as a result of their triumphs in battle at Mistick and the Great Swamp in 1637. Hundreds of Pequot men either died during the conflicts or were put to death in their aftermath. The survivors, consisting of a disproportionate number of women and children, were divided among the soldiers, given to Narragansett allies, or assigned to the Connecticut or Massachusetts colonies. It was in this context that seventeen Pequot Indians—fifteen boys and two women—were sold or traded into slavery on Providence Island in 1637. There, the English transformed the Pequots into "cannibal negroes," and condemned them to spend the remainder of their days in slavery.[84]

Although this story has often been treated as a stepping-stone in the linear development of slavery, or even racism, it seems rather to be a particularly cloudy historical moment. On the one hand, even in the aftermath of the breakdown of Anglo-Indian relations in the Chesapeake in 1622 and New England in 1637, numerous Englishmen espoused their conviction that Indians were candidates for Christian instruction and inclusion in the Anglo-American community. Even though his was but one voice in the wilderness on this issue, Roger Williams was particularly concerned about the justice of Indian slavery because of the stark division it implied between the natives and newcomers. Williams wondered, for example, what guidance the Bible offered the English as they thought about captives. Certainly, he recognized that perpetual slavery was a legitimate fate for those who deserved the death penalty for their crimes. In addition, he accepted that "the enemy may lawfully be weakened and despoiled of all comfort of wife and children, &c., but I beseech you," he wrote to John Winthrop, "weigh it after a due time of training up to labor, and restraint [whether] they ought not to be set free: yet so as without danger of adjoining to the enemy." Despite the war, Williams continued to believe that the enslavement of Indians made sense only when it was directed toward redemption. That John Winthrop himself had an Indian servant named "Reprieve" would seem to indicate that Williams was hardly alone in his views.[85] Hundreds of Indians could be found in English households in the 1630s and 1640s, although it is difficult to determine their precise legal status. A 1643 promotional tract indicated that "Divers of the Indians Children, Boyes and Girles, we have received into our houses . . . and in subjection to us." Regardless, John Mason claimed that although the English had divided a number of Indians among themselves after the war, "intending to keep them as Servants," they soon found that "they could not endure that Yoke; few of them of them continuing any time with their masters."[86]

Mason chose his words carefully. The unwillingness of Anglo-Americans to label Indians as slaves, even after their capture in a just war, is indicative of the English tendency to tread lightly on this subject. Already, by the late 1630s, many Europeans associated slavery in the broader Atlantic world primarily with bound African laborers. In this regard, the characterization of the captured Pequots as "Cannibal negroes" once they arrived in the West Indies was a significant, although exceptional, choice of words. Cannibalism fascinated Europeans during the era of overseas expansion and often served as a way of measuring the degree of civility or barbarity of various native groups. Writing to John Winthrop in early 1637, Roger Williams invoked this imagery when he wrote that the Pequots had "entered league . . . with the Mauquawogs or Mohawks which signifies man-eaters in their language; These cannibals have been all the talk these ten days." Williams worried, in particular, that "if the Lord please to let loose these mad dogs, their practice will render the Pequots cannibals too." Not only was cannibalism recognized as a particularly degenerate practice, it justified the conquest and enslavement of Indians who otherwise may have been offered friendship or protection.[87]

The use of the word *negro* was no accident either. First, as "cannibal negros" the New England Indians were distinguished from the Moskito Coast natives with whom the English hoped to maintain amicable relations. Second, as "negros" they were condemned to a recognized status—slavery—that was increasingly contingent in the Atlantic world upon a particular identity. It is therefore worth remembering here Morgan Godwyn's observation from later in the century: "These two words, *Negro* and *Slave*, being by Custom grown Homogenous and Convertible; even as *Negro* and *Christian, Englishman* and *Heathen*, are by the like corrupt Custom and Partiality made *Opposites*; thereby as it were implying, that the one could not be *Christians*, nor the other *Infidels*." Thus, the Pequots could become "negros" not because of confusion about their physical appearance or the absence of even the most basic understanding of national or ethnic characteristics, but because the definitive slave in the broader Atlantic world was becoming the "negro." In an important sense, then, as the ultimate punishment for their capture in a just war, the Pequots ceased to be Indians and instead became "negros," that is, "slaves."[88]

Events in Virginia and New England were highly localized, but Indian slavery during the first half of the seventeenth century was a problem that challenged the English throughout the Americas. Indians were often quite valuable trading partners and many English settlers continued to think of them as useful military allies. Nowhere was this truer than on Providence Island. Located as they were in the heart of Spain's American empire, the Puritan settlers on this distant and lonely outcrop could ill afford to foster enmity with the indigenous peoples. Thus, the enslavement of Indians, particularly the nearby Moskito Coast natives with whom they did business, was forbidden. It was perhaps this precedent that underlay the suggestion from the Providence Island Company in London to the governor and ruling council on the island itself that special care be taken of the New England Indians.[89] The English could ill afford to antagonize the indigenous peoples from whom they profited in trade and with whom they shared a dislike and fear of the nearby Spanish.

Of course, the Pequots were originally bound for Bermuda, not for Providence Island, and it is from Bermuda that we have some of the most intriguing evidence that Indian slavery may have been valued less at this time for its ability to provide laborers and more for its ability to facilitate Anglo-American colonialism. Reverend Patrick Copeland informed John Winthrop late in 1639 that if the original shipment had arrived, "I wold have had a care of them, to have disposed them to such honest men as should have trained them up in the principles of religion." When they were ready, Copeland imagined, they could be shipped back to New England in order to "doe some good upon their countrymen." If others could be procured, Copeland wrote to Winthrop, "or if you send mee a couple, a boy and a girle for my selfe, I will pay for their passage, so they be hopefull." Copeland's language in this exchange is striking and demonstrates the ability of at least one Englishman to imagine that slavery could serve the same purpose for Indians that other Englishmen hoped enslavement would serve *among* the English themselves during the sixteenth century and even into the seventeenth century. Copeland, after all, did not place any emphasis on slavery as a labor system; rather, he suggested that slavery was a means to a different end. In this case, slavery might even be an agent of conversion and would last until such time as the Indians were ready to return to New England as, theoretically, examples for their brethren to emulate. Slavery would redeem the Pequots, but this was conceptually possible only because Copeland was able to imagine that Indians were not so different from the English themselves.[90]

But even as Copeland was imagining how slavery might lead Indians out of the darkness, other Bermudians were on the prowl for chattel. Indian slaves were an increasingly common sight on the island in the 1630s and 1640s. Between 1644 and 1672, at least forty-seven Indian slaves appeared in local records. Of course, Bermudians did not actually call them "slaves." Recognizing in 1646 that there may have been some reluctance on the island to holding Indians in perpetuity, Captain Bartholomew Preston and members of his crew sold sixteen Indian women to local Bermudians. In each case, the woman was sold for a period of "fourscore & nineteen yeares If shee shall so long live." Technically, then, Indians were indentured servants, but the ninety-nine-year indenture was really only the barest pretense. When John Wainwright purchased an Indian servant named Anne from John Quick in January 1646, she came with the predictable ninety-nine-year indenture. Those years should have diminished over time, but when Wainwright resold Anne two years later to a local doctor, once again her contract stipulated that her new owner was entitled to ninety-nine years of service.[91] Indentured servitude, as English servants themselves were among the first to recognize, was an attractive innovation because it allowed masters to control their human property without actually practicing slavery. But, in some important ways, there was little to separate servitude from slavery in the early English Atlantic world.

The commodity value of Indian servants *as slaves* in Bermuda was clearly demonstrated in a case from 1651, when Philip Lee and William Williams agreed to allow their Indian servants—James and Frances—to marry. According to the arrangement, Williams would receive the first child and Lee the second if the couple produced offspring. In recognition of the fact that Williams owned Frances, however, the contract established that he would be responsible for all children for a year and a day after birth. Similarly, because childbirth would limit Frances's ability to work, Lee would pay for a midwife and provide a substitute servant "for the tyme the mother of the child lyeth inn." Presumably there were at least two children, as Philip Lee would later be in the possession of a young girl "by the name of Francis[,] the produce of my Indian man James & his wife an Indian belonging to Capt. Williams." In 1657, Lee sold this child to Lazarus Owen, who subsequently presented young Francis as a gift to his daughter Elizabeth. Leaving nothing to chance, Owen established that if Elizabeth were to die prematurely, his other daughter, Sarah, would become Francis's new owner "for ever." Assuming that Elizabeth (and young Francis) survived, however, Owen's plan was for Francis's first child to go to Sarah and "after that all such children: as shalbe borne of the body of the said Indian Francis shalbe equally devided betweene my saide daughters."[92] At no time were any of the Indian "servants" in these contracts referred to as "slaves," but as the passing reference to Sarah possibly owning young Francis in perpetuity would indicate, the Bermudian men who bought and sold the members of this Indian family were willing to deal in human property, even as they may have been simultaneously uncomfortable with Indian slavery.

Still, Indian slavery could not be transformed overnight and many people continued to worry about the circumstance under which some Indians found themselves in bondage. In April 1655, Captain Richard Jennins took up the cause of enslaved Indians before the Bermuda Company in England. Jennins declared that "about 11 yeares past 30 or 40 Indians which were freeborn people" were "made perpetual slaves to the great dishonor of God." According to Jennins, Captain Bartholomew Preston and others had taken them "by deceipt" in 1645 and, effectively, transformed a previously free people into slaves. The Company therefore requested that "some course may be taken for the restoring of this freeborne people to their form[er] libertyes." Bermudians almost certainly ignored this request, for six years later the Company again declared that they had received multiple complaints "touching the Indians for so manie yeares in bondage." Once again, they requested the General Assembly "to consider of a way and manner for the enfranchiseing of these people."[93] A similar sentiment emanated from Barbados during the 1650s when the plight of a group of nonnative Indians encouraged Captain Henry Powell to go to the Governor and ask for their liberation after nearly thirty years of "slavery and bondage." Powell had recruited thirty-two natives from Guiana in 1627 with promises of land and freedom, but the subsequent "Government of this Iland hath taken them by force and made them slaves."[94] It was one thing to condone slavery, or to treat human beings as slaves when they had done something to deserve the punishment, quite another to actually turn people into slaves indiscriminately.

Thus, despite the slowly growing willingness to treat Indians more like Africans and less like Englishmen, Indians were rarely made part of an undifferentiated class of bondmen before midcentury. Colonial records, official and unofficial, typically distinguished African slaves from Indian slaves.[95] Upon Richard Ligon's arrival in Barbados in 1647, he noted that Colonel Modyford purchased the property of Major William Hubbard, which contained "[h]ouses for Negroes and Indian slaves, with 96 Negroes, and three Indian women." Although both Indians and Africans were slaves, Ligon distinguished them by virtue of their intellectual capacity and physical appearance. Indians were "very active men, and apt to learn any thing, sooner than the Negroes; and as different from them in shape, almost as in colour." In a manner consistent with earlier pronouncements, however, Ligon also concluded that Indians were "much craftier, and subtiler then the Negroes; and in their nature falser." Decades of interaction with the natives, including frequent conflicts over land, religion, and government, had conditioned otherwise optimistic Englishmen to view Indians, in the words of John Smith, as "[c]raftie, timerous, quick of apprehension and very ingenious." They were thought by some to be "covetous" and "soone moved to anger, and so malitious, that they seldome forget an injury." These notions, however, were rooted in the recognition that Indians, unlike African slaves, were to be feared for the power they were able to exercise in the Americas. During the first half of the seventeenth century, English observers easily conceived of Indians as members of identifiable political entities and therefore, unlike African slaves, English settlers needed to approach them with much greater caution.[96]

Indigenous rights played an important role in how the English situated themselves in the New World. Colonial promotion required thoughtful Englishmen to pay special attention to Indian peoples, in part because the Spanish (so they claimed) had not. Even when Indians were largely absent, as in the case of Jamaica when the English invaded the island in 1655, many English propagandists thought carefully about the natives. When Thomas Gage, a former Dominican friar who had lived in Guatemala for more than a decade, dedicated his *New Survey of the West-Indies* in 1648, he emphasized that the Spanish had no legitimate claim to their American possessions except for force of conquest. And although legal scholars might emphasize the justness of Spanish actions, particularly in the light of "the inhumane butchery which the *Indians* did formerly commit in sacrificing of so many reasonable Creatures to their wicked Idols . . . ; The same argument may by much better reason be enforced against the *Spaniards* themselves, who have sacrificed so many millions of Indians to the Idol of their barbarous cruelty." As Gage and others would repeatedly emphasize, the English could more justly lay claim to lands in the Americas, like Jamaica, because "the just right or title to those Countries appertains to the Nations themselves; who if they shall willingly and freely invite the *English* to their protection, what title soever they have in them, no doubt but they may legally transfer it to others." [97] In this light, it is particularly interesting and crucially symbolic that upon the restoration of Charles II in 1660, the king "hounoured this Island with Arms, and with a publick Broad Seal, on one side of it his Majesty is seated on his Throne, with two *Indians* on their knees, presenting him *Fruits*." On the other side appeared "a Cross charged withe five Pines; two *Indians* for the *Supporters*, and for the Crest an *Alligator*."[98] Jamaica may have been a Spanish possession, but the island's essential indigenous heritage gave the English a reason to be there.[99]

The imagined relationship between English colonizers and the native inhabitants of the Americas therefore necessarily shaped the English experience with, and ideas about, slavery during the early seventeenth century. Fanciful notions about how slavery might be used to reconstruct society, or rehabilitate a given individual or group, were both an extension of English thoughts on the subject and a product of early modern colonialism. When compared with the willingness of the English to categorize their own countrymen as slaves, there was nothing particularly remarkable about the capture and enslavement of a handful of Indians in Virginia and Massachusetts in the aftermath of violent conflicts. It must be remembered that, on a global perspective, early modern Englishmen were more than willing to sell human beings into slavery.[100] But the enslavement of the indigenous inhabitants of the Americas was more complicated and Indians were therefore rarely enslaved indiscriminately. Certainly, the European notion that "Just Wars" legitimately allowed the victors to hold their captives as slaves was endorsed by a long line of distinguished political theorists.[101] Early modern English law continued to allow for the use of bondage as a form of punishment and Anglo-American officials did not hesitate to condemn criminals to slavery. Thus, for Englishmen inclined to imagine that they would be able to coexist with Indians or perhaps even construct an inclusive society, traditional modes of human bondage were easily extended to Indians. Once any pretense that there was a natural affinity between Indians and Englishmen exploded in their faces, however, Englishmen in America were free to rearticulate the logic of Indian slavery. By the end of the seventeenth century, Englishmen would be less concerned about Indians as allies, less optimistic about forging ties with Indian peoples, and less interested in whether Indian slavery was justified. During the first half century of Anglo-American colonialism, however, Indian slavery was a tricky business.

*   *   *

Early seventeenth-century English colonists thought about slavery in a variety of ways that appear, on the surface, to have been almost entirely subjective and arbitrary. In the light of their own English heritage, however, and the contemporary experience of so many Englishmen in the early modern Atlantic world, the willingness to condone a form of domestic slavery and apply it to Europeans and Indians alike makes a great deal of sense. America seemed to be a place wanting order and early modern Englishmen tended to articulate their ideas about the justice and the utility of human bondage at precisely those times when order was deemed necessary. Within the early modern English-speaking world, slavery was a mechanism for achieving coherence and order. It was, of course, inevitably punitive, whether exacted upon criminals or prisoners of war, but it would not have been condoned in England or English America unless officials could characterize slavery as fundamentally redemptive. That some people believed that bondage somehow made freeborn Englishmen more free might seem paradoxical, but it is nonetheless how many Tudor intellectuals and even some government officials thought about human progress. As historian David Brion Davis has artfully demonstrated, how Europeans thought about progress would change over time and it would become almost impossible to think of slavery as a progressive institution (at least among Europeans).[102] But the early years of Anglo-American colonialism reveal that there was still plenty of room for flexibility when it came to the subject of slavery.

Indian slavery, too, should be neither taken for granted nor simply viewed as either an early example or an extension of the enslavement of African peoples. Indian slavery, in which Indians were remade in the form of their oppressors, was a hopelessly idealistic enterprise that occupied the attention of just a few people. And it was arguably not nearly as desirable to most colonists as simply eliminating Indians. Still, it was an organizational and a promotional necessity and should be taken seriously as something that reveals what some English were willing to imagine as theoretically possible and, for our purposes, sheds considerable light on what early Anglo-Americans believed slavery meant. Indian slavery was rarely considered to be a viable labor system during the first half of the seventeenth century and the enslavement of indigenous peoples typically needed to be justified by the actions of Indians themselves. Early English colonial leaders preferred to avoid holding Indians as slaves, but Indian slavery made perfect sense if native bellicosity (from the English perspective) created a state of war. In other words, Indian slavery was viable in Virginia, New England, Bermuda, and the West Indies, but it does not seem to have been sought after or rationalized in the light of existing labor demands stemming from cash-crop agriculture.

The existence of multiple variants of slavery in seventeenth-century American colonies ultimately proved untenable. Englishmen became increasingly uncomfortable with labeling their own countrymen as slaves and less willing to think about Indians as possessing equal rights and shared qualities with Europeans. Arguments advanced at midcentury, especially that slavery was not simply unjust but represented a threat to the freedoms possessed by all Englishmen, had great rhetorical power, particularly in the American colonies where Englishness seemingly needed to be guarded even more jealously than in England itself. A century before, in 1547, when Parliament had declared that Englishmen could be enslaved, or when the Tudor government proclaimed that wayward Englishmen should be condemned to galley slavery, there was never any danger that by suffering such a fate these slaves would cease to be English. Indeed, their punishment was supposed to make them better Englishmen. This argument, however, was not so easily made in America. Seventeenth-century Anglo-America was a place where national identity was insecure and even elites felt compelled to guard their rights and prerogatives tenaciously. That colonial legislators gradually began to introduce legislation designed to protect their fellow countrymen from any and all abuses that might be exacted upon English servants was an outgrowth of this concern and could conceivably be thought of as some of the first anti-slavery legislation.

Finally, there was the problem of Anglo-Americans' eager embrace of plantation slavery and the subjugation of African peoples in the Atlantic world. Englishmen bragged about their cherished liberties to anyone who would listen and boasted that they were quite unlike other Europeans—and other people around the globe—by virtue of the fact that they did not treat human beings as either brute beasts or cheap commodities. They could make this argument, to some degree, when they considered their initial relationships with Indians and how they governed their own people in the colonies. But the standards by which Anglo-Americans measured the legitimacy of slavery among themselves and Indians were different than those they applied to Africans. Moreover, world-wise Englishmen were aware that the most common slave in the early modern Atlantic world was the displaced African, not Indians or fellow Europeans. Still, it is clear that there was a certain level of discomfort with African slavery, as when English authors hesitated to use the word "slave" with reference to their "negro servants" even as they applied the term loosely to other groups of people. Anglo-Americans understood that slavery served different purposes in different contexts. Yet, it was intellectually, legally, and culturally difficult to juggle discrete systems of slavery that were variously conceived and rationalized to preserve *Englishness*, redefine *Indianness*, and, as we shall see in the next chapter, isolate *Africanness*. The transatlantic plantation complex (with all that such a loaded phrase implies) did not immediately condemn Africans or predetermine the triumph of a singular, monolithic system of slavery in the Anglo-Atlantic world, but it certainly made it difficult for other forms of slavery to survive much beyond the first few decades of English overseas expansion.

CHAPTER 6

Slavery before "Slavery" in Pre-Plantation America

"wee are naturally inclin'd to love neigros if our purses would endure it."[1]

Nobody was particularly interested in Jamaica in the 1650s. As a result of high mortality rates among Indians in the aftermath of the conquest, slave raiding, and Spanish indifference, barely 1,500 people could be found on the island at this time and most of them were huddled around the city of St. Jago de la Vega, a few miles inland from the southern coast. The Spanish reaped few benefits from Jamaica, beyond using it as a place to raise cattle and produce hides for local and foreign markets.[2] European interlopers had occasionally raided the island during the preceding century, but everyone knew there were greater rewards to be found in other places, like Cuba and Hispaniola. However, as a result of Oliver Cromwell's "Western Design"—a grand imperial plan to destroy Spain's colonial empire in order to achieve both the economic and geopolitical ambitions of England and, perhaps, to help usher in a new age of Protestant ascendancy in the Americas—Jamaica's importance changed dramatically. In 1655, the English sent an expeditionary force to invade and capture Hispaniola from the Spanish Empire and begin the process of Anglicizing the New World. Their efforts ended disastrously and the English survivors were forced to lick their wounds on the coast of the ill-regarded but, as it turned out, lightly defended island of Jamaica. In just a few years, Spain would recognize English authority in Jamaica. As unexpected as this turn of events may have been, it laid the groundwork for the long-term expansion of England's sugar industry in the eighteenth century. In the short run, however, the English takeover of Jamaica proved to be a valuable opportunity for the northern Europeans to engage African peoples in the Americas and to experiment anew with racial slavery.[3]

The English conquest of Jamaica began simply, with a formal Spanish surrender in 1655, but it dragged on for nearly six years as the remnants of the local Spanish population, runaway slaves, and new invasion forces from other Spanish colonies contested English authority. Not until 1661 would Spain formally cede the island to the English. Beginning in 1656, though, English immigrants/invaders came to establish plantations along Jamaica's southern coast, but high mortality rates on the island ensured that the English population would remain low.[4] Although there were serious difficulties, English settlers did their best to transplant English laws and institutions into Jamaican soil and began the construction of settler societies that mirrored existing West Indian settlements.[5] Getting rid of Spain and all things Spanish was certainly one objective of the Protestant English invaders, but early Anglo-Jamaicans (like their forebears in other English colonies) willingly adapted themselves to the exigencies of a decidedly non-English Atlantic world, particularly when dealing with the resident African population.[6]

Many of the first Africans in England's new colony were runaway slaves—Maroons—who resisted the English invaders just as they had resisted the Spanish before them. If, as Governor Edward D'Oyley estimated, as many as 2,000 Africans "infested" the interior highlands then forming an alliance made much more sense than trying to root them out.[7] Spain had done much the same thing in some of its colonies in earlier decades and the policy had proven effective. But the English did more than simply try to neutralize Afro-Jamaicans with peace treaties, they tried to incorporate them into their emerging colonial society. Subsequent eighteenth-century treaties between the English and Maroons, such as the articles concluded in 1738, imagined the two sides as fixed entities that must necessarily remain far apart. In 1661, however, English authorities characterized Juan de Bolas and his 150 followers as "being much our friends, having their freedom as other planters" and living nearby, just "[o]ver the river." Two years later, Sir Charles Lyttelton suggested that the inclusion of Africans in the incipient Anglo-Jamaican society could be formalized when he invited "Juan Lubola [Juan de Bolas] and the rest of the Negroes of his Palenque" to be "in the same state and freedom as the English enjoy." Lyttelton's draft treaty also suggested that free blacks should receive a thirty-acre headright and "bring up their Children to the English Tongue" so "that by such Communitie of Language a better Societie, Correspondence and Commerce may be gotten between us and them."[8] Some Africans seem to have accepted the terms of this proposal. During the 1660s, there was a perceptible free African presence among the inhabitants of the island's principle town, St. Jago de la Vega. An African identified as "Mr De Camp" owned a residence in the city, as did "Anthony Rodrigues a Negro Soldier of the English Army." Some Englishmen had even more intimate relations. Cary Helyar, a merchant and prospective planter, had two children with a mulatto mistress during the 1660s.[9]

Jamaica would appear to be a strange place to begin the story of Anglo-African encounters and the early history of African slavery in the early modern Americas. Certainly, by the 1660s, Barbados, Virginia, and other English colonies were all well on their way to solidifying the slave-based plantation complex by purchasing an ever increasing number of African slaves and by enacting laws to provide legal cover for what they had been doing informally for decades. Thus, when historians want to know about the place of African peoples in the early English Atlantic world, they usually start much earlier with Virginia in the 1610s. The arrival of "20. and Odd Negroes" in the Chesapeake in 1619 is one of the most familiar episodes in the history of early Anglo-America. Yet, for all the attention this incidental exchange between a passing Dutch ship and some Virginia planters has attracted—representing, as it does to many scholars, the beginnings of the English embrace of racial hierarchies and a commitment to plantation slavery, depending on how you tell the story—it is not an especially transparent moment in the early history of the English Atlantic world.[10] If historians are to be believed, 1619 represents the beginning of all that America would come to be in subsequent decades and centuries. It was a historical watershed of the first order. Looked at from the perspective of the participants themselves, however, the arrival of a few Africans in the Chesapeake was rather unremarkable. Englishmen and Africans alike had been floating about the Atlantic world for more than a half century—the Africans, indeed, for much longer—and they frequently found themselves in contact with each other at sea and on shore in Europe, Africa, and the Americas. As a result, it is parochial at best and misleading at worst to imply that 1619 was all that new. The arrival of a small shipload of Africans, much like the occasion of an accidental English invasion of an unwanted island, merely created another opportunity for Anglo-Americans to build on their previous experiences with slavery and African peoples in the early modern Atlantic world.

Englishmen held Africans as slaves without shame or any sense of con-flict, but the newcomers also willingly integrated themselves into preexisting colonial frameworks that offered Africans considerable mobility and the op-portunity to be free. English mariners and merchants typically exploited Af-ricans for their labor and expertise and had rarely balked at opportunities to treat them as slaves. Unlike English or Indian slaves, very few people (beyond the Africans themselves) were interested in how African slaves came to be. What they cared about was the simple fact that African slaves could be made to work. In that regard, it was far easier to use and abuse African peoples than it was either other Europeans or Native Americans. This pattern had been true before 1619 and it would continue to hold after. During the first half of the seventeenth century, African slavery in the English Atlantic was certainly ill-defined, unsupported by positive law, and often without an obvious eco-nomic rationale, but that did not mean English settlers in the Americas had any intention of standing in the way of the organic expansion of this most Atlantic of institutions. Englishmen were no different from other European colonizers in their willing and sometimes even eager embrace of the callous commodification of African peoples as slaves. Positive law may not have initially supported English efforts in this regard, but the absence of a legal framework did nothing to stand in the way of Anglo-Americans who sought out bound African laborers.

But if Englishmen in the Americas were more than happy to buy and sell, or sometimes simply steal, African peoples, that willingness did not nec-essarily mean they automatically structured their colonial societies in a fash-ion that would be recognizable to later generations of colonists. Slavery in the pre-plantation era—roughly through the 1660s—functioned in English col-onies much as it did in other parts of the Atlantic world. African peoples were routinely held as slaves, but they were not the only ones to suffer such a fate and there were few barriers that stood in the way of them finding their way to freedom.[11] Most Englishmen living in the late sixteenth and early sev-enteenth centuries encountered Africans in the Americas as a people whose lives were almost totally defined by slavery, even as the boundary between slavery and freedom was far from absolute.[12] Not surprisingly, then, if Ja-maica's English invaders were willing to negotiate with Afro-Jamaicans in order to secure control of the colony, that did not mean they were opposed to slavery. In 1664, the Jamaican Council demonstrated its dexterity on the is-sue when it simultaneously continued to extend overtures to a band known as the "Varmahaly Negroes" just as it announced that if a servant or slave captured or killed any maroon, "he shall from thence forth be free." Moreover, the Council declared that "if any number of persons shall find out the Pallenque of the said Negroes; they shall have and enjoy to their uses all the weomen and Children, and all the Plunder they can find there for their reward."[13] In the same breath, and without any sense of irony or confusion, English officials embraced Africans in Jamaica as free residents within the new English colony, allies in an ongoing struggle, individuals who could be rewarded for their service, enemies of Anglo-American colonialism, legitimate victims, and ideal candidates for enslavement.

Since as early as the 1550s, the Africans that Englishmen encountered throughout the Atlantic world had been regarded and treated as slaves, ex-slaves, or runaway slaves. The English usually called them "negros," but there was no confusion about how Africans could and should be used once they moved beyond African shores. Europeans throughout the early modern Atlantic world thought about Africans primarily as slaves.[14] If some people became free over time, whether because of the actions of their former owners or because of their own initiative, they were the exceptions that proved the rule. If some African slaves became Christians or formed intimate bonds with Europeans, the presumptive status of African peoples as slaves in the Americas remained unchanged. These things would trouble Anglo-Americans more as the institution of slavery came to full fruition in later decades, but just as slavery varied in how it might be deployed in different contexts with different peoples, so too was slavery in the specific case of African peoples more fluid than the more rigid slave systems that would emerge in English colonies in the late seventeenth and early eighteenth centuries. It was to the benefit of a few notable individuals but the misfortune of many, many more nameless souls that slavery worked as well as it did during the first half of the seventeenth century, in the years before slavery *actually* existed.

* * *

Anglo-American colonists willingly adopted and adapted slavery to their specific circumstances before it was legal for them to do so.[15] Early Anglo-American slave-holding was consistent with the prevailing customs of the Atlantic world as established during the previous century, primarily by the Iberian powers. This similarity is not especially surprising because early Africans

often arrived in the English colonies not from Africa but instead from the
Iberian Atlantic world—typically the West Indies—where African peoples
were valued primarily for their labor.[16] Even when Africans did arrive directly
from their homeland, the Iberian powers were inevitably involved as slave
traders. It was much easier to trade with, or plunder from, the Spanish and
Portuguese in America than it was to contest them and other European powers for supremacy on the coast of Africa; in fact, the English had been shop-
lifting Africans from Spanish America, for all sorts of uses, for at least a
half-century before enslaving them in their own colonies. As a result, the West
Indies was arguably a much more influential arena than coastal West Africa
for informing and shaping popular English conceptions about the nature and
proper role of African peoples in the Atlantic world.[17]

Early English colonists willingly transplanted slavery onto Anglo-American
soil not simply because of supply considerations, but also because they were
fully aware from their privateering days that enslaved Africans were valuable
laborers and, perhaps even more important, highly skilled, technical crafts-
men and knowledgeable authorities about a variety of potentially valuable
commodities. Some of the first Africans in English colonies were therefore
sought out and acquired from Iberian sources not just because of their labor
value or geographic proximity, but because African slaves with special knowledge and experience could help the English develop their own colonial economies. The earliest and clearest example of this practice occurred in Bermuda,
where Africans were present beginning in 1616 as a direct result of the recruit-
ment efforts of the Somers Island Company, an offshoot of the Virginia Company of London. In order to develop a profitable local economy, the Company
commissioned Daniel Tucker to gather provisions for Bermuda from the West
Indies, including "negroes to dive for pearles." By May, "an Indian and a Negroe, the first these Ilands ever had," arrived on the island. Already in 1617,
Robert Rich, Bermuda's largest landholder, reported to his brother Nathaniel
that tobacco was being cultivated successfully on the island, thanks in great
part to the "good store of neggars which Mr Powell brought from the West
Indies."[18]

Like numerous of his English brethren, Captain John Powell acquired
his African commodities in a manner designed to offend the Spanish, as they
were part of the booty he and his men had looted from three Spanish ships.
Unfortunately, at least for the profit-minded Powell, Governor Daniel Tucker
seized the slaves for the Company's use and immediately set them to work on

the island cultivating sugar and tobacco. In subsequent years, English ships continued to deposit Africans on the island in small numbers. In 1619, "one Kirby a notorious rober in these parts," according to James Butler, traded fourteen Africans to Miles Kendall in exchange for a large quantity of corn and naval supplies. Daniel Elfrith, another piratical Englishman who had given Kendall eight slaves in 1618, extracted a group of Africans from what he claimed to be "an empty Angola ship" in 1619 and eventually landed twenty-nine of them in Bermuda. Elfrith repeated his exploits in 1620, delivering another unknown number of Africans to the Earl of Warwick's agent, John Dutton. Thus, between 1616 and 1620, and in a manner wholly consistent with English activities that had been occurring in the West Indies since at least the mid-1560s, as many as a hundred Africans arrived in Bermuda and quickly became the backbone of the tiny island's emerging tobacco economy. As Governor Nathaniel Butler made clear in January 1621 in a letter to Sir Nathaniel Rich, whatever other disagreements Anglo-Bermudians might have about their labor pool, "thes[e] Slaves are the most proper and cheape instruments for this plantation that can be."[19]

Although Anglo-Bermudians were the first to recognize the value of African laborers, they were not the only ones to rely on captured booty from Iberian sources in order to acquire African laborers. Every indication suggests that the first Africans to arrive in Virginia were similarly embedded in the Iberian market and, almost certainly, West Africa itself. Daniel Elfrith, captain of the *Treasurer*, acquired his cargo while sailing with another ship, the *White Lion*, under the command of Captain John Jope, a man most English sources describe as being either a Dutch or Flemish privateer.[20] Elfrith and Jope sailed with foreign commissions, issued out of Italy and the Netherlands, respectively, to do as much damage to Spanish shipping as possible as a result of ongoing European conflicts. Elfrith also had some important connections in Virginia. During the summer of 1618, he had been in Virginia where the deputy governor, Samuel Argall, commissioned him to "raunge the Indies." Only then had he sailed to Bermuda and met up with Jope. The two privateers then sailed for the West Indies where, off Campeche, they captured and plundered the Portuguese slave ship the *San Juan Batista*, which had only recently arrived in the region with a cargo of slaves from Angola. With roughly thirty beleaguered captives in each of their holds, the two captains charted a course for friendly waters. With his commission from Argall, Elfrith sailed for Virginia but found the colony now under the control of a new governor, Sir George Yeardley.[21] The change in leadership dampened his business prospects, so he sailed on to Bermuda, where he found in Miles Kendall a colonial official more receptive to the slave trade.[22]

Jope's travails, however, turned out to be much more central to the early history of Virginia than did Elfrith's, for it was Jope's "Dutch man of Warr" that "arrived at Point-Comfort" in late August 1619 and subsequently offered "20. and odd Negroes, w[hich] the Governo[r] and Cape Marchant bought for victualle."[23] Jope had actually been in Virginia several days before Elfrith's arrival and Governor Yeardley and the Company's chief merchant, Abraham Peirsey, willingly took control of the Africans, reserving most of them for either the Company's or their own personal use. Within a few months, in the spring of 1620, the presence of thirty-two Africans (fifteen men and seventeen women) was recorded in a census, suggesting that there were either already a few Africans in Virginia before the arrival of the *White Lion* or that Elfrith's *Treasurer* managed to deposit a few Africans ashore before fleeing to Bermuda.[24] The case of "Angelo a Negro Woman" makes speculation on this matter worthwhile because she reportedly arrived in Virginia "in the *Treasurer*." In addition to 1619, the *Treasurer* had been in Virginia on five separate occasions between 1613 and 1618. After Elfrith's 1619 expedition, the ship was described as "weather-beaten and tourne, as never likely to put to sea againe." According to one account, however, the *Treasurer* made a final trip to Virginia sometime before 1623—perhaps in early 1620—where the hulk was overturned and sunk in a creek. Considering the ship's frequent involvement in West Indian piracy, there were more than a few opportunities for a few Africans, like Angelo, to seep into the colony.[25]

Regardless of how and when the earliest Africans arrived in Virginia, their population grew slowly as they trickled into the colony during the 1620s. Antonio arrived in the *James* in 1621; Mary, "a Negro Woman," came in the *Margarett and John* in 1622; and John Pedro, "a Negar aged 30," reportedly arrived in 1623. "*John Phillip* A Negro Christened in *England* 12 yeers since," and likely a crewman on an English vessel, may not have lived in Virginia, but he was allowed to testify in a suit against an English colonist in 1624. A year later, surviving records show the presence of a "negro caled by the name of *brase*," who may have been the unnamed man who arrived in Virginia during the summer of 1625. In September of that year, the General Court ordered "the negro [that] came in w[i]th Capt Jones" to remain with Lady Yeardley "till further order be taken for him and that he shalbe allowed . . . forty pound waight of good merchantable tobacco for his labor and services so lange as he remayneth with her." Unlike John Phillip, who was exempted from bondage because he was a Christian, this African was presumably deemed worthy of personal liberty because he and a Frenchman "came away willingly" out of the West Indies. Not until 1628 did another relatively large shipment of Africans arrive in Virginia, when the *Fortune* took "an Angola man with many Negroes, which the Capt. bartered in Virginia for tobacco." The *Straker* brought yet another unknown number of enslaved Africans (probably fewer than five) to Virginia.[26] Between 1619 and 1628, then, at least seventy-five and maybe even as many as a hundred Africans found their way to the Chesapeake.[27]

The African population grew more rapidly elsewhere. Although Englishmen did not begin their attempt at establishing a permanent foothold in Barbados until the 1620s, Anglo-Barbadians eagerly absorbed Africans into their midst and embraced plantation slavery. Ten Africans were with the first Barbadian settlers when they arrived on the island in 1627 and there seems to have been little doubt about their status. Less than a decade later, Barbadian officials were able to declare with confidence that "*Negroes* and *Indians*, that came here to be sold, should serve for Life, unless a Contract was before made to the contrary."[28] Although doubts soon arose about the legal enslavement of some Indians, Barbadians held Africans as slaves with confidence, emboldened by their deep familiarity with, and pragmatic acceptance of, the important role played by chattel slavery in the West Indies during the previous decades. Writing a generation later, George Gardyner described Barbados as being "thoroughly inhabited with English, and Negroes their servants."[29] More famously, George Downing averred in a letter to John Winthrop Jr. that "[i]f you go to Barbados, you shal see a flourishing Iland" where, in 1645 alone, the inhabitants had purchased "no lesse than a thousand Negroes." In less than a generation, Downing could state confidently that enslaved Africans were "the life of this place."[30]

By all accounts, Africans arrived slowly but purposefully in English colonies in the early decades of the seventeenth century. In the absence of a reliable supply system and because (in the case of the mainland colonies) they were located some distance away from the most heavily traveled sea lanes, Anglo-Americans could not supply themselves with as many African laborers as they would have liked. The intentional acquisition of African slaves, though, is clear. English officials interfered with the efforts of would-be slave owners only if there was strong evidence that the Africans may have been acquired illegally. Otherwise, there was nothing to stand in the way of would-be slave owners in early English America. If a Dutch ship or an English privateer happened to show up in an English colony, the captain found plenty of people who were willing to purchase slaves.

Yet the difficulty in teasing out the precise status of the earliest generation of African peoples (who, it must be remembered, were rarely called slaves) in English colonies attests to the conscious strategy of many Anglo-Americans to remain circumspect on the matter. Clearly, the Barbados evidence and the acquisitive spirit of early Bermudians in particular leaves little room for doubt about the English willingness to construct societies with slaves in the Americas. But the sources tend to obfuscate rather than illuminate on the question of legal slavery. For example, much of what has been argued about the earliest African population in Virginia has been based on the events of 1619 and two censuses dating from the mid-1620s. The census materials, however, are as much a revealing testament to the general disregard English record-keepers had for Africans during this period as they are an insight into the lives of the earliest African inhabitants of Virginia. Beyond noting their existence, census takers recorded very little information about the twenty-two Africans living in Virginia in early 1624 or the twenty-three who were living there in 1625. If Africans had once numbered in the thirties, nobody bothered to comment here or elsewhere on the fate of the dozen or so individuals who had disappeared since 1619. In addition, none of the Africans from the first census was accorded a surname and nearly half were listed simply as "negar" or, in the case of those who resided at Flowerdew Hundred, six "negors."[31] The 1625 census, a household-by-household muster, is equally vague, with very little information about the names or date of arrival of the resident Africans. The absence of any record of arrival date in the latter census is a valuable piece of information that undermines the questionable assertion that Africans in early Virginia should be thought of as indentured servants.[32] Considering the novelty of indentured servitude in the Anglo-Atlantic world, not to mention slavery's familiarity, the logical default category for undocumented Africans was perpetual bondage.

Indifference to the precise legal status of early Africans is only part of the story when looking at the census records. Equally problematic is that, although the two censuses were compiled less than twelve months apart, the total number of Africans and their precise locations is a matter of great confusion. The additional African resident may be attributable to the birth of a child. Anthony and Isabella, recorded as living in Elizabeth City in 1624, reappear in 1625 with "William Their Baptised Child." "Edward a negro" appears in both 1624 and 1625 as living at the "Neck-of-Land neare James Citty." Otherwise, there is little correlation between the two sources and no acknowledgment of deaths or new arrivals.[33] The discrepancies between the two censuses suggest that some significant internal migration or movement among Africans had taken place between 1624 and 1625 or some important, and unrecorded, changes had occurred in the African population.[34] In the first census, for example, three Africans were living at James City; one year later, nine (three men and six women) were living there. Four Africans could be found at "Warwick's Squrak" in 1624, but only two lived at "Wariscoy-ack" in 1625. Sir George Yeardley had only two African women attributed to him in 1624, but by 1625 he seems to have been in possession of three men and five women, all of whom were living at James City. In 1624, the largest concentration of Africans had been the eleven men and women who resided at "Flowerdieu" Hundred on the south side of the James River. In 1625, the largest concentration were the eight men and women with Yeardley at James City; only seven Africans (four men, two women, and "a yong Child") were recorded as living with Abraham Peirsey at Flowerdieu (renamed Peirseys) Hundred at that time.[35]

No matter where one looks in early Anglo-America, it is difficult to get a sense of the precise number of Africans living in English colonial settlements.[36] This problem may be attributable to the nature of the sources, but English record-keepers were also either reluctant to document the presence of Africans living in their settlements or they simply did not care enough to record precise details. Africans were often as invisible in the colonies during the first few decades of the seventeenth century as they had been during late sixteenth-century English West Indian enterprises. No "negroes" were recorded in the first Bermudian census taken during the 1620s. Instead, the end of the tally stated simply: "Persons in all uppon the Tribes besides those which are uppon the publick Land besides the Negroes: 806."[37] Accounting for this historical silence is difficult, but in the case of Bermuda and early Virginia there were good reasons to overlook resident Africans. For one, most of the early African arrivals had been obtained through illegal channels, stolen from the Spanish and Portuguese by English pirates and privateers. During 1619 and 1620, there was a dispute concerning the ownership of the Africans brought into Bermuda by Captains Kirby and Elfrith. Kirby arrived during the summer of 1619 and gave then-governor Miles Kendall "14 Negars" in exchange for 50,000 ears of corn. Elfrith, who arrived just a few weeks later with his own pilfered Africans, acquired 100,000 ears of corn for his

29 Africans. By January 1620, the new governor, Nathaniel Butler, was writing to Sir Nathaniel Rich condemning his predecessor on the grounds that Kendall's exchange meant that "hereof wee are unfurnished of such a quantitie of corn . . . so that we are likely to live without bread two or three months." A year later, Butler continued to rail against Kendall when the former governor tried to argue that the 14 Africans he had purchased from Kirby were his personal property, not the Company's. Butler acquiesced for the moment, but informed Rich that "the truth is, that it wer fitter that he wer rewarded . . . some other way" because "slaves" were so valuable to the health and well-being of the colony and therefore "not safe to be any wher but under the Governours eye."[38]

Although the growing number of Africans appearing in English colonies supports the assertion that they were actively sought after, the trepidation with which they were treated in official records would indicate that there was some uncertainty about how to deal with them under the law. The illegal acquisition of Africans and their subsequent smuggling into Bermuda and Virginia was a problem that reappeared in other young colonies. The African presence in New England, for example, can be documented as early as 1637, when Captain Peirce returned from Providence Island after depositing his cargo of Pequot Indians. According to one source, however, Samuel Maverick, who arrived in Plymouth in 1624, had African slaves in his possession even before Puritan settlers established themselves at Massachusetts Bay.[39] By the 1640s, New England ships were actively engaged in a private transatlantic slave trade, although they did not always return to their home port with African cargoes. John Winthrop recorded in his journal in 1645 that "one of our ships . . . returned now and brought wine, and sugar, and salt, and some tobacco, which she had at Barbadoes, in exchange for Africoes, which she carried from the Isle of Maio." That same year, the case of Thomas Keyser and James Smith revealed the difficulty of importing Africans who may have been acquired through suspect channels. Keyser and Smith had been on the African coast, sailing in consort with another English ship, when they participated in an attack on a village that led to the capture of some of its inhabitants. When they returned to New England with two Africans, they were brought before the General Court and charged with murder, man-stealing, and Sabbath-breaking. The Court therefore decided to send the Africans back because "the negars" were not theirs, "but stolen."[40] If slavery was perfectly acceptable, making slaves was not.

English settlers on Providence Island, largely because of their advantageous location in the western Caribbean, routinely acquired Africans in large numbers as a result of their own clandestine activities during the 1630s. After more than a decade of experience with African laborers in the Chesapeake and Bermuda, as well as recent experience in newer colonies like Barbados, the members of the Providence Island Company in London and settlers alike took it for granted that enslaved Africans were necessary to ensure both the immediate and long-term success of English colonial ventures. Philip Bell, the colony's first governor, brought African slaves with him when he relocated to Providence from Bermuda in 1630. During the island's initial years, the Providence Island Company repeatedly empowered English ship captains to acquire African slaves whenever possible and informed Governor Bell in 1633 of its belief that "20 or 40 negroes might be very useful for public works," although "too great a number in the island might as yet be dangerous."[41] In 1636, the privateer William Rous arrived on the island with some pilfered Africans, some of whom were "to be conveyed to the Somers Island," while "those who can dive for pearls" were to be "so employed at Providence." Repeatedly, the Providence Island Company issued similar directives, making sure that Africans would be distributed in an appropriate fashion and addressing the complications that arose when English privateers unloaded their cargos of plundered Africans on the island. Indeed by 1637, the number of Africans on the island began to alarm company officials so much that they tried to limit their importation "with exceptions, until Providence be furnished with English." This policy proved difficult to implement and within a year the Providence Island Company set aside its concerns and authorized the governor to purchase "100 negroes for the public works."[42]

If there were legal and, perhaps, ethical reasons for circumspection, there were also some incentives to record African arrivals assiduously. Nowhere was this more true than in the Chesapeake, where, by the 1620s, fifty-acre headrights were granted to individuals who imported laborers into Virginia. Captain Henry Browne received a large headright in 1634 for importing twenty-one laborers, including "Mingo, a negro," "France a negro, Jon. a negro, [and] two women negroes." Charles Harner brought eight others into the colony in 1635, whose names were recorded as Alexander, Anthony, John, Sebastian, Polonia, Jane, Palatia, and Cassanga. The enslavement of Africans would not even begin to be formalized into law until the 1660s, but already by the 1630s slaves began to appear in significant numbers in Chesapeake headright records. Richard Kemp, writing to Lord Baltimore in 1638, noted that he had received his "Commands of the second of August last for the buying of Fortye neate Cattle, ten Sowes, Forty Henns and Ten Negroes to be Transported to St. Maryes for yo'r use." Four years later, John Skinner "covenanted and bargained to deliver unto the said Leonard Calvert, fourteene negro men-slaves, and three women slaves, of between 16 and 26 yeare old able and sound in body and limbs." Before mid-century, Virginia planters claimed more than 300 headrights. By the 1640s, Virginia and Maryland planters did not shy away from the purchase of Africans and, as Skinner's comments reveal, accepted that when they purchased Africans they were purchasing slaves.[43] Enslaving Africans may have been dicey business in the early Anglo-Atlantic world. Buying and holding Africans as slaves was another matter entirely.

Regardless of the absence of a positive law of slavery in the English colonies, then, Anglo-Americans accepted the commodity value of bound African slaves. Remarkably, considering the tenor of English assertions about their commitment to the principle of personal liberty and their general dislike of human bondage, early slave owners routinely conducted their business ventures openly and without apology. Early slave owners did not hesitate to sell their slaves, bequeath them to their heirs when they died, or use them as collateral in their local economic exchanges. As early as 1628, John Ellzeye, in a letter to Edward Nicholas, secretary to the Duke of Buckingham, openly acknowledged that he had received "85 hodsh'ds and 5 buts of tobacco" for the "Negroes sold in Virginia." In Maryland, Job Chandler, bequeathed his "negro woman Morratous to his wife, Francisco to his daughter Ann, and multiple Africans to his sons William and Richard. In a similar vein, officials in Providence Island wrote back and forth with agents of the Providence Island Company about the buying and selling of Africans and even broached the subject of doing so in order to generate revenue for the cash-strapped enterprise. By 1639, regardless of the difficulties that arose from keeping slaves, the Company could no longer afford to send large numbers of English servants and conceded that it might even be able to raise funds by selling excess Africans to buyers in Virginia and New England. Throughout English America the story was much the same.[44]

Although there is some indication that English settlers were uncomfortable enslaving Africans and that they needed to be careful when it came to describing how they acquired African slaves, scant evidence exists to suggest that they either were troubled by slavery itself or found it difficult to manage even in the absence of a solid legal foundation or a rudimentary statutory framework.[45] Their ability to buy and sell enslaved Africans was hampered by the absence of a regular supply chain, an obstacle that would take decades to overcome, and the small size of the early settlements meant that, as enterprising as they may have been, early slaveholders required only small numbers of slaves.[46] But these sorts of logistical matters in no way prevented early planters from taking full and complete advantage of Africans as slaves whenever they had the good fortune to take possession. Africans appeared in all of the early English colonies because they were ubiquitous in the early modern Atlantic world. It would have been remarkable for Africans to remain apart from Anglo-America, particularly in the West Indies but on the mainland as well. Moreover, the prevailing customs of the Atlantic world demanded that early English colonists find ways to accommodate themselves to the practice of holding African peoples in a state of perpetual and inheritable bondage. To do otherwise required the English colonists to imagine and create a genuinely new world premised on an anachronistic conception of liberty, necessitated that they adhere to ideological principles that still awaited full articulation, and demanded that they put their abstract and often untested historical celebration of freedom ahead of their lives and fortunes. The English were nothing if not pragmatic and African slaves were a tried-and-true solution to the labor problems that plagued the early Atlantic world.

*   *   *

Anthony Johnson was not the first African to arrive in Virginia, but he has certainly attracted the most scholarly interest. Johnson first appeared in the colony in 1621 and subsequently labored on the Bennett family's plantation at Warresqueak on the south side of the James River. In 1622, his future wife Mary arrived and the two of them were listed as "Antonio a Negro" and "Mary a Negro" in the 1625 census.[47] By 1640, Anthony and Mary had married, were the parents of four children, and had moved across the Chesapeake Bay to Virginia's Eastern Shore. At this juncture, nearly twenty years after their arrival, the Johnsons were still either in the employ of or bound in service to the Bennett family. By 1651, however, Anthony Johnson received a 250-acre headright for purchasing and importing five servants into the colony. Thirty years after his arrival, then, and regardless of more than twenty years of servitude or slavery, Johnson became a man of some importance and economic standing. Johnson expected, for example, to receive fair treatment in the local courts. When his plantation burned in 1653, he petitioned the government for, and received, tax relief to help him recover from the tragedy. Johnson and his heirs, especially his sons John and Richard, prospered in a Virginia where, regardless of the family's humble origins, they were able to own land, servants, and slaves and become acknowledged and respected members of the local community.[48]

Anthony Johnson's story is deceptive. On the one hand, he lived a remarkable life and his rags-to-riches story highlights all that was possible in the Americas for even the most disadvantaged of individuals. His story would also seem to caution scholars against treating early Africans in the Americas as slaves or framing their story too rigidly in the light of the practice of slavery as it operated in the broader Atlantic world. That, however, would be a mistake. We have already seen that the commodity value of African peoples framed the way Englishmen thought about African peoples in the Americas (although not necessarily in early modern England or Africa) during both the last half of the sixteenth century and the first few decades of the settlement era. Englishmen in the Americas were perfectly content to treat Africans as slaves. During the pre-plantation era, however, Anglo-American slavery often involved social and cultural practices at odds with how slavery was imagined in England and how plantation slavery would be organized when it fully matured during the eighteenth century. As much as anything else, pre-plantation slavery was premised on the prevailing customs of the Atlantic world and functioned according to the rules and traditions of Spain and Portugal. Normative slavery, as the English understood it and tried to implement it, therefore often involved high manumission rates, the toleration of the free black population, the tacit acceptance of racial intermixture, and even some willingness to think about incorporating African peoples into the Christian community.[49] None of these things would be particularly common later on, once lawmakers were allowed to define slavery to suit their particular needs. During the first half of the seventeenth century, the English embraced and creatively adapted the race-based plantation slave system that already defined the lives of the vast majority of African peoples in the Atlantic world.[50]

Certainly, one of the most interesting things about Anthony Johnson was, by the 1650s, his freedom. Free blacks were an important, or at least identifiable, part of Anglo-American society during the pre-plantation period. Yet, the presence of a free black population does not tell us much about what Anglo-Americans thought about slavery or whether they were fully committed to it. Indeed, a case can be made for the argument that free blacks appeared in early Anglo-America precisely because early modern Englishmen appreciated and respected the fact that manumission was a constituent part of slavery, not because they were hesitant to enslave. One distinguishing characteristic of Atlantic slavery, as well as of the institution as it existed in both the Iberian Peninsula and North Africa, was the opportunity for, and ready access to, freedom for enslaved peoples. Rather than weakening the system, or suggesting that the institution of slavery was not fully formed, high rates of manumission and the presence of a large number of free blacks in other places implied the existence of a lively, fully articulated, and secure slave society.[51] Whether it was rationalized as an act of benevolence, an act of piety, or simply yet another way of profiting from bondmen (by making them pay for their freedom), manumission was an effective social mechanism that facilitated masters' control over their slaves and freedmen. The master's power to negate slavery was as important as his power to enslave.[52]

Africans who were able to find their way to freedom within Anglo-American colonial societies were able to do so because of the willingness of their English owners to accept manumission as a legitimate aspect of a slave system. Of course, it also helped a great deal if Africans themselves had some knowledge about how to navigate the narrow pathways that led to freedom. Stories can easily be found in surviving records of self-purchase and of former slaves negotiating with white masters to redeem their wives and children out of slavery. Early English settlers of all stations accepted that slaves could be freed as a reward for faithful service because it was their Christian duty or because they were uncomfortable with the permanence of slavery. In Virginia, for example, Francis Payne famously negotiated with his owner to secure his freedom over the course of several years by purchasing new servants to replace his and his family's labor. John Graweere purchased his child out of slavery by making an arrangement with his wife's owner, Robert Sheppard, to accept payment in livestock that Graweere was allowed to cultivate in accordance with a relationship he had established with William Evans. In New England, Governor Theophilus Eaton facilitated a similar arrangement in 1646 when he freed his slave, John Wham, and proceeded to settle the man and his wife on a nearby farm.[53]

As these examples would suggest, the willingness of some English slave owners to release their slaves from perpetual and inheritable obligations was often premised on the promise of compensation, but it was also accompanied by a genuine interest in the long-term welfare of the newly freed. A sense of benevolence, possibly grounded in paternalistic considerations, featured prominently in these patron-client relationships. Richard Vaughan of Virginia freed his slaves when he died in 1656, leaving them land and instructing that they should be taught to read and make their own clothing. Mihill Gowen, along with "his Sonne William," was set free by Anne Barnehouse in 1657, even though the infant William was "of the body of my negro Rosa." In his 1647 will, Nathaniel Bacon promised to give "the mulatto Kate her freedom . . . , it being formerly promised by my deceased wife." In an interesting twist on manumission, when John Indecott Cooper of Boston prepared to sell a "Spanish Mulatto by name Antonio" in 1678, he asserted his "full power to Sell for his life time," but he acceded to "the request of William Taylor [that] I doe Sell him But for Tenn Yeares."[54]

The path to freedom was sometimes fraught with legal difficulties and the belief of some Englishmen that Africans could not, or should not, be fully functioning members of colonial society. In one especially striking case from Bermuda, a white sailor named Francis Jennyns acknowledged that he was "the trewe father of a child" soon to be born to "one Sarah a negroe Woeman." Because he was "outward bound," Jennyns chose to "freely and absolutly give the said child unto Mr. Hooper . . . to be forever for the use of . . . Hooper his heires and Assignes as his or their owne." English owners often gave mixed-race children the opportunity to improve their situation by apprenticing them to a trade, teaching them to read and write, or simply promising them their freedom after twenty or thirty years. Jennyns, for his part, requested that Hooper "doe bringe and nurture upp the same in the faith of Christ, and in the principles of the true protestant Religion."[55] At the other end of the spectrum, colonial officials did not prefer for the children of Englishmen to be condemned to a state of perpetual or inheritable slavery simply because of the physical appearance of one of the parents—particularly if it was the mother. Thus, the governor of Bermuda in 1649 determined that William Johnston was entitled "to enjoy A mallatto child: reputed to be the child of John Browne begotten of Mr. Johnstons negro," but only "untill that child attaines the age of thirtie yeares and then the said child is to be free."[56] Similar rulings were reached during the mid-seventeenth century in order to ensure that the stain of slavery did not blight the progeny of freeborn Englishmen.

Anglo-Virginians and Bermudians were interested in the lives and welfare of their slaves and servants for a number of reasons. In some cases, a very real sense of attachment led some English owners to make sure that Africans would not, by default, be treated as slaves but would instead have a chance at freedom. In 1649, the former governor of Bermuda, Roger Wood, "apointed my negroe boye Roger, the Sonn of Lewis and Maria, to be in the Possession and Service of my Cousen John Stowe, and be by him Instructed, and taught the trade he nowe useth, of boate makinge." By this date, Wood had been in possession of large numbers of Africans for nearly twenty years. Wood not only knew Roger, he had likely known Roger's parents since they, too, had been children in the 1630s. It is perhaps for this reason that Wood took special interest in young Roger. Thus, Wood specified that Roger was "to be freed" when he turned thirty and was to receive freedom dues, including "such apporcion of Tooles as are usually delivered to Boate Wrights, or boate Carpenters Servants at the expiracion of their tymes of Service of Indenture."[57] Because Africans were often, by default, condemned to lives of perpetual servitude during this period, Wood made certain that Roger's term of service would resemble that of English servants or apprentices. Bermudians might try to avoid the accusation that they dealt in slavery, largely by avoiding the word "slave," but local practice revealed otherwise. As with Indians, for example, Bermudians routinely bought and sold Africans as "servants" for the outrageous "tearme of fowerscore and Nineteene yeeres."[58] To paraphrase and likely abuse the intended meaning of the English poet Samuel Taylor Coleridge, Anglo-Americans did not hesitate to engage in a willing suspension of disbelief when it allowed them to achieve their material goals. But Wood's eagerness to see to the well-being and eventual freedom of a young African boy named Roger clearly points to something else. Wood sought not to undermine the customary practice of holding Africans in a state of slavery. Rather, he used traditional English legal mechanisms to bridge the gap between slavery and freedom for one individual.

There might also have been something to the fact that Governor Wood was dealing with a young African who was also his namesake. Manumission was not entirely random. English masters generally chose to free individuals with whom they had a relationship. It may also have been a process that was made possible by the ability of some Africans to tap into patron-client relationships that had been built up over time and would, presumably, continue after freedom. The structure of this relationship might even be traced directly to Hispanic precedents in the way it paralleled specific customs, like ritual godparentage. The most vivid example of this scenario occurred in Bermuda in the 1630s when James Sarnando, "Commonly Called olde James the Nigro," and his wife engaged Hugh Wentworth in a ceremony designed to cement a fictive familial bond. At the time, Sarnando and his wife were the parents of a seven-year-old girl named Hanna. The Sarnandos appeared at the Wentworth home sometime in 1639, whereupon "the sayd James did take the Childe by the hand & delivered it into the hande of Mr. Wentworth saying heere Master mee give you this Childe take her & bring her up & mee give her to you freely." The ritual was repeated once again with Sarnando placing his daughter's hand into that of Wentworth's wife and with Sardando's wife placing Hanna's hand into that of Hugh Wentworth. At the end of the ceremony, the Sarnandos believed that they had formed a bond that would enable them and their daughter to live fuller lives and, perhaps, might open the door to certain advantages at a later date.[59]

This episode, however, was more than a simple "touching" ceremony. As members of a generation of African peoples with close ties to Spanish or Portuguese America, the Sarnandos were enacting a ritual that closely paralleled the *compadrio*, or ritual godparentage. If James Sarnando and his wife had any familiarity with Catholic practice, they would have known that they were forging both a spiritual and temporal kinship with Wentworth. And Wentworth made a particularly good choice for a benefactor. James Sarnando and his wife were owned by the Earl of Warwick; Hugh Wentworth was a former indentured servant who had risen high enough to refer to himself as a gentleman. By the late 1630s, Wentworth was also serving as Warwick's agent and was, by one measure, Bermuda's most important dealer in African and Indian slaves. In Wentworth, Sarnando may have hoped to engage the protection of an influential free Bermudian to ensure the sanctity of his family's tenuous union.[60] In the end, though, things did not work out as Hanna's parents had hoped. Hanna continued to be a company slave until January 1646 when, to satisfy a debt, the Earl of Warwick gave Hanna to Nathaniel White "from the day of the date hereof to the end & terme of fourscore & nineteen yeares If shee shall so long live." Hanna obviously did not live that long, but she was still alive and in White's possession when he crafted his will in 1666. At that time, White determined conclusively that there would be no freedom for Hanna or her children when he declared that, upon his death, she would pass to "my dearly beloved wife" along with "Samuel her youngest sonne, with all those children that shalbe borne of her bodie which belong unto mee after my decease."[61]

Manumission, then, appears to have been an avenue to freedom that Englishmen and Africans on the mainland and, especially, in Bermuda recognized as being consistent with slavery. The story may have been quite different in Barbados, where the early and dramatic emergence of the sugar economy during the 1640s promoted a much more rapid and decidedly defensive com-modification of African labor than in any other English colony. As such, just as West Indian planters opened themselves up to criticisms that suggested they held their white servants as slaves, so too were there fewer incentives to manumit African slaves. Yet, there were still a few free blacks on the island—at least 123 individuals were manumitted between 1650 and 1700—and several of them even managed to maintain their free condition even after manumission ceased to be either socially or legally acceptable. In 1654, An-thony Iland petitioned for his freedom on the grounds that he had arrived on the island as a free person and of his own accord. In accepting Iland's argu-ment that he had subsequently been illegally detained by William Leachy, a local sugar planter, Barbadian officials sided with the plaintiff and remained true to the English ideal that they did not make slaves without cause. Thirty years later, in 1687, several other African slaves were ordered to "be freed and [to] be able to dispose of themselves as they shall see fit" on similar grounds. As a percentage of the overall population, however, the free black population in Barbados was minuscule. It is perhaps unsurprising that the profoundly curious and thorough observer Richard Ligon failed to mention any free blacks in his account of the island during the late 1640s.[62]

Manumission was an important part of pre-plantation slavery and some-thing that distinguished early slavery in the English Atlantic world from the system that would cohere in the late seventeenth century because it allowed for the greater incorporation of non-European peoples into Anglo-American societies. In this regard, manumission represented a continuation of the way Englishmen had been dealing with African peoples since the mid-sixteenth century and foreshadowed initial English efforts in Jamaica. So, too, did the use of Africans for colonial defense. English settlers in New England, the Chesapeake, and the West Indies all broached the idea of arming slaves for colonial defense during the 1640s and 1650s. Providence Islanders, in partic-ular, celebrated "with due gratitude and wonder" the "loyalty in adversity of the negroes who had often rebelled in times of prosperity" when they helped fend off a Spanish invasion in 1640. In 1652, the Massachusetts General Court ordered "that all Scotsmen, Negeres and Indians . . . shal be listed, and are hereby enjoyned to attend traynings as well as the English." Even in Virginia, free blacks possessed arms and were eligible for the militia during much of the seventeenth century. When the General Assembly passed an act requiring "all masters of families" to furnish "themselves and all those of their families which shall be capable of arms (excepting negroes) with arms both offensive and defensive" in 1640, it clearly chose not to arm slaves but it did not necessarily disarm the small free black population.[63]

Like the Spanish before them, Anglo-Americans armed Africans for a number of reasons. Neither the English nor Spanish inhabitants of the Americas were particularly fond of the Africans who lived in their midst, but Africans—free or enslaved—were routinely viewed with less fear and suspicion than either indigenous peoples or the European marauders who periodically threatened colonial outposts. Africans were armed, quite often, as a simple matter of expediency and self-preservation. Whether Africans could be found in large numbers and regardless of the relative structural importance of slavery in a given locale, Anglo-Americans continued a practice that dated back to the end of the sixteenth century: They put their trust in African allies. Normally, doing so merely meant employing them in construction projects, using them as personal servants, or deploying them in any number of other auxiliary functions. But throughout the late seventeenth century and even into the eighteenth century, Englishmen in Bermuda, Saint Christopher's, Jamaica, Barbados, and Antigua also all armed "stout Negroes, [who were] dextrous at handling a Pike" or "with good Firelocks and a good sharp Bill" during heightened periods of alarm. On the mainland, South Carolinians relied heavily on armed blacks for colonial defense. In 1672, Governor John Yeamans of South Carolina called on a small force of several dozen armed African slaves to defend his home plantation from Spanish and Indian assaults.[64] Arming Africans was clearly a matter of expediency in these cases, but it was a practice that blurred the lines between slavery and freedom and opened doors for African peoples to participate as equal members in England's colonial societies.

In the larger scheme of things, however, the willingness to arm Africans was a relatively small matter for the English during the early seventeenth century. There was little danger in arming a few Africans when Africans as a group were still only a small percentage of the overall population. But even a small number of Africans could force Englishmen to confront the challenge of transplanting English society and culture in the new world in other ways. Whether it was either appropriate or desirable to introduce African peoples to Protestant Christianity for the purpose of religious conversion was an especially tricky question. The Catholic powers and Islam had long since moved beyond this particular problem, but incipient Protestant traditions, combined with the peculiarities of English common law, mitigated against holding coreligionists as slaves. Or so some people thought. The Puritan Samuel Rishworth created quite a stir in Providence Island during the 1630s when he challenged the legality of human bondage on Christian principles and was accused by other island leaders of encouraging slaves to run away. The Providence Island Company especially condemned Rishworth for espousing the dangerous and "groundless opinion that Christians may not lawfully keep such persons in a state of servitude, *during their strangeness from Christianity.*" By the mid-seventeenth century, however, some Englishmen (typically metropolitan and church officials) had comfortably adopted the idea that Africans, free or enslaved, should be welcomed into the Christian community without impinging on the ability of Anglo-Americans to hold them as slaves. King Charles II espoused precisely this position in 1660 when he encouraged the Council of Foreign Plantations "to consider how the natives and slaves may be invited and made capable of baptism in the Christian faith." As it turned out, this was more easily said than done.[65]

Some colonial leaders attempted to follow through with the king's wishes, although the metropolitan position on the subject signaled a departure from English common law as it was understood in the colonies. It looked (suspiciously, many colonists thought) like the king, church officials, and some colonial elites were trying to get English settlers to reaffirm Spanish precedents and the customary practices of the Atlantic world. In 1663, an act appeared before the Assembly of Barbados "recommending the christening of negro children and instruction of all adult negroes." In 1667, in Virginia, the House of Burgesses avowed that the "conferring of baptisme doth not alter the condition of the person as to his bondage or Freedome," while the *Fundamental Constitutions of Carolina*, published in 1670, stipulated that religion "ought to alter nothing in any Man's Civil Estate" and therefore although Africans were free to "be of what *Church* or *Profession* any of them shall think best, . . . [n]o *Slave* shall hereby be exempted from that *Civil Dominion* his Master hath over him." A generation later, in 1696, the Jamaica Assembly similarly urged slave owners to baptize "all such as they can make sensible of a Deity and the Christian Faith."[66] Protestant ministers added their thoughts on the subject when they harangued planters about their unwillingness to spread Christianity among their slaves. John Eliot, more famous for his missionary efforts with Indians, urged slave owners in New England to "no more be guilty of such prodigious wickedness, as to deride, neglect, and oppose all due means of bringing their poor negroes unto the Lord." For many Protestants, the matter was simple. "*Bondage,*" the Anglican minister Morgan Godwyn famously, and bluntly, tried to convince planters in Virginia and Barbados, "is not *inconsistent* with *Christianity*."[67]

Seventeenth-century Englishmen were inclined to think of sub-Saharan African peoples in the Americas as slaves. That Africans were not Christians and did not come from a part of the world the English typically imagined as being inhabited by Christians made it easier to accept the idea that one particularly unfortunate group of people might even be thought of as natural slaves. Africans' distance from Christianity and their reputed idolatry did not justify slavery, but it certainly made holding them in bondage easier. Conversion to Christianity therefore roiled the waters. Regardless of what colonial officials and Protestant ministers—few of whom actually owned slaves—said, slave owners could not reconcile their cherished sense of themselves as genuine liberty-loving Englishmen with the practice of holding coreligionists in bondage. Richard Ligon, upon his arrival from England, believed that African slaves could be Christianized and continue to toil as slaves in Barbados. He was particularly taken with an African slave named Sambo who demonstrated (in Ligon's opinion) a remarkable intellect compared with other slaves on the island. When Sambo declared his intention to become a Christian, Ligon took the slave's case to his owner. The slave owner, however, informed Ligon that "the people of that Island were governed by the Lawes of *England*, and by those Lawes, we could not make a Christian a Slave." Ligon responded that it was not his intention to enslave Christians, rather he "desired . . . to make a Slave a Christian." The Barbadian sugar planter agreed that there was a difference, but continued to object on the grounds that "being once a Christian, he could no more account him a Slave, and so lose the hold they had of them as Slaves, by making them Christians; and by that means should open such a gap, as all the Planters in the Island would curse him."[68]

Where Anglo-Americans were sometimes willing to ameliorate the condition of Indian slaves, particularly when it came to their potential conversion, they were much less likely to accommodate the wishes of English officials and, sometimes, Africans themselves who sought to bridge the religious divide. Upon his arrival in Barbados in early 1655, General Isaac Birkenhead digressed from his military observations in order to make Secretary of State John Thurloe aware of a recent trial involving "a man [who] brought from other parts a certain number of Indian Christian protestants." Upon his death, and "haveing found them faithful in his life . . . he left them all freemen." But this was remarkable to Birkenhead because, as a rule, "the intollerable basenes of this island is such in that point, that they rather strive to keepe their slaves in ignorance, thereby thinking to make them hopelesse of freedom." But because the Indians managed to find "an honest man," they were set free. Typically, the newcomer observed, things went differently. "It would greeve your heart to talke with the nigor slaves in the island," Birkenhead wrote, "and especially with thos that are most ingenious, with whom I have had some discourse; and asking them, whether they know God, they sayd noe." Birkenhead could only conclude that "they are absolute atheists, worshipping nothing, being taken off their owne naturall superstitious worshipps. I asked them, why they would not be Christians? They sayd, they could get no body to teach them. I asked them, whether they were willing to learne? They said, with all their hearts, which I must confess strucke me to the heart."[69] But, despite their willingness and Birkenhead's palpable frustration, Anglo-Barbadians had little interest in pursuing the matter.

This difficulty was emblematic of the confusion that existed in a world where no one was really sure whose customs and legal traditions carried more weight—those of England or of the Atlantic world?[70] In New England and Bermuda, the two places that seemingly endorsed the prevailing customs of the Atlantic world when it came to reconciling slavery with religious conversion, colonists themselves were more eager to offer Christian instruction to African slaves and baptism to their children.[71] Just a few years after the arrival of the first African slaves in Massachusetts, "a Negro woman belonging to Rev. Stoughton of Dorchester, Massachusetts . . . was received into the Church and baptized." Considering that John Winthrop also reported that this event took place after "divers years experience," one suspects that this particular woman may have arrived from England or had been in Reverend Stoughton's employ for a longer period of time than extant records can verify. Baptisms were recorded more often in Bermuda during the 1630s and 1640s, although a 1647 legislative act outlawed the "baptizing of Bastards or Negroes children."[72] Some Englishmen attempted to encourage the baptism of African children and the conversion of Africans in every colony, but the New England colonies and Bermuda were exceptional in the extent of their efforts.

Baptism and conversion were equally contentious issues in the Chesapeake, where some Africans were able to exploit their adoption of Christianity as an avenue toward freedom. Afro-Bermudians would put the matter directly in 1669 when they petitioned for their freedom on the grounds that "the Gospel allowes noe bondmen."[73] This presumption had a powerful impact on Anglo-Americans and appeared quite early in the seventeenth century in Virginia when "John Phillip, A negro Christened in *England* 12 yeeres since," was able to assert his freedom when he visited in 1624 as a crew member on an English privateer.[74] It was even more the case with Elizabeth Key—who sued for her freedom during the 1650s, partly on the grounds that she had been baptized—and Fernando who tried the same thing and failed in the subsequent decade. Although the cases of Fernando and Elizabeth Key demonstrate "increasing intolerance," they also highlight an awareness among African slaves of a tension that existed in English colonial societies between the prevailing customs of Atlantic slavery and the English belief in their own exceptionalism. English colonists, in other words, hesitated when it came to incorporating Africans into their Protestant Christian communities not only because it raised doubts in their own minds about the legitimacy of the emerging race-based slave system, but also because they were called to task by the Africans living in their midst who tried to exploit Protestantism to achieve their liberty.[75]

Africans and Europeans alike recognized that the relationship between slavery and Christianity was more than a matter of theological confusion, it was a symbolic and visible way they could conduct a debate over the meaning of Englishness in the Americas. Yet, there were even more ways in which Anglo-Americans confronted the problem of maintaining a sense of themselves as real English men and women in an unstable and a dynamic colonial setting. Racial intermixture between people of African and European descent—"whites" and "blacks"—exposed the reality that Europeans and Africans were not so different from each other. Intimate bonds between people of different racial, ethnic, and religious backgrounds were common in the early Anglo-Atlantic world, as they had been throughout the Mediterranean beforehand. Only because it was something familiar could George Best make a specific reference to the offspring of an African man and an English woman in sixteenth-century England as part of his effort to prove that skin color was not determined by environmental factors. But if it was not especially odd to think about Europeans and Africans engaging in sexual unions, at least from an abstract perspective, the actual practice did run somewhat counter to one of the most important strains of early English colonial rhetoric: the emphasis on purity of blood.[76] When Africans and English engaged in sexual relations that produced mixed-race children, they made it very difficult for anybody to argue that there were immutable differences between people whose ancestors happened to originate in different parts of the world.[77] More immediately pressing, however, was the question of status: Would the child of someone from Africa and someone from England suffer the presumed fate of African peoples in the Atlantic world or reap the rewards of being heir to a legal culture that celebrated the rights and privileges of being "freeborn"?

Mulattos were an early visible outgrowth of overseas settlement and dramatic evidence of the willingness of many English and Africans to form intimate bonds. As a component of the emerging free black population, mulattos were disproportionately large in number. This situation was most evident early on in Bermuda where by the 1640s the second generation of Africans appeared. In 1640, Sarah Layfield, "a muletto gyrle" was among the first to appear in Bermuda records when she was admonished in an Assize for "Follish and dangerous words touching the person of the king's majesty." Because she was "but of the age of seaven or eight," however, she was discharged. If Sarah was a remarkable individual for her brashness, she was typical of the mulatto population of the 1640s in that she was young.[78] She was also common in that she was a source of problems for English magistrates. Because most of these children were the product of illicit relationships, a number of efforts to curb fornication were enacted in a fashion consistent with the common law. Yet, in most places, racial intermixture was problematic not because it was perceived as immoral or illegitimate but because it complicated property considerations. In the December 1660 assize, the Court addressed this problem when it ruled that John Davis was "permitted to marry Penelope Strange one of the Companys molatto women upon condition that every other child born of the marriage shall be the property of the Company—reserving to the said Davis the right to put in a negro child in lieu of any one of those so falling to the company." Davis was also allowed to pay for Penelope's freedom, "but in the interim he is to pay 40s per annum for her wages." This solution was not very satisfactory and Bermudian officials determined in 1664 that, to prevent "the great mischiefe & anger which otherwise is like to happen by the multyplication of malattoes," in the future "if any mallato shall be made free, such p[er]son doe within twelve months after depart the Islands."[79]

This pattern was repeated elsewhere. The potential growth of a mixed-race population was not initially viewed as a problem in and of itself. Instead, colonial officials viewed it in light of English common law and, specifically, the familiar crime of fornication. In 1630 in Virginia, when officials ordered Hugh Davis to be "soundly whipped, before an assembly of negroes and others for abusing himself to the dishonor of God and shame of Christians, by defiling his body in lying with a negro," Virginia officials were more concerned with questions related to marriage and property than they were in ensuring that Europeans and Africans would remain forever and always apart. The language of the court in this case suggests that Davis's crime may have been more opprobrious because it involved at least one African, but other courts punished English violators in much the same fashion throughout the Atlantic world.[80] Ten years later, Robert Sweat would be punished for getting "a negro woman servant belonging unto Lieutenant Sheppard" pregnant. In his case, he was ordered to do public penance while the unfortunate woman would be whipped.[81] Had they been married, as African men and English women were able to do during the seventeenth century, or had the African woman been Sweat's property, the court would not have been forced to intervene. Racial intermixture, such as it was, would be tolerated if unions were formalized and there were no complications concerning the labor obligations of the parties involved.[82] Africans, free or enslaved, would be held to English standards.

The status of mulatto children, particularly when either parent was a servant or slave, was a secondary but equally important consideration when it came to policing interracial sex. This issue had been at the heart of the case of Elizabeth Key, who was born in Virginia around 1630 as the illegitimate child of Thomas Key and an unnamed slave woman. At the age of six, she was bound out by her father to her godfather Humphrey Higginson for a nine-year term. Sometime later, however, she became the property of Colonel John Mottrom. Because of his death in 1655, Elizabeth Key had the opportunity to bring suit, as members of the Mottrom estate seemingly intended to keep her in bondage. Key won her case but not before working her way through at least three levels of Virginia justice and surviving several appeals on both sides.[83] After years of struggling with the problem of mixed-race children, Virginia officials tried to address the problem in a comprehensive fashion in 1662 when they determined that "all children borne in this country shalbe held bond or free only according to the condition of the mother." Moreover, they declared that "if any Christian shall commit fornication with a Negro man or woman, he shall pay double the fines of a former act."[84] Interracial marriages would not be banned outright in Virginia until 1691 (although other colonies began to do so earlier), but officials given the responsibility of maintaining a clear distinction between the free and enslaved moved closer to that position as part of their larger effort to determine the status of any offspring produced outside of marriage.[85]

Whether they were dealing with Christian conversion or interracial unions, Anglo-Americans were presented with new problems in the middle of the seventeenth century that forced them to think more carefully about how they could maintain control of African peoples as slaves. It had been relatively easy during the first few decades of the seventeenth century to keep Africans in bondage based solely on the fact that they had been purchased. But the line between slavery and freedom became much less clear once Africans became a larger and more visible part of colonial societies as coreligionists and even sexual partners. What it meant to be English in the Americas, in particular, became an increasingly important issue for many people as African peoples became free members of colonial societies, took up arms to defend settlements, broached the preexisting religious divide between Christians and non-Christians, and combined with European partners to produce mulatto children. English legislators would gradually enact laws in order to define slavery in the colonies (after the 1640s in the Caribbean and the 1660s on the mainland) not because they were trying to do something new but because they were forced to address a series of unanticipated problems. Slavery, in other words, was not created anew by colonial elites who were trying to construct a system that would give them absolute control over their laborers, although the ability to compel labor mattered a great deal. Slavery did not happen because Anglo-Americans were driven by racial antipathy to isolate African peoples, although many English people subscribed to an early modern version of racial ideology. African peoples were held in bondage by new, ever more rigid slave laws beginning during the second half of the seventeenth century because Englishmen in the Americas were forced by demographic and economic changes to enact a positive law to buttress what they had already been doing as a matter of custom for more than a hundred years.

* * *

It is worth revisiting here the story of Jamaica during the 1660s, for no single colony demonstrates both the constancy of English practices and the new challenges faced by Anglo-Americans during the final decades of the seventeenth century. As we saw at the outset, Anglo-Jamaicans initially embraced the African inhabitants on the island and made efforts to integrate them into English colonial society. In doing so, they were following in the footsteps of their countrymen who had tried much the same thing, in varying ways, in the Chesapeake, Bermuda, Barbados, Providence Island, and elsewhere. Working with Africans as allies had also been the order of the day for English pirates and privateers during the previous century. And, as the example of Spanish colonialism had taught them, the English found that Africans could also be useful allies in colonial defense and integral to the construction of new American societies whether they were held in slavery or granted their freedom.

But whatever the English may have tried to do in Jamaica, only a small number of Africans were inclined to accept the English as either allies or overlords. Not until early 1668 did the English begin to believe they were making progress with the Maroons, when they employed the recently pardoned "Varmahaly Negro Domingo Henriques" and two other Africans, Paul and another Domingo, "to carry a Charter of pardon and Freedom to all the Varmahaly Negroes to be enjoyed by them on their submission to his Majesties Authority."[86] A month later, the Governor and Council examined the emissary Paul when he returned to St. Jago de la Vega. Upon receiving the Governor and Council's message, Paul reported, the Varmahaly leader declared that "all of them did acknowledge themselves Subjects and Soldiers to the King of England." Subsequently, the Governor and Council ordered the English inhabitants to recognize Varmahaly rights and "to permitt the Said Varmahaly Negroes to pass and repass about their affaires in any part of this Island, . . . and on all occasions to treat and use them, as other his Majesties Loveing Subjects are treated and used."[87] As it turned out, nothing came of this effort and the Varmahalys ultimately chose to remove themselves to the more secluded northeastern section of the island. Although they were small in number, the group succeeded in frustrating the English. By 1670, Governor Thomas Modyford's Council ordered that no Englishmen should deal any longer with "ye said Traitors." They also began to encourage individuals to hunt down and destroy the "perfidious villaines," promising to reward them for their efforts.[88]

There were good reasons why initial English efforts to work with Jamaica's African inhabitants bore such small fruit. By 1670, as a result of a growing commitment to both plantation agriculture and the transatlantic slave trade, the English were increasingly dealing with Africans not as allies or trading partners but as commodities whose value rested in their labor and exchange value.[89] Prior to 1670, there had been little agreement among Anglo-American officials and colonists about how Jamaica should look. Numerous officials accepted that Jamaica's value rested primarily in its ability to foil Spanish ambitions by diminishing the ability of Spanish ships to sail into and out of the Caribbean with ease.[90] When Spain and England agreed to peace terms in 1670 with the Treaty of Madrid, however, the argument that "the true interest of England in that island" rested in plantation agriculture gained traction and fewer people were willing to condone the notion that any Africans should have the same rights and liberties as Englishmen. As long as England and Spain were at war, it seems, it was possible for Afro-Jamaicans to live in some measure of peace.[91]

English colonists initially embraced and adapted slavery to suit their needs during the pre-plantation era because it made sense at the time to keep doing what they had been doing since the mid-sixteenth century. Seventeenth-century Anglo-Americans therefore made a good-faith effort to construct their incipient "societies with slaves" in a fashion consistent with how slavery operated in other parts of the early modern Atlantic world. Although they were often critical of the Iberian world, Catholicism, and the nature of the conquest during the first half of the sixteenth century, the English rarely questioned the Spanish and Portuguese use of enslaved Africans. Beyond offering the occasional barb about Spanish cruelty toward slaves in general, the English actually found much to emulate. It would have been remarkable were it otherwise. What other examples did the English have to guide them when they thought about how to rule over non-European peoples, how to get work done, or how to generate wealth? Ireland, perhaps. But during the first half of the seventeenth century, English newcomers were heavily engaged in the difficult processes of establishing viable colonies in the New World. The Spanish and Portuguese had done this before them and were therefore largely responsible for establishing precedents, creating patterns, and developing formulas for addressing a wide array of problems.

In contrast to a few famous individuals, like Richard Ligon while he was on the coast of Africa in the 1620s, Anglo-Americans did not hesitate to buy and hold slaves whenever they had the chance. Although the separate colonies had different characteristics, Anglo-Americans everywhere held Africans in slavery even in the absence of a legal structure to buttress their actions. What they did have were the customary practices of the Atlantic world—patterns of behavior, traditions, and laws that enabled Europeans to dominate Africans and Indians alike even as they created space for non-Europeans to improve their condition over time. When Anglo-Americans began taking possession of enslaved Africans in their own colonies, they did so in a fashion that resembled the way things operated in the Spanish American colonies they had been frequenting and reading about for more than a half century. Englishmen accepted slavery and quickly came to believe that Africans were valuable commodities in and of themselves and slavery was the best way to achieve economic prosperity and independence in the new world. Whether they thought about African peoples in derogatory terms—and clearly many Englishmen did—was largely irrelevant. Africans had been taken or purchased, transported long distances, and put to work for generations (as were many other people throughout the world) and very few Englishmen seem to have cared much at all. Rigid social, legal, and cultural barriers would eventually be constructed to fortify the mature Anglo-American slave system. In the meantime, there were compelling reasons for the earliest generation of English settlers to follow the lead of those who came before them and to exploit the Africans in their midst as slaves.

Conclusion

By the dawn of the eighteenth century, race-based plantation slavery would be one of the defining characteristics of the English Empire in the Americas. By that time, tens of thousands of enslaved Africans would be imported into the English colonies, bound into a state of perpetual slavery by labor-starved planters, and compelled to work under threat of physical violence. Anglo-American legislators passed new laws in all of the colonies between 1661 and 1705 to enhance their ability to control this growing population in order to maximize productivity and guarantee security. Indentured servitude would continue to be an important institution in the Americas, but slavery gradually replaced it during these years as the definitive labor system in the plantation colonies. Indian slavery would also continue to be important, especially in the southeastern region of North America, but Indian slaves were much less likely to be viewed as a distinctive—or redeemable—cohort by the English as indigenous peoples increasingly came to be seen as an impediment to colonial expansion and potentially useful workers. By the early eighteenth century, Indian and African slaves alike were valued for their ability to produce cash crops for English markets. This kind of slavery, which served as the primary engine of economic production and an all-encompassing mechanism for social control in the Anglo-Atlantic world, was born during the last half of the seventeenth century.[1]

There is considerable merit in beginning the story of slavery in the English colonies with the demographic, economic, and legal transformations that took place during the late seventeenth century. Slavery is certainly much easier to characterize once the institution began to assume some structural coherence and Africans started appearing in larger numbers. But if we focus our gaze too narrowly on the period after 1660—or 1619, for that matter—we might mistakenly assume that slavery was unimportant before it manifested itself in familiar fashion.[2] As we have seen, what early modern English observers considered worth characterizing as slavery varied greatly between the mid-sixteenth and mid-seventeenth centuries. Sometimes they accepted slavery as natural or even desirable, even as they were often critical of it under certain circumstances. How the English encountered slavery and whether they were its likely victims or potential beneficiaries played an important role in the construction of increasingly well-defined English ideas about the proper place for slavery in the emerging Atlantic world. Few people bothered to challenge the propriety of human bondage, but what they may have thought about it in specific terms depended a great deal on what they thought slavery meant. And that was no simple thing.

This book began with a few stories to set the stage, so perhaps a couple more would be appropriate to wind things up. Consider, first, the observations of Fynes Moryson, who traveled throughout Europe and famously published the first volume of his itinerant travels in 1617.[3] Moryson was most well-known in his own time for his observations on Ireland, where he had served as part of the English force tasked with putting down Tyrone's Rebellion, but he wrote even more about Europe and the Mediterranean world. In so doing, he made frequent and predictably commonplace references to slavery. Writing about Poland, for example, Moryson noted without any sense of injustice or sympathy that many of the people are "meere slaves, (as in Bohemia) the Lord having power over their bodyes and goods, and over their Children to make them servants in their household." At the same time, when writing about Naples, Moryson struck a slightly different tone when he observed that "[m]ore miserable men cannot be found than those who are condemned to Rowe chayned in the Gallyes." Slavery in this instance was certainly lamentable, but it was hardly unfamiliar: Galley slaves were men who "for Capitall Crimes are condemned to this slaverye for life" while "others guilty of lesse Crimes are condemned to this service for certayne years, and some are so foolish as to sell their liberty for mony."[4] Fellow Englishmen had been saying much the same thing for more than fifty years by this time.

In a third instance, however, Fynes Moryson was absolute in his condemnation of slavery. "Nothing can be imagined more miserable," he wrote, "then a Towne taken by the Turkes" because they not only would lay waste to everything before them but also would not "spare the life of any whose age or lamenes makes him worth litle mony to be sold for a slave." Those who were not put to death were even "more miserable" because they were "reserved as slaves for base service and filthy Lusts." The fate of the enslaved was deplorable: "The faire women and boyes suffer fowle prostitutions, the strong men are used to grinde in mills, to beare heavy burthens and to doe all base and laborious woorkes." Slavery, in this telling, was horrifying, involving as it did being "bound one to another in Chaynes," the sick being forced "with whips to march as fast as the rest, or els cutt their throates if they be not able to goe," and the "women and boyes so prostituted to lust, as their miserable outcryes yield a wofull sound to all that are neere them."[5] This iteration of slavery was the one, Moryson no doubt knew, that would frighten his English readers because it was precisely how they imagined things might go for anyone whose misfortune led them into a state of bondage in the Mediterranean world. Considering the content of English slave narratives published during the early modern era, it would have been nearly impossible to imagine otherwise.

But think, too, about another Englishman. Thomas Gage, who lived in Mexico and Guatemala between 1625 and 1637, also had a great deal to say on the subject of slavery. Gage was born in England in 1603, joined the Jesuit order as a young man, and traveled to the New World, returning to England and the Puritan fold during the 1640s. As part of his retrospective condemnation of the Catholic Church and Spain, Gage published *The English-American, or A New Survey of the West India's* soon after his conversion. A few other full-length works about New Spain had been translated into English before Gage, but his was the first significant treatment authored by an Englishman to appear in print. In it, Gage sought to encourage further English colonization by emphasizing what the Spanish had wrought in the Americas. An important part of this program was to demonstrate to English audiences that Indians and Africans had been exploited by both the Catholic Church and the land-owning elite. Because they suffered from Spanish cruelty, Gage argued, the native inhabitants and other oppressed peoples of the region would be waiting for the English as liberators. In this highly polemical piece, then, Gage shed considerable light on the role of Africans in a New World society.[6]

According to Gage, the most basic fact of life for Africans and their descendants in Mexico and Guatemala was slavery. Gage never bemoaned the existence of slavery. For him, it was a simple and obvious fact that slavery existed and that some people were bound to serve others. Indeed, the casualness of his depiction of slavery suggests a level of disinterestedness. Near Tlaxcala, Mexico, Gage marveled at the wheat and sugar farms and took special note of one in particular (owned by the Dominicans) that "maintained in my time above two hundred blackamoor slaves, men and women, besides their little children." Gentlemen "have their train of blackamoor slaves . . . waiting on them, in brave and gallant liveries." The merchants on the island of Margarita (Pearl Island) "have thirty, forty, or fifty blackamoor slaves only to fish pearls out of the sea about the rocks." In another passage, Gage confirmed that the ability to own slaves was a sign of status and wealth when he told the story of Sebastián de Zavalata, who had been born into poverty in Spain but made his fortune in sugar and rose to possess "at least threescore slaves of his own for the work of his farm." As Gage's narrative revealed, African slaves were both a form of wealth and a necessity for the maintenance of that wealth through the production of goods.[7]

Despite the significance of slavery in Mexico and Guatemala, Gage characterized social relations among the Spanish and Africans as relatively fluid. At one level, this meant that free Africans and mulattoes could be found everywhere. Many were peasants or laborers, like the "company of poor and ordinary people most of them mestizoes, and mulattoes, who live in thatched houses" along the Río de la Vacas in Guatemala. Others, however, were quite remarkable. At a place Gage referred to as El Agua Caliente, there lived "a Blackamoor in an *estancia* of his own, who is held to be very rich, and gives good entertainment to the travellers that pass that way." This individual was thought to be so exceptional that it was rumored that his wealth did not "increase from his farm and cheeses, but from this hidden treasure, which credibly is reported to be known unto him." Because this man had once been a slave, local officials had even questioned him about his wealth, but he replied that "when he was young and a slave, he had a good master, who let him get for himself what he could" and "God hath since given [him] a blessing with a greater increase of stock." At another juncture of his narrative, Gage remarked positively on the mulatto captain of a ship, whose experience emphasized the larger purpose of the publication. The mulatto was a native of Cuba who, in his youth, ran away from his native Havana and threw himself on the mercy of some Dutch ships he found off shore. According to Gage, he promised to "serve them faithfully against his own nation, which had most injuriously and wrongfully abused, yea, whipped him." His skill as a seaman so impressed the Dutch that they eventually made him a captain.[8]

Taken together, the musings of these two Englishmen during the first half of the seventeenth century reveal considerable appreciation for the vagaries and subtleties of early modern slavery. Early modern Englishmen knew a great deal about slavery, were curious about its different manifestations, and were able to characterize it with considerable nuance. Their own domestic history had taught them much about human bondage. They gained considerable knowledge about the subject from textual sources, but firsthand experience revealed even more. The English knew that slavery could be an institution, a condition, an idea, or even a labor system. It could be permanent or impermanent, harsh or benign, geared toward punishment or improvement, concerned with ensuring the social order or fulfilling labor demands. It could even just be about sex. Somebody might become a slave because they were born to it, but it was more likely the result of a crime, warfare, piracy, kidnapping, or simple bad luck. Slavery could be central to the social organization of a given society or it could be incidental. Whatever the specific circumstances may have been, whatever its key characteristics were, though, Englishmen were clearly fascinated by it. As the inhabitants of a nation that generally set itself in opposition to slavery and that claimed to be distinctive by virtue of its commitment to personal liberty, the varieties of slavery throughout the world only strengthened the English in the resolve that they were a truly exceptional people.

But the English participated in slavery more than they would have liked to admit. It was common knowledge that many unfortunate Englishmen had fallen victim to captivity and slavery in the Mediterranean and Atlantic worlds. The plight of English slaves became part of the social and cultural landscape during the late sixteenth century and the driving force behind economic, diplomatic, and military endeavors. Less discussed were the activities of individual Englishmen who themselves bought and sold slaves. The English were less likely than others to hold their enemies in slavery and did not have the ability to transport large numbers of enslaved Africans throughout the Atlantic world, but that was not for lack of effort. Would-be English slavers also seem to have bought into the idea that one group of people in particular—Africans—could be exploited. Slavery had traditionally been thought of as the unfortunate plight of individuals who had done something specific and therefore suffered in bondage as punishment for their own actions. By the late sixteenth century, however, Europeans worried less about justifying slavery in the Americas and were increasingly likely to seek out Africans simply because they needed laborers. The English, although they might express reservations about the practice of "making slaves" and sometimes cooperated with African peoples in the Atlantic world, proved to be equally willing to exploit African slaves for material gain.

England's domestic background and global experiences combined to shape the way slavery was imagined and implemented in the American colonies. Early Anglo-Americans did not stop thinking about the meaning of slavery and whether it might be implemented once they established their own settlements in the Americas. What many English men and women knew about slavery provided disgruntled servants and other colonists with a powerful vocabulary to complain about their unjust treatment and the abuses of colonial authorities. Former servants were able to make a compelling argument that indentured servitude often had more in common with the way slavery operated in the Atlantic world than with apprenticeships or English labor contracts. Anglo-American concerns about slavery were grounded in the assumption that *if* an English man or woman were to be a slave, there needed to be a reason. The understanding that slavery was purposeful, punitive, and potentially even rehabilitative not only underlay how slavery could be applied to English subjects but also was at the heart of early Indian slavery. Because English colonial promoters argued that the English were not callous invaders and Indian societies needed to be treated as legitimate polities, they were obligated to rationalize Indian slavery just as slavery had traditionally been understood in European society and culture.

Africans were viewed differently and the enslavement of African peoples, often for no other reason than to generate revenue, was a characteristic feature of the early modern Atlantic world that most English colonists were eager to embrace. Englishmen encountered Africans in Africa as members of identifiable communities with territorial and political integrity. The Africans they met in the Americas, however, appeared to be rootless and moveable. They could be exploited because they had nobody to protect them. So despite the absence of a positive law of slavery and a routinized transatlantic slave trade, English colonists took advantage of every opportunity that came their way to buy and hold African peoples in a state of perpetual slavery. They might have allowed some Africans the opportunity to try to bridge the divide between slavery and freedom, based largely on how they understood the system to operate in other parts of the Atlantic world, but that did not mean they had doubts about slavery. As long as the number of enslaved Africans was relatively small and as long as the English could get away with it, Anglo-Americans let slavery operate according to the conventions of the Atlantic world. In doing so, they laid the groundwork for the expansion of the race-based, plantation labor system that would eventually triumph throughout much of the Anglo-Atlantic world.

In 1664, Anglo-Jamaican lawmakers would observe that they lacked a "guide by where to walke" on the question of slavery. Based on the experiences of countless English men and women at home and abroad for more than a century, this assertion should be taken with a grain of salt. If anything, there were too many guides. Early modern Englishmen liked to tell themselves that they did not know much about slavery because it was something that was foreign to them. They prided themselves on the idea that slavery was antithetical to Englishness. But slavery pervaded the early modern English world, influenced the way the English thought about society and culture, colored their encounters with non-English peoples across the globe, and increasingly factored into how they imagined they might themselves benefit from a more active engagement in the Atlantic world. Anglo-Jamaicans might have argued in 1664 that English common law provided no help on the subject of slavery, but they had plenty of touchstones, precedents, examples, and experiences to invoke. How else would they have learned that "the right rule of reason & ord[er]" necessitated that they needed to protect "Negroes" from the "arbitrary cruell and outrageous will of every evill disposed p[er]son"? Their solution in this instance was much the same as the one already reached in Barbados and one that would soon be enacted in other colonies—African slaves would be protected "as wee doe mens other goods & chattels."[9] The law of slavery, in this formulation, could even be imagined as something that would be good for slaves. But the English were really only protecting themselves and thereby ensuring their ability to continue doing what other Englishmen had already been doing for the better part of a hundred years.

NOTES

INTRODUCTION

1. John Rolfe to Sir Edwyn Sandys, January 1619/20, cited in Engel Sluiter, "New Light on the '20. and Odd Negroes' Arriving in Virginia, August 1619," *William and Mary Quarterly* 54:2 (April 1997): 395. This event (and those that follow) will be discussed in greater detail elsewhere.

2. The details of this story appear in a number of sources, but see Richard S. Dunn, James Savage, and Laetitia Yeandle, eds., *The Journal of John Winthrop, 1630–1649* (Cambridge, MA: Belknap Press, 1996), 237; Almon Wheeler Lauber, *Indian Slavery in Colonial Times within the Present Limits of the United States* (New York: Columbia University Press, 1913), 122–25; and Alison Games, "'The Sanctuarye of our rebell negroes': The Atlantic Context of Local Resistance on Providence Island," *Slavery & Abolition* 19:3 (December 1998): 7.

3. Thomas Burton, *Parliamentary Diary, 1656–1659*, 4 vols. (London, 1828), 4:255, 260–62, 268.

4. Ira Berlin, *Many Thousands Gone: The First Two Centuries of Slavery in North America* (Cambridge, MA: Belknap Press, 1998), 32.

5. In addition to Berlin, *Many Thousands Gone*, see T. H. Breen and Stephen Inness, *"Myne Owne Ground": Race and Freedom on Virginia's Eastern Shore, 1640–1676* (New York: Oxford University Press, 1980), and Linda M. Heywood and John K. Thornton, *Central Africans, Atlantic Creoles, and the Foundation of the Americas, 1585–1660* (New York: Cambridge University Press, 2007).

6. The image of the African and the meaning of blackness in early modern England have often been directed toward understanding the articulation of British identity. See, esp., Kim F. Hall, *Things of Darkness: Economies of Race and Gender in Early Modern England* (Ithaca, NY: Cornell University Press, 1995), and Alden T. Vaughan and Virginia Mason Vaughan, "Before *Othello*: Elizabethan Representations of Sub-Saharan Africans," *William and Mary Quarterly* 54:1 (January 1997): 45–64. More recently, see Ania Loomba and Jonathan Burton, eds., *Race in Early Modern England: A Documentary Companion* (New York: Palgrave Macmillan, 2007); Imtiaz Habib, *Black Lives in the English Archives, 1500–1677: Imprints of the Invisible* (Burlington, VT: Ashgate, 2008); and Catherine Molineaux, *Faces of Perfect Ebony: Encountering Atlantic Slavery in Imperial Britain* (Cambridge, MA: Harvard University Press, 2012).

7. Some of the more important works produced in just the last decade include Juliana Barr, "From Captives to Slaves: Commodifying Indian Women in the Borderlands," *Journal of American History* 92:1 (June 2005): 19–46; James F. Brooks, *Captives & Cousins: Slavery, Kinship, and Community in the Southwest Borderlands* (Chapel Hill: University of North Carolina Press, 2002); Alan Gallay, *The Indian Slave Trade: The Rise of the English Empire in the American South, 1670–1717* (New Haven, CT: Yale University Press, 2002); Alan Gallay, ed., *Indian Slavery in Colonial*

America (Lincoln: University of Nebraska, 2009); Brett Rushforth, " 'A Little Flesh We Offer You': The Origins of Indian Slavery in New France," *William and Mary Quarterly* 60:4 (October 2003): 777–808; and Rushforth, *Bonds of Alliance: Indigenous and Atlantic Slaveries in New France* (Chapel Hill: University of North Carolina Press, 2012).

8. Certainly this notion of the justice of enslavement that followed from legitimate warfare was essential to Emanuel Downing's determination in the 1640s that captured Narragansetts could also be taken to the West Indies and sold as slaves. See George H. Moore, *Notes on the History of Slavery in Massachusetts* (New York, 1866), 10; Lorenzo Johnston Greene, *The Negro in Colonial New England* (New York: Atheneum, 1942), 60–61; and Winthrop D. Jordan, *White over Black: American Attitudes toward the Negro, 1550–1812* (Chapel Hill: University of North Carolina Press, 1968), 68–69.

9. Betty Wood, *The Origins of American Slavery: Freedom and Bondage in the English Colonies* (New York: Hill & Wang, 1997), 20–39. More precisely, see Edmund Morgan's argument that "it was easy for Virginians to extend to blacks some of the bad feelings they harbored toward Indians" in the 1680s. According to this logic, Indians and Africans were both "seen as slaves," as "outlanders," and it was therefore natural "for their owners . . . to lump them together in a lowest common denominator of racist hatred and contempt." Morgan, *American Slavery, American Freedom: The Ordeal of Colonial Virginia* (New York: W. W. Norton, 1975), 330. Morgan's view of slavery follows from David Brion Davis, *The Problem of Slavery in Western Culture* (Ithaca, NY: Cornell University Press, 1966). According to Davis, "In spite of a widespread tendency to differentiate the Negro from the Indian and to associate the latter with the freedom of nature, Negro slavery was actually imposed on top of a pre-existing Indian slavery; in North America, at least, the two never developed as distinct institutions" (176).

10. Hilary McD. Beckles, *White Servitude and Black Slavery, 1627–1715* (Knoxville: University of Tennessee Press, 1989); Don Jordan and Michael Walsh, *White Cargo: The Forgotten History of Britain's White Slaves in America* (New York: New York University Press, 2007); and John Donoghue, " 'Out of the Land of Bondage': The English Revolution and the Atlantic Origins of Abolition," *American Historical Review* 115:4 (October 2010): 943–74.

11. Carla Gardina Pestana, *The English Atlantic in an Age of Revolution, 1640–1661* (Cambridge, MA: Harvard University Press, 2004), esp. 205–12. A similar perspective can be found in Abbot Emerson Smith, *Colonists in Bondage: White Servitude and Convict Labor in America, 1607–1776* (Chapel Hill: University of North Carolina Press, 1947), 159–61. Another more textured treatment appears in Susan Dwyer Amussen, *Caribbean Exchanges: Slavery and the Transformation of English Society, 1640–1700* (Chapel Hill: University of North Carolina Press, 2007), 126–29.

12. See, for example, David Eltis, *The Rise of African Slavery in the Americas* (Cambridge: Cambridge University Press, 2000), 51–52; Russell R. Menard, *Sweet Negotiations: Sugar, Slavery, and Plantation Agriculture in Early Barbados* (Charlottesville: University of Virginia Press, 2006), 29–48; and Robert J. Steinfeld, *The Invention of Free Labor: The Employment Relation in English & American Law and Culture, 1350–1870* (Chapel Hill: University of North Carolina Press, 1991), 44–54.

13. Jordan, *White over Black*, viii.

14. A glance at several recent titles reveals the continuing tendency to enshrine "1619." For example, Peter Kolchin, *American Slavery, 1619–1877* (New York: Hill and Wang, 1993); Thomas D. Morris, *Southern Slavery and the Law, 1619–1860* (Chapel Hill: University of North Carolina Press, 1996); John B. Boles, *Black Southerners, 1619–1869* (Lexington: University of Kentucky Press, 1983); and Nell Irvin Painter, *Creating Black Americans: African-American History and Its Meanings, 1619 to the Present* (New York: Oxford University Press, 2007).

15. These concepts are usually attributed to the influential work of Moses Finley, especially his *Ancient Slavery and Modern Ideology* (New York: Viking, 1980). More recently, they have been popularized by Berlin, *Many Thousands Gone*, esp. 7–14.

CHAPTER 1

1. Thomas Massinger, *The Bondman* (1624), Act 1, scene 3.

2. The complications faced by the English in this period are familiar, but see D. M. Palliser, *The Age of Elizabeth: England under the Later Tudors, 1547–1603*, 2nd ed. (London: Longman, 1992), 15–34; Lisa Ferraro Parmalee, "Printers, Patrons, Readers, and Spies: Importation of French Propaganda in Late Elizabethan England," *Sixteenth Century Journal* 25:4 (1994): 853–72; Nicholas Canny, *Making Ireland British, 1580–1650* (New York: Oxford University Press, 2001), 121–64; and Simon Adams, "Elizabeth I and the Sovereignty of the Netherlands, 1576–1585," *Transactions of the Royal Historical Society* 14 (2004): 309–19. The best source on Walsingham continues to be Conyers Read, *Mr. Secretary Walsingham and the Policy of Queen Elizabeth*, 3 vols. (Oxford: Clarendon Press, 1925).

3. Richard Hakluyt, *Divers Voyages Touching the Discovery of America* (London, 1582). Significantly, Hakluyt's first major publication was dedicated to Sir Philip Sidney, Walsingham's son-in-law. On the range of Hakluyt's career and interests, see David B. Quinn, ed., *The Hakluyt Handbook*, 2 vols. (London: Hakluyt Society, 1974). For more specific treatment of these issues, see Richard Helgerson, *Forms of Nationhood: The Elizabethan Writing of England* (Chicago: University of Chicago Press, 1992), esp. 151–91, and Peter C. Mancall, *Hakluyt's Promise: An Elizabethan's Obsession for an English America* (New Haven, CT: Yale University Press, 2007), esp. 102–27. For a slightly different view, see Mary C. Fuller, "Writing the Long-Distance Voyage: Hakluyt's Circumnavigators," *Huntington Library Quarterly* 70:1 (2007): 37–60, and "Richard Hakluyt's Foreign Relations," in *Travel Writing, Form, and Empire: The Poetics and Politics of Mobility*, ed. Julia Kuehn and Paul Smethurst (New York: Routledge, 2009), 38–52.

4. Eden and Willes will be discussed more fully in other places. On the Tudor polymath John Dee, see Charlotte Artese, "King Arthur in America: Making Space in History for *The Faerie Queene* and John Dee's *Brytanici Imperii Limites*," *Journal of Medieval and Early Modern Studies* 33:1 (2003): 125–41, and Glyn Parry, "John Dee and the Elizabethan British Empire in its European Context," *Historical Journal* 49:3 (2006): 643–75. On Sidney, see Roger Kuin, "Querre-Mahau: Sir Philip Sidney and the New World," *Renaissance Quarterly* 51:2 (Summer 1998): 549–85.

5. Richard Hakluyt, *A Discourse of Western Planting*, ed. David B. Quinn and Alison M. Quinn (London: Hakluyt Society, 1993), quotations taken from 60, 40, 119, and 52. Hakluyt included in his manuscript a lengthy Latin excerpt drawn from a largely unrelated work by Johannes Metellus Sequanus [Jean Matal] concerning Emmanuel the Fortunate, in which the author castigates the Spanish, in particular, for the cruelty they exercised toward their slaves, regardless of national origin or even gender. For an English translation by Neil M. Cheshire, see pp. 163–64.

6. William S. Maltby, *The Black Legend in England: The Development of Anti-Spanish Sentiment, 1558–1660* (Durham, NC: Duke University Press, 1971).

7. All biblical citations taken from *The Geneva Bible: A Facsimile of the 1560 Edition* (Madison: University of Wisconsin Press, 1969). The Geneva Bible of 1560 was inexpensive and widely available. Between 1560 and the publication of the Authorized Version in 1611, it went through sixty editions. Palliser, *The Age of Elizabeth*, 387. See also Alister E. McGrath, *In the Beginning: The Story of the King James Bible and How It Changed a Nation, a Language, and a Culture* (New York: Doubleday, 2001),

and David Brion Davis, *Inhuman Bondage: The Rise and Fall of Slavery in the New World* (New York: Oxford University Press, 2006), esp. 95 and 353 n. 43.

8. The translators of the Geneva Bible invariably use the words "servant," "servitude," and "bondage," though the context and marginal notations leave little room for doubt when they mean "slavery." Leviticus 25:42, for example, reads: "For they are my servants, whome I broght out of the land of Egypt: they shal not be sold as bonde men are solde." The marginal notation for this passage reads: "Unto perpetual servitude." Likewise, a marginal note to Leviticus 25:46 notes: "For thei shal not be boght out at the Jubile."

9. David Brion Davis, *The Problem of Slavery in Western Culture* (Ithaca, NY: Cornell University Press, 1966), 63–66.

10. St. Augustine, Bishop of Hippo, *Of the Citie of God* (London, 1610), 772–73 [Book 19, Chapter 15]. On St. Augustine, see Peter Garnsey, *Ideas of Slavery from Aristotle to Augustine* (Cambridge: Cambridge University Press, 1996), 206–19, and Stephen Jablonski, "Ham's Vicious Race: Slavery and John Milton," *Studies in English Literature, 1500–1900* 37:1 (Winter 1997): 173–90. Jablonski points out that Augustine neither linked slavery with deficiency of reason nor identified any particular group of people as more appropriate for slavery than others and therefore lacked a conception of natural slavery. Augustine's conception, however, certainly admits slavery as a natural pattern and consequence of a fallen world. Slavery was, in essence, a natural condition in an unnatural world.

11. For a good introduction to the literature on this subject (which typically delves into the question of "race" in addition to slavery), see William McKee Evans, "From the Land of Canaan to the Land of Guinea: The Strange Odyssey of the 'Sons of Ham'," *American Historical Review* 85:1 (February 1980): 15–43; Benjamin Braude, "The Sons of Noah and the Construction of Ethnic and Geographical Identities in the Medieval and Early Modern Periods," *William and Mary Quarterly* 54:1 (January 1997): 103–43; Jonathan Schorsch, *Jews and Blacks in the Early Modern World* (Cambridge: Cambridge University Press, 2004), esp. 135–65; and David M. Goldenberg, *The Curse of Ham: Race and Slavery in Early Judaism, Christianity, and Islam* (Princeton, NJ: Princeton University Press, 2003).

12. See, for example, Dominic Baker-Smith, "Who Went to Thomas More's Lectures on St. Augustine's *De Civitate Dei?*" *Church History & Religious Culture* 87:2 (April 2007): 145–60, and Robert Dodare and Michael C. Questier, "Strategies in Jacobean Polemic: The Use and Abuse of St. Augustine in English Theological Controversy," *Journal of Ecclesiastical History* 44:3 (July 1993): 432–49.

13. Aristotle, *The Politics*, trans. T. A. Sinclair (Middlesex: Penguin Books, 1981), 66–69; Davis, *The Problem of Slavery in Western Culture*, 69–72, and Peter Garnsey, *Ideas of Slavery*, 23–52. Perhaps Aristotle's notion that slaves might be readily identifiable by their physical characteristics alarmed some Englishmen who, in the traditional European mode of human description, were often described by their contemporaries as "tall of stature, strong of body" or "blockish, uncivil, fierce, and warlike." According to William Harrison, "[F]or that we dwell northward, we are commonly taken by the foreign historiographers to be men of great strength and little policy, much courage and small shrift." Harrison, *The Description of England: The Classic Contemporary Account of Tudor Social Life*, ed. Georges Edelen (New York: Dover Publications, 1994). This point will be examined in greater detail below.

14. See, for example, Thomas Cranmer, "An Exhortation to Obedience," in *Certain Sermons, or homelies, apoynted by the kinges Majestie, to be declared and read, by all Persones, Vicars, or Curates, every Sondaie in their Churches, where thei have cure* (London, 1551), and *An Homelie Against Disobedience and wylfull rebellion* (London, 1570).

15. St. Thomas Aquinas, *Summa Theologica*, pt. 1, question 96. See also John B. Killoran, "Aquinas and Vitoria: Two Perspectives on Slavery," in *The Medieval Tradition of Natural Law*, ed. Harold J. Johnson (Kalamazoo: Western Michigan University, 1987), 87–101. Davis, *The Problem of Slavery in Western Culture*, 93–97, and Jablonski, "Ham's Vicious Race," 183.

16. See, for example, the sample curriculums in David Cressy, *Education in Tudor and Stuart England* (New York: St. Martin's Press, 1975), 80–85. On Cicero's ideas about slavery, see Garnsey, *Ideas of Slavery*, 38–43.

17. *The Romane Historie Written by T. Livius of Padua*, trans. Philemon Holland (London, 1600); Cornelius Tacitus, *The Description of Germanie: and Customes of the People*, trans. Richard Greneway, and *The Agricola*, trans. Henry Savile (London, 1598).

18. *The Digest of Justinian*, 1:2 (bk. 1, pt. 1, no. 4); Henri de Bracton, *On the Lawes and Customes of England*, 4 vols., trans. Samuel E. Thorne, ed. George E. Woodbine (Cambridge, MA: Harvard University Press, 1968), 2:29–30. As Quentin Skinner has argued, classical Roman writers and, especially, the *Digest* of Roman law, were central to the developing "neo-Roman" discourse of slavery in early Stuart England. Skinner, *Liberty before Liberalism* (Cambridge: Cambridge University Press, 1998), 36–57. The "neo-Roman" influence on Tudor and early Stuart political culture is also emphasized in David Armitage, *The Ideological Origins of the British Empire* (Cambridge: Cambridge University Press, 2000). Alan Watson, however, makes the salient point that slavery was essentially an abstract issue for jurists, who tended to emphasize its more benign aspects. Watson, "Seventeenth-Century Jurists, Roman Law, and the Law of Slavery," *Chicago-Kent Law Review* 68 (1993): 1343–54.

19. *The Digest of Justinian*, 4 vols., Latin text ed. Theodor Mommsen, English translation ed. by Alan Watson (Philadelphia: University of Pennsylvania Press, 1985), 1:2 (bk. 1, pt. 1, no. 4). It is interesting, in this context, that the first definition provided for "freedom" in the *Oxford English Dictionary* is "exemption or release from slavery or imprisonment."

20. From another perspective "freedom" was something much more closely connected to the traditional world and has, over time, been diminished by the imposition of the state and statute law. Here, the issue is that of civil rather than personal liberty. On the slippery meaning of words like "freedom" and "liberty" in early modern England, see Christopher Hill, *Liberty against the Law: Some Seventeenth-Century Controversies* (London: Penguin Press, 1996), 242–51.

21. Jean Bodin, *The Six Bookes of a Commonweale*, ed. Kenneth Douglas McRae (Cambridge, MA: Harvard University Press, 1962), 33–34. On Bodin's influence in England, see Leonard F. Dean, "Bodin's Methodus in England before 1635," *Studies in Philology* 39:2 (April 1942): 160–66.

22. Thomas More, *A fruteful pleasaunt, & wittie work, of the best state of a publique weale, and of the newe yle, called Utopia*, trans. Raphe Robynson (London, 1556), 74v–75r [L2v–L3r]. Thomas More's *Utopia* will be treated in greater depth below.

23. G. J. R. Parry, "William Harrison and Holinshed's Chronicles," *Historical Journal* 27:4 (1984): 789–810. Holinshed's *Chronicles* were the realization of a collaborative enterprise, initially coordinated by the London printer Reginald Wolfe, to produce a "Universal cosmographie" (789).

24. Raphael Holinshed, *The First and Second Volumes of Chronicles* (London, 1587), 5–8. Holinshed's *Chronicles* were originally published in 1577. For broader context, see Annabel Patterson, *Reading Holinshed's* Chronicles (Chicago: University of Chicago Press, 1994).

25. On Tudor history writing and the debates about the origins of the English people, see F. J. Levy, *Tudor Historical Thought* (San Marino, CA: Huntington Library, 1967); May McKisack, *Medieval History in the Tudor Age* (Oxford: Clarendon Press, 1971); and Richard Helgerson, *Forms of Nationhood: The Elizabethan Writing of England* (Chicago: University of Chicago Press, 1992). As

Andrew Escobedo puts the problem, however, "[a]s the urgency for national unity deepened during the sixteenth century, the anxiety about heterogeneity in England's past increased"; some Englishmen were torn "between the etiological impulse to remember the past and the suspicion that the national present may require certain aspects of this past to be forgotten." Escobedo, *Nationalism and Historical Loss in Renaissance England: Foxe, Dee, Spenser, Milton* (Ithaca, NY: Cornell University Press, 2005), 4–5.

26. John Bale, *The Epistel Exhortatory* (1544), cited in Andrew Hadfield, *Politics and National Identity: Reformation to Renaissance* (Cambridge: Cambridge University Press, 1994), 61, and John Aylmer, *An Harborowe for Faithfull and Trewe Subjectes*, in *British Pamphleteers*, ed. George Orwell and Reginald Reynolds (London: A. Wingate, 1948), 32.

27. *Tudor Royal Proclamations* [hereafter *TRP*], 3 vols., ed. Paul L. Hughes and James F. Larkin (New Haven, CT: Yale University Press, 1964–69), 3:13–17. Predictably, the rhetoric of political slavery would prove to be an especially powerful device for a whole catalog of disparate grievances during the years of the English Civil War, when evocatively titled works such as *England's Lamentable Slaverie* (1645) and *Liberty Vindicated against Slavery* (1646), were published. On the use and meaning of the rhetoric of liberty and slavery in this period, see Rachel Foxley, "John Lilburne and the Citizenship of Free-born Englishmen," *Historical Journal* 47:4 (2004): 849–74; Hugh Jenkins, "Shrugging Off the Norman Yoke: Milton's *History of Britain* and the Levellers," *English Literary Renaissance* 29:2 (1999): 306–25; and Quentin Skinner, "John Milton and the Politics of Slavery," *Prose Studies* 23:1 (2000): 1–22.

28. Geoffrey of Monmouth, *The History of the Kings of Britain*, trans. Lewis Thorpe (London: Penguin Books, 1966), 55–56, and Michael Drayton, *Poly-Olbion*, vol. 4 of *The Works of Michael Drayton*, ed. J. William Hebel (Oxford: B. Blackwell, 1933), 10. Drayton's work first appeared in 1612, but the first complete edition did not appear until 1619.

29. Geoffrey of Monmouth, *History*, 107–8, 117. Geoffrey also recounted that after the Britons repelled the Roman forces the first time, Caesar returned to Gaul where he had to soothe further opposition in order to avoid fighting a war on two fronts. To this end, Geoffrey noted, "[H]e even went so far as to promise liberation to the slaves" (111). This tactic would be common well into the modern era. William Camden's choreographical history of Britain included a number of epigrams, several of which were concerned with the Roman conquest, such as "Britain that hath a wintry clime alotted for her seat, / Where cold North-Beare shines alway bright with stars that never set / Even at thy sight and first approach o[f] Caesar soone subdu'd, / Submitted hath her necke to beare strange yoke of servitude." Camden, *Remaines Concerning Britain* (London, 1870), 47.

30. Geoffrey of Monmouth, *History*, 233, 248–49.

31. Camden, *Britain*, 12; William Lambarde, *A Perambulation of Kent: Conteining the Description, Hystorie, and Customes of that Shire* (1570; reprinted, 1970), 7, 323. Christopher Hill's reconsideration of his own failure to appreciate the significance of the "Norman yoke" is indicative of the escalating attention being granted to the theme of anti-bondage in Tudor–Stuart political culture. See Hill, *Intellectual Origins of the English Revolution Revisited* (Oxford: Clarendon Press, 1997), ch. 17: "The Norman Yoke," 361–65. The patriotic assertion of natural liberties and a political culture shaped by an anti-slavery framework was not unique to the British. See, for an example from a later era, Sue Peabody, *"There are no slaves in France": The Political Culture of Race and Slavery in the Ancien Régime* (New York: Oxford University Press, 1996).

32. Drayton, *Poly-Olbion*, 381. John Selden's commentary on Drayton's lyric retelling of the Norman Conquest recounted Kentish efforts to avoid "bondage to the *Normans*," and their resolve "rather to die then lose their freedome." According to this account, Archbishop Stigand and Abbot

Egelsin met with the Conqueror, with the inhabitants of Kent lined up for battle behind them, and successfully offered to receive William as their liege lord, "upon condition, that they may for ever enjoy their ancient Liberties and Laws used among their ancestors; otherwise, . . . being readie rather to die, then undergoe a yoake of Bondage." Drayton continued with this theme in his account of resistance to King John, which resulted in a virtual Civil War and led to the rise of Henry III, "[b]y his more forcefull friends: who, wise and puissant growe, / The General Charter seiz'd: that into slavery drew / The freest borne *English* blood. Of which such discord grew." Drayton, *Poly-Olbion*, 385, 333.

33. William Camden, *Britain, or a Chorographicall Description of the most flourishing Kingdomes, England, Scotland, and Ireland*, trans. Philemon Holland (London, 1610), 49−50. The original Latin edition of this work appeared in 1586.

34. Richard Verstegan, *A Restitution of Decayed Intelligence* (Antwerp, 1605), 43. Verstegan's family name was Rowlands, but he assumed his grandfather's name to emphasize his German ancestry. See also Hugh A. MacDougall, *Racial Myth in English History: Trojans, Teutons, and Anglo-Saxons* (Montreal: Harvest House, 1982), esp. 7−27.

35. Sir Thomas Smith, *De Republica Anglorum*, ed. Mary Dewar (Cambridge: Cambridge University Press, 1982), bk. 2, ch. 24, 118, and William Harrison, *The Description of England: The Classic Contemporary Account of Tudor Social Life*, ed. Georges Edelen (New York: Dover Publications, Inc., 1994), 147, 118. Dewar's translation is based on a reading of the six extant manuscripts from the original work completed in the 1560s. The Harrison passage dates from 1587. On the context of Smith's project, see Anne McLaren, "Reading Sir Thomas Smith's *De Republica Anglorum* as Protestant Apologetic," *Historical Journal* 42:3 (December 1999): 911−39.

36. Scholars have noted that England was in the midst of an "education revolution" during the late Tudor and early Stuart eras, but only a small percentage of English society benefited substantively from the elementary and grammar schools, much less the two universities or the Inns of Court where many of the most important texts on the subject were read. Moreover, in this era when a significant amount of important scholarship was only available in Latin, more Englishmen were engaged in learning to read and write English. To be sure, an increasing number of people were coming into possession of books, building libraries, and engaging in a nascent print culture, but the dissemination of ideas through manuscripts, letters, and books involved a narrow band of exceptional, perhaps even atypical, individuals in early modern England. See Lawrence Stone, "The Educational Revolution in England, 1560−1640," *Past and Present* 28 (1964): 41−81; Joan Simon, *Education and Society in Tudor England* (Cambridge: Cambridge University Press, 1966), esp. 369−403; Keith Wrightson, *English Society, 1580−1680* (New Brunswick, NJ: Rutgers University Press, 1982), 183−99; and Palliser, *The Age of Elizabeth*, 411−28.

37. F. W. Maitland, *Domesday Book and Beyond: Three Essays in the Early History of England* (Cambridge: Cambridge University Press, 1897), 26−36, and R. Welldon Finn, *An Introduction to the Domesday Book* (London: Longman, 1963). On the enduring significance of slavery in England in the light of parallel developments on the continent, see Marc Bloch, *Slavery and Serfdom in the Middle Ages: Selected Essays* (Los Angeles: University of California Press, 1975), 25−26. On Scandinavia, see Ruth Mazo Karras, *Slavery and Society in Medieval Scandinavia* (New Haven, CT: Yale University Press, 1988). For a more recent treatment of medieval English slavery, see David A. E. Pelteret, *Slavery and Early Medieval England from the Reign of Alfred to the Early Twelfth Century* (Woodbridge: Boydell Press, 1995).

38. David Pelteret, "Slave Raiding and Slave Trading in Early England," *Anglo-Saxon England* 9 (December 1980), 99−114; Bede, *The Ecclesiastical History of the English People* (New York:

Oxford University Press, 1999), 70–71 [bk. II, ch. 1]; and Robert Bartlett, *The Making of Europe: Conquest, Colonization and Cultural Change, 950–1350* (Princeton, NJ: Princeton University Press, 1993), 78–79.

39. Ross Samson has outlined the five traditional explanations for the end of early medieval slavery: semantic, natural demography, economic, class struggle, and the influence of the Church. Samson dismisses the first three possibilities in favor of the last two. See Samson, "The End of Medieval Slavery," in *The Work of Work: Servitude, Slavery, and Labor in Medieval England*, ed. Allen J. Frantzen and Douglas Moffat (Glasgow: Cruithne Press, 1994), 95–124. Marc Bloch and Moses Finley have been the most well-known proponents of the economic reason, which boils down to the premise that the slave lacked motivation and was therefore a poor worker. More recently, Ruth Mazo Karras, drawing on the work of David Pelteret, concluded that "demesne slavery in England probably came to an end because it was not as productive as domiciling the slaves and working the demesne by means of labor dues from free and unfree tenants." See Karras, *Slavery and Society in Medieval Scandinavia* (New Haven, CT: Yale University Press, 1988), 32, esp. ch. 1; and Pelteret, *Slavery and Early Medieval England*.

40. According to R. H. Hilton, slaves were legally "the chattels of their masters, employed as instruments of production in agriculture or industry, receiving food, clothing and shelter from the master" while serfs "possessed, even if they did not own, the means of production of their own livlihood." Hilton, *The Decline of Serfdom in Medieval England* (London: Macmillan, 1969), 10.

41. Andrew Horn, *The Mirror of Justices*, ed. William Joseph Whittaker (London: Selden Society, 1895), 79. My comments on the subject are drawn for the most part from R. H. Hilton, "Freedom and Villeinage in England," *Past & Present* 31 (1965): 3–19; Paul Hyams, "The Proof of Villein Status in the Common Law," *English Historical Review* 89 (1974): 721–49; and John Hatcher, "English Serfdom and Villeinage: Towards a Reassessment," *Past & Present* 90 (1981): 3–39. On the legal history of unfreedom in England, see Sir Frederick Pollock and Frederic William Maitland, *The History of English Law*, 2nd ed., 2 vols. (Cambridge: Cambridge University Press, 1898), 1:412–32.

42. Paul R. Hyams, *Kings, Lords, and Peasants in Medieval England: The Common Law of Villeinage in the Twelfth and Thirteenth Centuries* (Oxford: Clarendon Press, 1980), 1–79; Chris Given-Wilson, "Service, Serfdom and English Labour Legislation, 1350–1500," in *Concepts and Patterns of Service in the Later Middle Ages*, ed. Anne Curry and Elizabeth Matthew (Woodbridge: Boydell Press, 2000), 21–37; and Paul Vinogradoff, *Villeinage in England: Essays in English Mediaval History* (Oxford, 1892), 67. Vinogradoff notes that "there was absolutely nothing to prevent a villein from acting in every respect like a free man if he was so minded and was not interrupted by his lord" (68). This point is also discussed by Hatcher, "English Serfdom and Villeinage," 6–14. For a useful treatment of the structural and legal relationship between slavery and serfdom, see the essays in Bush, *Serfdom & Slavery*, esp. Stanley L. Engerman, "Slavery, Serfdom and Other Forms of Coerced Labour: Similarities and Differences" (18–41). My understanding of villeinage as an institution usefully conceptualized as "slave-like"—which runs counter to most contemporary scholarship—has been influenced by Orlando Patterson, who refers to English serfdom in his own work as, essentially, "recombinant slavery." See Patterson, *Freedom and the Making of Western Culture*, 349–50.

43. *The Works of Geoffrey Chaucer*, 2nd ed., ed. F. N. Robinson (Boston: Houghton Mifflin, 1933), 252.

44. John Fitzherbert, *The Boke of Surveying and Improvements* (London, 1523), 26–27. Tudor monarchs were generally unwilling to overstep their prerogative when it came to bondmen held in private or ecclesiastical hands and they were occasionally refused when they requested subjects to manumit their human property. For a useful study of Tudor villeinage, see Diarmaid MacCulloch,

"Bondmen under the Tudors," in *Law and Government under the Tudors*, ed. Claire Cross, David Loades, and J. J. Scarisbrick (Cambridge: Cambridge University Press, 1998).

45. *Select Cases of the Court of Requests, 1497–1569*, ed. I. S. Leadam (London: Selden Society, 1898), lxix–lxxi, 42–46, and G. R. Elton, *The Tudor Constitution: Documents and Commentary* (Cambridge: Cambridge University Press, 1960), 184–95.

46. *Select Cases of the Court of Requests, 1497–1569*, lxxi–lxxii, 48–59.

47. *Select Cases before the King's Council in the Star Chamber, A.D. 1477–1509*, ed. I. S. Leadam (London: Selden Society, 1909), 118–29, and Vinogradoff, *Villeinage in England*, 83–84. Hyams, "The Proof of Villein Status in the Common Law," suggests, however, that this "suit of kin" process was fraught with difficulty. It had been used at an earlier time as part of the process that held many in a continued state of villeinage because of divergent legal opinions about whether status followed from the mother or the father. In the thirteenth century, "tenemental influence," or residency, was often more useful in establishing the status of an individual.

48. Smith, *De Republica Anglorum*, bk. III, ch. 8, 135–36.

49. Anthony Fletcher, *Tudor Rebellions*, 3rd ed. (Essex: Longman, 1983), 54–68, 120–23, quote on 122; Diarmaid MacCulloch, "Kett's Rebellion in Context," in *Rebellion, Popular Protest, and the Social Order in Early Modern England*, ed. Paul Slack (New York: Cambridge University Press, 1984), 36–59; and Andy Wood, *Riot, Rebellion and Popular Politics in Early Modern England* (New York: Palgrave, 2002), esp. 54–70.

50. Unlike the western counties, where many of the manors that continued to hold bondmen into the sixteenth century were controlled by ecclesiastics, most East Anglian manors with bondmen were controlled by lay lords. Diarmaid MacCulloch, "Bondmen under the Tudors," in *Law and Government under the Tudors*, ed. Claire Cross, David Loades, and J. J. Scarisbrick (Cambridge: Cambridge University Press, 1988), 94 (Table 10). MacCulloch's numbers indicate that in 1485 Gloucestershire and Somersetshire contained a total of 89 manors with serfs, 61 of which (69 percent) were monastic and secular cathedral chapters or manors owned by monasteries or nunneries. By 1560, only 18 manors with bondmen remained. In contrast, in 1485 the shires of Norfolk and Suffolk contained a total 115 manors with serfs, 88 of which (77 percent) were held by lay lords. By 1560 only 35 manors continued to possess bondmen.

51. Cited in MacCulloch, "Bondmen under the Tudors," 99.

52. MacCulloch, "Kett's Rebellion in Context," 55–56, and Dairmaid MacCulloch, *Suffolk and the Tudors: Politics and Religion in an English County, 1500–1600* (Oxford: Clarendon Press, 1986), 75, 308.

53. *Letters and Papers, Foreign and Domestic of the Reign of Henry VIII*, 21 vols., ed. J. S. Brewer, J. Gardiner, R. H. Brodie, et al. (London, 1862–1932), 13:1 (January–July 1538), 465; 12:2 (June–December 1537), 214; 13:1 (January–July 1538), 108.

54. See MacCulloch, "Bondmen under the Tudors," 99–100. See also J. H. Baker, ed., *The Reports of Sir John Spelman*, 2 vols. (London: Selden Society, 1976–77), 2:192.

55. *Calendar of the Patent Rolls: Edward VI*, 6 vols. (London, 1924–29), 3 (1549–51), 215–16, 316; 5 (1547–53), 407. The financial incentive to manumit bondmen, especially those who were so in name only, should not be ignored. In 1538 the Prior of Leominster wrote Cromwell to inform him of the abbot's pattern of manumitting the richest bondmen and then keeping the profits, rather than paying them into the priory's coffers. The prior then went on to tempt Henry's minister by mentioning that "my predecessors have had the authority to 'manumys' them; and if you will comfort me to use the same, you shall have half the profits." *Letters and Papers*, 13:2 (August–December), 1538.

56. *Select Statutes and Other Constitutional Documents Illustrative of the Reigns of Elizabeth and James I*, 4th ed., ed. G. W. Prothero (Oxford: Clarendon Press, 1913), 173–74; Alexander Savine,

"Bondmen under the Tudors," *Transactions of the Royal Historical Society* 17 (1903): 268–72; Mac-Culloch, "Bondmen under the Tudors," 107–8; E. K. Chambers, *Sir Henry Lee: An Elizabethan Portrait* (Oxford: Clarendon Press, 1936), 43–46. If any villeins declined to enter into an agreement with Lee, he was authorized to seize their lands anyway.

57. On the Earl of Bath, see *Select Cases of the Court of Requests*, lxxi–lxxii, 48–59. On Lord Stafford and his villeins, see the *Acts of the Privy Council of England, 1542–1604*, 32 vols., ed. John Roche Dasent (London, 1924–29), 14:48–49, 100, 153, 205–6, and 15:69, 303–4; Helen Tunnicliff Catterall, ed., *Judicial Cases Concerning American Slavery and the Negro* (Washington, DC: Carnegie Institution, 1926), 1:9. "Cartwright's Case" is also cited (and discussed) in Jonathan A. Bush, "The First Slave (and why he matters)," *Cardozo Law Review* 18 (November 1996): 610, 614.

58. Or "Much Nonsense," according to Robert M. Adams in his translation of Thomas More, *Utopia*, 2nd (New York: W. W. Norton, 1992), 15. More was famously playful in the names he chose for places and people, but his wordplay may have been quite purposeful. See, for example, Eric Nelson, "Greek Nonsense in More's *Utopia*," *Historical Journal* 44:4 (December 2001): 889–917. On the larger problem of determining what is meant by, or wanted from, *Utopia*, see Joseph M. Levine, "Thomas More and the English Renaissance: History and Fiction in *Utopia*," in *The Historical Imagination in Early Modern Britain: History, Rhetoric, and Fiction, 1500–1800*, ed. Donald R. Kelley and David Harris Sacks (Cambridge: Cambridge University Press, 1997), 69–92.

59. Thomas More, *A fruteful pleasaunt, & wittie work, of the best state of a publique weale, and of the newe yle, called Utopia*, Raphe Robynson, trans. (London, 1556), 20v–24r [D5v–E1r]. Because it was the more popular of the two, I have chosen to quote from Robinson's second edition. The two texts do not vary in their treatment of human bondage, minus some spelling variations. The 1556 edition is also mispaginated. There are, however, other important differences in tone. See David Weil Baker, "Topical Utopias: Radicalizing Humanism in Sixteenth-Century England," *Studies in English Literature, 1500–1900* 36:1 (Winter 1996): 1–30.

60. More, *Utopia*, 21r. "Hythloday" means "Talker of Nonsense."

61. In both the 1551 and 1556 English editions, Ralph Robinson generally uses the word "bondman" rather than "slave." Robinson's desire to play down the existence of slavery in More's *Utopia* is further indicated by his choice to water down the stark section heading in the 1518 Latin edition ("De Servis") to "Of Bondemen, sicke persons, wedlocke, and divers other matters." Although this section heading more accurately reflects the contents of what follows, it also effectively draws the reader's attention away from the subject of slavery. More, *Utopia*, 91r [N3r].

62. More, *Utopia*, 91v–92r [N3v–N4r].

63. More, *Utopia*, 55r [H8r], 64r [K1r], 96r [N8r], 92r [N4r].

64. More, *Utopia*, 64r [K1r], 63v [I7v], 96r [N8r]. Orlando Patterson discusses these issues in terms of "liminal incorporation." As in the case of the slave in the Anglo-Saxon epic *Beowulf*, Patterson argues that even though the slave was socially a nonperson, he was not an outsider. As More's butcher-slaves demonstrate, slavery involved contradictory principles of marginality and integration. See Patterson, *Slavery and Social Death: A Comparative Study* (Cambridge, MA: Harvard University Press, 1982), 45–51. On the link between slavery and the animal kingdom, see Keith Thomas, *Man and the Natural World: Changing Attitudes in England, 1500–1800* (New York: Oxford University Press, 1983), 41–50.

65. On the relationship between shame and honor, see Stephen Greenblatt, *Renaissance Self-Fashioning: From More to Shakespeare* (Chicago: University of Chicago Press, 1980), 39–58, and Patterson, *Slavery and Social Death*, 79ff.

66. C. S. L. Davies, "Slavery and Protector Somerset; the Vagrancy Act of 1547," *Economic History Review* 2nd ser. 9 (1966): 533–49, and Armitage, *The Ideological Origins of the British Empire*, 51. It should be reemphasized that neither Thomas More nor the 1547 legislation constructed a model of slavery that had much to do with the need for a bound labor force. Robin Blackburn, *The Making of New World Slavery: From the Baroque to the Modern, 1492–1800* (New York: Verso, 1997), suggests that the measure proved impossible to implement, "being opposed not only by those at whom it was directed but also by labourers who did not wish to be undercut by convict labour and magistrates who thought it provocative" (57). Unfortunately, there is no evidence to support these conclusions.

67. *CSPV* 5 (1534–54), 351–52, 548 (May 1551 and 1554); *APC* 3:209 (5 February 1551); John Francis Guilmartin Jr., *Gunpowder and Galleys: Changing Technology and Mediterranean Warfare in the Sixteenth Century* (Cambridge: Cambridge University Press, 1974); *British Naval Documents, 1204–1960*, ed. John B. Hattendorf, R. J. B. Knight, M. W. H. Pearsall, N. A. M. Rodger, and Geoffrey Till (Aldershot: Scolar Press for the Navy Records Society, 1993), 77–78; R. C. Anderson, "Henry VIII's 'Great Galley,'" *Mariner's Mirror* 6 (1920): 274–81; and J. E. G. Bennell, "English Oared Vessels of the Sixteenth Century," *Mariner's Mirror* 60:1 (1974): 9–26 and 60:2 (1974): 169–86.

68. *TRP* 1:326–27, 352, 456, and 3:86–92; *Report from the Lost Notebooks of Sir James Dyer*, 2 vols., ed. J. H. Baker (London: Selden Society, 1994), 1:135; and *The Egerton Papers*, ed. J. Payne Collier (London: Camden Society, 1840), 116–17.

69. Sir Henry Mainwaring, "Of the Beginnings, Practices, and Suppression of Pirates," in *The Life and Works of Sir Henry Mainwaring*, 2 vols., ed. G. E. Mainwaring and W. G. Perkin (London: Navy Records Society, 1922), 2:18–20; *The Naval Tracts of Sir William Monson*, 6 vols., ed. M. Oppenheim (London: Navy Records Society, 1902–14), 4:107–9. A roughly contemporaneous draft of a bill in Parliament reveals that penal slavery was not a far-fetched idea. Thus, it was proposed that "beinge adjudged to die for smale faultes they maie be saved and Condemned as Slaves duringe lief and be used as in other Cuntreys unto anie Publique workes in the Kingdome, Givinge power after eight yeares service to the Master of those workes if they become newe men, and Demeane themselves well, to Release them of theire boundadge and Slaverie, into their former libertie and fredome." *Commons Debates 1621*, 7 vols., ed. Wallace Notestein, Frances Helen Relf, and Hartley Simpson (New Haven, CT: Yale University Press, 1935), 7:54–55.

70. Hawkins's memorandum is published as an appendix to J. E. G. Bennell, "English Oared Vessels of the Sixteenth Century," *Mariner's Mirror* 60 (1974): 185. E. R. Adair, "English Galleys in the Sixteenth Century," *English Historical Review* 35 (1920): 497–512, makes the intriguing assertion that Hawkins's estimate was based on the potential use of African slaves, in the light of his slave-trading exploits and the rather incongruous statement that England did not have any experience in the employment of galley slaves.

71. *Letters and Papers, Foreign and Domestic of the Reign of Henry VIII*, 21 vols., ed. J. S. Brewer, J. Gardiner, R. H. Brodie, et al. (London, 1862–1932), 21:1, 636–37 (15 July 1546). The slaves were apparently not returned with the galley in 1547, but whether they were set free or continued to serve on another galley remains in question. See Adair, "English Galleys in the Sixteenth Century," 500–502.

72. Indeed, it would continue to resonate among a select group of British elites into the eighteenth century. Michal J. Rozbicki, "To Save Them from Themselves: Proposals to Enslave the British Poor, 1698–1755," *Slavery & Abolition* 22:2 (August 2001): 29–50.

CHAPTER 2

1. Richard Hakluyt, *The Principall Navigations, Voiages and Discoveries of the English Nation* (London, 1589), 2v.

2. Richard Willes, *The History of Travayle in the West and East Indies* (London, 1577), B3v.

3. Jean Bodin, *The Six Books of a Commonweale*, ed. Kenneth Douglas McRae (Cambridge: Harvard University Press, 1962), 34.

4. Pierre Charron, *Of Wisdome Three Bookes*, trans. Samson Lennard (London, ca. 1612), 194. Charron was careful to identify four kinds of slavery: "Natural, that is slave borne; Enforced, and made by right of warre; Just, termed slaves by punishment by reason of some offence, or debt, whereby they are slaves to their Creditors, at the most for seven yeeres . . . ; [and] Voluntaries, whereof there are many sorts."

5. See, esp., David A. Armitage, "The New World and British Historical Thought: From Richard Hakluyt to William Robertson," in *America in European Consciousness, 1493–1750*, ed. Karen Ordahl Kupperman (Chapel Hill: University of North Carolina Press, 1995), 52–75, and Peter Mancall, *Hakluyt's Promise: An Elizabethan's Obsession for an English America* (New Haven: Yale University Press, 2007). Scholars continue to be fascinated by the challenges faced by Hakluyt as both editor and translator. See, for example, David A. Boruchoff, "Piety, Patriotism, and Empire: Lessons for England, Spain, and the New World in the Works of Richard Hakluyt," *Renaissance Quarterly* 62:3 (Fall 2009): 809–58; Julia Schleck, " 'Plain Broad Narratives of Substantial Facts': Credibility, Narrative, and Hakluyt's *Principall Navigations*," *Renaissance Quarterly* 59:3 (Fall 2006): 768–94; and the voluminous scholarship and invaluable insights of Mary C. Fuller, much of which can be gleaned from her *Remembering the Early Modern Voyage: English Narratives in the Age of European Expansion* (New York: Palgrave Macmillan, 2008).

6. Samuel Purchas is often treated by scholars as an afterthought or a tangential consideration of their primary interest in Richard Hakluyt, but see Linda McJannet, "Purchas His Pruning: Refashioning the Ottomans in Seventeenth-Century Travel Narratives," *Huntington Library Quarterly* 74:2 (June 2011): 219–42, and L. E. Pennington, ed., *The Purchas Handbook: Studies of the Life, Times, and Writings of Samuel Purchas, 1577–1626*, 2 vols. (London: Hakluyt Society, 1997). Protestantism, it has been argued, also informed Hakluyt's *Principal Navigations*. See David Harris Sacks, "Discourses of Western Planting: Richard Hakluyt and the Making of the Atlantic World," in *The Atlantic World and Virginia, 1550–1624*, ed. Peter Mancall (Chapel Hill: University of North Carolina Press, 2007), 410–53.

7. Samuel Purchas, *Hakluytus Posthumus, or Purchas His Pilgrimes*, 20 vols. (Glasgow: James MacLehose and Sons, 1905–7), 1:17, 29.

8. William D. Phillips, *Slavery from Roman Times to the Early Transatlantic Trade* (Minneapolis: University of Minnesota Press, 1985), 97–113; Daniel Evans, "Slave Coast of Europe," *Slavery & Abolition* 6:1 (May 1985): 41–58; Sergio Tognetti, "The Trade in Black African Slaves in Fifteenth-Century Florence," in *Black Africans in Renaissance Europe*, 213–24; and Juan María de la Obra Sierra, "Protocolos Notariales, Fuentes Para el Estudio de la Esclavitud en El Esclavo Extranjero en la Granada de Principios del Siglo XVI," *Anuario de Historia Contemporánea* 12 (1985): 5–27. James H. Sweet, "The Iberian Roots of American Racist Thought," *William and Mary Quarterly* 54:1 (January 1997): 143–66, has suggested that Iberian Christians "became acquainted with the Muslim system of black slavery and adopted the same set of symbols and myths, with additional arguments" (149). On the medieval frontier, see Robert Bartlett and Angus McKay, eds., *Medieval Frontier Societies* (Oxford: Clarendon Press, 1989), esp. Manuel González Jiménez, "Frontier and Settlement in the

Kingdom of Castile (1805–1350)," and José Enrique López de Coca Castañer, "Institutions on the Castilian-Granadan Frontier, 1369–1482."

9. Robert Brenner, *Merchants and Revolution: Commercial Change, Political Conflict and London's Overseas Traders, 1550–1653* (Princeton, NJ: Princeton University Press, 1993), 13. Because the company's records were largely destroyed in the Great Fire of London in 1666, Richard Hakluyt is responsible for preserving the most complete record of the early expeditions. On the trade and extant sources, see T. S. Willan, "Trade between England and Russia in the Second Half of the Sixteenth Century," *English Historical Review* 63:248 (July 1948): 307–21.

10. On the Muscovy Company, see T. S. Willan, *The Early History of the Russia Company, 1553–1603* (Manchester: Manchester University Press, 1956). On slavery in Russia, see Richard Hellie, *Slavery in Russia, 1450–1725* (Chicago: University of Chicago Press, 1982).

11. *Early Voyages and Travels to Russia and Persia by Anthony Jenkinson and Other Englishmen*, 2 vols., ed. E. Delmar Morgan and C. H. Coote (London: Hakluyt Society, 1896), 1:52, 72, 95.

12. Giles Fletcher, *Of the Russe Commonwealth, or, The manner of government by the Russe emperor . . . with the manners, and fashions of the people of that country* (London, 1591), 17r, 37v, 46r, 13r–v. Although Fletcher's work was excerpted by both Hakluyt and Purchas, it seems that the Muscovy Company was interested in suppressing it so as not to offend the Russian government with which they preferred to do business. In his dedication to the Queen, Fletcher made clear his perspective when he celebrated that "you are a Prince of subjectes, not of slaves, that are kept within duetie by love, not by feare" (A4r).

13. Fletcher, *Of the Russe commonwealth*, 69r. On Fletcher's negative impression of the Tartars, see Richard W. Cogley, "'The most vile and barbarous nation of all the world': Giles Fletcher the Elder's *The Tartars or, Ten Tribes* (ca. 1610)," *Renaissance Quarterly* 58:3 (2005): 781–814.

14. It is perhaps less common than it once was to argue that England's overseas ventures were modeled on earlier efforts in Ireland, but Ireland's centrality to English imperial concerns should not be underestimated. See, esp., two works by Nicholas P. Canny, *The Elizabethan Conquest of Ireland: A Pattern Established, 1565–1576* (New York: Harvester Press, 1976), and *Making Ireland British, 1580–1650* (New York: Oxford University Press, 2001). See also Jane H. Ohlmeyer, "'Civilizinge of those Rude Partes': Colonization with Britain and Ireland, 1580s-1640s," in *The Oxford History of the British Empire*, vol. 1: *The Origins of Empire*, ed. Nicholas Canny (Oxford: Oxford University Press, 1998), 124–47. The contrasting view, that Ireland is best seen within an insular European rather than an Atlantic context, has been most effectively argued by a number of scholars. For examples, see Brendan Bradshaw, "Sword, Word and Strategy in the Reformation in Ireland," *Historical Journal* 21 (1978): 475–502, and Steven G. Ellis, *Tudor Ireland: Crown, Community and the Conflict of Cultures, 1470–1603* (Harlow: Longman, 1985). Regardless, there is an emerging consensus that Ireland was fundamentally a "British" problem in the early modern era. Among literary scholars, this point has been made by Andrew Hadfield in *Shakespeare, Spenser and the Matter of Britain* (New York: Palgrave Macmillan, 2004).

15. Robert Bartlett, *The Making of Europe: Conquest, Colonization and Cultural Change, 950–1350* (Princeton, NJ: Princeton University Press, 1993), 78, 80.

16. In Andrew Hadfield's words, "Gerald was indeed the 'ghost in the machine' of English representations of Ireland for at least four-and-a-half centuries." See Hadfield, "Rethinking Early-Modern Colonialism: The Anomalous State of Ireland," *Irish Studies Review* 7:1 (1999): 14. See also John Brannigan, "'A Particular Vice of That People': Giraldus Cambrensis and the Discourse of English Colonialism," *Irish Studies Review* 6:2 (1998): 121–30. On the pervasiveness of negative stereotypes, see Brendan Bradshaw and Andrew Hadfield, eds., *Representing Ireland: Literature and the*

Origins of Conflict, 1534–1660 (Cambridge: Cambridge University Press, 1993). David Beers Quinn, *The Elizabethans and the Irish* (Ithaca, NY: Cornell University Press, 1966), is still worth reading but usefully augmented by Bradshaw, "The Elizabethans and the Irish: A Muddled Model," *Studies* 70 (1981): 233–44. On Gerald, more generally, see Robert Bartlett, *Gerald of Wales, 1146–1223* (Oxford: Clarendon Press, 1982).

17. *State Papers Concerning the Irish Church in the Time of Queen Elizabeth*, ed. W. Maziere Brady (London, 1868), 48–55; Edmund Spenser, *A View of the Present State of Ireland* (1596), in *Elizabethan Ireland: A Selection of Writings by Elizabethan Writers on Ireland*, ed. James P. Myers Jr. (Hamden, CT: Archon Books, 1983), 101. Spenser was willing to grant that they "are very valiant and hardy" and "great endurers of cold, labor, hunger, and all hardness, very active and strong of hand, very swift of foot, very vigilant and circumspect in their enterprises, very present in perils, [and] very great scorners of death." With that in mind, he was willing to concede that the Irish made good soldiers. On Spenser, and Ireland in his time, see Canny, *Making Ireland British*, esp. 1–58.

18. Barnabe Rich, *A New Description of Ireland, together with the Manners, Customs, and Dispositions of the People* (1610), in Myers, *Elizabethan Ireland*, 130; Rich, *A Short Survey of Ireland* (London, 1609). John P. Harrington, "A Tudor Writer's Tracts on Ireland, His Rhetoric," *Eire-Ireland: A Journal of Irish Studies* 17:2 (1982): 92–103.

19. On the relationship between the peoples of the English marchlands and the question of identity in the medieval era, see Bartlett, *The Making of Europe*; Jeffrey Jerome Cohen, *Hybridity, Identity, and Monstrosity in Medieval Britain: On Difficult Middles* (New York: Palgrave Macmillan, 2006); and Hugh M. Thomas, *The English and the Normans: Ethnic Hostility, Assimilation, and Identity, 1066–c. 1220* (New York: Oxford University Press, 2003). For the early modern period, see Kathleen M. Noonan, "'The Cruell Pressure of an Enraged, Barbarous People': Irish and English Identity in Seventeenth-Century Policy and Propaganda," *Historical Journal* 41:1 (1998): 151–77.

20. And there was plenty of worry that the English were losing some important battles, as evidenced by the shocking revelation that in Ireland the problem was not the native Irish, but that many of the Old English inhabitants had "degenerated and grown almost mere Irish, yea, more malicious to the English than the Irish themselves." Edmund Spenser, *A View of the Present State of Ireland* (1596), in Myers, *Elizabethan Ireland*, 78. It was this problem that prompted Edward III to issue an ordinance in the mid-fourteenth century "that no one of English descent shall speak in the Irish tongue with other Englishmen . . . but every Englishman should study the English language." Language was a potent indicator of English identity, but this attempt to prevent cultural declension was augmented by other statutes that outlawed marriages between immigrants and natives and that required Englishmen to use English names, ride in the English way (i.e., with saddles), and wear English apparel. Bartlett, *The Making of Europe*, 201–3, 239, Edward III quotation on p. 203.

21. G. A. Hayes-McCoy, "The Completion of the Tudor Conquest, and the Advance of the Counter-Reformation, 1571–1603," in *A New History of Ireland*, vol. 3: *Early Modern Ireland, 1534–1691*, ed. T. W. Moody, F. X. Martin, and F. J. Byrne (Oxford: Clarendon Press, 1976), 94–141; William Palmer, *The Problem of Ireland in Tudor Foreign Policy, 1485–1603* (Woodbridge: Boydell Press, 1994); and Hiram Morgan, "Hugh O'Neill and the Nine Years War in Tudor Ireland," *Historical Journal* 36 (1993): 21–37.

22. Fynes Moryson, *An Itinerary* (unpublished excerpt ca. 1617), in Myers, *Elizabethan Ireland*, 201; Sir Philip Sidney, *Discourse on Irish Affairs* (1577), in Myers, *Elizabethan Ireland*, 36; *Calendar of the State Papers relating to Ireland* [hereafter *CSP: Ireland*], 11 vols. (London, 1860–1912),

NOTES TO PAGES 50–53

1:330 (20 April 1567), and 4:458 (20 February 1592); and Sir John Davies, *A Discovery of the True Causes Why Ireland Was Never Entirely Subdued* (1612), in Myers, *Elizabethan Ireland*, 159–60.

23. Barnabe Rich, *A New Description of Ireland*, in Myers, *Elizabethan Ireland*, 133 (both citations), and Morgan, "Hugh O'Neill and the Nine Years War," 24.

24. *CSP: Ireland* 11:287; Hayes-McCoy, "The Completion of the Tudor Conquest," 96–97; Raphael Holinshed, *The First and Second Volumes of Chronicles* (London, 1587), 2:15. In another passage, Holinshed told the story of St. Patrick who, at the age of sixteen, "became slave to an Irish lord . . . , from whome after six yeares terme he redeemed himself with a peece of gold which he found in a clod of earth" (2:53). It was this act, his divine deliverance from bondage, that turned him from his previous secular pursuits to a more sacred path.

25. Purchas, *Hakluytus Posthumus*, 1:14. The breadth and rationale of human bondage in the region can be gleaned from Géza Dávid and Pál Fodor, eds., *Ransom Slavery along the Ottoman Borders (Early Fifteenth–Early Eighteenth Centuries)* (Leiden: Brill, 2007). On English and European engagement with the Ottoman Empire and, more generally, the Mediterranean world, during this era, see Nabil Matar, *Britain and Barbary, 1589–1689* (Gainesville: University Press of Florida, 2005), and Robin W. Winks, *Europe in a Wider World, 1350–1650* (New York: Oxford University Press, 2003). For a slightly later period, see Daniel Goffman, *Britons in the Ottoman Empire, 1642–1660* (Seattle: University of Washington Press, 1998).

26. Richard Hakluyt, *The Principal Navigations, Voyages, Traffiques, & Discoveries of the English Nation*, 12 vols. (New York: AMS Press, 1965), 5:80; Purchas, *Hakluytus Posthumus*, 8:151. The account by George Sandys was originally published in 1615 as *A Relation of a Journey begun an: Dom: 1610* (London, 1615). It was reprinted eight more times before 1670. On Sandys, see James Ellison, *George Sandys: Travel, Colonialism and Tolerance in the Seventeenth Century* (Rochester, NY: D. S. Brewer, 2002).

27. Hakluyt, *Principal Navigations*, 5:106; Purchas, *Hakluytus Posthumus*, 8:257, 281–82, 381. On the larger history of military slavery in Islam, particularly the important roles played by the Mamluks (literally meaning "owned" or "slave"), see David Ayalon, *Islam and the Abode of War: Military Slavery and Islamic Adversaries* (Aldershot, Great Britain: Variorum, 1994); Godfrey Goodwin, *The Janissaries* (London: Saqi Book Depot, 1997); and Bernard Lewis, *Race and Slavery in the Middle East: An Historical Enquiry* (New York: Oxford University Press, 1990), 62–71. Although Janizaries originated in the fourteenth century as the elite personal bodyguards to the Ottoman Sultan, Mamluks emerged as the tip of the spear through which the expansion of Islam was achieved during the ninth century. It is also worth noting that most military slaves in Islam were, by subsequent definitions, white (i.e., from southeastern Europe and modern-day Turkey).

28. Purchas, *Hakluytus Posthumus*, 8:135, 5:335. On Leo Africanus, see Natalie Zemon Davis, *Trickster Travels: A Sixteenth-Century Muslim Between Worlds* (New York: Hill and Wang, 2006).

29. Although the idea of voluntary slavery was familiar to early modern Englishmen—it was one of the legitimate forms of bondage in Thomas More's *Utopia*—the concept came under increasing philosophical attack during the seventeenth century. The most famous critique of self-enslavement was generated by John Locke in his *Second Treatise on Government*: "Freedom," he notes, "is to have a standing rule to live by, common to every one of that Society . . . and not to be subject to the inconstant, uncertain, unknown, Arbitrary Will of another Man." Freedom from arbitrary rule was so fundamental, he added, that man "cannot, by Compact, or his own Consent, enslave himself to anyone." Indeed, to Locke slavery could only be justified as something that was exacted from people who had already lawfully been sentenced to death or as a continuation of a state of war "between a lawful Conquerour, and a Captive." John Locke, *Two Treatises of Government* (London, 1690), 241–42. On

Locke's rejection of voluntary slavery and its antecedents in the writings of Hugo Grotius, see Stephen Buckle, *Natural Law and the Theory of Property: Grotius to Hume* (Oxford: Clarendon Press, 1991), 48–52, 174–80.

30. Purchas, *Hakluytus Posthumus*, 8:262, 151–52; 9:269. On the law of slavery in Islam, see Lewis, *Race and Slavery in the Middle East*; Shaun E. Marmon, ed., *Slavery in the Islamic Middle East* (Princeton, NJ: Marcus Wiener Publishers, 1999); and Ronald Segal, *Islam's Black Slaves: The Other Black Diaspora* (New York: Farrar, Straus and Giroux, 2001), 35–66. An interesting case study of the way both masters and slaves could use the law to their own advantage can be found in Ahman Alawad Sikainga, "Slavery and Muslim Jurisprudence in Morocco," *Slavery & Abolition* 19:2 (1998): 57–72.

31. It is worth remembering that the slave system described by Thomas More in *Utopia* was an almost entirely male institution.

32. Hakluyt, *Principal Navigations*, 3:165. On the larger subject of women and slavery, see Judy Madro, *Veiled Half-Truths: Western Travelers' Perceptions of Middle Eastern Women* (London: I. B. Tauris, 1996), and Amira El-Azhary Sonbol, ed., *Beyond the Exotic: Women's Histories in Islamic Societies* (Syracuse, NY: Syracuse University Press, 2005).

33. Purchas, *Hakluytus Posthumus*, 8:147, 151–52.

34. *William of Malmesbury's Chronicle of the Kings of England, from the Earliest period to the Reign of King Stephen*, trans. J. A. Giles (London, 1847), 279, 222. Susan Mosher Stuard, "Ancillary Evidence for the Decline of Medieval Slavery," *Past and Present* 149 (November 1995): 3–28, has argued that linguistic evidence suggests that the medieval traffic in slaves was overwhelmingly a traffic in women. Thus, although male slaves were often freed or transformed into serfs, female slaves remained important in the medieval European textile industry and as domestics in wealthy households. In a sense, Stuard argues, even though they were few in number, domiciled female slaves "kept the idea of slave labour alive" (27). See also Kirsten A. Seaver, "Thralls and Queens: Female Slavery in the Medieval Norse Atlantic," in *Women and Slavery: Africa, the Indian Ocean World, and the Medieval North Atlantic*, ed. Gwyn Campbell, Suzanne Miers, and Joseph C. Miller (Athens: Ohio University Press, 2007), 147–68.

35. Ruth Mazo Karras, "Desire, Descendants, and Dominance: Slavery, the Exchange of Women, and Masculine Power," in *The Work of Work: Servitude, Slavery, and Labor in Medieval England*, ed. Allen J. Frantzen and Douglas Moffat (Glasgow: Cruithne Press, 1994), 17.

36. Purchas, *Hakluytus Posthumus*, 8:152 (Sandys), 9:368–69 (Withers). Ronald Segal, *Islam's Black Slaves: The Other Black Diaspora* (New York: Farrar, Straus and Giroux, 2001), 111–14. Withers, it has been argued, was not the author of the treatise attributed to him by Purchas but rather the translator of an Italian manuscript. See Warner G. Rice, "The Grand Signiors Serraglio: Written by Master Robert Withers," *Modern Language Notes* 43:7 (November 1928): 450–59.

37. Purchas, *Hakluytus Posthumus*, 9:32. On Terry, see Ram Chandra Prasad, *Early English Travellers in India* (Delhi: Montilal Banarsidass, 1965), 267–310.

38. D. F. Lach, "The Far East," in *The Hakluyt Handbook*, 2 vols., ed. D. B. Quinn (London: Hakluyt Society, 1974), 1:214–22. Other accounts of the region, however, were translated and published by John Frampton (who translated from Spanish a copy of Marco Polo in 1579), Thomas Nicholls (who translated a pilfered Spanish dispatch from China and published it in 1578), and Robert Parke (who translated from Spanish an edition of Mendoza's *China* in 1588). The Englishman Ralph Fitch was an important source for Hakluyt, though Lach suggests that Fitch's work may not be as reliable as the others' because it apparently was written for money and was mildly plagiarized.

39. Michael Strachan, "India and the Areas Adjacent" and S. Arasaratnam, "Southeast Asia," in *The Purchas Handbook*, 2 vols., ed. L. E. Pennington (London: Hakluyt Society, 1997), 1:242–54, 255–67. On the East India Company, see P. J. Marshall, "The English in Asia to 1700," in *The Oxford History of the British Empire*, vol. 1: *The Origins of Empire*, ed. Nicholas Canny (Oxford: Oxford University Press, 1998), 264–85; Philip Lawson, *The East India Company: A History* (London: Longman, 1993); and K. N. Chaudhuri, *The English East India Company: The Study of an Early Joint-Stock Company, 1600–1640* (London: F. Cass, 1965).

40. Although the English were generally uninterested in the regional slave trade, there does survive an entry in an early East India Company letterbook noting that on the "Iland of Botonar [there] are some good *slaves* but noe good of their owne but what are thither brought from Java for *Slaves* for heare the[y] buie and sell *Slaves* as a good m[er]chandize *China dishes* or *Puselen* of [or?] all sorte of the finest *Clothes.*" See *The Register of the Letters & c. of the Governour and Company of Merchants of London Trading into the East Indies, 1600–1619*, ed. Sir George Birdwood and William Foster (London, 1893), 77.

41. There are a number of important exceptions to this rule, as when the English complained that either the Dutch or the Portuguese (their main competitors in the region) held them in bondage. Writing in 1619, Martin Pring reported that the Dutch had taken four English ships in the Moluccas and "keep our people in chains like slaves," something he found particularly offensive because the English had "spilt so much of their own blood to keep them from slavery" to the Spanish. Writing three years later, Thomas Johnson claimed that "the English are curbed like slaves, so that flesh and blood cannot endure it." *CSP:CS* 3 *(East Indies, China, and Japan, 1617–1621)*, 265, 467. Numerous other examples of this sort of rhetoric can be gleaned easily from the State Papers.

42. Purchas, *Hakluytus Posthumus*, 2:440–41, 443, 12:454–55. On female slavery in Asia, see Barbara Watson Andaya, "From Temporary Wife to Prostitute: Sexuality and Economic Change in Early Modern Southeast Asia," *Journal of Women's History* 9:4 (1998): 11–34, and Maria Jashok, *Concubines and Bondservants: A Social History* (London: Zed Books, 1988).

43. Purchas, *Hakluytus Posthumus*, 9:547; 3:327, 332, 104–6. Peter William Floris was the cape merchant on the seventh EIC voyage to the East Indies. David Middleton was a mariner and brother to the more famous captain Sir Henry Middleton, who commanded the second EIC expedition. See also W. H. Moreland, ed. *Peter Floris: His Voyage to the East Indies in the Globe, 1611–1615* (London: Hakluyt Society, 1934).

44. Anthony Farrington, ed., *The English Factory in Japan, 1613–1623*, 2 vols. (London: British Library, 1991), 1:72; Purchas, *Hakluytus Posthumus*, 3:458. For a nice collection of contemporary maps and images, see Farrington, *Trading Places: The East India Company and Asia, 1600–1834* (London: British Library, 2002). William Adams's fascinating story has been detailed in both fact and fiction numerous times. See, for example, Giles Milton, *Samurai William: The Englishman Who Opened Japan* (New York: Farrar, Straus & Giroux, 2003).

45. Purchas, *Hakluytus Posthumus*, 3:447–48. For fuller treatment of the subject, see Thomas Nelson, "Slavery in Medieval Japan," *Monumenta Nipponica* 59:4 (2004): 463–92.

46. The dependency of English merchants on local realities, their willingness to adapt themselves to local circumstances, and the generally neutral or even sometimes quite enthusiastic characterizations of the peoples and places beyond the Indian Ocean is part of an emerging consensus among scholars. See, for example, Alison Games, *The Web of Empire: English Cosmopolitans in an Age of Expansion, 1560–1660* (New York: Oxford University Press, 2008), and Robert Markley, "Riches, Power, Trade, and Religion: The Far East and the English Imagination, 1600–1720," *Renaissance Studies* 17:3 (2003): 494–516.

47. "A journal kept on board the Hosiander," in *The Voyage of Thomas Best to the East Indies, 1612–1614*, ed. Sir William Foster (London: Hakluyt Society, 1934), 174–75, and Farrington, *The English Factory in Japan*, 1:140. Best's own journal, kept aboard the *Dragon*, makes no mention of the purchase. Cocks, Wickham, and another merchant (William Nealson) were open about their sexual dalliances, which may have been common at the Hirado trading fort. Richard Watts would later write to Sir Thomas Smythe that the place was "more liker a puteree [a brothel] than a m'chantes' factory." Cited in Farrington, *The English Factory in Japan*, 2:843. Giles Cole was particularly direct in his recommendation, even arguing that the purchase price of two slaves would be recovered in only one year. *CSP:CS* 3 *(East Indies, China, and Japan, 1617–1621)*, 488–89. Following up on his own advice, Cole bought a slave named Sallamat in 1622, which he subsequently delivered to his colleague Thomas Johnson. *CSP:CS* 4 *(East Indies, China, and Japan, 1622–1624)*, 24. On this subject more generally, with more of an emphasis on the role of women as interlocutors, see Games, *The Web of Empire*, 104–9.

48. Three thirteenth-century encyclopedias containing important geographical information were published before 1500 by the English printer William Caxton and his protégé Wynkyn de Worde: Gautier of Metz, *The Mirrour of the World* (Westminster, 1481) [reprinted 1490]; Ranulf Higden, *Polichronicon* (Westminster, 1482) [reprinted 1495], and Bartholomaeus Anglicus, *Proprietatibus rerum* (Westminster, 1495). John Parker, *Books to Build an Empire: A Bibliographical History of English Overseas Interests to 1620* (Amsterdam: N. Israel, 1965), 14–15. On these early English printers and their trade, see Seth Lerer, "William Caxton," in *The Cambridge History of Medieval English Literature*, ed. David Wallace (Cambridge: Cambridge University Press, 1999), 720–38.

49. *Mandeville* was printed in 1496, 1499, 1501, 1503, 1568, and 1583. In addition, at least thirty editions appeared on the continent before 1500. See Parker, *Books to Build an Empire*, 16–17. On the availability of *Mandeville*, see C. W. R. D. Moseley, "The Availability of Mandeville's Travels in England, 1356–1750," *The Library* 30:2 (1975): 125–33. As Benjamin Braude argues in "The Sons of Noah and the Construction of Ethnic and Geographical Identities in the Medieval and Early Modern Periods," *William and Mary Quarterly* 54:1 (January 1997): 103–42, Mandeville's "book not only represents a summa of medieval European knowledge and prejudices about the rest of the world, but it is also essential for tracking the transformation of European understanding of the Other" (116).

50. The 1566, 1585, and 1587 translations of Pliny the Elder's *Historia Naturalis* were abstracted abbreviations of an earlier French translation. Pomponius Mela was a first-century Roman geographer and author of *De situ orbis*. Lesley B. Cormack, *Charting an Empire: Geography at the English Universities, 1580–1620* (Chicago: University of Chicago Press, 1997), 39–42.

51. *Of the newe landes and of ye people founde by the messengers of the kynge of portyngale named Emanuel* ([Antwerp], ca. 1510), and Damião de Góis, *The legacye or embassate of the great emperour of Inde prester Iohn, vnto Emanuell kynge of Portyngale, in the yere of our lorde M. v.C.xiii. Of the fayth of the Indyans, ceremonyes, relygyons [&]c. Of the patryarche [and] his offyce. Of the realme, state, power, maiesty, and order of the courte of prester Iohn* ([London], 1533).

52. Johann Boemus, *The discription of the contrey of Aphrique* (London, 1554), D2v, D6r, and George Abbot, *A briefe description of the whole worlde* (London, 1600), F2r. Boemus was originally published in 1520. Prat's translation was from one of the French translations that appeared in 1540 and 1542. Parker, *Books to Build an Empire*, 42. John Speed argued that "Terra Nigritarum" took its name "either from the colour of the people which are blacke, or from the River *Niger*." Speed, *A Prospect of the Most Famous Parts of the World* (London, 1627), 6.

53. *The Historie of the world: Commonly called, the naturall historie of C. Plinius Secundus*, 2 vols., trans. Philemon Holland (London, 1601), 1:96, and *The Travels of Sir John Mandeville*,

trans. C. W. R. D. Moseley (London: Penguin, 1983), 64, 117–18, 137. See also Iain Macleod Higgins, *Writing East: The "Travels" of Sir John Mandeville* (Philadelphia: University of Pennsylvania Press, 1997), esp. 101–2 and 143–49. On English interest, see Lesley B. Cormack, *Charting an Empire: Geography at the English Universities, 1580–1620* (Chicago: University of Chicago Press, 1997), 129–62.

54. Johann Boemus, *The Fardle of Facions* (London, 1555), B3v–B4r, and John Leo [Leo Africanus], *A Geographical Historie of Africa*, trans. John Pory (London, 1600), 6.

55. *Book of the Knowledge of All the Kingdoms, Lands, and Lordships That Are in the World . . .* , ed. and trans. Sir Clements Markham (London: Hakluyt Society, 1912), 35–36.

56. Charles E. Nowell, "The Historical Prester John," *Speculum* 28:3 (July 1953): 435–45; J. R. S. Phillips, *The Medieval Expansion of Europe* (New York: Oxford University Press, 1988), 59–62; L. N. Gumilev, *Searches for an Imaginary Kingdom: The Legend of the Kingdom of Prester John*, trans. R. E. F. Smith (Cambridge: Cambridge University Press, 1987 [orig. 1970]); *The Prester John of the Indies: A True Relation of the Lands of Prester John, being the narrative of the Portuguese Embassy to Ethiopia in 1520 written by Father Francisco Alvares*, ed. C. F. Beckingham and G. W. B. Huntingford (London: Hakluyt Society, 1961); Bailey W. Diffie and George D. Winius, *Foundations of the Portuguese Empire, 1415–1580* (Minneapolis: University of Minnesota Press, 1977), esp. 162–65, 349–59; and David Northrup, "Vasco da Gama and Africa: An Era of Mutual Discovery, 1497–1800," *Journal of World History* 9:2 (1998): 189–211.

57. Boemus, *The discription of the contrey of Aphrique* (1554), E2r. Regardless of whether it was a measure of his eminence, Boemus also noted that Prester John was "not blacke as other of the people of Ethiope be." Instead, he was "bothe of face and body whyte" (E3r).

58. Jean Devisse and Michel Mollat, *Image of the Black in Western Art*, vol. 2, pt. 2, 281 n. 176; Phillips, *The Medieval Expansion of Europe*, 143–63; Duarte Lopes, *A Report of the Kingdom of Congo, a region of Africa* (London, 1597), translator's note "To the Reader." This work had been written in Italian by Filippo Pigafetta in 1591. Whether there was an original, now lost, Portuguese manuscript or Pigafetta authored the work based on oral evidence from Lopes is unclear. There has been some consideration of its contribution to the European departure from classical models of the world. See Francesc Relaño, "Against Ptolemy: The Significance of the Lopes-Pigafetta Map of Africa," *Imago Mundi* 47 (1995): 49–66.

59. Edward Webbe, *The Rare and most wonderful things which Edw. Webbe an Englishman borne, hath seene and passed in his troublesome travailes* (London, 1590), B4r–v. Webbe apparently knew how to attract attention. Three simultaneous editions of the work were issued by three different publishers. H. W. L. Hine, "The Travels of Edward Webbe," *English Historical Review* 31:123 (July 1916): 464–70.

60. Abbot, *A briefe description of the whole world*, F2v–F3v. Abbot's source here is a passage from Pliny's *Historia Naturalis*, in which he observes "Africa haec maxime spectat, inopia aquarum ad paucos amnes congregantibus se feris. ideo multiformes ibi animalium partus, varie feminis cuiusque generis mares aut vi aut voluptate miscente: unde etiam vulgare Graeciae dictum semper aliquid novi Africam adferre." Interestingly, this passage was not included in the abbreviated 1566, 1585, or 1587 English translations. It did appear, however, in Philemon Holland's authoritative 1601 translations as "This, Affricke knoweth best, and seeth most: and especially in time of a great drought, when for want of water, a number of wild beasts resort by troups to those few rivers that be there, and meet together. And hereupon it is, that so many strange shaped beasts, of a mixt and mungrell kind are there bred, while the males either perforce, or for pleasure, leape and cover the females of all sorts. And hereupon it is also, that the Greekes have this common proverbe, *That Affricke*

evermore bringeth forth some new strange thing or other." The Historie of the World, 200 [bk. 8, ch. 16]. I thank Keyne Cheshire for identifying this reference.

61. Parker, *Books to Build an Empire*, 46, 68, 78; *Voyages of Cadamosto*, xlii–xlv. Richard Hakluyt's passing references to Barros in his *Principal Navigations* (7:170, 176, and 8:442), though in the context of his consideration of China, would indicate that he was more familiar with Portuguese sources concerning their activities in Africa than P. E. H. Hair indicates in "Guinea," in *The Hakluyt Handbook*, 2 vols., ed. D. B. Quinn (London: Hakluyt Society, 1974), 1:197–207. Samuel Purchas was more forthcoming in his use of Portuguese sources. See *The Purchas Handbook*.

62. *John Huighen van Linschoten his Discours of Voyages into ye Easte & West Indies* (London, 1598). Benjamin Schmidt, *Innocence Abroad: The Dutch Imagination and the New World, 1570–1670* (Cambridge: Cambridge University Press, 2001), argues that Linschoten's *Itinerario* "instantly launched Dutch trade to the East, and it rapidly vaulted its author to the heights of patriotic prominence" (154).

63. Speed, *A Prospect of the Most Famous Parts of the World*, 6; Abbot, *A briefe description of the whole world*, F2r. As a measure of the declining influence of classical and medieval authorities in favor of firsthand accounts, it is worth observing that Hakluyt included Mandeville in his first edition but omitted the work from his more comprehensive second edition. I thank Peter Mancall for this observation.

64. The image of Africa as a dynamic world and Africans as active agents in control of events on the continent has been emphasized by John Thornton, *Africa and Africans in the Making of the Atlantic World, 1400–1800*, 2nd ed. (Cambridge: Cambridge University Press, 1998), esp. 13–71; David Northrup, "The Gulf of Guinea and the Atlantic World," in *The Atlantic World and Virginia*, 170–93; and Linda M. Heywood and John K. Thornton, *Central Africans, Atlantic Creoles, and the Foundation of the Americas, 1585–1660* (Cambridge: Cambridge University Press, 2007).

65. Thornton, *Africa and Africans*, 74.

66. Direct European involvement in the slave trade, and its relationship to preexisting patterns and eventual implications, continues to be a source of some controversy. See Paul Lovejoy, *Transformations in Slavery: A History of Slavery in West Africa* (Cambridge: Cambridge University Press, 1983), and Patrick Manning, *Slavery and African Life: Occidental, Oriental, and African Slave Trades* (Cambridge: Cambridge University Press, 1990). See also Suzanne Miers and Igor Kopytoff, eds., *Slavery in Africa: Historical and Anthropological Perspectives* (Madison: University of Wisconsin Press, 1977), and Herbert S. Klein, *The Atlantic Slave Trade* (Cambridge: Cambridge University Press, 1999), 7–9.

67. Perhaps a dozen expeditions numbering not more than twenty ships traversed the seas between England and Guinea between 1553 and 1565. Only another six Guinea voyages took place during what turned out to be a particularly quiet period between 1565 and 1588. Between 1588 and 1600, however, English activity increased somewhat with another dozen or so voyages. Thus, even by the most generous estimate, one that counts the Cape Verde Islands as part of Guinea, perhaps thirty expeditions and only twice as many ships made the trip between England and Guinea (and, in some cases, on again to the Americas) between 1553 and 1600. P. E. H. Hair, "The Experience of Sixteenth-Century English Voyages to Guinea," *Mariner's Mirror* 83:1 (February 1997): 3–13. It is revealing that to Richard Hakluyt, in his *Principal Navigations*, "Guinea" is largely synonymous with "Africa." On this point, see P. E. H. Hair, "Guinea," in the *Hakluyt Handbook*, 1:197–207.

68. Hakluyt, *Principal Navigations*, 11:23–24; John W. Blake, *Europeans in West Africa, 1450–1560*, 2 vols. (London: Hakluyt Society, 1942), 2:301; P. E. H. Hair and Robin Law, "The English in Western Africa to 1700," in *The Oxford History of the British Empire*, vol. 1: *The Origins of Empire*, ed. Nicholas Canny (Oxford: Oxford University Press, 1998), esp. 242–44.

69. For the context of these voyages, see Kenneth R. Andrews, *Trade, Plunder, and Settlement: Maritime Enterprise and the Genesis of the British Empire, 1480–1630* (Cambridge: Cambridge University Press, 1984), 101–10; P. E. H. Hair, "The Experience of the Sixteenth-Century English Voyages to Guinea," *Mariner's Mirror* (February 1997): 3–13; P. E. H. Hair and J. D. Alsop, *English Seamen and Traders in Guinea, 1553–1565: The New Evidence of Their Wills* (Lewiston, NY: Edwin Mellon Press, 1992); Blake, *Europeans in West Africa*, 2:320.

70. Between 1550 and 1600, 209,347 Africans were transported, but only about 60,000 of that number shipped before 1575. By comparison, 667,893 enslaved Africans endured the middle passage between 1601 and 1650 and another 1,207,738 suffered this fate in the half century after 1651. *Voyages: The Trans-Atlantic Slave Trade Database*, www.slavevoyages.org/tast/assessment/estimates.faces (accessed 26 May 2011).

71. Hakluyt, *Principal Navigations*, 6:200. Additional evidence in Towerson's account would suggest that some local inhabitants harbored deep suspicions about the intent of the English "because that foure men were taken perforce last yeere from this place," including "the Captaines sonne and three others . . . with their golde, and all that they had about them" (205, 207).

72. Hakluyt, *Principal Navigations*, 6:217. With regard to the importance of language and communication, see P. E. H. Hair, "The Use of African Languages in Afro-European Contacts in Guinea, 1440–1560," *Sierra Leone Language Review* 5 (1966): 7–17.

73. Blake, *Europeans in West Africa*, 2:355–58.

74. Hakluyt, *Principal Navigations*, 10:7–8 (first Hawkins voyage), and 6:263–65 and 10:9–63 (second Hawkins voyage). The details of the Hawkins and Lovell slave-trading expeditions have been recounted in numerous sources. Two recent works are Harry Kelsey, *Sir John Hawkins: Queen Elizabeth's Slave Trader* (New Haven, CT: Yale University Press, 2003), and Nick Hazelwood, *The Queen's Slave Trader: John Hawkyns, Elizabeth I, and the Trafficking in Human Souls* (New York: Harper Perennial, 2004).

75. PRO, State Papers, Domestic, Elizabeth [SP 12/44] (16 September 1567), cited in Hazelwood, *The Queen's Slave Trader*, 173; Hakluyt, *Principal Navigations*, 10:64–65 (third Hawkins voyage). On English investors, see Ronald Pollitt, "John Hawkins' Troublesome Voyages: Merchants, Bureaucrats, and the Origin of the Slave Trade," *Journal of British Studies* 12:2 (May 1973): 26–40.

76. Hakluyt, *Principal Navigations*, 10:65–73. The fate of many of those left behind will be detailed in Chapter 4.

77. John Hawkins, *A true declaration of the troublesom voyadge of M. John Hawkins to the parties of Guynea and the west Indies, in the yeares of our Lord 1567 and 1568* (London, 1569). This text was copied, with punctuation and spelling corrections, by Hakluyt for his account of the third voyage. On the reasons for the English abandonment of the slave trade, see Andrews, *Trade, Plunder, and Settlement*, 127–28.

78. G.V. Scammell, "The English in the Atlantic Islands, c. 1450–1650," *Mariner's Mirror* 72:3 (1986): 310; John C. Appleby, "A Guinea Venture, c. 1657: A Note on the Early English Slave Trade," *Mariner's Mirror* 79:1 (February 1993): 84–87; and Appleby, " 'A Business of Much Difficulty': A London Slaving Venture, 1651–54," *Mariner's Mirror* 81:1 (February 1995): 3–14.

79. Andrews, *Trade, Plunder, and Settlement*, 113; Hair and Law, "The English in Western Africa to 1700," 250–53; John W. Blake, "The English Guinea Company, 1618–1660," *Proceedings of the Belfast Natural History and Philosophical Society* 3:1 (1945–46): 14–27; and Robert Porter, "The Crispe Family and the African Trade in the Seventeenth Century," *Journal of African History* 9 (1968): 57–77.

80. Purchas, *Hakluytus Posthumus*, 4:2, and Hakluyt, *Principal Navigations*, 7:98. On the uncertain provenance of the Rainolds manuscript, see *The Hakluyt Handbook*, 1:194–95, 2:425.

81. About lands farther to the south, Purchas had several recent English eyewitness accounts to rely on, particularly that of Andrew Battell, but he also reprinted Abraham Hartwell's 1597 translation of Duarte Lopes's experiences in the Congo. On Marees and Ruiters, see Schmidt, *Innocence Abroad*, 157–58. On Dierick Ruiters as the possible author of the brief entry on Benin, see Albert van Dantzig and Adam Johns, ed. and trans., *Description and historical account of the Gold Kingdom of Guinea (1602), by Pieter de Marees* (Oxford: Oxford University Press, 1987). Schmidt also emphasizes here the Dutch obsession with "wonders" in this body of literature (157–58). On this subject, see Stephen J. Greenblatt, *Marvelous Possessions: The Wonder of the New World* (Chicago: University of Chicago Press, 1991). On the Dutch, slavery, and their attitudes toward Africans, see P. C. Emmer, *The Dutch Slave Trade, 1500–1850*, trans. Chris Emery (New York: Berghahn Books, 2005), esp. 10–16.

82. Purchas, *Hakluytus Posthumus*, 6:353–54.

83. Richard Jobson, *The Golden Trade: Or, a discovery of the River Gambra, and the Golde Trade of the Aethiopians* (London, 1623), 89. It seems, however, that Jobson was being offered "comfort women" rather than laborers. As the passage continues, the African remarks that "it was the only marchandize, they carried downe into the countrey, where they fetch all their salt, and that they were solde there to white men, who earnestly desired them, especially such young women, as hee had brought for us: we answered, They were another kinde of people different from us." For insight into this passage, see the modern reprint edition, *The Discovery of River Gambra (1623)*, ed. David P. Gamble and P. E. H. Hair (London: Hakluyt Society, 1999), 31–32, esp. n. 1, and 140.

84. Purchas, *Hakluytus Posthumus*, 4:373–74, 421–22.

85. Sir Edward Coke, *The first part of the Institutes of the lawes of England: Or, A commentarie upon Littleton, not the name of a lawyer onely, but of the law it self* (London, 1628), 116; Thomas More, *A frutefull pleasaunt, & wittie work, of the best state of a publique weale, and of the newe yle, called Utopia*, trans. Raphe Robynson (London, 1556), 91v.; and John Wheeler, *A Treatise of Commerce* (London, 1601), 6–7.

86. "The first voyage of Robert Baker," in Hakluyt, *Principall Navigations* (1589), 134. The two modern reprint editions of the poem are Boies Penrose, *Robert Baker: An Ancient Mariner of 1565* (Boston: Club of Odd Volumes, 1942), and *The Travails in Guinea of an unknown Tudor poet in verse*, ed. P. E. H. Hair (Liverpool: Liverpool University Press, 1990). Neither Penrose nor Hair can offer much in the way of a biography, except to suggest that Baker's work may have originally been published in 1568.

87. Hakluyt, *Principall Navigations* (1589), 139. On Portuguese trade in the region, see Northrup, "The Gulf of Guinea and the Atlantic World," 170–93.

88. Hakluyt, *Principall Navigations* (1589), 139.

89. Hakluyt, *Principall Navigations* (1589), 141. Baker's poem has been a frequent touchstone for scholars interested in determining what early modern Englishmen thought about Africa and Africans, with most scholars concluding that it offers strong evidence that English seafarers were prone to characterize African peoples in derogatory terms, and skin color was difficult to ignore. To Baker, the argument goes, sub-Saharan Africans were "wilde" men, "blacke beast[s]," "brutish blacke people," "blacke burnt men," "beastly savage people," and "fiends more fierce than those in hell." For examples, see Winthrop D. Jordan, *White over Black: American Attitudes Toward the Negro, 1550–1812* (Chapel Hill: University of North Carolina Press, 1968), 4; Alden T. Vaughan and Virginia Mason Vaughan, "Before *Othello*: Elizabethan Representations of Sub-Saharan Africans," *William and Mary Quarterly* 54:1 (January 1997): 32; and Andrews, *Trade, Plunder, and Settlement*,

115. Although negative assessments can be plucked from the poem, the use of more neutral and occasionally even positive language was equally common.

90. Hakluyt, *Principal Navigations*, 6:200, 277; 7:94, 99. It was by the "vile trecherous meanes of the Portugals," Rainolds also reported, that "about forty Englishmen [were] cruelly slaine and captived" (7:91). For a less jaundiced view, see Peter Mark, "The Evolution of 'Portuguese' Identity: Luso-Africans on the Upper Guinea Coast from the Sixteenth to the Early Nineteenth Century," *Journal of African History* 40 (1999): 173–91.

91. Hakluyt, *Principal Navigations*, 6:457, 7:93; Thornton, *Africa and Africans*, 43–71; P. E. H. Hair, "Attitudes to Africans in English Primary Sources on Guinea up to 1650," *History in Africa* 26 (1999): 43–68; and Andrews, *Trade, Plunder, and Settlement*, 41–63, 101–15.

CHAPTER 3

1. Archivo General de la Nación, Inquisición, tomo 52 (Cambridge University Library, Add. 7230–31): proceedings against William Collins, 1572, cited in P. E. H. Hair, "Protestants as Pirates, Slavers, and Proto-Missionaries: Sierra Leone 1568 and 1582," *Journal of Ecclesiastical History* 21:3 (July 1970): 223.

2. For simplicity and because of the lack of clarity in the sources, I have generally chosen to use the word *African* as a generic referent to Africans, African Americans, and/or people of African descent, free and enslaved. The distinctions among these categories matter greatly, but the English sources, in particular, are often elusive and English writers typically glossed over them with their use of the less satisfactory word: "negro."

3. Kenneth R. Andrews, ed., *The Last Voyage of Drake & Hawkins* (London: Hakluyt Society, 1972), 94, 190, 192.

4. Richard Hakluyt, *The Principal Navigations, Voyages, Traffiques, & Discoveries of the English Nation*, 12 vols. (New York: AMS Press, 1965), 10:149; Hakluyt, *A Discourse of Western Planting*, ed. David B. Quinn and Alison M. Quinn (London: Hakluyt Society, 1993), 43. The idea that there existed an eternal conflict between the Spanish and cimarrons has, of course, important historiographical implications. Edmund Morgan claimed that Drake and "the Cimarrons evidently took to one another or recognized that they had common or complementary interests." Morgan also suggests that the English began to "indoctrinate the Cimarrons with a hatred of Catholicism." Their alliance, Morgan concludes, reveals "a camaraderie that went beyond the mutual benefits of the alliance." From this perspective, the English were not simply base privateers looking for gold, they were freedom fighters. Edmund S. Morgan, *American Slavery, American Freedom: The Ordeal of Colonial Virginia* (New York: W. W. Norton, 1975), 11–13.

5. John King, *Lectures upon Jonas, delivered at Yorke in the yeare of our Lorde 1594* (Oxford, 1597), 179. Girolamo Benzoni's work was published in Italian in 1565, Latin in 1578, and French in 1579. No English version appeared until Samuel Purchas included a small fragment of the work in the 1625 edition of his *Hakluytus Posthumus*.

6. Sir William Alexander, *An Encouragement to Colonies* (London, 1624), 7; *The Drake Manuscript (in the Pierpont Morgan Library)—Histoire Naturalle des Indes*, trans. Ruth S. Kraemer (London: André Deutsch, 1996), f. 57, 97–97v, 98–98v, 10–100v, 106–106v; *The Observations of Sir Richard Hawkins Knight, in his Voyage to the South Sea, Anno Domini 1593* (London, 1622), reprinted in I. A. Wright, ed., *Documents Concerning English Voyages to the Spanish Main, 1569–1580* (London: Hakluyt Society, 1932), 339; Hakluyt, *Principal Navigations*, 9:407.

7. Andrews, *The Last Voyage of Drake & Hawkins*, 217, 207, 209.

8. Kenneth R. Andrews's arguably definitive *Trade, Plunder, and Settlement: Maritime Enterprise and the Genesis of the British Empire, 1480–1630* (Cambridge: Cambridge University Press, 1984), provides one paragraph on the entire expedition.

9. On England's changing attitudes about piracy, see Claire Jowitt, "Piracy and Politics in Heywood and Rowley's *Fortune by Land and Sea* (1607–9)," *Renaissance Studies* 16:2 (2002): 217–33, and Barbara Fuchs, "Faithless Empires: Pirates, Renegadoes, and the English Nation," *English Literary History* 67:1 (2000): 45–69.

10. Between 1562 and 1568, 4 slave-trading expeditions took place, involving perhaps 15 ships. Between 1570 and 1585, 14 expeditions (30 ships) set sail. Between 1585 and 1603, 76 expeditions involving 235 vessels plundered Spanish shipping and coastal enclaves. Two of these expeditions, Drake's grand voyage of 1585 and 1586 and the 1595 armada co-commanded by Drake and Hawkins, account for 52 ships. See Kenneth R. Andrews, *The Spanish Caribbean: Trade and Plunder, 1530–1630* (New Haven, CT: Yale University Press, 1978), and Andrews, *Elizabethan Privateering: English Privateering During the Spanish War, 1585–1603*. (Cambridge: Cambridge University Press, 1964). According to Andrews, extant records likely reveal only half of the total number of actual voyages and ships during this era.

11. Hakluyt, *Principal Navigations*, 10:7–74; I. A. Wright, ed., *Spanish Documents Concerning English Voyages to the Caribbean, 1527–1568* (London: Hakluyt Society, 1929), esp. 95–112. The most useful account of these slave-trading voyages is Andrews, *Trade, Plunder, and Settlement*, esp. 116–34.

12. Andrews, *Trade, Plunder, and Settlement*, 129; Wright, *Documents*, 9, 33.

13. Wright, *Documents*, 50, 69. It seems unlikely that the English would have handed over Spanish subjects to cimarrons to be used as slaves. In fact, John Oxenham earned the ire of cimarrons when he allowed some Spaniards to go free during his 1577 expedition. The English were not beyond treating other Europeans badly; during an expedition to Brazil beginning in 1594, James Lancaster captured a ship with sixty Africans, ten Portuguese women, and forty Portuguese men. Accordingly, "the women and the Negros we turned out of the towne, but the Portugals our Admiral kept to draw the carts when they were laden, which to us was a very great ease." It was one thing for Englishmen to use other Europeans as slaves, but quite another for them to allow cimarrons to do the same. Wright, *Documents*, 172–73, 176; Hakluyt, *Principal Navigations*, 11:57.

14. Richard Hakluyt, "A Discourse of the Commodity of the Taking of the Straight of Magellanus" (ca. 1579–80), in *The Original Writings & Correspondence of the Two Richard Hakluyts*, 2 vols., ed. E. G. R. Taylor (London: Hakluyt Society, 1935), 1:142–43.

15. Wright, *Documents*, 176–77. For more concerning the specifics and larger context of the Oxenham expedition, see Andrews, *The Spanish Caribbean*, 134–46.

16. I use the word "imperial" here under advisement. Although scholars generally distinguish between early English colonialism (or "colonial enterprises") and later British imperialism, largely as a result of the absence of any real bureaucratic infrastructure or coherent ideology to buttress an empire in the early modern period, some individuals, under certain circumstances, were clearly thinking in a purposeful and comprehensive fashion about empire in this early period. For a lucid consideration of the problem, see David Armitage, *The Ideological Origins of the British Empire* (Cambridge: Cambridge University Press, 2000), esp. 1–23.

17. Ruth Pike, "Black Rebels: The Cimarrons of Sixteenth-Century Panama," *The Americas* 64:2 (2007): 243–66; David M. Davidson, "Negro Slave Control and Resistance in Colonial Mexico, 1519–1650," *Hispanic American Historical Review* 46:3 (1966): 235–53, reprinted in Richard Price, ed., *Maroon Societies: Rebel Slave Communities in the Americas*, 2nd ed. (Baltimore: Johns Hopkins

University Press, 1979), 82–103; and Edgar F. Love, "Negro Resistance to Spanish Rule in Colonial Mexico," *Journal of Negro History* 52:2 (April 1967): 91. For an informative treatment of the cooperative relationships that were forged in Spanish America, often out of mere necessity, see Matthew Restall, *The Black Middle: Africans, Mayas, and Spaniards in Colonial Yucatan* (Stanford, CA: Stanford University Press, 2009).

18. Andrews, *The Last Voyage of Drake & Hawkins*, 211, 212, and Andrews, *Trade, Plunder, and Settlement*, 134. The two cimarron communities were actually somewhat small. The town of Santiago del Principe numbered fewer than thirty houses, while Santa Cruz la Real was home to about a hundred people. And although both settlements were supposedly loyal to the Crown, Spanish authorities continued to be wary. A 1587 report on the defenses in Panama, for example, remarked that "there is no trust or confidence in any of these Negroes, and therefore we must take heede and beware of them, for they are our mortall enemies." It may be significant that this observation fell into English hands and was published in the final edition of Richard Hakluyt's *Principal Navigations*. As Kenneth Andrews notes, Drake probably had access to this document before his departure in 1595. See Andrews, *The Last Voyage of Drake & Hawkins*, 193 n. 2.

19. The Spanish were likely naïve to conclude that cimarrons were loyal, as famously evoked in Lope de Vega's celebratory *La Dragontea* (1598). For a discussion of this point, see Antonio Sánchez Jiménez, "Raza, identidad y rebelión en los confines del Imperio hispánico: los cimarrones de Santiago del Príncipe y *La Dragontea* (1598) de Lope de Vega," *Hispanic Review* 75:2 (Spring 2007): 113–33.

20. Wright, *Documents*, 259; Hakluyt, *Discourse of Western Planting*, 60, 43.

21. John Hale, *The Civilization of Europe in the Renaissance* (New York: Atheneum, 1994), 43–45; William B. Cohen, *The French Encounter with Africans: White Responses to Blacks, 1530–1880* (Bloomington: Indiana University Press, 1980), 5; and A. C. de C. M. Saunders, *A Social History of Black Slaves and Freedmen in Portugal, 1441–1555* (Cambridge: Cambridge University Press, 1982). Similar comments about the extraordinary number of "Ethiopians" in Portugal were recorded by the Bohemian baron Leo of Rozmital in 1466 and Hieronymus Münzer in 1494. See A. J. R. Russell-Wood, "Before Columbus: Portugal's African Prelude to the Middle Passage and Contribution to the Discourse on Race and Slavery," in *Race, Discourse, and the Origin of the Americas: A New World View*, ed. Ver Lawrence Hyatt and Rex Nuttleford (Washington, DC: Smithsonian Institution Press, 1995), 148.

22. W. G. Hoskins, *The Age of Plunder: The England of Henry VIII, 1500–1547* (New York: Longman, 1976), 39; Heather Dalton, "Negotiating Fortune: English Merchants in Early Sixteenth-Century Seville," in *Bridging the Early Modern Atlantic World: People, Products, and Practices on the Move*, ed. Caroline A. Williams (Burlington, VT: Ashgate, 2009), 57–74, esp. 64–65. I thank Alison Games for this reference.

23. William D. Phillips Jr., *Slavery from Roman Times to the Early Transatlantic Trade* (Minneapolis: University of Minnesota Press, 1985), 160–63; Ruth Pike, *Enterprise and Adventure: The Genoese in Seville and the Opening of the New World* (Ithaca, NY: Cornell University Press, 1966), 55; Hakluyt, *Principal Navigations*, 9:338; Pauline Croft, *The Spanish Company* (London: London Record Society, 1973); Croft, "English Trade with Peninsular Spain, 1558–1625" (D.Phil. diss., Oxford University, 1969); Croft, "Trading with the Enemy, 1585–1604," *Historical Journal* 32:2 (1989): 281–302; and V. M. Shillington and A. B. Wallis Chapman, *The Commercial Relations of England and Portugal* (New York: Burt Franklin, 1907).

24. G. V. Scammell, "The English in the Atlantic Islands, c. 1450–1650," *Mariner's Mirror* 72:3 (August 1986): 295–317; L. De Alberti and A. B. Wallis Chapman, eds., *English Merchants and the Spanish Inquisition in the Canaries* (London: Camden Society, 1912); Eduardo Aznar Vallejo, "The

Conquests of the Canary Islands," in *Implicit Understandings: Observing, Reporting, and Reflecting on the Encounters Between Europeans and Other Peoples in the Early Modern Era*, ed. Stuart B. Schwartz (Cambridge: Cambridge University Press, 1994), 134–56; and Hakluyt, *Principal Navigations*, 6:124–31, 10:7–8.

25. Croft, "English Trade with Peninsular Spain," 351–54; Albert J. Loomie, S.J., *The Spanish Elizabethans: The English Exiles at the Court of Philip II* (New York: Fordham University Press, 1963). On Bodenham's 1550 voyage, see Hakluyt, *Principal Navigations* 5:71–76.

26. On the development of anti-Jewish and anti-Moorish attitudes in the Iberian world, as well as related social implications, see David Nirenberg, *Communities of Violence: Persecution of Minorities in the Middle Ages* (Princeton, NJ: Princeton University Press, 1996), and Bernard Lewis, *Cultures in Conflict: Christians, Muslims, and Jews in the Age of Discovery* (New York: Oxford University Press, 1995).

27. Frank Tannenbaum, *Slave and Citizen: The Negro in the Americas* (New York: Knopf, 1946). Tannenbaum's broader thesis, concerning the connection between Roman law and Catholicism and the significance of racism in Latin America, has been justly criticized. On the continuing relevance of Tannenbaum, see Alejandro de la Fuente, "Slave Law and Claims-Making in Cuba: The Tannenbaum Thesis Revisited" (with commentaries by María Elena Díaz and Christopher Schmidt-Nowara), *Law and History Review* 22:2 (2004): 339–69.

28. Phillips, *Slavery from Roman Times to the Early Transatlantic Trade*, 107–13, 154–70; Ruth Pike, "Sevillian Society in the Sixteenth Century: Slaves and Freedmen," *Hispanic American Historical Review* 47:3 (August 1967): 344–59; and Miguel Gual Camarena, "Una cofradía de negros libertos en el siglo XV," *Estudios de la Edad Media en la Corona de Aragón* 5 (1952): 457–66.

29. Herman L. Bennett, *Africans in Colonial Mexico: Absolutism, Christianity, and Afro-Creole Consciousness, 1570–1640* (Bloomington: Indiana University Press, 2003); Patrick J. Carroll, *Blacks in Colonial Veracruz: Race, Ethnicity, and Regional Development*, 2nd ed. (Austin: University of Texas Press, 2001); Robinson A. Herrera, " 'Por que no sabemos firmar': Black Slaves in Early Guatemala," *The Americas* 57:2 (2000): 247–67; Rodolfo Pastor F., "De Moros en la Costa a Negros de Castilla: Representación y Realidad en las Crónicas del Siglo XVII Centroamericano," *Historia Mexicana* 44:2 (1994): 195–235; and Frederick P. Bowser, "Africans in Spanish American Colonial Society," in *The Cambridge History of Latin America*, vol. 2: *Colonial Latin America*, ed. Leslie Bethell (Cambridge: Cambridge University Press, 1984), 357–79. More recently, see Alejandro de la Fuente, *Havana and the Atlantic in the Sixteenth Century* (Chapel Hill: University of North Carolina Press, 2008), esp. 147–85.

30. Hakluyt, *Principal Navigations*, 9:338, 341, 347, 350, 10:6–7.

31. Hakluyt, *Principal Navigations*, 9:354, 361, 368, 389. The possible exception to this pattern was the interest Robert Tomson took in a few of the Africans he encountered. He noted, for example, that there was a "kind of small worme which creepeth into the soles of mens feet & especially of the black Moores and children which use to go barefoot, & maketh their feet to grow as big as a mans head" (342). Tomson's mild curiosity was aroused even more by the plight of "a woman black Moore," who fell into the ocean after a shipwreck while trying to get into the rescue boat. Tomson related how the woman was "caught by the coat & pulled into the boate having still her child under her arme, both of them halfe drowned, and yet her naturall love towards her child would not let her let the childe goe" (344–45).

32. "The *Primrose* Journal," in Mary Frear Keeler, ed., *Sir Francis Drake's West Indian Voyage, 1585–86* (London: Hakluyt Society, 1981), 188–89. A similar offhand comment regarding the presence of African slaves appears on page 191. One other main source for this expedition, hereafter

NOTES TO PAGES 97–103

known as "The *Leicester* Journal," contains the simple remark that "the generall and most of his Captens with 700 men went into the Illand. They went in the night from Saint Iacomo having 2 or 3 Moores for there guides." *Sir Francis Drake's West Indian Voyage*, 148.

33. The term "go-between" comes from Stephen Greenblatt, *Marvelous Possessions: The Wonder of the New World* (Chicago: University of Chicago Press, 1991), 119–51. On the notion of cultural brokers among the earliest generation of Africans in the Atlantic world, see esp. Ira Berlin, "From Creole to African: Atlantic Creoles and the Origins of African-American Society in Mainland North America," *William and Mary Quarterly* 53:2 (April 1996): 251–88.

34. *New Light on Drake: A Collection of Documents Relating to His Voyage of Circumnavigation, 1577–1580*, trans. and ed. Zelia Nuttall (London: Hakluyt Society, 1914), 102.

35. *New Light on Drake*, 27 n. 1, 94, 106, 171, 325. If Diego had been with Drake since 1573, he may be the same "Diego a Negro" recorded in *Sir Francis Drake Revived* (London, 1628). The Diego recorded in this work came to Drake's men upon their arrival in Panama and continually appeared in the record for his help in locating gold and silver, facilitating relations with cimarrons, and working on small-scale construction projects. See Wright, *Documents*, 264–65, 269, 275, 278.

36. Harry Kelsey, *Sir Francis Drake: The Queen's Pirate* (New Haven, CT: Yale University, 1998), 141, 149, 152, 154–56.

37. Wright, *Documents*, 278.

38. Hakluyt, *Principal Navigations*, 11:222; Purchas, *Hakluytus Posthumus*, 16:102–3.

39. E. G. R. Taylor, ed., *The Troublesome Voyage of Captain Edward Fenton, 1582–1583* (Cambridge: Cambridge University Press for the Hakluyt Society, 1955), 209. Further details may be found in Elizabeth Story Donno, ed., *An Elizabethan in 1582: The Diary of Richard Madox, Fellow of All Souls* (London: Hakluyt Society, 1976).

40. Hakluyt, *Principal Navigations*, 6:284.

41. Kenneth R. Andrews, ed., *English Privateering Voyages to the West Indies, 1588–1595* (London: Hakluyt Society, 1959), 234, 249. This collection also contains further documentation relating to Newport's and King's voyages.

42. Kenneth R. Andrews, "English Voyages to the Caribbean, 1596–1604: An Annotated List," *William and Mary Quarterly* 31 (1974): 248.

43. Irene A.Wright, ed., *Further English Voyages to Spanish America, 1583–1594* (London: Hakluyt Society, 1951), 7, 2. William Hawkins, brother to John, led an expedition of seven ships to the West Indies, which included stops in the Cape Verde Islands, Margarita, and Puerto Rico, that returned in 1583. Apparently with him upon his return was a man named Bastien, about whom little is known beyond his death and burial in December of that year. See M. C. S. Cruwys, ed., *The Register of Baptisms, Marriages & Burials of the Parish of St. Andrew's, Plymouth, Co. Devon, A.D. 1581–1618, with Baptisms 1610–1633* (Exeter: Devon & Cornwall Record Society, 1954), 292.

44. Hakluyt, *Principal Navigations*, 10:184–85. Other instances of English ships capturing a Portuguese slave ship and landing the cargo can be found in Purchas, *Hakluytus Posthumus*, 16:293.

45. If Drake had been concerned about criticism upon his return regarding the condition of the African woman, he was partly justified. William Camden later wrote that Drake had "most inhamanely" left the "Black-more-Maide who had been gotten with Child in his Ship" to her own fate on a deserted island. Cited in Kelsey, *Sir Francis Drake*, 201.

46. For the evidence of those who returned with Lovell, see Robert Barrett's testimony, in Kelsey, *Sir Francis Drake*, 473 n. 73. For those who returned with Hawkins in 1568, see Hair, "Protestants as Pirates," 220.

47. Hakluyt, *Principal Navigations*, 10:191; Wright, *Documents*, 264, 269, 283.

48. The best general treatments of this history can be found in the early pages of James Walvin, *Black and White: The Negro in English Society, 1555–1945* (London: Penguin, 1973); Folarin Shyllon, *Black People in Britain, 1555–1833* (London: Oxford University Press, 1977); and Peter Fryer, *Staying Power: The History of Black People in Britain* (London: Pluto Press, 1984).

49. William Cuningham, *The Cosmographical Glasse, conteinyng the pleasant Principles of Cosmographie, Geographie, Hydrographie, or Navigation* (London, 1559), 66–67.

50. Marika Sherwood, "Black People in Tudor England," *History Today* 33:10 (2003): 40–42. The Derby Household Books contain "Orders touching the government of My lord's house," which state that "no *slaves* nor boyes shall sitt in the hall, but in the place therefore appoynted convenyent. . . . That the yemen of horses and groomes of the stable shall not suffre any boyes or *slaves* to abye about the stables nor lye in them." *Stanley Papers*, pt. 2 (Chetham Soc., 1843), 9, cited in Alexander Savine, "Bondmen under the Tudors," *Transactions of the Royal Historical Society* 17 (1903): 251. Savine, along with C. S. L. Davies and James Walvin, suggests that these slaves may have been Africans, but Peter Fryer argues that they were probably "the villeins regardant of the manor."

51. Fryer, *Staying Power*, 8–9, and Walvin, *Black and White*, 8; and *The Register of Baptisms, Marriages & Burials of the Parish of St. Andrew's, Plymouth, Co. Devon, A.D. 1581–1618, with Baptisms 1610–1633*, ed. M. C. S. Cruwys (Exeter: Devon & Cornwall Record Society, 1954), 305, 292.

52. For some indication of these faint traces, see Paul Edwards, "The Early African Presence in the British Isles," in *Essays on the History of Blacks in Britain*, ed. Jagdish S. Gundara and Ian Duffield (Aldershot: Ashgate, 1992), 9–29; Imtiaz Habib, "*Othello*, Sir Peter Negro, and the Blacks of Early Modern England: Colonial Inscription and Postcolonial Excavation," *Literature Interpretation Theory* 9 (1998): 15–30; and Gustav Ungerer, "Recovering a Black African's Voice in an English Lawsuit: Jacques Francis and the Salvage Operation of the *Mary Rose* and the *Sancta Maria* and *Sanctus Edwardus*, 1545–ca. 1550," *Medieval and Renaissance Drama in England* 17 (2005): 255–71.

53. Little is known about the precise location of the African inhabitants in Tudor England, but the surviving evidence and much of the previously cited scholarship would indicate that the highest concentrations could be found in the port cities that served as the main points of entry during the era.

54. *Calendar of State Papers: Domestic Series, of the Reigns of Edward VI, Mary, Elizabeth, and James I (1547–1625)* [hereafter *CSP:DS*], 12 vols. (London, 1856–72), 4:381 and 5:199; *Notes and Queries*, n.s., 8:4 (April 1961): 138; and E. M. Leonard, *The Early History of English Poor Relief* (Cambridge, 1906), 297n, cited in Walvin, *Black and White*, 8.

55. Alison Grant, "Breaking the Mould: North Devon Maritime Enterprise, 1560–1640," in *Tudor and Stuart Devon: The Common Estate and Government*, ed. Todd Gray, Margery Rowe, and Audrey Erskine (Exeter: University of Exeter Press, 1992), 126–27; and *The Register of Baptisms, Marriages & Burials of the Parish of St. Andrews Plymouth Co. Devon A.D. 1581–1618 . . .*, ed. M. C. S. Cruwys (Exeter: Devon & Cornwall Record Society, 1954), 57, cited in Fryer, *Staying Power*, 9.

56. George Best, *A True Discourse of the late voyages of discoverie, for the finding of a passage to Cathaya, by the Northwest, under the conduct of Martin Frobisher, Generall* (London, 1578), 19–35; and Hakluyt, *Principal Navigations*, 7:262. The St. Andrew's parish records record only one possible example of a marriage in 1599 when "Blackmore *alias* Hellier, John & Anstice Light, *wid*" were married in October. *Register of Baptisms, Marriages & Burials of the Parish of St. Andrew's*, 242. Best's *Discourse* will be given greater consideration below.

57. Literature on "anti-blackness" and color prejudice and early modern England generally takes its cue from Winthrop D. Jordan, *White over Black: American Attitudes Toward the Negro, 1550–1812* (Chapel Hill: University of North Carolina Press, 1968), esp. 4–11.

58. Reginald Scot, *The Discoverie of Witchcraft* (London, 1584), 152–53 [bk .7, cap. 15]. See also Keith Thomas, *Religion and the Decline of Magic* (New York: Charles Scribner's Sons, 1971). Thomas suggests that "contemporary assumptions as to what was displeasing and perverted" were revealed through such descriptions of demons. Thus, one apparent victim of possession described Satan as "an ugly black man with shoulders higher than his head" (480).

59. *The Drake Manuscript*, f. 111–111v and 269. For examples of woodcuts, see *The Euing Collection of English Broadside Ballads . . . in the Library of the University of Glasgow* (Glasgow: University of Glasgow Publications, 1971), 108, 402, 522.

60. Roy Strong, *The Cult of Elizabeth: Elizabethan Portraiture and Pageantry* (London: Thames and Hudson, 1977). The scholarship on this subject is rich, particularly among literary scholars who have been inclined to emphasize the instability of categories of whiteness and blackness. See, for example, Mary Floyd-Wilson, "Temperature, Temperance, and Racial Difference in Ben Jonson's *The Masque of Blackness*," *English Literary Renaissance* 28:2 (1998): 183–209, and Bernadette Andrea, "Black Skin, The Queen's Masques: Africanist Ambivalence and Feminine Author(ity) in the Masques of *Blackness* and *Beauty*," *English Literary Renaissance* 29:2 (1999): 246–81.

61. *Biblioteca Eliotae* (London, 1545) cited in Carolyn Prager, " 'If I be Devil': English Renaissance Response to the Proverbial and Ecumenical Ethiopian," *Journal of Medieval and Renaissance Studies* 17 (1987): 259. Several continental examples are included in Ladislas Bugner, general ed., *The Image of the Black in Western Art*, vol. 2, pt. 2: Jean Devisse and Michel Mollat, *From the Early Christian Era to the "Age of Discovery": Africans in the Christian Ordinance of the World (Fourteenth to Sixteenth Century)*, trans. William Granger Ryan (Lausanne: Office du Livre, 1979), 59–61.

62. Geffrey Whitney, *A Choice of Emblemes, and other devises, for the moste parte gathered out of sundrie writers, Englished and moralized* (Leiden, 1586), 57. The power of this commonplace was implied in Marochitanus Samuel, *The Blessed Jew of Marocco or, a Blackamoor made White* (London, 1648), a work that appeared first in Arabic and Latin.

63. Richard Percevale, *A Spanish Grammar, first collect and published by Richard Percivale Gent: Now augmented and increased . . . by John Minsheu* (London, 1599), 83; *The Geneva Bible: A Facsimile of the 1560 Edition* (Madison: University of Wisconsin Press, 1969). Interestingly, the header for this page (312) reads "The blacke More" although the reference is buried in the middle of the page.

64. Literary scholar Kim F. Hall has argued that " 'black' in Renaissance discourses is opposed not to 'white' but to 'beauty' or 'fairness,' and these terms most often refer to the appearance or moral states of women." In Hall, *Things of Darkness: Economies of Race and Gender in Early Modern England* (Ithaca, NY: Cornell University Press, 1995), 9.

65. George Whetstone, *An Heptameron of Civill Discourses* (London, 1582), R3r–v; William Shakespeare, *Hamlet*, Act 1, scene 2. See Louis Montrose, *The Purpose of Playing: Shakespeare and the Cultural Politics of the Elizabethan Theatre* (Chicago: University of Chicago Press, 1996). Much the same observation was made by Edmund Spenser in *The Faerie Queene* (London, 1590), 527 [bk. 3, cant. 9], where he wrote, "Never let the en'sample of the bad / Offend the good: for good by paragone / Of evil, may more notably be rad, / As white seemes fairer, macht with black attonce." Subsequent editions use the word "attone" (at one) rather than "attonce" (at once).

66. *Archivo General de Indias*, 51–3–81/5 (C.U.L., Add. 7258): depositions of Walter Jones, Richard Temple, and Michael Sole, Seville, November–December 1569; cited in P. E. H. Hair, "Protestants as Pirates, Slavers, and Proto-missionaries: Sierra Leone 1568 and 1582," *Journal of Ecclesiastical History* 21:3 (July 1970): 220.

67. Hakluyt, *Principal Navigations*, 6:436, 7:122, 9:319; 10:191, 243, 11:144, 175; Ralph Lane, "Discourse of the First Colony," in *The Roanoke Voyages*, ed. David Beers Quinn (London: Hakluyt Society, 1955), 1:235, 268, 272–74, cited in Carole Shammas, "The Elizabethan Gentlemen Adventurers and Western Planting" (Ph.D. diss., Johns Hopkins University, 1971), 143.

68. *The Register of Baptisms, Marriages & Burials of the Parish of St. Andrew's*, 292, and Wright, *Further English Voyages*, 2, 7.

69. Hakluyt, *Principal Navigations*, 10:216, and Purchas, *Hakluytus Posthumus*, 16:6.

70. "The *Primrose* Journal," 187; Wright, *Further English Voyages*, 212. No single English source makes more mention of Africans than "The *Primrose* Journal." Indeed, the unknown author of this invaluable record occasionally expressed some anti-Spanish vitriol, which led him to reserve a certain compassion for those Africans subjected to Spanish cruelty. For example, he mentioned in passing that while the English forces occupied Santo Domingo "there came 3 or 4 nigros whom wee succored & gave vittles unto," but little else was said in this regard (190).

71. Wright, *Further English Voyages*, 104, 127–29. It was recorded in one deposition that "the negroes of Santo Domingo, armed with nicking knives and swords, seriously harass these English continuously and kill many, and do daring things" (30–31). See also, Andrews, *The Last Voyage of Drake & Hawkins*, 94, 112, for evidence of Africans fighting on the side of the Spanish. For the larger American context, see Matthew Restall, "Black Conquistadors: Armed Africans in Early Spanish America," *The Americas* 57:2 (October 2000): 171–205; Ben Vinson III, *Bearing Arms for His Majesty: The Free-Colored Militia in Colonial Mexico* (Stanford, CA: Stanford University Press, 2001); and Peter M. Voelz, *Slave and Soldier: The Military Impact of Blacks in the Colonial Americas* (New York: Garland Publishing, 1993).

72. "The *Primrose* Journal," 193.

73. Wright, *Further English Voyages*, 35, and "The *Primrose* Journal," 195. Fewer than twenty of the galley slaves seem to have been French. See Louis Lacour, ed., *Mémoire du Voiage en Russie Fait en 1586 par Jehan Sauvage Suivi de L'Expedition de Fr. Drake en Amérique a la Même Epoque* (Paris, 1855), cited in Keeler, *Sir Francis Drake's West Indian Voyage*, 195 n. 3. According to at least one report, some German and French slaves did indeed make it safely back to Europe. See Keeler, *Sir Francis Drake's West Indian Voyage*, 32 n. 1. A handful of Moors also made it home. For the most complete treatment of the Spanish galley slaves, see David Wheat, "Mediterranean Slavery, New World Transformations: Galley Slaves in the Spanish Caribbean, 1578–1635," *Slavery & Abolition* 31:3 (2010): 327–44.

74. Wright, *Further English Voyages*, 35, and Kelsey, *Sir Francis Drake*, 263.

75. Wright, *Further English Voyages*, 51, 124, 135, 159. There is no indication as to whether those who ran to the English were therefore free or kept as slaves. Diego Mendes Torres wrote from Panama that the English brought with them "twelve negroes for the road—these are from Río de la Hacha" (217). Whether they were enslaved or freed, it seems likely that the English kept them around in order to work, in this case as porters.

76. "The *Leicester* Journal," 169. Kelsey contends that the restrictions on slave-holding were an outgrowth of the much larger problems that were incurred by the practice of taking female slaves for sexual partners. According to Kelsey's sources, Englishmen engaged in an "unrightous intercourse" with captured African and Indian women. This, Kelsey suggests, may have been the root of the tensions that existed among the English. See Kelsey, *Sir Francis Drake*, 270–71.

77. Wright, *Further English Voyages*, 52; Keeler, *Sir Francis Drake's West Indian Voyage*, 30 n. 3; and Kelsey, *Sir Francis Drake*, 261. The assertion that Drake sought out cimarrons in Hispaniola dates back to the classic work of Julian S. Corbett, *Drake and the Tudor Navy*, 2 vols. (London, 1898, 1899), esp. 2:33–35.

78. For a useful narrative of this part of the expedition, see Kelsey, *Sir Francis Drake*, 275–79.

79. Wright, *Further English Voyages*, 181, 204, 173, 212; see also pp. 206 and 230.

80. Hakluyt, *Principal Navigations*, 8:342.

81. Hakluyt, *Principal Navigations*, 8:343–44. The myth of England's unique commitment to freedom and anti-slavery principles has been enabled, in part, by the record of English privateering activity in the West Indies during the last half of the sixteenth century. In particular, much has been made of the "liberated" slaves of 1585–86. According to David Beers Quinn, *The Roanoke Voyages, 1584–1590*, 2 vols. (London: Hakluyt Society, 1955), Drake arrived at Roanoke with numerous "negro domestic slaves to whom he promised their freedom, and a substantial number of South American Indians (about 300, including women)." Quinn claims Drake intended to dispose of them as "free labour for the Roanoke settlers" (1:251, 254). In a later collection of documents, edited with Alison Quinn, *First Colonists: Documents on the Planting of the First English Settlements in North America, 1584–1590* (Raleigh: North Carolina Department of Cultural Resources, 1982), we have the statement that "[i]t is unfortunate that we have not the precise terms of Drake's offer, since in it he would have referred to liberated Indians and Negroes who were intended as reinforcement to the colony's labour force" (149). Karen Ordahl Kupperman, *Roanoke: The Abandoned Colony* (Savage, MD: Rowman & Littlefield, 1984), states merely that Drake's men "rescued a very large number of slaves and Indians from Spanish clutches. The few European galley slaves among them he intended to keep, but he decided to offer the three hundred to five hundred others to the colony, probably as a labor supply" (88). When the English decided to abandon the colony, "the several hundred freed slaves and Indians collected by Drake for the colony were probably left in Carolina. . . . If they succeeded in melting into the Indian population," Kupperman adds, "then they began a tradition that was to have a long history in that part of America" (92). Edmund Morgan, in *American Slavery, American Freedom*, offers the most melodramatic interpretation. For him, Drake's expedition took "hundreds of liberated slaves" from Santo Domingo; Drake "made it clear that he would return no slaves, 'except when the slaves themselves desired to go'" from Cartagena; Drake arrived at Roanoke "with his load of Indians and Negroes freed from their Spanish oppressors; and, finally, "What, then, of the liberated slaves and Indians? The saddest part of the story and perhaps the most revealing is that no one bothered to say. . . . Thus casually and ignominiously ended the first attempt to join the planting of English gentle government in North America with the liberation of the Caribbean and South America from Spanish tyranny" (34–35, 41–42).

Based on the pattern of English involvement with Africans in the Atlantic world, it is a dubious assertion that Drake or any other Englishman believed that he had "freed" or "liberated" as many as five hundred Africans and Indians from Spanish America. Most likely, Drake hoped to leave the Roanoke settlers these several hundred laborers (probably as lifetime slaves) and then, had everything gone as planned, received payment from the colony's sponsor, Sir Walter Raleigh, or the Queen for his service to his country's overseas enterprise.

82. Job Hortop remarked on his return to England in 1591 (after having been abandoned along with a number of other Englishmen in the wake of John Hawkins's disastrous final slave-trading voyage) that "many misliked that he left us so behind him, & broght away Negros." The reason, Hortop recalled, was "for them he might have had victuals, or any other thing needfull, if by fowle weather he had beene driven upon the Ilands, which for gold nor silver he could not have had." [Job Hortop], *The travailes of an English man* (London, 1591),18. Hortop's account was reprinted in Hakluyt, *Principal Navigations*, 9:455.

83. For those who returned with Baskerville, see the reference in *Acts of the Privy Council of England . . . New Series, 1542–1604* [hereafter *APC*], 32 vols., ed. John Roche Dasent (London,

1890–1907), 26:16 (1596–97), that one Edward Banes should "take of those blackamoores that in this last voyage under Sir Thomas Baskervile were brought into this realme the nomber of tenn, to be transported by him out of the realme."

84. Great Britain, Public Record Office [hereafter PRO], Privy Council [PC] 2/21, f. 304. Also in *APC* 26:16 (1596–97).

85. PRO, PC 2/21, f. 306. Also in *APC* 26:16–17 (1596–97).

86. *Tudor Royal Proclamations*, 3 vols., ed. Paul L. Hughes and James F. Larkin (New Haven, CT: Yale University Press, 1964–69), 3:221–22. Miranda Kaufmann has argued that there is good reason to believe that the 1601 "proclamation" was never made official and that we should be cautious about attributing its words and sentiments to Elizabeth. See Kaufmann, "Caspar van Senden, Sir Thomas Sherley, and the 'Blackamoor Project,'" *Historical Research* 81 (May 2008): 266–71. I sympathize with Kaufmann's argument that the van Senden project was primarily a business matter, perhaps energized by van Senden himself, and that there is little evidence to support the idea that it came to pass because of racist motives. Yet, the fact that these proposals were not only considered but also implemented, at least in 1596 and quite possibly again in 1601, suggests that the commodification of African peoples was in evidence decades before the first Africans appeared in English American colonies. I would like to thank Miranda Kaufmann for her generous and insightful comments on this material.

87. In Ania Loomba's words, "From Elizabeth I's communiqué deporting blacks . . . to today's British immigration laws, the 'preservation' of the white race is seen to be at stake" (Loomba, *Gender, Race, and Renaissance Drama* [Manchester: Manchester University Press, 1989], 52). See also Fryer, *Staying Power*, 10–12, and Kim F. Hall, "Guess Who's Coming to Dinner?: Colonization and Miscegenation in *The Merchant of Venice*," *Renaissance Drama* n.s. 23 (1992): 87–111. The relevant literature has been summarized by Emily C. Bartels, "Too Many Blackamoors: Deportation, Discrimination, and Elizabeth I," *Studies in English Literature, 1500–1900* 46:2 (2006): 305–22.

88. PRO, PC 2/21, f. 304, 306.

89. Imtiaz Habib has produced an invaluable study that identifies 448 records from English sources documenting the history of Africans in England during the sixteenth and seventeenth centuries. See his *Black Lives in the English Archives, 1500–1677: Imprints of the Invisible* (Aldershot: Ashgate, 2008).

CHAPTER 4

1. "An Admirable New Northern Story," in *The Euing Collection of English Broadside Ballads . . . in the Library of the University of Glasgow*, ed. J. O. Halliwell-Phillipps (Glasgow: University of Glasgow Publications, 1971), 10.

2. William Gouge, *A Recovery from Apostacy* (London, 1639), 2–5. Although the sermon upon which the story of Vincent Jukes is based was published in 1639, Gouge delivered it in October 1638.

3. Gouge, *A Recovery from Apostacy*, 12, 26, 41, 62–63.

4. William Davies, *True Relation of the Travailes and most miserable Captivitie of William Davies, Barber-Surgion of London . . .* (London, 1614), E4, and Samuel Purchas, *Hakluytus Posthumus, or, Purchas His Pilgrimes*, 20 vols. (Glasgow: James MacLehose and Sons, 1905), 1:52–53. See below for the context in which Davies believed people should give thanks to God for their freedoms.

5. Davies, *True Relation*, E4.

6. And historians have been increasingly inclined to tell these stories. See, for example, Giles Milton, *White Gold: The Extraordinary Story of Thomas Pellow and Islam's One Million White Slaves* (New York: Farrar, Straus and Giroux, 2004); Linda Colley, *Captives: The Story of Britain's Pursuit of Empire and How Its Soldiers and Civilians Were Held Captive by the Dream of Global Supremacy, 1600–1850* (New York: Pantheon Books, 2002); and Nabil Matar, *Turks, Moors, and Englishmen in the Age of Discovery* (New York: Columbia University Press, 1999).

7. It is worth noting that historians often go to great lengths to distinguish between the experience of Englishmen as slaves and that of contemporary and subsequent generations of Africans. To make the distinction clear, authors choose to describe their English subjects as captives rather than as slaves and accounts of their ordeals as "captivity narratives" rather than as "slave narratives." See, for example, Paul Baepler, "The Barbary Captivity Narrative in Early America," *Early American Literature* 30 (1995): 95–120, and *White Slaves, African Masters: An Anthology of American Barbary Captivity Narratives* (Chicago: University of Chicago Press, 1999). This perspective is implicit in the works of several other scholars, especially Nabil Matar and Linda Colley, who conceptualize the *corpus captivus*, in Matar's words, primarily as a lens on either the emerging British Empire or the perception of the Muslim world in seventeenth- and eighteenth-century Britain. Matar, "Introduction: England and Mediterranean Captivity, 1577–1704," in *Piracy, Slavery, and Redemption: Barbary Captivity Narratives from Early Modern England*, ed. Daniel J. Vitkus (New York: Columbia University Press, 2001), 1–52; Colley, *Captives*; Kenneth Parker, "Reading 'Barbary' in Early Modern England, 1550–1685," *Seventeenth Century* 19:1 (2004): 87–115; and Joe Snader, *Caught Between Worlds: British Captivity Narratives in Fact and Fiction* (Lexington: University Press of Kentucky, 2000). In the index of Lisa Voigt's *Writing Captivity in the Early Modern Atlantic: Circulations of Knowledge and Authority in the Iberian and English Imperial Worlds* (Chapel Hill: University of North Carolina Press, 2009), the reader will find the following entry: "Slavery. *See* Captivity" (338). A refreshing exception is Catherine M. Styer, "Barbary Pirates, British Slaves, and the Early Modern Atlantic World, 1570–1800" (Ph.D. diss., University of Pennsylvania, 2011).

8. For some insight into the problem of experiential evidence, upon which much of this section is based, see Joan W. Scott, "The Evidence of Experience," *Critical Inquiry* 17 (Summer 1991): 773–97.

9. Richard Hakluyt, *The Principal Navigations, Voyages, Traffiques, & Discoveries of the English Nation*, 12 vols. (New York: AMS Press, 1965), 5:62; Fernand Braudel, *The Mediterranean and the Mediterranean World in the Age of Philip II*, 2 vols. (New York: Harper & Row, 1972–73), 1:612–29. See also Kenneth R. Andrews, *Trade, Plunder, and Settlement: Maritime Enterprise and the Genesis of the British Empire, 1480–1630* (Cambridge: Cambridge University Press, 1984), 87–100; Robert Brenner, "The Social Basis of English Commercial Expansion, 1550–1650," *Journal of Economic History* 32:1 (1972): 361–84; and Lee Eysturlid, " 'Where Everything Is Weighed in the Scales of Material Interest': Anglo-Turkish Trade, Piracy, and Diplomacy in the Mediterranean during the Jacobean Period," *Journal of European Economic History* 22:3 (1993): 613–26.

10. Purchas, *Hakluytus Posthumus*, 6:108, 114. In the words of the historian G. A. Starr, North Africa was "a lively emblem of Hell—a Hell as credible as the newly discovered Paradises, and no less fascinating." Starr, "Escape from Barbary: A Seventeenth-Century Genre," *Huntington Library Quarterly* 29:1 (November 1965): 35.

11. The general European characterization of North African slavery, particularly documents authored by former captive slaves, should be read with a cautious eye. Many of these works are suffused with rhetoric and are not even remotely concerned with presenting slavery in the Muslim

world accurately. See, for example, Ehud R. Toledano, "Representing the Slave's Body in Ottoman Society," *Slavery & Abolition* 23:2 (2002): 57–74.

12. According to W. Laird Clowes, *The Royal Navy: A History from the Earliest Times to the Present*, 7 vols. (London, 1897–1903), at least 466 English ships with perhaps 5,600 Englishmen were taken between 1609 and 1616 (2:22). David Delison Hebb, *Piracy and the English Government, 1616–1642* (Aldershot: Scolar Press, 1994), estimates that more than 400 ships and 8,800 Englishmen were taken by Barbary pirates between 1616 and 1642 (139–40). Linda Colley, "Britain and Islam, 1600–1800: Different Perspectives on Difference," *Yale Review* 88 (October 2000): 1–20, offers the more conservative estimate that there may have been 15,000 "British captives" between 1600 and 1800 (5). Her estimate for the period rises to "20,000 or more" in her monograph, *Captives* (44). For a comprehensive effort to determine the total number of Christian captives in North Africa—a number that Robert C. Davis places in excess of one million people between 1530 and 1780—see Davis, "Counting European Slaves on the Barbary Coast," *Past and Present* 172 (August 2001): 87–124. More recently, see Davis, *Christian Slaves, Muslim Masters: White Slavery in the Mediterranean, the Barbary Coast, and Italy, 1500–1800* (New York: Palgrave Macmillan, 2003), esp. 3–26.

13. *Briefe Abstracts out of Divers Letters of Trust* (London, 1622), 5, 6.

14. On the ideological context of the publication of early narratives, see Nabil Matar, "English Accounts of Captivity in North Africa and the Middle East: 1577–1625," *Renaissance Quarterly* 54 (2001): 553–72.

15. Linda Colley, "Britain and Islam," notes the survival of more than twenty "substantial captivity narratives" for the period between the 1630s the and early nineteenth century" (11). In her monograph, she is more specific: "As far as Barbary is concerned, only fifteen narratives by Britons who were unquestionably captives there appear to have survived from the seventeenth and eighteenth centuries" (*Captives*, 88–89). My intent, however, is to highlight information and ideas about slavery available to a relatively broad spectrum of English society in the early modern era. Therefore, this section, with notable exceptions, is based on the relation in print of roughly a dozen separate incidents published before 1640. Several of these, such as the tale of John Fox, the *Jacob*, John Rawlins, and Edward Webbe appeared in print more than once. (Webbe's account ran through five editions between 1590 and 1610.) Additional details have been extracted from several later publications, particularly when the events of the narrative occurred before 1650.

16. Hakluyt, *Principal Navigations*, 5:154–55. In Hakluyt's telling, the English mariners took the dying boatswain's words to heart, except for the "masters mate, who shrunke from the skirmish, like a notable coward, esteeming neither the value of his name, nor accounting the present example of his fellowes, nor having respect to the miseries, whereunto he should be put."

17. Edward Webbe, *The Rare and most wonderful things* (London, 1610), A4, and A. Roberts, *The Adventures of (Mr T.S.) an English Merchant, Taken Prisoner by the Turks of Argiers* (London, 1670), 9.

18. Hakluyt, *Principal Navigations*, 5:292–97.

19. Purchas, *Hakluytus Posthumus*, 8:334–35, and John Smith, *The True Travels, Adventures, and Observations of Captaine John Smith* (London, 1630), in *The Complete Works of Captain John Smith (1580–1631)*, 3 vols., ed. Philip Barbour (Chapel Hill: University of North Carolina Press, 1986). On Smith's slavery, see Alden T. Vaughan, *American Genesis: Captain John Smith and the Founding of Virginia* (Boston: Little, Brown, 1975), 6–10.

20. Hakluyt, *Principal Navigations*, 5:62; Purchas, *Hakluytus Posthumus*, 8:337, 141 (Sandys), and [Anthony Munday], *The Admirable Deliverance of 266. Christians by John Reynard* (London, 1602), B2. Orlando Patterson, *Slavery and Social Death: A Comparative Study* (Cambridge, MA:

Harvard University Press, 1982), suggests that not only has hair, or lack thereof, been singularly important in setting slaves apart in all slave societies, but also that the shorn beard was a symbol of castration (60).

21. Hakluyt, *Principal Navigations*, 7:126–27, 5:155; Munday, *The Admirable Deliverance of 266. Christians*, B2; Francis Knight, *A Relation of Seaven Yeares Slaverie under the Turkes of Argiere, suffered by an English Captive Merchant* (London, 1640), 28; Davies, *True Relation*, C1.

22. Purchas, *Hakluytus Posthumus*, 6:155, and Ellen G. Friedman, *Spanish Captives in North Africa in the Early Modern Age* (Madison: University of Wisconsin Press, 1983), 55–56.

23. James Wadsworth, *The English Spanish Pilgrime*, 2nd ed. (London, 1630), reported that after his capture, "[W]e were carried to the Castle, and crammed like Capons, that wee might grow fatter and better for sale" (36); Emanuel D'Aranda, *The History of Algiers and It's Slavery with Many Remarkable Particulars of Africk*, trans. John Davies (London, 1666), 9; and Purchas, *Hakluytus Posthumus*, 8:151, 9:280, 392. On the resemblance between the sale of slaves and beasts of burden in English society, see Keith Thomas, *Man and the Natural World: Changing Attitudes in England, 1500–1800* (New York: Oxford University Press, 1983), 41–50.

24. Munday, *The Admirable Deliverance of 266. Christians*, B3; Ellen G. Friedman, "Christian Captives at 'Hard Labor' in Algiers, 16th–18th Centuries," *International Journal of African Historical Studies* 13:4 (1980): 624–26; Knight, *A Relation of Seaven Yeares Slaverie*, 28; Hakluyt, *Principal Navigations*, 5:301, and Purchas, *Hakluytus Posthumus*, 9:280.

25. Hakluyt, *Principal Navigations*, 5:302; Knight, *A Relation of Seaven Yeares Slaverie*, 28; and Purchas, *Hakluytus Posthumus*, 9:280.

26. Hakluyt, *Principal Navigations*, 5:302–3; Webbe, *The Rare and most wonderful thinges*, A4; and Friedman, "Christian Captives," 619–20. In reality, ship owners had no interest in incapacitating their oarsmen, especially if they were about to engage the enemy in combat, and conditions were little different on Christian and Muslim galleys.

27. Hakluyt, *Principal Navigations*, 5:156; Roberts, *The Adventures of an English Merchant*, 28ff; and Friedman, "Christian Captives," 620–24.

28. *The Estate of Christians living under the subjection of the Turke* (London, 1595), 2–3, and Purchas, *Hakluytus Posthumus*, 9:280–81.

29. This theme, and its implied threat to the future of Christianity, became commonplace in late sixteenth-century England. Remarkably, however, there are few examples of the inverse—a Turk turned Christian. See Meredith Hanmer, *The Baptizing of a Turke* (London, [1586]), which recounts the story of "Chinano, a Turke, born at Nigropontus," who returned to England with Drake's fleet after twenty-five years in Spanish slavery. Chinano subsequently confessed his sins and took the name William. Nabil Matar, *Islam in Britain, 1558–1685* (Cambridge: Cambridge University Press, 1998), esp. 120–52.

30. Proclamation, James I, 29 June 1624; Charles Fitz-Geffrey, *Compassion towards Captives, chiefly Towards our Brethren and Countrymen who are in miserable bondage in the Barbaries* (Oxford, 1637), 35.

31. Purchas, *Hakluytus Posthumus*, 6:153–55, and Davies, *True Relation*, B4.

32. Purchas, *Hakluytus Posthumus*, 1:14, 17, 29.

33. *A Returne from Argier* [2 sermons by Edward Kellet and Henry Byam preached at Minhead in the County of Somerset the 16 of March, 1627, at the re-admission of a relapsed Christian into our Church] (London, 1628), 16–17, 65, 76–77.

34. As Roslyn Knutson and Carolyn Prager demonstrate, few Englishmen in this era directly criticized the institution of slavery. Although they may have looked with horror at the violence of

the Mediterranean world, civic and religious leaders seem to have believed that mariners and merchants should have been aware that they were placing themselves in harm's way. John Aylmer wrote to the Privy Council that it was "very strange and dangerous, that the desier of worldly and transitori things shold carry men so farr with such kinde of traficke, which neither our auncestors before us knewe of, nor can be attempted with selling of sowles for purchasing of pelf to the great blemishe of our religion and the shame of our Country." Churchmen quite often took the opportunity to focus their parishioners' attention on the effect of bondage on the soul and even suggested that enslavement could be a spiritual benefit that provided an occasion for the soul to triumph over the body. In support of this notion, Prager cites the prayer for a galley slave in Thomas Dekker's *Four Birds of Noahs Arke*, in which the captive prays for relief but promises to endure if it is God's will that he continue "longer to grone under this heavie yoake of servitude and slaverie for the triall of [his] faith." Corporation of London Record Office [CLRO], *Remembrancia*, I, item 403, cited in Roslyn Knutson, "Elizabethan Documents, Captivity Narratives, and the Market for Foreign History Plays," *English Literary Renaissance* 26:1 (Winter 1996): 93–94, and Carolyn Prager, " 'Turkish' and Turkish Slavery: English Renaissance Perceptions of Levantine Bondage," *Centerpoint* (Fall 1976): 57–64.

35. Giles Fletcher, *The Policie of the Turkish Empire* (London, 1597), 19v. Daniel J. Vitkus, *Turning Turk: English Theater and the Multicultural Mediterranean, 1570–1630* (New York: Palgrave Macmillan, 2003); Jonathan Burton, *Traffic and Turning: Islam and English Drama, 1579–1624* (Newark: University of Delaware Press, 2005); and Matthew Dimmock, *New Turkes: Dramatizing Islam and the Ottomans in Early Modern England* (Aldershot: Ashgate, 2005). Thomas Stukely was also the source for another popular play, *The Famous History of the Life and Death of Captain Thomas Stukeley* (ca. 1605). Daborne's *A Christian Turned Turke* and Massinger's *Renegado* are reprinted in Vitkus, *Three Turk Plays in Early Modern England* (New York: Columbia University Press, 2000).

36. Knight, *A Relation of Seaven Yeares Slaverie*, 50; Wadsworth, *The English Spanish Pilgrime*, 35; and Roberts, *The Adventures of an English Merchant*, 28. In J. B. Gramaye's otherwise graphic diatribe, printed by a sympathetic Purchas, the author balked on this particular subject: "Now for the Sodomiticall lusts to Boyes, and their damnable services, and sending them for Presents to the Turke or his Bassas, I abhorre to mention." Purchas, *Hakluytus Posthumus*, 9:281.

37. Death rates were alarming. Of 237 Irish men and women taken in a raid on Baltimore in 1631, no more than two or three were ransomed and returned to their homeland. Davis, "Counting European Slaves," 110.

38. The surviving ransom lists from the period before 1640 are exceptional and indicate that most slaves came from London and the southern coastal areas, although there were individuals from all over England, Scotland, and Ireland. Matar, "England and Mediterranean Captivity," 15–16.

39. Hakluyt, *Principal Navigations*, 5:187–88, 6:40, 429; *Acts of the Privy Council* [hereafter, *APC*], 14:205–6 (August 1586). As a result of the intended amity between the Turks and English, Elizabeth received a petition from "Hamed, a distressed Turk," who wrote to the queen describing his ten years of "most miserable slavery" in the Spanish galleys before he eventually escaped. Hamed desired a passport and assistance in order to come to England out of France so that he could find a way to return to his homeland. See *Calendar of State Papers: Domestic Series, of the Reigns of Edward VI, Mary, Elizabeth, and James I (1547–1625)* [hereafter *CSP:DS*], 12 vols. (London, 1856–72), 3:109–10. At least two other passes were issued in 1622 and 1623 for twelve "Turkes to returne to their countrey, by speciall order from the Boarde," or the Privy Council. See *APC* 38:329 (10 October 1622), 38:467 (14 April 1623).

40. *CSP:DS: Edward VI, Mary, Elizabeth*, 1:295. The reference to "most cruel slavery" comes from the daybook of Thomas Harridance, clerk of St. Botolph Aldgate, 1583–1600. This record from the Guildhall Library, London, records more than twenty-five collections for the period between 1587 and 1597, and are reprinted in Knutson, "Elizabethan Documents," 75–110. In 1581, the Privy Council requested that the Lord Mayor of London reimburse Edward Cotton for redeeming captives with his own funds. See *APC*, 13:265–66 (27 November 1581).

41. *APC*, 18:375 (1 April 1582), 21:281 (13 July 1591), 31:270–71 (7 April 1601). Other references to the use of funds gathered at St. Mary Spital for the redemption of English slaves can be found in *APC*, 24:207–8 (29 April 1593), 28:408 (18 April 1598), 30:157 (10 March 1599/1600).

42. Matar, "England and Mediterranean Captivity," 5. See also Matar, "Wives, Captive Husbands, and Turks: The First Women Petitioners in Caroline England," *Explorations in Renaissance Culture* 23 (1997): 111–29.

43. *James by the grace of God King of England, Scotland, France and Ireland, and defender of the faith, &c* [5 February 1624] (London, 1624).

44. John Stow, *A Survey of London* (Oxford: Clarendon Press, 1908), 167–68. This edition is a reprint of the 1603 edition. V. M. O'Mara, *A Study and Edition of Selected Middle English Sermons* (Leeds: University of Leeds, 1994), 32–38. References to St. Mary Spital preaching between 1550 and 1563 can be found in *The Diary of Henry Machyn*, ed. J. G. Nichols (London: Camden Society, 1847), 33, 131–32, 192, 231, 254, 299, 304–5. *The Diary of Samuel Pepys*, 11 vols., ed. Robert Latham and William Matthews (Berkeley: University of California Press, 1970–83), 3:58. Philip Massinger's play, *The Bondman* (1623) is a tale about a slave revolt in the Greek city of Syracuse.

45. *Diary of Samuel Pepys*, 3:33–34.

46. *CSP:DS: James I*, 9:542, 10:12, 11:350 and 430. On the English expeditions to the Mediterranean, see Hebb, *Piracy and the English Government*, ch. 5: "The Algiers Expedition" (77–104) and ch. 11: "The Sallee Expedition of 1637" (237–65). For an analysis of similar episodes later in the seventeenth century, see G. E. Aylmer, "Slavery under Charles II: The Mediterranean and Tangier," *English Historical Review* 114 (April 1999): 378–88.

47. *James by the grace of God King of England, Scotland, France and Ireland, and defender of the faith, &c* [29 June 1624] (London, 1624); *CSP:DS: James I*, 11:287; and Fitz-Geffrey, *Compassion towards Captives*, 4, 11, 17.

48. Fitz-Geffrey, *Compassion towards Captives*, 35, and Gouge, *A Recovery from Apostacy*, 3. Another Englishman named Abraham Brown, who had been captured in 1655 and later emigrated to Massachusetts, recalled that the physical labor of slavery bothered him less than "being commanded by a negro man, who had been a long time in his patron's house a freeman, at whose beck and command he was obliged" to serve. "Thus I, who had commanded many men in several parts of the world," he recounted, "must now be commanded by a negro, who, with his two countrywomen in the house, scorned to drink out of the water pot I drank of, whereby I was despised of the despised people of the world." Cited in Charles Sumner, *White Slavery in the Barbary States* (Boston, 1853), 125.

49. Hakluyt, *Principal Navigations*, 5:177–78, 187–88; Andrews, *Trade, Plunder, and Settlement*, 88–93; and Daniel Goffman, *The Ottoman Empire and Early Modern Europe* (New York: Cambridge University Press, 2002), 194–96.

50. *Calendar of State Papers: Foreign, Elizabeth, 1558–1589* [hereafter *CSP: Foreign*], 23 volumes (London, 1863–1950), 7:98, 157 (Elizabeth), 202, 53, 96 (Challoner).

51. *CSP: Foreign*, items 1084 and 2019, "British History Online," www.british-history.ac.uk (accessed 2 November 2011).

52. *CSP:DS*, 2:535–38, 586–87; *CSP:DS*, 7:572; and Cecil Roth, *The Spanish Inquisition* (New York: W. W. Norton, 1964), 180.

53. Job Hortop, who counted himself among the unfortunate, defended Hawkins for this act when he later wrote that the commander asked for volunteers and that "fourscore and sixteen of us were willing to depart." Hakluyt, *Principal Navigations*, 9:454.

54. Scholars have made good use of Philips in order to address the question of the permeability of English national identity in the late sixteenth century. See, for example, Barbara Fuchs, "An English *Pícaro* in New Spain: Miles Philips and the Framing of National Identity," *CR: The New Centennial Review* 2:1 (2002): 55–68, and Richard Helgerson, "'I Miles Philips': An Elizabethan Seaman Conscripted by History," *PMLA* 118 (2003): 573–80.

55. Hakluyt, *Principal Navigations*, 9:410–13.

56. Hakluyt, *Principal Navigations*, 9:414.

57. G. R. G. Conway, ed., *An Englishman and the Mexican Inquisition, 1556–1560* (Mexico City, 1927), 159, 161; Hakluyt, *Principal Navigations*, 9:421–23.

58. Hakluyt, *Principal Navigations*, 9:423.

59. L. De Alberti and A. B. Wallis Chapman, eds., *English Merchants and the Spanish Inquisition in the Canaries* (London: Camden Society, 1912), xiv–xv, and Conway, *An Englishman and the Mexican Inquisition*, 70–71.

60. Philips stated that the "bloodie and cruell Inquisition" appeared in Mexico in 1574, but he likely confused the organization of the formal tribunal with the large *autos de fe* that occurred in 1574 and again in 1575. Hakluyt, *Principal Navigations* 9:424; José Luis Soberanes Fernández, "La Inquisición en México durante el siglo XVI," *Revista de la Inquisición* 7 (1998): 283–95; Richard E. Greenleaf, *The Mexican Inquisition of the Sixteenth Century* (Albuquerque: University of New Mexico Press, 1969); and Martin Austin Nesvig, *Ideology and Inquisition: The World of the Censors in Early Mexico* (New Haven, CT: Yale University Press, 2009).

61. Hakluyt, *Principal Navigations*, 9:426–27.

62. Hakluyt, *Principal Navigations*, 9:428–29; Lu Ann Homza, ed., *The Spanish Inquisition, 1478–1614: An Anthology of Sources* (Indianapolis, IN: Hackett, 2006), esp. 258–66; and Conway, *An Englishman and the Mexican Inquisition*, 161. Philips may have confused John Martin (who appears in the records as Guillermo Cornelius) with a Frenchman named Martin Cornu when he named one of the three condemned men as "Cornelius the Irishman." Cornu was sentenced the same year as Philips, Martin a year later.

63. Hakluyt, *Principal Navigations*, 9:429; Wright, *Documents, 1569–1580*, 93; "The Primrose Journal," in *Sir Francis Drake's West Indian Voyage, 1585–86*, ed. Mary Frear Keeler (London: Hakluyt Society, 1981), 199; Kenneth R. Andrews, ed., *The Last Voyage of Drake & Hawkins* (London: Hakluyt Society, 1972), 107 n. 1.

64. See Chapter 3 for a more in-depth treatment of Drake's 1585–86 privateering expedition.

65. "The Primrose Journal," in Keeler, *Sir Francis Drake's West Indian Voyage*, 202 n. 3; Irene A. Wright, ed., *Further English Voyages to Spanish America, 1583–1594* (London: Hakluyt Society, 1951), 173 (Suarez), 212 (Sanchez); and Hakluyt, *Principal Navigations*, 6:40. For greater treatment, see David B. Quinn, "Turks, Moors, Blacks, and Others in Drake's West Indian Voyage," *Terrae Incognitae* 14 (1982), 97–104, reprinted in Quinn, *Explorers and Colonies: America, 1500–1625* (London: Hambledon Press, 1990), 197–204.

66. Hakluyt, *Principal Navigations*, 9:430.

67. Purchas, *Hakluytus Posthumus*, 16:144; Hakluyt, *Principal Navigations*, 9:422–23, 431.

68. Hakluyt, *Principal Navigations*, 9:432, 434, 438, 441, 444–45.

69. *A Declaration of His Highnes, By the Advice of His Council; Setting forth . . . the Justice of their Cause against Spaine* (London, 1655), 115. See also Thomas Scott, *The Spaniards cruelty and treachery to the English in time of peace and war* (London, 1656).

70. Richard Blome, *A Description of the Island of Jamaica* (London, 1672), 51–54.

71. *A Declaration of His Highnes*, 125, 140. Two pamphlets were published in 1655 that similarly accused the French of having invaded St. Christopher Island and Martinique, "at which time they became Masters thereof, and subdued the English, keeping them as Vassals and slaves." See *Three Great and Bloody Fights between the English and the French* (London, 1655), 3, and *A great and wonderful victory* (London, 1655).

72. For several examples of seventeenth-century ballads, see "The Algerian Slave's Releasement; or, The Unchangeable Boatswain," and "The Lamentable Cries of at Least 1500 Christians: Most of Them Being Englishmen . . ." in Vitkus, *Piracy, Slavery, and Redemption*, 341–46, and "An Admirable New Northern Story," in *The Euing Collection*, 10.

CHAPTER 5

1. Extract from George Chapman, Ben Jonson, and John Marston, "Eastward Hoe," Act 3, scene 2 (1605); reprinted in Alexander Brown, ed., *The Genesis of the United States*, 2 vols. (New York, 1890), 1:31.

2. Two important collections speak to these issues in much greater depth and breadth. See Robert Appelbaum and John Wood Sweet, eds., *Envisioning an English Empire: Jamestown and the Making of the North Atlantic World* (Philadelphia: University of Pennsylvania Press, 2005), and Peter C. Mancall, ed., *The Atlantic World and Virginia, 1550–1624* (Chapel Hill: University of North Carolina Press, 2007). See also the several articles in *The Oxford History of the British Empire*, vol. 1: *The Origins of Empire: British Overseas Enterprise to the Close of the Seventeenth Century*, ed. Nicholas Canny (Oxford: Oxford University Press, 1998), esp. Canny, "The Origins of Empire: An Introduction" (1–33), Anthony Pagden, "The Struggle for Legitimacy and the Image of Empire in the Atlantic to c. 1700" (34–54), and Canny, "England's New World and the Old, 1480s–1630s" (148–69). For an effort at comparing rather than contrasting England with Spain, see J. H. Elliott, *Empires of the Atlantic World: Britain and Spain in America, 1492–1830* (New Haven, CT: Yale University Press, 2006).

3. See, for example, Don Jordan and Michael Walsh, *White Cargo: The Forgotten History of Britain's White Slaves in America* (New York: New York University Press, 2007); Peter Linebaugh and Marcus Rekiker, *The Many-Headed Hydra: Sailors, Slaves, Commoners, and the Hidden History of the Revolutionary Atlantic* (Boston: Beacon Press, 2000); Theodore W. Allen, *The Invention of the White Race*, vol. 1: *Racial Oppression and Social Control*, and vol. 2: *The Origin of Racial Oppression in Anglo-America* (London: Verso, 1994, 1997); and Hilary McD. Beckles, *White Servitude and Black Slavery in Barbados, 1627–1715* (Knoxville: University of Tennessee Press, 1989).

4. See, esp., Joyce Chaplin, *Subject Matter: Technology, the Body, and Science on the Anglo-American Frontier, 1500–1676* (Cambridge, MA: Harvard University Press, 2001).

5. In addition to works cited previously, other works that set aside the slavery-as-labor paradigm include Michael L. Fickes, "'They Could Not Endure That Yoke': The Captivity of Pequot Women and Children after the War of 1637," *New England Quarterly* 73:1 (March 2000): 58–81; Joyce E. Chaplin, "Enslavement of Indians in Early America: Captivity Without the Narrative," in *The Creation of the British Atlantic World*, ed. Elizabeth Mancke and Carole Shammas (Baltimore:

Johns Hopkins University Press, 2005), 45–70; and Owen Stanwood, "Captives and Slaves: Indian Labor, Cultural Conversion, and the Plantation Revolution in Virginia," *Virginia Magazine of History and Biography* 114:4 (2006): 434–63.

6. Michael Drayton, "Ode to the Virginian Voyage," December 1606, cited in Hugh T. Lefler, "Promotional Literature of the Southern Colonies," *Journal of Southern History* 33:1 (February 1967): 5.

7. George Alsop, *A Character of the Province of Maryland* (London, 1666), reprinted in *Narratives of Early Maryland, 1633–1684*, ed. Clayton Colman Hall (New York: Charles Scribner's Sons, 1910), 378, 357, and George Gardyner, *A Description of the New World* (London, 1651), 8–9.

8. Alexander Whitaker, *Good Newes from Virginia* (London, 1613), D1; *Records of the Virginia Company of London* [hereafter *RVC*], 4 vols., ed. Susan Myra Kingsbury (Washington, DC: Government Printing Office, 1906–35), 4:41, 58, 61, 235, 473. On Frethorne, see Emily Rose, "The Politics of Pathos: Richard Frethorne's Letters Home," in Appelbaum and Sweet, *Envisioning an English Empire*, 92–108.

9. *Calendar of State Papers: Colonial Series, 1574–1660* [hereafter *CSP:CS*], 2:28–29 (12 April 1622), 2:38–40 (February 1623), 3:58 (28 February 1624). For the political context of these disputes, see Wesley Frank Craven, *Dissolution of the Virginia Company: The Failure of a Colonial Experiment* (Gloucester, MA: Peter Smith, 1964; orig. 1932), 245–58, 279–83.

10. William Strachey, *For the Colony in Virginea Britannia: Lawes Divine, Morall and Martiall*, ed. David H. Flaherty (Charlottesville: University of Virginia Press, 1969); *Journals of the House of Burgesses of Virginia*, vol. 1: *1619–1658/59*, ed. H. R. McIlwaine (Richmond, VA, 1915), 31. Despite his ignoble reputation, Dale has had his defenders. According to Ralph Hamor, *A True Discourse of the Present Estate of Virginia* (London, 1615), "more deserved death in those daies, then do now the least punishment, so as if the law should have restrained by execution, I see not how the utter subversion and ruine of the Colony should have bin prevented. . . . Sir Thomas Dale hath not bin tyranous, nor severe at all; Indeed the offences have bin capitall, and the offenders dangerous, incurable members" (27). See Edmund S. Morgan, *American Slavery, American Freedom: The Ordeal of Colonial Virginia* (New York: W. W. Norton, 1975), esp. 71–91, for the context of Dale's Laws (although Morgan fails to mention galley slavery).

11. *RVC*, 3:69, 93 (2).

12. *Memorials of the Discovery and Early Settlement of the Bermudas or Somers Islands, 1515–1685*, 2 vols., ed. J. H. Lefroy (Toronto: University of Toronto Press, 1981), 1:127.

13. *Records of the Governor and Company of the Massachusetts Bay in New England*, 5 vols., ed. Nathaniel B. Shurtleff (Boston, 1853–54), 1:246, 269 (Andrews); other cases appear at 1:284, 297, 300, and 2:21. *Records of the Court of Assistants of the Colony of Massachusetts Bay, 1630–1692*, 3 vols., ed. John Noble and John F. Cronin (Boston, 1901–28), 2:78–79 (Andrews); other cases appear at 2:86, 87, 90, 94, 97, and 118 (2).

14. European observers, when it suited their needs, also commented on the existence of human bondage among the English. The Spanish Ambassador to England, Don Diego de Molina, highlighted the instability in early Virginia when he reported to Don Alonso de Velasco in 1613 not only that the English were struggling to maintain a settlement but also that many settlers believed they were "treated like slaves, with great cruelty." A half-century later, Peter Stuyvesant reported that the Dutch settlers at New Amstel (Delaware) had been "stripped, utterly plundered and many of them sold as slaves to Virginia" by callous English invaders. Alexander Brown, *Genesis of the United States*, 2 vols. (New York, 1890), 2:648, and Peter Stuyvesant, "Report on the Surrender of New Netherland, 1665," in *Narratives of New Netherland, 1609–1664*, ed. J. Franklin Jameson (New

York: Charles Scribner's Sons, 1909), 465. On the changing fortunes of Spain and England in Dutch writings, see Benjamin Schmidt, *Innocence Abroad: The Dutch Imagination and the New World, 1570–1670* (Cambridge: Cambridge University Press, 2001), 298–303.

15. *Commons Debates 1621*, 7 vols., ed. Wallace Notestein, Frances Helen Relf, and Hartley Simpson (New Haven, CT: Yale University Press, 1935), 7:54–55.

16. D. M. Palliser, *The Age of Elizabeth: England under the Later Tudors, 1547–1603*, 2nd ed. (London: Longman, 1992), 139–51; Paul Slack, *Poverty and Policy in Tudor and Early Stuart England* (London: Longman, 1988); David Thomas Konig, "'Dale's Laws' and the Non-Common Law Origin of Criminal Justice in Virginia," *American Journal of Legal History* 26:4 (October 1982): 354–75; Konig, "Colonization and Common Law in Ireland and Virginia, 1569–1634," in *The Transformation of Early American History: Society, Authority, and Ideology*, ed. James A. Henretta, Michael Kammen, and Stanley Katz (New York: Alfred A. Knopf, 1991), 70–92; and Warren M. Billings, "The Transfer of English Law to Virginia, 1606–1650," in *The Westward Enterprise: English Activities in Ireland, the Atlantic, and America, 1480–1650*, ed. Kenneth R. Andrews, Nicholas P. Canny, and P. E. H. Hair (Liverpool: Liverpool University Press, 1978), 215–44.

17. *The Rich Papers: Letters from Bermuda, 1615–1646*, ed. Vernon A. Ives (Toronto: University of Toronto Press, 1984), 237–39

18. *Book of General Lawes and Libertyes Concerning the Inhabitants of the Massachusetts* (facsimile reprint of the 1648 ed.; San Marino, CA: Huntington Library, 1975), 4.

19. Historians are correct to point out that the early use of the language of slavery does not correspond to the manifestation of the race-based labor institution that would appear later in the century. Nonetheless, we should be careful about imprinting later developments and definitions on the words that appear in our sources. Robert McColley, "Slavery in Virginia, 1619–1660: A Reexamination," *New Perspectives on Race and Slavery in America*, ed. Robert H. Abzug and Stephen E. Maizlish (Lexington: University Press of Kentucky, 1986), 13, and Edmund S. Morgan, *American Slavery, American Freedom: The Ordeal of Colonial Virginia* (New York: W. W. Norton, 1975), esp. 127–30.

20. *Newes from Sally: Of a Strange Delivery of Foure English-Captives from the slavery of the Turkes* (London, 1642). See also Henry Robinson, *Libertas, or Reliefe to the English captives in Algier: Briefly discoursing hovv such as are in slavery may be soonest set at liberty, others preserved therein, and the great Turke reduc'd to renue and keepe the peace inviolate, to a greater enlargement of trade and priviledges than ever the English nation hitherto enjoy'd in Turkie* (London, 1642).

21. In addition to the titles mentioned in Chapter 3, see Richard Overton, *The commoners complaint: or, A dreadful warning from Newgate, to the commons of England. Presented to the honourable committees for consideration of the commoners liberties. Wherein (as in a glasse) every free-man of England may clearly behold his own imminent insufferable bondage and slavery under the Norman-prerogative men of this kingdom* . . . (London, 1647), and *A Brief Discourse of the Present Miseries of the Kingdome: Declaring by what practices the people of England have been deluded, and seduced into Slavery* (London, 1648). For the other end of the spectrum, see Edward Mathews, *King Charles the II his restitution: The best cure for Englands confusion; or A most soveraigne salve for healing the sores of the three nations. Being an alarme to the nobility, gentry, clergie, and commonalty to bend and lend their hearts, heads and hands unanimously for the speedy and peaceable restitution of their liedge, lord and King to his crown and dignity, and recovery of their native countrey from ruine and slavery* . . . (London, 1660), and James Warwell, *Votiva tabula; or, A solemn thanksgiving offered up to God the mighty protector of kings, for the wonderful protection, and happy restauration of our gracious soveraign Charls the II unto the exercise of his just right and authority of governing his three kingdoms of England,*

Scotland, & Ireland Thereby delivering these three nations from a miserable slavery, and restoring them to their ancient liberty, peace and glory (London, 1660).

22. Richard Hubberthorn, *The Real Cause of the Nations Bondage and Slavery* (London, 1659), and Richard Younge, *The seduced soul reduced and rescued from the subtilty and slavery of Satan* (London, 1660).

23. *A pittifull Remonstrance, or just Complaint made To all free-born true-hearted Englishmen, sensible of the Kingdoms miserable slavery* (London, 1648). This perspective was echoed in 1654 when Parliament received a petition from "a great number of Imprisoned Free-men for Debt" who complained that they were not merely being detained in prison, they were "under the cruell rigour of the *Norman* yoke of bondage and slavery, by the cruelty and oppression of their obdurate Creditors." *To the High court of Parliament of the Commonwealth of England, Scotland, and Ireland: The humble Petition of a great number of Imprisoned Free-Men . . .* (London, 1654).

24. John Lilburne, *Liberty Vindicated against Slavery: Shewing, That Imprisonment for Debt, Refusing to answer Interrogatories, long imprisonment, though for just causes. Abuse of Prisons, and cruell Extortion of Prison-keepers, are all destructive to the fundamentall Laws and common Freedoms of the people* (London, 1646), 8–9. Lilburne's comments should be understood in the light of the jealousy with which many Englishmen were beginning to defend their liberty in the era of the English Civil War. For context, see Karen Ordahl Kupperman, "Definitions of Liberty on the Eve of the Civil War: Lord Saye and Sele, Lord Brooke, and the American Puritan Colonies," *Historical Journal* 32:1 (1989): 17–23; Christopher Hill, *Liberty against the Law: Some Seventeenth-Century Controversies* (London: Penguin Books, 1996); and David Underdown, *A Freeborn People: Politics and the Nation in Seventeenth-Century England* (Oxford: Clarendon Press, 1996).

25. Christopher Tomlins suggests that roughly 80 percent of the English immigrants into the Chesapeake during the seventeenth century were servants. Tomlins, "Reconsidering Indentured Servitude: European Migration and the Early American Labor Force, 1600–1775," *Labor History* 42:1 (2001): 9–10. A revised version of this essay appears in Tomlins, *Freedom Bound: Law, Labor, and Civic Identity in Colonizing English America, 1580–1865* (Cambridge: Cambridge University Press, 2010), 21–66. The best economic analysis of indentured servitude is still David W. Galenson, *White Servitude in Colonial America: An Economic Analysis* (New York: Cambridge University Press, 1981). More recently, the literature has been ably summarized in Sharon V. Salinger, "Labor, Markets, and Opportunity: Indentured Servitude in Early America," *Labor History* 38 (1997): 311–38, and Kenneth Morgan, *Slavery and Servitude in Colonial North America: A Short History* (New York: New York University Press, 2001).

26. William Bullock, *Virginia Impartially Examined* (London, 1649), 13–14.

27. On servitude in English history, see Ann Kussmaul, *Servants in Husbandry in Early Modern England* (Cambridge: Cambridge University Press, 1981), and Robert J. Steinfeld, *The Invention of Free Labor: The Employment Relation in English and American Law and Culture, 1350–1870* (Chapel Hill: University of North Carolina Press, 1991). On the articulation of indentured servitude in the seventeenth-century Chesapeake, see Tomlins, *Freedom Bound*, 258–76.

28. Morgan Godwyn, *Trade preferr'd before Religion and Christ made to give place to Mammon* (London, 1685), 6.

29. *Journals of the House of Commons*, 9 May 1645, vol. 4 (1644–46), 135–36. C. H. Firth and R. S. Rait, *Acts and Ordinances*, vol. 1 (1645), 681–82. Cited in John Wareing, "Preventative and Punitive Regulation in Seventeenth-Century Social Policy: Conflicts of Interest and the Failure to Make 'stealing and transporting Children, and other Persons' a Felony, 1645–73," *Social History* 27:3 (October 2002): 291.

NOTES TO PAGES 166–168

30. *Acts of the Privy Council of England, Colonial Series* (Hereford, 1908), 1:296–97.

31. *Proceedings and Debates of the British Parliaments respecting North America*, 5 vols., ed. Leo Francis Stock (Washington, DC: Carnegie Institution of Washington, 1924), 1:303, 269.

32. Wareing, "Preventative and Punitive Regulation," 290. On the kidnapping problem, more generally, see Abbot Emerson Smith, *Colonists in Bondage: White Servitude and Convict Labor in America, 1607–1776* (Chapel Hill: University of North Carolina, 1947), 67–86.

33. Philip L. Barbour, ed., *The Complete Works of Captain John Smith (1580–1631)* (Chapel Hill: University of North Carolina Press, 1986), 2:268; *CSP:CS*, 2:28–29 (12 April 1622).

34. Barbour, *Complete Works*, 2:329–30.

35. Richard Ligon, *A True & Exact History of the Island of Barbadoes* (London, 1673), 43–45. For a useful discussion of the slave-like condition of indentured servants in Barbados, see Hilary McD. Beckles, "The concept of 'white slavery' in the English Caribbean during the early seventeenth century," in *Early Modern Conception of Property*, ed. John Brewer and Susan Staves (London: Routledge, 1996), 572–84. To place Ligon and his written work in context, see Susan Scott Parrish, "Richard Ligon and the Atlantic Science of Commonwealths," *William and Mary Quarterly* 67:2 (April 2010): 209–48.

36. Servant rebellions were a constant concern in the colonies, particularly in the West Indies where other European powers threatened English settlements. As early as 1631, Sir Henry Colt lamented that, although St. Christopher's could be defended if servants fought, the "servants of ye planters rather desyer ye Spaniards might come, [that] by itt they might be freed." Cited in *Colonising Expeditions to the West Indies and Guiana, 1623–1667*, ed. V. T. Harlow (London: Hakluyt Society, 1925), 87–88.

37. Although the absence of European competition and the wider availability of land tempered the relationship between masters and indentured servants on the mainland, there was no shortage of complaints, abuses, and threats of insurrection in places like Virginia and Maryland, either. See, for example, the sources excerpted in *The Old Dominion in the Seventeenth Century: A Documentary History of Virginia, 1606–1700*, rev. ed., ed. Warren M. Billings (Chapel Hill: University of North Carolina Press, 2007), 144–72, 296–355. On early indentured servitude in the Chesapeake, particularly colonial adaptations, see Lois Green Carr, Russell R. Menard, and Lorena S. Walsh, *Robert Cole's World: Agriculture & Society in Early Maryland* (Chapel Hill: University of North Carolina Press, 1991), and John Ruston Pagan, *Anne Orthwood's Bastard: Sex and Law in Early Virginia* (New York: Oxford University Press, 2003).

38. Carla Gardina Pestana, *The English Atlantic in an Age of Revolution, 1640–1661* (Cambridge, MA: Harvard University Press, 2004), 210.

39. Thomas Burton, *Parliamentary Diary, 1656–1659*, 4 vols. (London: Henry Colburn, 1828), 4:255–58. The petition of Rivers and Foyle was printed in full as *Englands Slavery, or Barbados Merchandize; Represented in a Petition to the High and Honourable Court of Parliament, by* Marcellus Rivers *and* Oxenbridge Foyle *Gentlemen, on the behalf of themselves and threescore and ten more Freeborn English-men sole (uncondemned) into slavery* (London, 1659).

40. Burton, *Parliamentary Diary*, 4:260–62, 301–8. Members of Parliament were not being disingenuous when they expressed concern that these types of petitions were a Cavalier plot designed to divide them. Oliver Cromwell had died the previous September and Richard Cromwell's position as Lord Protector was not wholeheartedly embraced by everyone, especially those in the army. On Thurloe's parliamentary affairs at this time and his efforts to balance opposing factions, see Philip Aubrey, *Mr. Secretary Thurloe: Cromwell's Secretary of State, 1652–1660* (London: Athlone Press, 1990), esp. 129–63.

41. *England's Slavery*, 5, 11, 3, 4, 22, 17, 9, 15, 7, 20, 21, 10, and 12. The idea that freeborn Englishmen were threatened by slavery appears in many different contexts. Frequent references were made in the Parliamentary session of 1628 to the possible enslavement of Englishmen when the body considered King Charles I's demand for funds to continue his naval war against France. In response, Parliament issued the *Petition of Right*, which argued, among other things, that there should be no taxation without Parliamentary consent and there should be no imprisonment without cause. In the course of the debates, Sir Roger North claimed that he was guided by a simple but fundamental principle: "I consider the condition of us all—who sent us, and to what purpose. We are parliament men; [and] may speak freely. We are sent by the public to save them and ourselves from being slaves." *Commons Debates, 1628*, 6 vols., ed. Robert C. Johnson, Mary Frear Keeler, Maija Jansson Cole, and William B. Bidwell (New Haven, CT: Yale University Press, 1977), 3:280. Similar references invoking the language of slavery can be found throughout. On the meaning that different constituencies attached to the *Petition of Right*, see Jess Flemion, "A Savings to Satisfy All: The House of Lords and the Meaning of the *Petition of Right*," *Parliamentary History* 10:1 (1991): 27–44.

42. Burton, *Parliamentary Diary*, 4:262–64, 268. "Paul's Case" refers to Acts 22:25, wherein Paul was arrested and strapped down for punishment, at which time he questioned the Centurion on duty whether it was "legal for you to flog a man who is a Roman citizen and has not been brought to trial." In 1621, Parliament debated how Edward Floyd, who had been accused of libel, should be punished. When it was suggested that he should be whipped, Edward Alford responded that there was indeed a precedent: "I have knowne whippinge inflicted by this house, and then it was saide it was for slaves not for gentlemen. And lett us take head what presedentes wee make; wee knowe not how farre it maye be extended against us and our posteritie." Sir Edwin Sandys concurred, noting that a "good cause doth sometimes breed a badde president. Lett not our affections transport us to farr. I can not consent to whipping unless he were first degraded. It is the punishment of a slave." *Commons Debates*, 5:129–30.

43. *Bermuda Colonial Records* [microfilm; hereafter BCR], 3:63–64 (Assize 11, 22 November 1650). It is unclear whether these examples from 1650 are exceptional cases or part of a consistent pattern of punishment because the 1631–38 and 1640–47 records are missing.

44. Michael Jarvis, "'In the eye of all trade': Maritime Revolution and the Transformation of Bermudian Society, 1612–1800" (Ph.D. diss., College of William and Mary, 1998), 276.

45. Morgan Godwyn, *The Negro's and Indians Advocate* (London, 1680), 36.

46. Burton, *Parliamentary Diary*, 4:270.

47. Richard Hakluyt, *Virginia Richly Valued* (London, 1609).

48. Alexander Whitaker, *Good Newes from Virginia* (London, 1613), 24. On the idea that Indians lived, to an exceptional degree, under Satan's influence, see Alfred A. Cave, "Richard Hakluyt's Savages: The Influence of 16th-Century Travel Narratives on English Indian Policy in North America," *International Social Science Review* 60:1 (1985): 3–24.

49. The idea that Indians and Africans were generally part of an undifferentiated class of bondmen is common. Several examples of this emphasis can be found in older works, such as Geoge H. Moore, *Notes on the History of Slavery in Massachusetts* (New York: D. Appleton & Co., 1866), 15–41, and Almon Wheeler Lauber, *Indian Slavery in Colonial Times within the Present Limits of the United States* (New York: Columbia University Press, 1913), esp. 48–102, 105–17, 211–16, 222–29, and 250–82. More conventional examinations of Indian slavery include John A. Sainsbury, "Indian Labor in Early Rhode Island," *New England Quarterly* 48:3 (1975): 378–93; Donald Grinde Jr., "Native American Slavery in the Southern Colonies," *Indian History* 10:2 (1977): 38–42; Rodney M. Baine, "Indian Slavery in Colonial Georgia," *Georgia Historical Quarterly* 79:2 (1995): 418–24; and

Hilary McD. Beckles, "The Colours of Property: Brown, White and Black Chattels and their Responses on the Caribbean Frontier," *Slavery & Abolition* 15:2 (1994): 36–51.

50. There were a few Indians in England at earlier dates. Three Indian men from Newfoundland were presented to the court of Henry VII in 1501, although they may have been in England as early as 1498. Henry VIII likewise met an Indian king from Brazil in the 1530s.

51. The best treatment of this disparate material is Alden T. Vaughan, *Transatlantic Encounters: American Indians in Britain, 1500–1776* (Cambridge: Cambridge University Press, 2006). On remaking Indians, see Kathleen M. Brown, *Good Wives, Nasty Wenches & Anxious Patriarchs: Gender, Race, and Power in Colonial Virginia* (Chapel Hill: University of North Carolina Press, 1996).

52. John Winthrop, "Reasons to Be Considered for Justifying the Undertakers of the Intended Plantation in New England . . . ," (1629), in *Envisioning America: English Plans for the Colonization of North America, 1580–1640*, ed. Peter C. Mancall (Boston: Bedford, 1995), 137; John T. Juricek, "English Territorial Claims in North America under Elizabeth and the Early Stuarts," *Terrae Incognitae* 7 (1976): 7–22; Karen Ordahl Kupperman, "Errand to the Indies: Puritan Colonization from Providence Island through the Western Design," *William and Mary Quarterly* 45:1 (January 1988): 70–99; Anthony Pagden, *Lords of all the World: Ideologies of Empire in Spain, Britain and France, c. 1500–c. 1800* (New Haven, CT: Yale University Press, 1995), 73–94; David Armitage, "The Cromwellian Protectorate and the Languages of Empire," *Historical Journal* 35:3 (September 1992): 531–55; Patricia Seed, *Ceremonies of Possession in Europe's Conquest of the New World, 1492–1640* (New York: Cambridge University Press, 1995), 16–40; and Joyce E. Chaplin, "Natural Philosophy and an Early Racial Idiom in North America: Comparing English and Indian Bodies," *William and Mary Quarterly* 54:1 (January 1997): 229–52.

53. Robert Johnson, *Nova Britannia* (London, 1609), C2, and "Philo-Caledon," *A Defence of the Scots Settlement in Darien with an Answer to the Spanish Memorial against it* (Edinburgh, 1699), 24. Both works cited in Pagden, *Lords of All the World*, 88.

54. [Edmund Hickeringill], *Jamaica Viewed*, 2nd ed. (London, 1661), 32–33, 34; *A Declaration of His Highnes, By the Advice of His Council; Setting forth . . . the Justice of their Cause against Spaine* (London, 1655), 117–18. See also Hans Sloane, *A Voyage to the Islands Madera, Barbados, Nieves, S. Christophers and Jamaica . . .* , 2 vols. (London, 1707 and 1725), 1:lxxxvii. English assertions of Spanish barbarism date back to the 1580s and the translation and publication of Bartolomé de las Casas's *Brevísima Relación de las Indias* as *The Spanish Colonie* (1583). Two useful general treatments of European perceptions of Spain are William S. Maltby, *The Black Legend in England: The Development of Anti-Spanish Sentiment, 1558–1660* (Durham, NC: Duke University Press, 1971), and J. N. Hillgarth, *The Mirror of Spain, 1500–1700: The Formation of a Myth* (Ann Arbor: University of Michigan Press, 2000).

55. Richard Eden, *The First Three English Books on America [1511?]–1555 A.D.*, ed. Edward Arbor (Birmingham, 1885), 50–55. Edmund Morgan has characterized English awareness of Spanish activities in the New World as a "horror story" from the first appearance of Peter Martyr's *De Orbo Novo* in 1511. Clearly, however, there was plenty of room for more positive assessments, at least through the 1550s, as evidenced by Eden's lavish praise. Morgan, *American Slavery, American Freedom*, 7. For a recent effort to complicate the role of Spain in early English colonial promotion, see David A. Boruchoff, "Piety, Patriotism, and Empire: Lessons for England, Spain, and the New World in the Works of Richard Hakluyt," *Renaissance Quarterly* 62:3 (Fall 2009): 809–58.

56. Smith, *A Description of New England* (London, 1616), in *Complete Works*, 1:348.

57. Hakluyt, *Principal Navigations*, 10:390–91. See the useful discussion of Raleigh's narrative in Louis Montrose, "The Work of Gender in the Discourse of Discovery," in *New World Encounters*,

ed. Stephen Greenblatt (Berkeley: University of California Press, 1993), 177–217. The Dutch, too, were not beyond characterizing the Spanish as exceptionally lascivious." Philip Marnix van St. Aldedonde argued in 1578 that the Spanish intended to steal their "wives and daughters to satisfy their unchaste desires." Cited in Schmidt, *Innocence Abroad*, 86.

58. *Certain Inducements to Well-Minded People* (London, 1643), 21; Daunce, *A Briefe Discourse of the Spanish State* (1590), cited in Hillgarth, *The Mirror of Spain*, 388. English authors paid special attention to the genealogical makeup of identifiable human populations during the early modern era in great part because they were engaged at home in an intellectual enterprise concerned with demonstrating the origins and purity of the English "race." That they were, as a nation, "not mixt with others," was as important to Richard Verstegan in *The Restitution of Decayed Intelligence* (Antwerp, 1605), 43, as it was to Reverend William Symonds when he reminded Virginia colonists that God promised Abraham to make him a great Nation, as long as "Abraham's posterity keep to themselves. They may not marry nor give in marriage to the heathen, that are uncircumcised. . . . The breakers of this rule may break the neck of all good success of this voyage." Cited in Robin Blackburn, *The Making of New World Slavery: From the Baroque to the Modern, 1492–1800* (London: Verso, 1997), 237.

59. Richard Eburne, *A Plaine Pathway to Plantations* (London, 1624), 28; Samuel Purchas, *Hakluytus Posthumus, or Purchas His Pilgrimes*, 20 vols. (Glasgow: James MacLehose and Sons, 1905–7), 19:263; and [William Castell], *A Petition of W.C. Exhibited to the High Court of Parliament now assembled* (London, 1641), 8.

60. Eburne, *A Plaine Pathway to Plantations*, 21; [Robert Johnson], *Nova Britannia: Offring Most Excellent fruites by Planting in Virginia* (London, 1609), B4r; [Robert Johnson], *The New Life of Virginea* (London, 1612), F4v. Of course, these impressions were closely associated with the efforts of the Virginia Company of London to keep the Chesapeake venture afloat. Regardless, similar claims had been made in earlier periods. George Peckham's 1583 account of America contained the observation that the English would find "all things that be necessarie profitable, or delectable for mans life" because the region was "neither too hotte nor too colde." Peckham cited in Chaplin, *Subject Matter*, 134.

61. John Smith, *A Description of New England* (London, 1616), in *Complete Works*, 1:330; Thomas Morton, *New English Canaan* (London, 1637), B2r–v.

62. John Brereton, *A Briefe and true Relation of the Discoverie of the North part of Virginia*, cited in Karen Ordahl Kupperman, "Presentment of Civility: English Reading of American Self-Presentation in the Early Years of Colonization," *William and Mary Quarterly* 54:1 (January 1997): 198; Purchas, *Hakluytus Posthumus*, 18:304, 319; William Strachey, *The Historie of Travaile into Virginia Britannia* (London: Hakluyt Society, 1849), 64. Strachey's manuscript was not published in his lifetime; it was likely written near the end of the 1610s.

63. Thomas Harriot, *A Briefe and True Report of the New Found Land of Virginia* (1590; Dover Reprint Edition, 1972), 75; Alden T. Vaughan, "Early English Paradigms for New World Natives," in *Roots of American Racism: Essays on the Colonial Experience* (New York: Oxford University Press, 1995), 45; Eburne, *A Plaine Pathway to Plantations*, 7, 28, 35; and Arthur H. Williamson, "Scots, Indians and Empire: The Scottish Politics of Civilization, 1519–1609," *Past and Present* 150 (February 1996): 46–83, esp. 56–66. The best treatment of how early modern English understandings of their own history fed into colonial efforts can be found in Karen Ordahl Kupperman, *Indians & English: Facing Off in Early America* (Ithaca, NY: Cornell University Press, 2000).

64. Hakluyt, *Principal Navigations*, 7:155; Purchas, *Hakluytus Posthumus*, 18:325; Morton, *New English Canaan*, 32; and Strachey, *The Historie of Travaile*, 63.

65. This interpretation contrasts somewhat with the argument that "[m]ost English writers did not dwell on these areas of similarity and exchange, however, but emphasized the 'wild' and ani-

malistic qualities of Tidewater peoples." See Brown, *Good Wives, Nasty Wenches & Anxious Patriarchs*, 64.

66. *RVC* 3:3, 27, 71.

67. It is worth emphasizing that the English were not the only ones to engage in anti-Spanish rhetoric. The plight of American Indians served the needs of Dutch polemicists in support of the rebellion against Hapsburg rule that had been ongoing since the 1560s. A crucial component of the anti-Spanish literature of the era, and root of the Black Legend, was the translation and publication of Bartolomé de las Casas's *Brevísima Relación de las Indias* into Dutch, French, and English after 1578. In his text, Las Casas claimed that the Spanish entered the New World "as wolves, as lions, & as tigres most cruel of long time famished" who, when they confronted the natives, chose to "teare them in peeces, kill them, martyr them, afflict them, torment them, & destroy them by straunge sortes of cruelties." Characterizations of this sort only encouraged the view that "[t]he Spaniard is very haughty, vengeful, and tyrannical." "Let us imagine the example of the Indians," Philip Marnix van St. Aldedonde urged in 1578, "and let us keep in mind that our descendants will be abused as are they." Dutch and English writers emphasized that Spanish barbarism should not be viewed as an aberration, rather as a natural attribute of the predatory Spanish. Pay attention to what the Spanish "have done to the poore Indians," William of Orange declared in 1581, for nothing more clearly revealed to the world "their perverse, naturall disposition, and tyrannous affection and will." Bartolomé de las Casas, *The Spanish Colonie, or Briefe chronicle of the acts and gestes of the Spaniardes in the West Indies* (London, 1583), A1v, and Schmidt, *Innocence Abroad*, 86–88. Schmidt argues convincingly that the changing political and constitutional situation in the Low Countries resulted in "a revolution in Dutch representations of America" (68).

68. Lauber, *Indian Slavery*, 212. The Powhatan perspective on these issues is treated by Helen Rountree, *Pocahontas's People: The Powhatan Indians of Virginia through Four Centuries* (Norman: University of Oklahoma Press, 1990). A number of instructive sources concerning the Anglo-Indian *détente* after 1646 are reprinted in Billings, *The Old Dominion in the Seventeenth Century*, 280–85.

69. *The Statutes at Large, being a collection of all the Laws of Virginia*, 18 vols., ed. William Waller Hening (Richmond, 1809), 1:396, 2:143, 404, 440. On Bacon's Rebellion, see Morgan, *American Slavery, American Freedom*, 250–79.

70. *True Declaration of the Estate of the Colonie in Virginia* (London, 1610), in *Tracts and Other Papers Relating Principally to the Origin, Settlement, and Progress of the Colonies in North America from the Discovery of the Country to the Year 1776*, 4 vols., ed. Peter Force (Washington: P. Force, 1836–46), 3:1.

71. Richard Blome, *A Description of the Island of Jamaica . . .* (London, 1672), 52; *A Declaration of His Highnes, By the Advice of His Council; Setting forth . . . the Justice of their Cause against Spaine* (London, 1655), 138–39.

72. On the events of 1622, see Alden T. Vaughan, " 'Expulsion of the Salvages': English Policy and the Virginia Massacre of 1622," *William and Mary Quarterly* 35:1 (1978): 57–84, and J. Frederick Fausz, "George Thorpe, Nemattenew, and the Powhatan Uprising of 1622," *Virginia Calvacade* 28:3 (1970): 110–17.

73. *RVC* 3:557–58, 672. On the Spanish debates concerning slavery and the nature of Indians, see Anthony Pagden, *The Fall of Natural Man: The American Indian and the Origins of Comparative Ethnology* (Cambridge: Cambridge University Press, 1982).

74. In so doing, Spanish precedents came to be viewed as more worthy of emulation. The broader issue of the relationship between Anglo-Virginia colonialism and information derived from Spanish precedents is the subject of April Lee Hatfield, "Spanish Colonization Literature,

Powhatan Geographies, and English Perceptions of Tsenacommacah/Virginia," *Journal of Southern History* 69:2 (2003): 245–82.

75. *RVC* 3:558–59, 706, 4:58.

76. *RVC* 3:672; "Virginias Verger," in Purchas, *Hakluytus Posthumous*, 19:246; and *RVC* 3:706.

77. Native resistance in Virginia prompted some Englishmen not only to reevaluate their impression of Indians but also to reconfigure the image of Spain and Spanish conduct in the West Indies. Edward Waterhouse noted that "the Spaniard made great use for his own turne of the quarrels and enmities that were amongst the Indians" and applied the principle: "*Diuide & impera*, Make divisions and take Kingdomes." He also reintroduced the impressions of Gonzalo Fernández de Oviedo y Valdés, whose *Summario de la Natural Historia de las Indias* and *Historia Natural y General de las Indias* had been partially available in English since first appearing in excerpted form in 1555. According to Waterhouse, Oviedo declared that Indians were "by nature slothfull and idle, vitious, malancholy, slovenly, of bad conditions, lyers, of small memory, [and] of no constancy or trust." Referring again to the wisdom of Oviedo, Waterhouse added that they "are lesse capable then children of sixe or seaven yeares old, and lesse apt and ingenious." In the opinion of at least one man, the patterns of Spanish ethnology and conquest were useful precedents for explaining the course of events in Virginia, as well as what the English might expect in the future if they were too lenient or too inclusive. *RVC* 3:562.

The use of Oviedo to demean Indians was, in reality, a significant departure from the prevailing trends in English publishing, where more favorable sources like Las Casas and José de Acosta were more well-known. Oviedo, for example, has only been translated into English in the twentieth century, while both Las Casas and Acosta were printed in English in 1583 and 1604, respectively. Moreover, Acosta was clearly central to Purchas's collections, whereas only "Extracts" concerning the physical landscape were translated and reprinted from Oviedo. See C. R. Steele, "Latin America," in *The Purchas Handbook*, 2 vols., ed. L. E. Pennington (London: Hakluyt Society, 1997), 1:303. Gonzalo Fernández de Oviedo y Valdés, *Natural History of the West Indies*, ed. Sterling A. Stoudemire (Chapel Hill: University of North Carolina Press, 1959), and José de Acosta, *The Natural & Moral History of the Indies*, trans. Edward Grimston (London, 1604).

78. *RVC* 2:397, 3:552. In his effort to explain what he believed to be the religious perversions of Virginia Indians, William Strachey had already proposed that they were the descendants of the "vagabond race of Cham," but he had little interest in using this assessment to justify Indian slavery. Strachey, *The Historie of Travaile*, 47.

79. *The Planters Plea, Or the Grounds of Plantations Examined, And usuall Objections answered* (London, 1630), in Peter Force, *Tracts and Other Papers*, 4 vols. (Washington, DC, 1836–47), vol. 2.

80. Jill Lepore, in a generally excellent treatment of the issue of Indian slavery in the context of King Philip's War, notes that the enslavement of Indians in the wake of that conflict was yet another "critical step in the evolution toward an increasingly racialized ideology of the differences between Europeans and Indians." She is surely correct, but it should be noted that this was an ongoing struggle throughout the seventeenth century and would not be resolved for several more generations. Lepore, *The Name of War: King Philip's War and the Origins of American Identity* (New York: Vintage Books, 1998), 166.

81. John Eliot, the noted Puritan missionary, lamented to a friend in a 1657 letter that the Spaniards had forced the Indians to convert and the French "would hire them to it by giving them coates and shirts." Thus far the English had tried neither tactic, by which "wee could have gathered many hundreds, yea thousands it may bee by this time, into the name of Churches." The failure to

follow a more productive pattern of conversion as demonstrated by England's Catholic rivals in the Americas frustrated Eliot. "[W]ee have not learnt yet," he bemoaned, "the art of coyning Christians, or putting Christs name and image upon copper mettle." Eliot to Richard Baxter, 7 October 1657, cited in Michael Leroy Oberg, *Dominion and Civility: English Imperialism and Native America, 1585–1685* (Ithaca, NY: Cornell University Press, 1999), 126.

82. Smith, "A Description of New England," in *Complete Works*, 1:352.

83. Shurtleff, *Records*, 1:83, 394.

84. *The Journal of John Winthrop, 1630–1649*, ed. Richard S. Dunn, James Savage, and Laetitia Yeandle (Cambridge, MA: Belknap Press, 1996), 237.

85. *The Complete Writings of Roger Williams*, 7 vols., ed. John Russell Bartlett (New York: Russell & Russell, 1963), 6:54–55. For "Reprieve," see 69, 78–79, and 82. See also Margaret Ellen Newell, "Indian Slavery in Colonial New England," in Alan Gallay, ed., *Indian Slavery in Colonial America* (Lincoln: University of Nebraska Press, 2009), 33–66. The Narragansett and Mohegan perspective on these matters is considered in Michael Leroy Oberg, *Uncas: First of the Mohegans* (Ithaca, NY: Cornell University Press, 2003), 72.

86. *New England's First Fruits* (London, 1643), 3, and Mason cited in Fickes, "'They Could Not Endure That Yoke,'" 73–74.

87. *The Complete Writings of Roger Williams*, 6:14. The literature on European conceptions of cannibalism is rich, but for a suggestive analysis, see Peter Hulme, *Colonial Encounters: Europeans and the Native Caribbean, 1492–1797* (London: Routledge, 1986), esp. ch. 1: "Columbus and the Cannibals" (13–42). On the tension between English conceptions of civility in the New World and cannibalism, see Michael Zuckerman, "Identity in British America: Unease in Eden," in *Colonial Identity in the Atlantic World, 1500–1800*, ed. Nicholas Canny and Anthony Pagden (Princeton, NJ: Princeton University Press, 1987), esp. 143–57.

88. Godwyn, *The Negro's and Indians Advocate*, 36. Godwyn's concerns about the plight of Africans and Indians is treated more fully in Alden T. Vaughan, "Slaveholders' 'Hellish Principles': A Seventeenth-Century Critique," in *Roots of American Racism*, 55–81. Games, "'The Sanctuarye of our rebell negroes,'" 7. On the significance of the use of the word "negro" in the colonial era, see Jack D. Forbes, *Africans and Native Americans: The Language of Race and the Evolution of Red-Black Peoples*, 2nd ed. (Urbana: University of Illinois Press, 1993).

89. Karen Ordahl Kupperman, *Providence Island, 1630–1641: The Other Puritan Colony* (Cambridge: Cambridge University Press, 1993), 166–67.

90. Lefroy, *Memorials*, 1:698, 700. Indian slavery in Bermuda is fairly well documented and is treated in passing in Virginia Bernhard, *Slaves and Slaveholders in Bermuda, 1616–1782* (Columbia: University of Missouri Press, 1999), esp. 56–66.

91. *BCR* 2:99, 110; Jarvis, "'In the eye of all trade,'" 160. Volume 2 of the *Bermuda Colonial Records* consists of various deeds and bills of sale recording 131 lifetime servants between 1636 and 1661. Twenty-six of these, or nearly 20 percent, were Indian slaves.

92. *BCR* 2:195, 299, 300, and Lefroy, *Memorials*, 1:669–70. The manuscript sources indicate that the two Indian women were both name Frances even though record keepers alternated randomly between "Frances" and "Francis" when spelling the name. For the sake of clarity, I have chosen to spell the mother's name as "Frances" and daughter's name as "Francis."

93. Lefroy, *Memorials*, 2:54–55, 154–55. One problem faced by the Company and the General Assembly was property rights. As officials wrote in 1655, "[W]ee doe asuer you that yt is farr from our purpose to take aways the servant of any man to whom any service doth belong of right, but in our care to relieve the oppressed & to execute Justice."

94. *Colonising Expeditions to the West Indies and Guiana, 1623–1667*, ed. V. T. Harlow (London: Hakluyt Society, 1925), 30, 32, 37–38. Brief mention and the context of the Barbados Indians can be found in Richard S. Dunn, *Sugar and Slaves: The Rise of the Planter Class in the English West Indies, 1624–1713* (Chapel Hill: University of North Carolina Press, 1972), 227.

95. The exception to this rule occurred when slaveowners purposely characterized all their bondmen as "negroes," perhaps in an effort to evade the greater opposition to Indian as opposed to African slavery. This occurred in sixteenth-century Spanish America, where the enslavement of indigenous peoples was condemned by the papal bull *Veritas Ipsa* in 1537, and generally prohibited after the promulgation of the New Laws in 1542. Indian slavery was outlawed in Brazil in 1570.

96. Ligon, *A True & Exact History*, 54, and John Smith, *A Map of Virginia* (Oxford, 1612), cited in Billings, *The Old Dominion in the Seventeenth Century*, 264. The ever-expanding slave population and the increasing significance of marronage would, by the last half of the century, reorient English apprehension in the general direction of their African slaves.

97. Thomas Gage, *A New Survey of the West-India's, or, the English American his travail by sea and land*, 2nd ed. (London, 1655), v.

98. *The Laws of Jamaica, Passed by the Assembly, And Confirmed by his Majesty in Council, April 17, 1684* (London, 1684), x. The imagery of the royal seal issued to Jamaica and the embedded mottos reveal a great deal about the story Englishmen liked to tell themselves about their relationship with the indigenous peoples of America and, more specifically, how they justified their possession of the island. Indians were regularly lionized in English colonial promotion. John Ogilby, a London geographer, reported that "the antient Natives of this Place [Jamaica] were a subtile and sharp-witted People, skilful in Handicrafts, and expert in warlike Affairs, above all the *Americans* besides." Ogilby, *America: Being the latest, and most accurate description of the New World* (London, 1671), 340.

99. The use of Indians, posed in such a way as to suggest both their supplication and the act of gift-giving, signified the willing cooperation of a people fully aware of the alliance they were making. The use of pineapples, a traditional symbol of hospitality, is also significant. On the seal, too, is written the motto "*Duro de Cortice fructus quam Dulces?*" (How sweet is the fruit from a hard rind?). Encircling the depiction of the male and female Indians supporting the cross, the inscription reads: "*Ecce alium Ramos porrexit in orbem Nect sterilis crux est*" (Behold! Another has offered its branches). Finally, the motto at the foot of the image: "*Indus Uterque serviet uni*" (Each Indian will serve one). In both words and images, then, the English government projected an image of Jamaica as a gift willingly given to the English nation by an indigenous people who had long since ceased to inhabit the island themselves. Patricia Mohammed, "Taking Possession: Symbols of Empire and Nationhood," *Small Axe* 11 (March 2002): 31–58. I thank Keyne Cheshire, Classics Department, Davidson College, for help in translating and discussing these Latin mottos with me.

100. The English privateer Sir Thomas Shirley, in his description of the Ottoman Empire during the first decade of the seventeenth century, even noted that in that part of the world "our English shyppes doe use to carye Christian slaves for the Turkes from porte to porte." Indeed, Shirley continued, "noe Christian shyppes that trade with the Turke . . . wyll carye anye of these, but onelye the English." "Discours of the Turkes by Sir Thomas Sherley," ed. E. Denison Ross (ca. 1607), in *Camden Miscellany, XVI*, 3rd series, 52 (London: Camden Society, 1936), 10–11.

101. The idea that slavery was legitimized by the prosecution of a just war can be traced backed to Aristotle's *Politics*, but the most important contemporary articulation of the just war doctrine was Hugo Grotius, *De juri belli ac pacis* (Amsterdam, 1625). For a classic treatment of the broader

subject, see Michael Walzer, *Just and Unjust Wars: A Moral Argument with Historical Illustrations*, 4th ed. (New York: Basic Books, 2006).

102. David Brion Davis, *Slavery and Human Progress* (New York: Oxford University Press, 1984).

CHAPTER 6

1. Charles Calvert to Lord Baltimore, 22 April 1664, cited in Lois Green Carr, Russell R. Menard, and Lorena S. Walsh, *Robert Cole's World: Agriculture & Society in Early Maryland* (Chapel Hill: University of North Carolina Press, 1991), 160.

2. Francisco Morales Padrón, *Spanish Jamaica*, trans. Patrick E. Bryan (Kingston, Jamaica: Ian Randle Publishers, 2003). In the roughly thirty-year period before 1610, Jamaican imports to Havana, the most important regional trade center, accounted for less than 1 percent of the value of all imports. Alejandro de la Fuente, *Havana and the Atlantic in the Sixteenth Century* (Chapel Hill: University of North Carolina Press, 2008), 15.

3. The new imperial policy, however, was generally unpopular with the emerging colonial plantocracy and merchants, many of whom more clearly recognized the tenuous nature of England's presence in the region and therefore feared reprisals. Spain's reconquest of Providence Island in 1641 was a recent cautionary tale of violence and instability that frightened many Anglo-Americans. See S. A. G. Taylor, *The Western Design: An Account of Cromwell's Expedition to the Caribbean* (Kingston: Institute of Jamaica and the Jamaica Historical Society, 1965); Stephen Saunders Webb, *The Governors-General: The English Army and the Definition of Empire, 1569–1681* (Chapel Hill: University of North Carolina Press, 1979), esp. 151–210; David Armitage, "The Cromwellian Protectorate and the Languages of Empire," *Historical Journal* 35:3 (1992): 531–55; and Karen Ordahl Kupperman, "Errand to the Indies: Puritan Colonization from Providence Island through the Western Design," *William and Mary Quarterly* 45 (January 1998): 70–99. For the unpopularity of the Western Design among English colonists, see Carla Gardina Pestana, *The English Atlantic in an Age of Revolution, 1640–1641* (Cambridge, MA: Harvard University Press, 2004), 177–82.

4. By one estimate, perhaps 12,000 English soldiers and settlers came to Jamaica in the six years after 1655, yet fewer than 3,000 Englishmen and roughly 500 Africans could be found on the island in 1661. Writing in November 1655, one early conqueror lamented: "[G]reater disapoyntments I never met with, having had noe provision allowed me in 10 weeks last past, nor above 3 biskets this 14 weeks." Worse still, the writer claimed, "Wee have lost halfe our armie from our first landing on Spaniola, where we were 8000. . . . Never did my eyes see such a sickly time, nor so many funerals." *The Narrative of General Venables*, ed. C. H. Firth (London: Camden Society, 1900), Appendix D, 142. See also Irene A. Wright, "The Spanish Resistance to the English Occupation of Jamaica, 1655–1660," *Transactions of the Royal Historical Society*, 4th ser., 13 (1930): 117–47, and Richard S. Dunn, *Sugar and Slaves: The Rise of the Planter Class in the English West Indies, 1624–1713* (Chapel Hill: University of North Carolina Press, 1972), 151–53.

5. The extent to which it was not possible is highlighted in Trevor Burnard, "A Failed Settler Society: Marriage and Demographic Failure in Early Jamaica," *Journal of Social History* 28:1 (Fall 1994): 63–82, and "'The Countrie Continues Sicklie': White Mortality in Jamaica, 1655–1780," *Social History of Medicine* 12:1 (1999): 45–72. On the creation of an Anglo-Jamaican colony, see David Barry Gaspar, "'Rigid and Inclement': Origins of the Jamaican Slave Laws of the Seventeenth Century," in *The Many Legalities of Early America*, ed. Christopher L. Tomlins and Bruce H. Mann

(Chapel Hill: University of North Carolina Press, 2001), 78–96, and James Robertson, "Re-writing the English Conquest of Jamaica in the Late Seventeenth Century," *English Historical Review* 117/473 (September 2002): 813–39.

6. Historians have typically emphasized that, "[o]n the whole the English started de novo in Jamaica. They rejected everything Spanish from the Catholic church to the plaster and tile bungalow houses." Like settlers on Barbados, who "endeavoured, as swiftly as circumstances permitted, to transplant English ways of living to the Caribbean," it is common currency that early Anglo-Jamaicans put aside the old and set about creating their own "Little England" in the former Spanish colony." Dunn, *Sugar and Slaves*, 151; Larry Gragg, *Englishmen Transplanted: The English Colonization of Barbados, 1627–1660* (Oxford: Oxford University Press, 2003), 10; and Gary A. Puckrein, *Little England: Plantation Society and Anglo-Barbadian Politics, 1627–1700* (New York: New York University Press, 1984). Some scholars, however, have argued that creolization was an inevitable component of transatlantic colonialism. See, for example, David Buisseret, "The Process of Creolization in Seventeenth-Century Jamaica," in *Creolization in the Americas*, ed. David Buisseret and Steven G. Reinhardt (College Station: Texas A&M University Press, 2000), 19–33; James Robertson, *"Gone Is the Ancient Glory!" Spanish Town, Jamaica, 1534–2000* (Kingston, Jamaica: Ian Randle Publishers, 2005); and Frederic G. Cassidy, "The Earliest Placenames in Jamaica," *Names* 36:3–4 (September–December 1988): 151–61.

7. *Calendar of State Papers: Colonial Series* [hereafter *CSP:CS*], 40 vols. (London, 1860–1939), 5:21. D'Oyley's estimate is almost certainly several times greater than the real number. Don Francisco de Leyba, lieutenant commander for the defense of Jamaica, reported in 1659 that there were "in three settlements about two hundred and fifty black men and women who govern themselves." Cited in Frank Cundall and Joseph L. Pietersz, *Jamaica under the Spaniards* (Kingston: Institute of Jamaica, 1919), 90.

8. Cited in D. J. Buisseret and S. A. G. Taylor, "Juan de Bolas and His Pelinco," *Caribbean Quarterly* 25 (1978), 5; Great Britain, Public Record Office [hereafter PRO], Colonial Office [CO] 140/1, 75–76 (1 February 1663); and "Beeston's Journal," 272; PRO, CO 140/1, 76 (1 February 1663). Lyttelton's successor, Sir Thomas Modyford, endorsed the idea in 1664 when he advised the Secretary of State that "His Majesty be prodigal in granting the first million of acres, allowing 30 acres per head to white or black." CSP:CS 5:207–8. See also Mavis C. Campbell, *The Maroons of Jamaica, 1655–1796: A History of Resistance, Collaborations & Betrayal* (Granby, MA: Bergin & Garvey Publishers, 1988), 17–23. For the eighteenth-century treaty, see "Articles of Pacification with the Maroons of Trelawney Town, concluded March the first, 1738," in *Maroon Societies: Rebel Slave Communities in the Americas*, 2nd ed., ed. Richard Price (Baltimore: Johns Hopkins University Press, 1979), 237–39.

9. Cited in James Robertson, *"Gone Is the Ancient Glory!"* 50, and J. Harry Bennett, "Cary Helyar, Merchant and Planter of Seventeenth-Century Jamaica," *William and Mary Quarterly* 21:1 (January 1964): 53–76.

10. There have been some excellent efforts in recent years to look anew at early Virginia. See, esp., John C. Coombs, "The Phases of Conversion: A New Chronology for the Rise of Slavery in Early Virginia," *William and Mary Quarterly* 68:3 (July 2011): 332–60, and Lorena S. Walsh, *Motives of Honor, Pleasure, & Profit: Plantation Management in the Colonial Chesapeake, 1607–1763* (Chapel Hill: University of North Carolina Press, 2010). Although not especially interested in the meaning and varied expressions of slavery, as in the present work, these studies share a similar interest in fleshing out slavery's history before it became as large-scale and widely embraced as it would be in the late seventeenth and early eighteenth centuries.

11. As a result, the tendency in recent years has been to try to make sense of the lives of the earliest African peoples arriving in the Americas by emphasizing their agency as historical actors in their own right. Certainly, there is a great deal to recommend this approach. Yet, the recent scholarly fascination with "Atlantic Creoles" should not allow us to lose sight of the more brutal reality that bondage, captivity, forced transportation, and other manifestations of unfreedom that defined the lives of the vast majority of African peoples in the Atlantic world (not including here the African littoral itself) from the late fifteenth century. See, for example, Ira Berlin, "From Creoles to African: Atlantic Creoles and the Origins of African-American Society in Mainland North America," *William and Mary Quarterly* 53:2 (April 1996): 251–88, and *Many Thousands Gone: The First Two Centuries of Slavery in North America* (Cambridge, MA: Belknap, 1998); and John Thornton and Linda Heywood, *Central Africans, Atlantic Creoles, and the Foundation of the Americas, 1585–1660* (Cambridge: Cambridge University Press, 2007). For a work that takes the "Atlantic Creole" paradigm into a slightly later period, see Jane G. Landers, *Atlantic Creoles in the Age of Revolutions* (Cambridge, MA: Harvard University Press, 2010).

12. As Alden Vaughan has pointed out, even those historians most inclined to emphasize the opportunities for freedom available to African peoples in the early Anglo-Atlantic world conclude that, under the best of circumstances, during the first half-century of colonization, at least 70 percent of Africans were enslaved. See, for example, Edmund S. Morgan, "Slavery and Freedom: The American Paradox," *Journal of American History* 59 (1972–73): 18 n. 39, and T. H. Breen and Stephen Innes, *"Myne Owne Ground": Race and Freedom on Virginia's Eastern Shore, 1640–1676* (New York: Oxford University Press, 1980), 66–69, 72. Moreover, it is also generally conceded that "most of the Africans, perhaps all of them," in Edmund Morgan's words, "came as slaves." Morgan, "Slavery and Freedom," 17. Alden T. Vaughan, "The Origins Debate: Slavery and Racism in Seventeenth-Century Virginia," in *Roots of American Racism: Essays on the Colonial Experience* (New York: Oxford University Press, 1995), 156–57, 305 n. 50, 309 n. 84.

13. This group proved to be especially troublesome to the English, as evidenced in particular in November 1663 by the revenge they exacted on the "colonel of the black regiment" in service to the English, Juan de Bolas, when they "cut him to pieces." In 1665 the Council announced its frustration with the "Varmahalys [who] dayly under notion of Freindshipp and fair Correspondence beguile many Hunters, and commit divers Murders." To resolve this problem, a thirty-pound bounty was placed on the head of "that Varmahaly Negro, commonly called the Serjent Major." PRO, CO 140/1, 121 (28 July 1664); "A Journal Kept by Col. William Beeston, From His First Coming to Jamaica," in *Interesting Tracts Relating to the Island of Jamaica* (St. Jago de la Vega [Jamaica], 1800), 281; and PRO, CO 140/1, 138–40 (1 September 1665).

14. Ironically, from the perspective of the study of Anglo-American slavery, those people historians have been most likely to designate as slaves (because they were held in perpetuity, because their status was inheritable, and because they were often consigned to plantation labors) were unlikely to be labeled as such in their own time. At the same time, Englishmen willingly, perhaps eagerly, talked and wrote about both slaves and slavery all the time, although when they did so they were rarely referring to either African peoples or a perpetual and inheritable status directed toward the production of some cash crop. Parallel arguments but with a greater emphasis on labor, trade, and ideological issues can be seen in Robert J. Steinfeld, *The Invention of Free Labor: The Employment Relation in English & American Law and Culture, 1350–1870* (Chapel Hill: University of North Carolina Press, 1991); Christopher Hill, *Liberty Against the Law: Some Seventeenth-Century Controversies* (London: Penguin Books, 1996); David Armitage, *The Ideological Origins of Empire* (Cambridge, MA: Harvard University Press, 2000); and Carla Gardina Pestana, *The English Atlantic in an Age of Revolution*.

288

NOTES TO PAGES 199–201

15. Although the emphasis in what follows is not on the legal realm, it is worth emphasizing that a great deal of scholarly attention has been devoted to the question of the evolution of the law of slavery in the Anglo-Atlantic world. See, esp., Warren M. Billings, "The Transfer of English Law to Virginia, 1606–50," in *The Westward Enterprise: English Activities in Ireland, the Atlantic, and America, 1480–1650*, ed. K. R. Andrews, N. P. Canny, and P. E. H. Hair. (Liverpool: Liverpool University Press, 1978); Thomas D. Morris, "'Villeinage . . . as it existed in England, reflects but little light on our subject': The Problem of the 'Sources' of Southern Slave Law," *American Journal of Legal History* 32:2 (April 1988): 95–137; Bradley J. Nicholson, "Legal Borrowing and the Origins of Slave Law in the British Colonies," *American Journal of Legal History* 38:1 (January 1994): 38–54; and Jonathan A. Bush, "The British Constitution and the Creation of American Slavery," in *Slavery and the Law*, ed. Paul Finkelman (Madison, WI: Madison House, 1997). Of all the legal arguments, I find Jonathan Bush's contributions to be the most compelling, particularly his assertion that, although common law did not address slavery in a systematic fashion, the "doctrine of prerogative governance . . . allowed the retention of local customs like slavery and the selective 'reception' of various usable common law doctrines that facilitated the retention and management of slavery." In other words, historians should pay less attention to what common law said and more to how it was constructed and legitimated over time. Anglo-American slavery is therefore easy to imagine as something that was similarly constructed during the seventeenth century "as a private matter, under local men and local custom." That it might have been done otherwise would have been innovative in the Anglo-Atlantic world (405).

16. A common practice has been to identify Spanish and Portuguese names among the first generation of African peoples in Anglo-American records. See, for example, Winthrop D. Jordan, *White over Black: American Attitudes toward the Negro, 1550–1812* (Chapel Hill: University of North Carolina Press, 1968), 73; Breen and Innes, *"Myne Owne Ground,"* 70; and Berlin, *Many Thousands Gone*, 39. On the active role of Portuguese merchants in the early modern Atlantic world, see Daviken Studnicki-Gizbert, *A Nation upon the Ocean Sea: Portugal's Atlantic Diaspora and the Crisis of the Spanish Empire, 1492–1640* (New York: Oxford University Press, 2007).

17. See, esp., April Lee Hatfield, *Atlantic Virginia: Intercolonial Relations in the Seventeenth Century* (Philadelphia: University of Pennsylvania Press, 2004), and Philip D. Morgan, "Virginia's Other Prototype: The Caribbean," in *The Atlantic World and Virginia, 1550–1624*, ed. Peter Mancall (Chapel Hill: University of North Carolina Press, 2007), 342–80.

18. *Memorials of the Discovery and Early Settlement of the Bermudas or Somers Islands, 1515–1685*, 2 vols., ed. J. H. Lefroy (Toronto: University of Toronto Press, 1981), 1:115–16; Nathaniel Butler, *The Historye of the Bermudaes or Summer Islands*, ed. Sir J. Henry Lefroy (London: Hakluyt Society, 1882), 84–85, and *The Rich Papers: Letters from Bermuda, 1615–1646*, ed. Vernon A. Ives (Toronto: University of Toronto Press, 1984), 25, 123–24, 125, 141–42, 202–3. Further details concerning the first enslaved Africans in Anglo-America can be found in Michael J. Jarvis, "'In the eye of all trade': Maritime Revolution and the Transformation of Bermudian Society, 1612–1800" (Ph.D. diss., College of William and Mary, 1998), 143–64, and Virginia Bernhard, *Slaves and Slaveholders in Bermuda, 1616–1782* (Columbia: University of Missouri Press, 1999), 1–48.

19. Jarvis, "'In the eye of all trade,'" 145–48, and *Rich Papers*, 229.

20. Tim Hashaw, *The Birth of Black America: The First African Americans and the Pursuit of Freedom at Jamestown* (New York: Carroll & Graf Publishers, 2007), has identified Jope as a native of Cornwall and the *White Lion* as an aged English ship that had been part of Sir Francis Drake's 1585–86 expedition to the West Indies and part of the fleet that defended Spain during the Armada (71).

21. On the political dynamics of the Virginia Company of London, see Wesley Frank Craven, *The Dissolution of the Virginia Company: Failure of a Colonial Experiment* (New York: Oxford University Press, 1932). See also Theodore K. Rabb, *Jacobean Gentleman: Sir Edwin Sandys, 1561–1629* (Princeton, NJ: Princeton University Press, 1998), 319–85, and Robert Brenner, *Merchants and Revolution: Commercial Change, Political Conflict, and London's Overseas Traders, 1550–1653* (Princeton, NJ: Princeton University Press, 1993), 93–102.

22. *Narratives of Early Virginia, 1606–1625*, ed. Lyon Gardiner Tyler (New York, 1907), 337; Vaughan, *Roots of American Racism*, 300 n. 17; Jarvis, "'In the eye of all trade,'" 148 n. 89. On the Africans and the Portuguese slave ship, see Engel Sluiter, "New Light on the '20. and Odd Negroes' Arriving in Virginia, August 1619," *William and Mary Quarterly* 54:2 (April 1997): 395–98; and John Thornton, "The African Experience of the '20 and Odd Negroes' Arriving in Virginia in 1619," *William and Mary Quarterly* 55:3 (July 1998): 421–34.

23. *Records of the Virginia Company of London* [hereafter *RVC*], 4 vols, ed. Susan Myr Kingsbury (Washington, DC: Government Printing Office, 1906–35), 3:243.

24. William Thorndale, "The Virginia Census of 1619," *Magazine of Virginia Genealogy* 33:3 (Summer 1995): 155–70, and Martha W. McCartney, "An Early Virginia Census Reprised," *Quarterly Bulletin of the Virginia Historical Society* 54 (1999): 178–96.

25. Alden T. Vaughan, "Blacks in Virginia: Evidence from the First Decade," in *Roots of American Racism*, 132; Jarvis, "'In the eye of all trade,'" 148. Heywood and Thornton, *Central Africans*, seem to be confident that Angelo was part of a shipment of more than a dozen Africans, originally part of Elfrith's cargo, transferred from Bermuda to Virginia in early 1620 (5–8). Several contemporary accounts from the High Court of Admiralty concerning these events appear in Peter Wilson Coldham, *English Adventurers and Emigrants, 1609–1660: Abstracts of Examinations in the High Court of Admiralty with Reference to Colonial America* (Baltimore: Genealogical Publishing Co., 1984), esp. 12–13, 181–82.

26. Annie Lash Jester and Martha Woodruff, eds., *Adventurers of Purse and Person: Virginia, 1607–1625* (Princeton, NJ: Princeton University Press,1956), 46, 62; *Minutes of the Council and General Court of Colonial Virginia, 1622–1632, 1670–1676*, ed. H. R. McIlwaine (Richmond: Virginia State Library, 1924), 33, 67–68, 71–73; Vaughan, "Blacks in Virginia," 134; and Heywood and Thornton, *Central Africans*, 7–8.

27. That these Africans were actively sought after, not simply accidental immigrants, is an important point of emphasis in Coombs, "The Phases of Conversion," esp. 338–41.

28. *Memoirs of the First Settlement of the Island of Barbados and Other the Carribbee Islands* (London, 1743), 20.

29. George Gardyner, *A Description of the New World* (London, 1651), 77. The classic treatment of early Barbados is Richard S. Dunn, *Sugar & Slaves: The Rise of the Planter Class in the English West Indies, 1624–1713* (Chapel Hill: University of North Carolina Press, 1972). But see also Gragg, *Englishmen Transplanted*, and Russell R. Menard, *Sweet Negotiations: Sugar, Slavery, and Plantation Agriculture in Early Barbados* (Charlottesville: University of Virginia Press, 2006).

30. "George Downing to John Winthrop, Jr." (26 August 1645), in *Documents Illustrative of the History of the Slave Trade to America*, vol. 1: *1441–1700*, ed. Elizabeth Donnan (Washington, DC, 1930), 125–26.

31. Alden Vaughan finds this remarkable, in part because by all accounts "most of them had been in America for five years" by the time of the census. Although this may have been true for many of these individuals, the absence of names could indicate not only indifference but also that some Africans had been imported only recently. Those named include four men at Flowerdew Hundred

(Anthony, William, John, and another Anthony), one man (John) living near James City, two men and two women at "Warwick's Squrak" (Peter, Anthony, Frances, and Margarett), and a man and a woman at Elizabeth City (Anthony and Isabella). Vaughan, "Blacks in Virginia," 130–31.

32. For the two censuses, see "Lists of the Livinge and Dead in Virginia Febr: 16th 1623," and "Muster of the Inhabitants in Virginia," in *The Original Lists of Persons of Quality . . . 1600–1700*, ed. John Camden Hotten (London, 1874), 169–96, 201–65. Specific references to Africans appear on 172–74, 178–79, 182, 185, 190, 217–18, 222, 224, 229, 241, 244, and 258. See also Irene W. D. Hecht, "The Virginia Muster of 1624/5 as a Source for Demographic History," *William and Mary Quarterly* 30:1 (January 1973): 65–92.

33. Another subject that should raise questions about just how little we know about the African presence in early Virginia is mortality rates. If it is possible to document the presence or arrival of roughly forty Africans before 1624, why does that document list only twenty-two blacks among the colonial population? The 1624 census indicates that one African had died during the spring of 1623, but there are no other records indicating that any Africans died in Virginia, even during the Powhatan Uprising of 1622.

34. Heywood and Thornton, *Central Africans*, suggest that the differences between the numbers from 1624 and 1625 were probably attributable to a population redistribution resulting from the ongoing war with the Powhatan confederacy. This assertion is highly speculative. If anything, Yeardley's sale of Flowerdew Hundred to Abraham Peirsey in 1624 probably accounts for the most important variations.

35. Yeardley and Peirsey appear to have owned fifteen of twenty-three Africans in 1625. In 1624, eleven Africans lived at Flowerdew and two others may have been with Yeardley at James City. Interestingly, however, no Africans appear in Peirsey's will in early 1627. Reprinted in *Virginia Carolorum: The Colony under the Rule of Charles the First and Second, A.D. 1625–A.D. 1685*, ed. Edward D. Neill (New York, 1886), 404–6. That Yeardley and Peirsey should account for a majority of the Africans inhabiting Virginia in the mid-1620s is not especially surprising. Yeardley had been deputy governor under the absent Thomas West, Lord De la Warr, between 1616 and 1617. Samuel Argall assumed his place at that time and Yeardley sailed to London, where he married Temperance Flowerdieu, was knighted by the king, and was appointed governor in his own right. In April 1619, Yeardley returned to Virginia and it was on his watch that the first shipment of Africans arrived soon thereafter. Abraham Peirsey, at the time, served as the Company's cape merchant. Perhaps more important, Peirsey purchased Flowerdew Hundred in 1624.

36. Heywood and Thornton, *Central Africans*, have done other scholars quite a service by providing a detailed list, in an appendix, of all the names they found in their research of Barbadoes, Bermuda, New Netherland, Chesapeake, and New England records (333–59).

37. *Rich Papers*, 244. The double "besides" is a telling indication of the length to which some Englishmen might go to ignore Africans.

38. *Rich Papers*, 157, 229; Jarvis, "'In the eye of all trade,'" 143–51. The relationship between privateering and early slavery was perhaps nowhere more crucial than in Bermuda. As Jarvis notes, once the Company clamped down on the West Indian privateers in 1621, Africans and Indians ceased arriving in the colony for more than a decade.

39. Robert Twombly and Robert H. Moore, "Black Puritan: The Negro in Seventeenth-Century Massachusetts," *William and Mary Quarterly* 24:2 (April 1967): 224–42.

40. George H. Moore, *Notes on the History of Slavery in Massachusetts* (New York: D. Appleton & Co., 1871), 29, 29–30, and Lorenzo Johnston Greene, *The Negro in Colonial New England* (New York: Atheneum, 1969), 16–17.

41. *CSP:CS* 1:162 (10 April 1633). See, esp., Karen Ordahl Kupperman, *Providence Island, 1630–1641: The Other Puritan Colony* (Cambridge: Cambridge University Press, 1993), 165–80, and Alison Games, "'The Sanctuarye of Our Rebell Negroes,': The Atlantic Context of Local Resistance on Providence Island, 1630–1641," *Slavery and Abolition* 19:3 (December 1998): 1–21.

42. *CSP:CS* 1:225 (19 March 1636), 1:249 (29 March 1637), and 1:271 (23 April 1638).

43. "Abstracts of Virginia Land Patents," *Virginia Magazine of History and Biography* 7:2 (October 1899): 191–92; *County Court Records of Accomack-Northampton, Virginia, 1632–1640*, ed. Susie M. Ames (Washington, DC: American Historical Association, 1954), 35; "Land Patents," *Virginia Magazine of History and Biography* 3:3 (January 1896): 273; and Elizabeth Donnan, ed., *Documents Illustrative of the History of the Slave Trade to America*, vol. 4: *The Border Colonies and the Southern Colonies* (Washington, DC: Carnegie Institute, 1935), 8, 9. See also *Cavaliers and Pioneers: Abstracts of Virginia Land Patents and Grants, 1623–66*, ed. Nell Marion Nugent (Baltimore: Genealogical Publishing Co., 1983), and John C. Coombs, "Building 'the Machine': The Development of Slavery and Slave Society in Early Colonial Virginia" (Ph.D. diss., College of William and Mary, 2003), 38.

44. *Virginia Magazine of History and Biography* [hereafter *VMHB*] 7:3 (January 1900): 265–66; *VMHB* 3:3 (January 1896): 322; and *CSP:CS* 1:296 (7 June 1639).

45. For this reason, some scholars have claimed that the first Africans to arrive in the American colonies, particularly the Chesapeake, were indentured servants. But as Lorena Walsh has recently asserted, little or no concrete evidence exists to support this claim. See Walsh, *Motives of Honor, Pleasure, and Profit*, 112–21, esp. n. 128.

46. On the intermittent involvement by the English in the early transatlantic slave trade, see Larry Gragg, "'To Procure Negroes': The English Slave Trade to Barbados, 1627–60," *Slavery and Abolition* 16:1 (1995): 65–84.

47. I am following the lead of Breen and Innes, *"Myne Owne Ground,"* 116 n. 9, in identifying this "Antonio" with the subsequently renown Anthony Johnson. In their eagerness to connect the early African population in Virginia with Christianity, Heywood and Thornton (*Central Africans*, 272) err when they argue that "Antoney Negro: Isabell Negro: and William their child bapitized," who were living with Captain William Tucker in Elizabeth City, is a record of "the same Anthony who became both free and prosperous in his later days" and "was sufficiently interested in the formal marks of Christian identity to offer his child for baptism."

48. There are numerous more detailed accounts of Johnson's life. See, esp., Breen and Innes, *"Myne Owne Ground,"* 7–18; J. Douglas Deal, *Race and Class in Colonial Virginia: Indians, Englishmen, and Africans on the Eastern Shore of Virginia During the Seventeenth Century* (New York: Garland Publishers, 1993), 217–50; and Berlin, *Many Thousands Gone*, 29–32. See also Brown, *Good Wives, Nasty Wenches & Anxious Patriarchs*, who usefully makes Mary Johnson as central to the story as her husband Anthony (107–13).

49. Although I have generally opted to use the word "African" as the least problematic identifier for the people of African descent found throughout the Atlantic world, in the specific case of free or freed peoples in the English colonies, I have typically chosen to use "free black." Although the term is suspect, for a number of reasons, it is generally preferable to the confusing "free African" alternative.

50. T. H. Breen, "Creative Adaptations: Peoples and Cultures," in *Colonial British America: Essays in the New History of the Early Modern Era*, ed. Jack P. Greene and J. R. Pole (Baltimore: Johns Hopkins University Press, 1984), 195–232.

51. As historian Frank Tannenbaum argued in the mid-twentieth century, "[T]he attitude toward manumission is the crucial element in slavery; it implies the judgment of the moral status of

the slave, and foreshadows his role in the case of freedom." Tannenbaum, *Slave & Citizen: The Negro in the Americas* (New York: Vintage Books, 1946), 69. Tannenbaum's comparative study is a bit overdrawn, but it is clear that there were both structural and ideological reasons for manumission's greater popularity in Latin America. For a recent discussion of the strengths, weaknesses, and continuing relevance of Tannenbaum's scholarship, see the forum in "What Can Frank Tannenbaum Still Teach Us about the Law of Slavery?" *Law and History Review* 22:2 (Summer 2004): 339–88.

52. For a useful discussion of manumission and its modes, see Orlando Patterson, *Slavery and Social Death: A Comparative Study* (Cambridge, MA: Harvard University Press, 1982), esp. 209–39. On Islam, see Bernard Lewis, *Race and Slavery in the Middle East: An Historical Enquiry* (New York: Oxford University Press, 1990). More recent works dealing with the Atlantic world in a comparative context include Marc Kleijwegt, ed., *The Faces of Freedom: The Manumission and Emancipation of Slaves in Old World and New World Slavery* (Leiden: Brill, 2006), and Rosemary Brana-Shute and Randy Sparks, eds., *Paths to Freedom: Manumission in the Atlantic World* (Columbia: University of South Carolina Press, 2009).

53. McIlwaine, *Minutes of the Council and General Court of Colonial Virginia*, 477; Breen and Innes, *"Myne Owne Ground,"* esp. ch. 4: "The Free Blacks of the Eastern Shore"; and Greene, *The Negro in Colonial New England*, 290–315.

54. *VMHB* 5 (1897–98), 40 and 2 (1894–95), 128 (Vaughan and Bacon); and Warren M. Billings, ed., *The Old Dominion in the Seventeenth Century: A Documentary History of Virginia, 1606–1700*, rev. ed. (Chapel Hill: University of North Carolina Press, 2007), 194. Concerning the case of Antonio, surviving records indicate that he witnessed and made his mark on the contract.

55. *Bermuda Colonial Records* [microfilm; hereafter *BCR*] 2:145 (September 1648).

56. *BCR* 2:168.

57. *BCR* 2:171, and Bernhard, *Slaves and Slaveholders in Bermuda*, 38–42. Bernhard argues here and elsewhere in her study that "*slave* was not synonymous with *Negro* in early Bermuda" (41). She is certainly correct if she is arguing that "slave" could and did mean many things during this period, but it is much harder to argue that "negro" meant many things other than "slave" to the English unless the word was somehow qualified (i.e., "negro servant" or "free negro").

58. *BCR*, 2:146.

59. *BCR*, 2:85.

60. As Stuart Schwartz has shown for Brazil, ritual godparentage "created a set of bonds, of spiritual kinship, between the godchild (*afilhado*) and his or her godfather (*padrinho*) and godmother (*padrinha*), and between the natural parents and the godparents." On ritual godparentage, see Stuart B. Schwartz, *Sugar Plantations in the Formation of Brazilian Society: Bahia, 1550–1835* (New York: Cambridge University Press, 1985), esp. 406–12 (quotation on 406), and Schwartz, "Opening the Family Circle: Godparentage in Brazilian Slavery," in *Slaves, Peasants, and Rebels: Reconsidering Brazilian Slavery* (Urbana: University of Illinois Press, 1992), 137–60. Virginia Bernhard tells a very different version of this story; see *Slaves and Slaveholders in Bermuda*, 76–80.

61. *BCR* 2:113, and Lefroy, *Memorials*, 2:278–80. Hugh Wentworth seems to have died in 1641.

62. Jerome S. Handler and John T. Pohlmann, "Slave Manumissions and Freedmen in Seventeenth-Century Barbados," *William and Mary Quarterly* 41:3 (July 1984): 390–408; Hilary McD. Beckles, *White Servitude and Black Slavery in Barbados, 1627–1715* (Knoxville: University of Tennessee Press, 1989), 86; Dunn, *Sugar & Slaves*, 255–56; and Richard Ligon, *A True & Exact History of the Island of Barbados* (London, 1673), esp. 46–54.

63. Games, "'The Sanctuarye of Our rebell negroes,'" 16; Moore, *Notes on the History of Slavery in Massachusetts*, 243; and Billings, *The Old Dominion in the Seventeenth Century*, 203. Breen and

Innes argue that the 1640 act was not intended to disarm all blacks, only those who resided in white households. According to their argument, "the law does not prohibit a black master such as Anthony Johnson from possessing a firearm, nor for that matter, does it order all blacks regardless of their status to surrender their weapons to the state. And finally, the law does not make it illegal for blacks to engage in offensive or defensive warfare." They conclude, however, that the law did separate "some blacks for special treatment, but little more can be said with authority about the act." See Breen and Innes, "Myne Owne Ground," 26. Of course, "some blacks" probably equaled roughly 80 percent of all Africans in Virginia.

64. Peter M. Voelz, Slave and Soldier: The Military Impact of Blacks in the Colonial Americas (New York: Garland Publishing, 1993), 25; Bernhard, Slaves and Slaveholders in Bermuda, 198–99; David Barry Gaspar, Bondmen and Rebels: A Study of Master-Slave Relations in Antigua (Durham, NC: Duke University Press, 1985), 120; and Peter H. Wood, Black Majority: Negroes in Colonial South Carolina from 1670 through the Stono Rebellion (New York: W. W. Norton, 1974), 23. It is an interesting aside that Irish Catholics were regularly excluded from seventeenth-century colonial militias, particularly in places like Barbados, while blacks were armed. See Robin Blackburn, The Making of New World Slavery: From the Baroque to the Modern, 1492–1800 (London: Verso, 1997), 317. For a broad comparative treatment, see the essays in Christopher Leslie Brown and Philip D. Morgan, eds., Arming Slaves: From Classical Times to the Modern Age (New Haven, CT: Yale University Press, 2006).

65. CSP:CS, 1:202–3; Kupperman, Providence Island, esp. 168–69; and CSP:CS 1:493 (1 December 1660). In addition to what follows, see, esp., Ruth Paley, Cristina Malcomson, and Michael Hunter, "Parliament and Slavery, 1660–c. 1710," Slavery and Abolition 31:2 (June 2010): 257–81.

66. CSP:CS 5:169 (23 November 1663); Billings, The Old Dominion in the Seventeenth Century, 204; [John Locke], The Fundamental Constitutions of Carolina (London, 1670), 25; and Acts of Assembly, Jamaica (1696), cited in Dunn, Sugar and Slaves, 249–50.

67. Mather, Life of John Eliot, 109, cited in Lorenzo Johnston Greene, The Negro in Colonial New England (New York: Atheneum, 1969), 263; Vaughan, "Slaveholders' 'Hellish Principles': A Seventeenth-Century Critique," in Roots of American Racism, 69.

68. Richard Ligon, A True & Exact History of the Island of Barbadoes (London, 1673), 50. Other important seventeenth-century proponents of conversion include the Quaker George Fox and the Anglican Morgan Godwyn. With the exception of the London merchant Thomas Tryon and a few others, however, few of these men can easily be characterized as decidedly "anti-slavery." See Phillipe Rosenberg, "Thomas Tryon and the Seventeenth-Century Dimensions of Antislavery," William and Mary Quarterly 61:4 (2004): 609–42, and Travis Glasson, Mastering Christianity: Missionary Anglicanism and Slavery in the Atlantic World (New York: Oxford University Press, 2012), esp. 47–50.

69. A Collection of the State Papers of John Thurloe, 7 vols. (London, 1742), 3:159.

70. Mary Sarah Bilder has argued convincingly, in the case of Rhode Island, that the absence of clarity about where English legal culture should apply in colonial matters was, in fact, "essential to the functioning of empire." What she characterizes as a transatlantic legal culture premised on "pragmatism and flexibility" is a useful framework for thinking about how early Anglo-Americans tried to work with slavery. Bilder, The Transatlantic Constitution: Colonial Legal Culture and the Empire (Cambridge, MA: Harvard University Press, 2004), quotations on 7.

71. On Bermuda's Atlantic orientation, see, esp., Michael J. Jarvis, In the Eye of All Trade: Bermuda, Bermudians, and the Maritime Atlantic World, 1680–1783 (Chapel Hill: University of North Carolina Press, 2010).

72. Greene, The Negro in Colonial New England, 257, and Bernhard, Slaves and Slaveholders in Bermuda, 137–39.

73. Cited in Philip D. Morgan, "British Encounters with Africans and African-Americans, circa 1600–1780," in *Strangers within the Realm: Cultural Margins of the First British Empire*, ed. Bernard Bailyn and Philip D. Morgan (Chapel Hill: University of North Carolina Press, 1991), 170.

74. John Phillip is discussed in several places, but for the most useful contextualization see, esp., Vaughan, "Blacks in Virginia," 130, and Berlin, *Many Thousands Gone*, 40.

75. Warren M. Billings, "The Cases of Fernando and Elizabeth Key: A Note on the Status of Blacks in Seventeenth-Century Virginia," *William and Mary Quarterly* 30:3 (July 1973): 467–74. Fernando claimed in 1667 that he "was a Christian and had been several yeares in England." The Court, however, ruled against Fernando, no doubt in part because of a recently enacted statute that declared neither baptism nor conversion altered the condition of slaves. Billings, *The Old Dominion in the Seventeenth Century*, 200.

76. In addition to sources cited elsewhere, see Michael J. Guasco, "Encounters, Identities, and Human Bondage: The Foundations of Racial Slavery in the Anglo-Atlantic World" (Ph.D. diss., College of William and Mary, 2000), 138–241.

77. Racism—what it was, where it came from, how it manifested itself, and whether it operated in different times and places—is a historical concept that has generated a large body of literature. Although the details of the subject are somewhat tangential to this study, and it is a topic generally treated with greater subtlety and sophistication for the period after the eighteenth century, it is worth considering the various arguments that appear in George F. Fredrickson, *Racism: A Short History* (Princeton, NJ: Princeton University Press, 2002), and Ivan Hannaford, *Race: The History of an Idea in the West* (Washington, DC: Woodrow Wilson Center Press, 1996).

78. Lefroy, *Memorials*, 1:565.

79. Lefroy, *Memorials*, 2:141, 178–79.

80. Billings, *The Old Dominion in the Seventeenth Century*, 190; Kathleen M. Brown, *Good Wives, Nasty Wenches & Anxious Patriarchs: Gender, Race, and Power in Colonial Virginia* (Chapel Hill: University of North Carolina Press, 1996), 195; and Kevin Mumford, "After Hugh: Statutory Race Segregation in Colonial America, 1630–1725," *American Journal of Legal History* 43:3 (July 1999): 280–305. As several scholars have noted, the case leaves room for the possibility that Davis was himself of African descent.

81. McIlwaine, *Minutes of the Council and General Court of Colonial Virginia*, 466. That the woman was punished by whipping and did not simply have her term of service extended would suggest that she was enslaved.

82. Elizabeth Key was somewhat unusual for marrying a white man, William Greensted, during the 1650s after he successfully pleaded for her freedom in Virginia courts. More often, Chesapeake marriages involved African men and English women, as with Francis Payne, who was married to an English woman named Aymey. As Ira Berlin has pointed out, at least one man from the three leading black families on the Eastern Shore (the Johnsons, Paynes, and Drigguses) married a white woman. This pattern of behavior was common in colonial societies where the number of Africans was small. See Edmund S. Morgan, *American Slavery, American Freedom: The Ordeal of Colonial Virginia* (New York: W. W. Norton, 1975), 333–37; Breen and Innes, *"Myne Owne Ground,"* 107; Berlin, *Many Thousands Gone*, 44–45; Morgan, "British Encounters with Africans and African Americans," 172–73; and A. Leon Higginbotham Jr., *In the Matter of Color: Race and the American Legal Process: The Colonial Period* (New York: Oxford University Press, 1978), 43.

83. Billings, *The Old Dominion in the Seventeenth Century*, 195–99. For a slightly different interpretation of the case of Elizabeth Key and its relationship to the development of racial slavery, see Theodore W. Allen, *The Invention of the White Race*, vol. 2: *The Origin of Racial Oppression in Anglo-*

America (London: Verso, 1997), 194–97. In contrast to my assertions, Allen contends that perpetual slavery was not normative for the earliest Africans in Anglo-America.

84. William Waller Hening, ed., *The Statutes at Large*, 13 vols. (Richmond and Philadelphia, 1809–23), 2:170.

85. Maryland, for example, banned interracial marriages in 1664. New England moved as slowly as Virginia. According to Lorenzo Greene, the term "mulatto" did not even appear in regional records until 1679. Even so, at least one accusation of an "improper" relationship between an Englishman and a slave women, which resulted in the birth of a mulatto child outside of marriage, occurred in 1663. Over the course of subsequent decades, fornication was punished similarly regardless of whether the offenders were English or African. Not until 1705 was racial intermarriage declared illegal in Massachusetts. Greene, *The Negro in Colonial New England*, 150, 204, and Twombly and Moore, "Black Puritan," 224–42. For the classic example of the way these issues have been framed in the light of the question of race rather than the question of status, see Jordan, *White over Black*, 78–80.

86. PRO, CO 140/1, 171–72 (29 February 1668). Henriques apparently had been captured and turned in by a slave—"Colonel Coape's Corimontee"—before he submitted to English authority. See PRO, CO 140/1, 173.

87. PRO, CO 140/1, 173–76 (28 March 1668). Animosity among different groups of Africans can be traced back to the presence of at least three main groups on the island at the time of the English Army's invasion: (1) those under Juan de Bolas who inhabited the hills above Guanaboa; (2) those at Los Vermejales under Juan de Serras, and (3) another, less well-known band in the valley between Mocho Mountains and Porus. Campbell, *The Maroons of Jamaica*, 17–18.

88. Campbell, *The Maroons of Jamaica*, 34–35. PRO, CO 140/1, 190–6 (2 May 1670).

89. Although nearly 10,000 enslaved Africans were already on the island by the early 1670s, the island previously had a much more diversified economy in cacao (which would be wiped out by a blight in 1671 and 1672), the logwood trade, and "entrepreneurial" privateering. By the mid-1670s, however, the island's landscape increasingly came to be dominated by sugar cultivation and its trade increasingly connected to slavery. Nuala Zahediah, "The Merchants of Port Royal, Jamaica, and the Spanish Contraband Trade, 1655–1692," *William and Mary Quarterly* 43:4 (October 1986): 570–93; "Trade, Plunder, and Economic Development in Early English Jamaica, 1655–89," *Economic History Review* 39:2 (May 1986): 205–22; and "'A Frugal, Prudential and Hopeful Trade': Privateering in Jamaica, 1655–89," *Journal of Imperial and Commonwealth History* 18:2 (May 1990): 145–68.

90. In early 1666, the governing council issued a comprehensive document appealing to the Crown "to have Letters of Mart granted against the Spaniards." Plundering the Spanish, they argued, was the most efficient way of supplying the colony with goods and bullion, which benefited everyone from merchant elites to poor planters. Continuing to ship out privateers from Jamaica would also help provide "seasonable Intelligence to the Governor of any evill intended ag[ainst] the English." PRO, CO 140/1, 144–46 (22 February 1666).

91. Ralph Nevil, "The Present State of Jamaica, in a Letter from Mr. Nevil to the Earl of Carlisle," *Interesting Tracts*, 106. Interestingly, the turn to sugar cultivation and commitment to transatlantic slavery effectively tied Jamaica's prospects even more closely to Spanish America. During the late 1670s and 1680s, the Royal African Company poured thousands of Africans into the island, partly in order to resell them in the Spanish market. Within the island, Anglo-Jamaicans routinely claimed that the failure of the Company to provide an adequate number of slaves "hurt ye nacon & ye Island" and would inevitably lead to higher levels of illicit trade. "People talk," Governor Lynch noted, "of having them by ye way [of] Holland & Curasoa Interlopers." Lynch promised to "do my

utmost to prevent al this" but urged the English government not to "let ye RC moralize the Dog in ye Manger." See K. G. Davies, *The Royal African Company* (London: Longman, 1957), 328–29, and Trevor Burnard, "Who Bought Slaves in Early America? Purchasers of Slaves from the Royal African Company in Jamaica, 1674–1708," *Slavery and Abolition* 17:2 (August 1996): 68–92. On Lynch, see the Colonial Williamsburg Foundation Library, *Blathwayte Papers* 28:3 (14 October 1682), 24:1 (15 June 1683), 24:2 (23 July 1683), and 24:4 (25 February 1684).

CONCLUSION

1. This crude summary oversimplifies the subtlety of a large body of scholarship. Beyond those works cited previously, the best examples of this narrative structure include Eric Williams, *Capitalism and Slavery* (Chapel Hill: University of North Carolina Press, 1944); Oscar and Mary Handlin, "Origins of the Southern Labor System," *William and Mary Quarterly* 7:2 (April 1950): 199–222; Lerone Bennett Jr., *Before the Mayflower: A History of the Negro in America, 1619–1964* (Chicago: Johnson Publishing Co., 1962); Russell Menard, "From Servants to Slaves: The Transformation of the Chesapeake Labor System," *Southern Studies* 16 (1977): 355–90; and Anthony S. Parent Jr., *Foul Means: The Formation of a Slave Society in Virginia, 1660–1740* (Chapel Hill: University of North Carolina Press, 2003).

2. It is also a product of the problematic search for "origins." Several generations ago, the French historian Marc Bloch warned scholars against the Sisyphean search for origins. Bloch recognized that history oriented toward the study of origins has often been put in the service of value judgments, as when past events are "assiduously used as an explanation of the present only in order that the present might be the better justified or condemned. So in many cases the demon of origins has been, perhaps, only the incarnation of that other satanic enemy of true history: the mania for making judgments." The search for the origins of racial slavery in the early English colonies is therefore a predictable enterprise because the history of slavery is undoubtedly a complicated and troubling proposition that speaks directly to the character of the nation and the integrity of the United States. Marc Bloch, *The Historian's Craft* (New York: Vintage Books, 1953), 29–35.

3. Fynes Moryson, *An Itinerary* (London, 1617). Three of five intended volumes were published during Moryson's lifetime. The material that would have made up the fourth volume was edited and published by Charles Hughes in 1903 as *Shakespeare's Europe: Unpublished Chapters of Fynes Moryson's Itinerary* (London, 1903). On Moryson's travels and writings, more generally, see Alison Games, *The Web of Empire: English Cosmopolitans in an Age of Expansion, 1560–1660* (New York: Oxford University Press, 2008), passim.

4. *Shakespeare's Europe*, 90, 137.

5. *Shakespeare's Europe*, 13–14.

6. Thomas Gage, *The English-American, his travail by sea and Land, or, A New Survey of the West India's* (London, 1648). This discussion of Gage relies on *Thomas Gage's Travels in the New World*, ed. J. Eric S. Thompson (Norman: University of Oklahoma Press, 1958). Gage's work was originally published in 1648, although it went through subsequent editions in 1655 (to coincide with the Venebles expedition to capture Hispaniola), 1677, 1699, 1702, 1711, and 1758. Other editions have continued to appear to the present time. On Gage's reliability as an observer, see Rodolfo Pastor F., "De Moros en la Costa a Negros de Castilla: Representación y Realidad en las Crónicas del Siglo XVII Centroamericano," *Historia Mexicana* 44:2 (1994): 195–235.

7. *Thomas Gage's Travels*, 51, 73, 97, 203.

8. *Thomas Gage's Travels*, 197, 315–16. A similarly well-to-do "free Negro of Nombre de Dios" named Ana Gómez was characterized by Spanish officials during Sir Francis Drake's 1595 raid on the Isthmus of Panama as a "rich trader" who was despoiled of "some Negro women" by the English. Gómez apparently even dined with Drake on one occasion soon after this incident. See Kenneth R. Andrews, ed., *The Last Voyage of Drake & Hawkins* (London: Hakluyt Society, 1972), 230, 211–12.

9. "An Act for the better ordering & Governing of Negro Slaves" (1664), PRO, CO 139/1, 55r.

INDEX

Page numbers in italics indicate figures.

Abbott, George, 62, 64, 65, 253n60
Acosta, José de, 282n77
Adams, William, 58–59
Aday, John, 100
Africa, literature on, 60–65, 252n49; English translations of Portuguese writing, 60, 64–65; recently translated geographical works of classical authors, 60; travelogues, 60, 252n49
African slave trade, English traders and, 65–77; and anti-slavery rhetoric, 72–77; Guinea expeditions, 66, 254n67; and Hawkins's disastrous 1567 expedition, 68–71; mortality rates, 66–67; traders' views of slavery itself, 71–77; transatlantic slave trade (after 1560), 67–71, *70*, 82, 255n70
African slavery, English travelers' encounters with, 60–77; and African climate, 61–62; and Africans' skin color, 62; and arrival of sub-Saharan African slaves in England, 67; characterizations of Africans, 76–77, 78–79; Christian interpretations/myths, 63–64; depictions of Africa's exoticism and mystery, 61–63; and English anti-slavery rhetoric, 72–77; and English embrace of African slavery, 65–71; literature on Africa, 60–65, 252n49; Prester John myth, 63–64, 253n57; traders' participation in African slave trade, 65–77
African slavery and Anglo-African encounters in pre-plantation America, 7, 195–226, 231–33; and Anglo-American ideas about slavery, 199, 208–9, 225–26, 231–33, 287n14; Barbados, 203, 215, 217–19; Bermuda, 200–201, 205–6,

212–14, 219–20, 221; census records and legal status of Africans, 204–6, 289n31, 290nn33–35; and England's new imperial policy, 195–96, 285n3; free blacks, 196–99, 209–16, 219–20, 224, 291n49; indentured servitude, 213; and Indian slavery, 190, 236n9, 284n95; Jamaica, 195–99, 217, 223–25, 233; legal status and circumspection regarding slave ownership, 204–9; New England, 206, 295n85; opportunities for freedom/manumission, 211–12, 291n51; and origins of racial slavery, 3, 5, 8, 163, 194, 225–26, 231–33; Protestant Christian baptism and conversion, 216–20, 293n68; Providence Island, 207, 208, 215–16, 217; racial intermixture, 220–23, 295n85; sales records, 208; scholarly attention to, 3, 5, 197, 286n10, 287nn11–12, 287n14, 288n15, 296n2; Virginia colony, 1–3, 8, 197–98, 201–5, 209–11, 217–18, 221–22
Africans in sixteenth-century England, 102–9, 115–18; arrivals by way of the Americas, 102–3, 108–9, 115; baptisms, 104–5; black servants in early decades of Elizabeth's reign, 103; burial records, 104; Elizabethan cult of whiteness, 105–8, *107*, 220, 263n58, 263nn64–65, 280n58; Elizabeth's 1601 royal proclamation, 117–18, 266n86; Elizabeth's supposed effort to expel African population, 115–18, 266nn86–87; late Elizabethan era, 103–5, 262n53; marriages, 105; Privy Council's 1596 directive, 115–16, 118
Africanus, Leo ("John Leo"/al-Hasan al-Wazzan), 52–53
Aldersey, Laurance, 151

Englishmen enslaved in the Mediterranean
  (*continued*)
  slavery, 144, 163; miseries and physical
  punishments, 133–35, *136*; and Muslim
  sexual deviancy, 138–39, 270n36; and
  notions of English freedom, 128–31, 139;
  process by which the newly captured were
  transformed into brutes, 131–33; public
  sales in the marketplace, 132–33; religious
  sermons and clergymen's commentaries,
  137–38, 141–42, 269–70n34; shaven heads
  and beards (and symbolism of), 131–32,
  268–69n20; stripping and reclothing of
  the newly captured, 131–32; theatrical
  productions depicting, 138; Tudor
  government efforts to secure freedom,
  139–47, 270n39; variations in treatment
  and fates, 132, 133
Eugenius III, Pope, 63
eunuchs, 55–56
Evans, William, 211

Fabian Robert, 179–80
female slaves: English slave-holding in
  Spanish America, 264n76; English
  travelers' accounts of, 53–55, 59–60, 72–73,
  256n83; Indian servants in Bermuda,
  188–89; Japanese concubines/sexual
  slavery, 59–60; Muslim world concubines/
  sexual slavery, 53–55; pre-Conquest
  medieval England, 54–55, 250n34; public
  sales of captive-slaves in Mediterranean
  marketplace, 133; Virginia colony ("Angelo
  a Negro Woman"), 202, 289n25
Fenner, George, 76, 100
Fernando (baptized African in seventeenth-
  century Virginia), 220, 294n75
Finch, William, 71
Fitz-Geffrey, Charles, 135, 143–44
Fitzgerald, Thomas, 48
Fitzherbert, John, 27
Fletcher, Giles, 45–46, 247n12
Floris, Peter William, 58, 251n43
Floyd, Edward, 278n42
Fowler, William, 92
Fox, George, 293n68
Fox, John, 127, 132, 134
Foyle, Oxenbridge, 168
France: English visitors witnessing Africans
  in, 91; Tudor government efforts to secure
  freedom of Englishmen enslaved in, 145–46

free blacks. *See* Anglo-American society, free
  blacks in
freedom. *See* manumission
freedom/liberty rhetoric, English: and
  African slavery in pre-plantation America,
  218; and bondmen/villeinage in Tudor
  England, 27–33; and "British History"
  (narrative identifying English forebears
  with ancient Greece), 21–24, 240n29; and
  depictions of unjust English enslavement,
  128–31, 139, 154, 163; and domestic slavery
  in pre-colonial England, 21–24, 29–33,
  38–39, 128–31, 163; and English exceptionalism, 40, 78, 220; and English national
  identity conceptions, 19–24, 39, 128–31,
  239–40n25; and English participation in
  African slave trade, 72–77; freedom and
  civil liberty, 18, 239n20; and Mediterranean slave narratives, 128–31, 139;
  pre-plantation Anglo-America, 170–72,
  194; Roman law, 18, 239n19
Frethorne, Richard, 159, 183
Frobisher, Martin, 11, 110, 174

Gabriel, Nicholas, 161, 162
Gage, Thomas, 191, 229–30; *New Survey of
  the West-Indies*, 191, 229
galley slavery: Drake's transportation of
  liberated galley slaves, 151; Hawkins's
  failed third slave-trading voyage (1567–68)
  and Englishmen in, 147–53; Moryson
  on, 228–29; narratives of Englishmen
  enslaved in the Mediterranean, 132,
  133–34; sixteenth-century domestic
  penal slavery, 36–38
Gardyner, George, 158–59, 203
Gates, Sir Thomas, 180
Gelofe, Juan, 80
Geneva Bible, 14–16, 106, 238n8
Geoffrey of Monmouth, *The History of the
  Kings of Britain*, 21–22, 240n29
Gerald of Wales, 47, 50, 247n16
Gilbert, Humphrey, 65
Godwyn, Morgan, 165, 171, 187, 217–18,
  293n68
Gómez, Ana, 297n8
Goodfreye, Thomas, 31
Gorge, Sir Edward, 27–28
Gosnold, Bartholomew, 178
Gouge, William, 121–22, 144
Gowen, Mihill, 212

ACKNOWLEDGMENTS

The finished work you hold in your hands is an unapologetic example of "big-picture" scholarship. I'll be the first to admit that there is a great deal more lumping than splitting going on here. In my effort to try to present an interpretive overview of the place of slavery in the English-speaking world during roughly 100 years of history—and to do so in a concise and readable fashion—I have had to leave some things out, move quickly where I would have preferred to linger, and generalize at the expense of the exceptions to the rule. My cutting-room floor is a mountainous testament to just how much more there is to say about this subject. As a result, I am sure that I've gotten some things wrong. I fully expect, and indeed hope, that my work will prompt others to elaborate on and even revise some of the lines of inquiry that I have only sketched here. Even so, I am equally confident that there is quite a lot in this book that makes perfect sense. And how could it be otherwise? For one, more scholars than I can count have a stake in all of this. I have relied heavily in places on the keen insights and amazingly thorough research of the individuals whose names pepper the notes. To them all, most of whom I've never met, I offer my heartfelt gratitude for their inspirational scholarship (and sincerest apologies if I have not done things well enough).

Even more, though, I am confident about this work because of the many people I do know who have read and commented on it either in its totality or in the bits and pieces that appeared in draft form, as conference papers, or in scholarly articles (real and imagined). First, I have to acknowledge Ron Hoffman, who bears some responsibility for my pursuing this line of inquiry and whose support for me and my research has been unwavering. I would not be here without him (although this may not be precisely the book he would have had me write) and will be forever thankful for all he has done for me. For offering me some of their time and considerable insights (and with apologies to those I may have forgotten to include), I would also especially like to thank Ira Berlin, Christopher L. Brown, Trevor Burnard, Dale Hoak, James

Horn, Michael Jarvis, Kris Lane, and Philip D. Morgan. All have served, at one time or another, as friends, colleagues, model scholars, and (lucky for me) willing readers of my work. Most recently, Peter Mancall offered keen criticism that helped me sharpen my argument and order my thoughts. Others who have had a finger in this pie (whether they realize it or not) include John Coombs, David Brion Davis, David Eltis, Alison Games, Christopher Grasso, Rhys Isaac, Karen Ordahl Kupperman, Sally Mason, Brett Rushforth, John Wood Sweet, Fredrika Teute, Alden and Virginia Mason Vaughan, and Walt Woodward. My friends and colleagues at Oberlin College—particularly Gary Kornblith and Carol Lasser—and Davidson College—not least Jonathan Berkey, Keyne Cheshire, Vivien Dietz, Earl Edmondson, Randy Ingram, Sally McMillen, Jane Mangan, Trish Tilburg, and Alan Michael Parker—have aided this project considerably with perfect measures of encouragement and patience. My students, on more than a few occasions over the years, have served as unwitting guinea pigs for my ideas and thoughtful readers of chapter drafts in seminar. I am indebted to them all. The staff of the E. H. Little Library at Davidson College, especially Susanna Boyleston and Joe Gutekanst, have provided more assistance to me than I'm sure they recognize. Last, but not at all least, I need to thank the University of Pennsylvania Press and, especially, Robert Lockhart. This book has evolved quite a bit since we started working together seven or eight years ago. I will never be able to thank Bob enough for his ability to be both critical and supportive of this project and for exercising more patience with me than any editor should ever be expected to demonstrate. I can't imagine a better shepherd.

I have benefited greatly from the financial support and generosity of a number of institutions, including Davidson College (where Clark Ross and Verna Case have been particularly helpful), the Henry E. Huntington Library, the Folger Shakespeare Library, and the John Carter Brown Library. Andy Gosling stepped in at the last minute and generously helped me out with a tricky international finance problem. In addition, I would like to thank the librarians and archivists who gave of their time at the British Public Record Office, the John D. Rockefeller, Jr. Library in Williamsburg, the Pierpont Morgan Library & Museum, the Earl Gregg Swem Library at the College of William and Mary, and the Oberlin College Library.

Bits and pieces of this book, often in highly altered forms, appeared previously as "Settling with Slavery: Human Bondage in the Early Anglo-Atlantic World," in *Envisioning an English Empire: Jamestown and the Invention of the North Atlantic World*, ed. Robert Appelbaum and John Wood Sweet (Philadelphia: University of Pennsylvania Press, 2005), 236–53; "To 'doe some good upon their countrymen': The Paradox of Indian Slavery in Early Anglo-America," *Journal of Social History* 41:2 (Winter 2007): 389–411; and "'Free from the tyrannous Spanyard'? : Englishmen and Africans in Spain's Atlantic World," *Slavery & Abolition* 29:1 (March 2008): 1–22. I would like to thank the publishers, editors, and myriad readers who helped to improve the material in these early efforts.

I would be remiss if I did not thank those people who made sure this project took much longer to complete than might otherwise have been the case by providing the kinds of joyous distractions that only friends and family can offer. So, to David Bishop, Rob Galgano, Joseph Kanofsky, and Scott Pell, I can only say "thank you!" To my parents (David Guasco and Judy Tweedy), Kevin Tweedy, Marlene Guasco, my brother Eddie and his wonderful family, and even the in-laws, my sincerest gratitude for delaying the completion of this book. And to everyone who has given me a reason not to go to work and do what I should have been doing, thank you, too.

Joseph Guasco and Amelia Guasco have not read a word of this book, but I'm pretty sure they will get a kick out of seeing their names in print. And just in case one or the other happens to be reading this right now, I'll put it directly: Thank you, Joseph, and thank you, Meals, for being who you are and making me who I am. That goes for your mom, too. Nobody has read this book more, in all its various manifestations, than Suzanne Cooper Guasco. An outstanding historian in her own right, with her own research and teaching interests, she has nonetheless given countless hours to this project. Because of her, this is a better book than it would have been otherwise. For that I will always be thankful. I hope she knows, though, that it's all the other stuff that really matters to me. I could easily bare my heart and plumb the depths of my soul here, but that would only embarrass her. So, I'll keep it simple. Thanks, Suz. This is for you.